SHOT IN MONTANA

A History of
Big Sky Cinema

BRIAN D'AMBROSIO

RIVERBEND
PUBLISHING

Shot in Montana: A History of Big Sky Cinema

Copyright © 2016 Brian D'Ambrosio

Published by Riverbend Publishing, Helena, Montana

ISBN: 978-1-60639-096-2

Printed in U.S.A.

1 2 3 4 5 6 7 8 VP 22 21 20 19 18 17 16

Cover and text design by Sarah Cauble, www.sarahcauble.com

Riverbend Publishing
P.O. Box 5833
Helena, MT 59604
1-866-787-2363
www.riverbendpublishing.com

All photos courtesy of the Montana Film Office except where noted.

To Sophia

Life is short; choose your friends and your films wisely.

Acknowledgments

For your inestimable help and assistance, thank you to John Ansotegui, Thomas Bezucha, Jeff Bridges, Tina Buckingham, Chaiken Films, Kaycee Cronk, Michael Dante, Danielle de Leon, Benicio Del Toro, Larry De-Waay, David Field, Lily Gladstone, Maribeth Goodrich, Brunson Green, Rachel Gregg, Curtis Hanson, Audrey Hall, Ron Howard, Sten Iversen, Margot Kidder, Alicia Knievel, Jim Kouf, Bill Kuney, Patrick Markey, Terri Mavencamp, Thomas McGuane, David Morse, Nick Nolte, Paramount Classics, Mark and Michael Polish, Bill Pullman, Mike Robe, Deny Staggs, Rob Story, Alex and Andrew Smith, Stan Smith, Lonie Stimac, James Woods, Allison Whitmer, Billy Wirth, Garry Wunderwald, and Markus Zetler.

Also by Brian D'Ambrosio

WARRIOR IN THE RING:
THE LIFE OF MARVIN CAMEL, NATIVE AMERICAN WORLD CHAMPION BOXER

MENACING FACE WORTH MILLIONS
A LIFE OF CHARLES BRONSON

RASTA IN THE RING
THE LIFE OF RASTAFARIAN BOXER LIVINGSTONE BRAMBLE

CONTENTS

INTRODUCTION

Montana is a realistic feast for filmmakers. It is not surprising that Hollywood selected Glacier National Park as the mythical setting to depict heaven in the 1998 Robin Williams movie, *What Dreams May Come*. Filmmakers captured the surreal beauty of one of the world's greatest treasures so vividly that critic Roger Ebert declared *What Dreams May Come* as "one of the great visual achievements in film history."

Montana's majesty and unspoiled beauty offer detailed delights and, at times, peace of mind. Such eye-dazzling assets are a filmmaker's paradise. For that reason, the motion picture industry has often hitched its journey to Big Sky Country. As filmmaker Arthur Penn (*Little Big Man*, *The Missouri Breaks*) noted, "It just doesn't get any better. Montana is the real thing." Penn first fell in love with the smell of sage and the whistle of the wind while vacationing and scouting locations in the late 1960s.

The movies *Thunderbolt and Lightfoot*, *Heaven's Gate*, *Firefox*, *Runaway Train*, *The Stone Boy*, and *The Slaughter Rule* have little in common. But one thing they all share: each was filmed in Montana. For more than 100 years, production companies have been coming to Montana to capture its elements. From the earliest known 1897 travel promotion film *Tourist Train Leaving Livingston* to major studio films such as *The Horse Whisperer*, *A River Runs Through It*, and *Nebraska*, Montana has hosted nearly 100 feature films.

In film and on the map, Montana covers a lot of soil. Montana has a land area of 93,157,952 acres, holds 10 National Forests, including fourteen Wilderness Areas, with 26,616,234 acres of National Forest and BLM Land. Approximately 1,000,000 people live in Montana (and 2.3 million cows). The fourth largest state, at 500 miles by 300 miles, there is a richness of diversity in Montana: from rolling prairies, cropland, and badlands in the east to forests, vast mountains and trout streams in the west. Filmmakers working on period pieces can often use Montana to effectively simulate the look of past or even ancient eras—thanks to the low population and tremendous amount of open space without impeding towns, roads or power lines.

The state is divided roughly into thirds. On one border there is Glacier National Park and three of the five entrances to Yellowstone National Park are in Montana. The east is rolling plains; the mid-section, high plains with isolated, towering mountain ranges, buttes, mesas, pristine river valleys and canyons; and the west is mountainous. In between is the stark beauty of the Missouri breaks and the high desert of Charlie Russell country. Central Montana's also a haven for independent filmmakers whose use of the landscape informs the narratives of thoughtful, introspective films—like *Northfork*, starring James Woods, Nick Nolte and Darryl Hannah, a film with Biblical undertones involving a young orphan, a hydroelectric dam and—perhaps—Noah's Ark. Sweeping Montana landscapes set a melancholy mood in *Northfork*, a surreal drama that boasts sumptuous cinematography.

Virtually every type of terrain is available to a filmmaker, with the exception of desert and ocean. Montana has vast stretches of forests, peaks rising to more than 12,000 feet, clean air, unobstructed views, irrigated farmland, badlands, alpine lakes and meandering cold-water streams. The absence of pollutants in the air allows for more sunlight to reach ground-level, a great advantage for filmmakers yearning to see and breathe freely. Special locations, such as a vacant prison that dates back to territorial days, and an abandoned B-52 air force base, can also be found in the state.

Location sites have been far-flung and varied. Director Steven Spielberg made his first cinematic foray into adult romance in Libby with *Always*. Montana filled the need for a flaming forest in Spielberg's story of forest fire retardant bomber pilots. For a while, those connected with *Always* thought they'd always be searching for the right location—it was over a year's time before Spielberg and company finally settled on Libby as the primary backdrop. The dramatic story was enhanced by the 1988 fires in Yellowstone National Park, which provided Spielberg the opportunity to capture footage of an actual fire.

The state has been the Midwest-Canadian border in *The Untouchables*; Morocco in the climactic ending of the horse and cowboy adventure *Hidalgo*. Hundreds of wild horses run free across the Montana prairie in the final scene of *Hidalgo*. It's a breathtaking scene in a beautiful movie. The spectacular sight lasts only four minutes in the film. But those four minutes took more than a month of preparation.

Montana doubled as China and San Francisco in *A Thousand Pieces of Gold*; Oklahoma in *Far and Away*. In *Far and Away*, the son of a tenant farmer (Tom Cruise) and a landowner's daughter (Nicole Kidman) set off together for America with hopes of prosperity—the Cherokee Strip Land Race is one of the movie's spectacular sequences. Depicting the 1893 Cherokee Strip Land Race in Oklahoma required the involvement of over 800 extras on 400 horses and 200 wagons, on a "set" that was more than a quarter-mile wide. Director Ron Howard, anxious about the safety of his cast and crew, had trouble getting to sleep the night before shooting began on a 12,000-acre ranch outside Billings. Fortunately, his fears turned out to be groundless—almost.

And then there was Norway in a popular Norwegian children's movie called *Wolf Summer*; an angler's paradise in *A River Runs Through It*; upstate New York and Connecticut in the low-budget thriller *Devil's Pond*. Montana has dished out a bit of its own history in *Son of the Morning Star*, a quadruple Emmy winner; an iconoclastic *Rancho Deluxe*; and a financially disastrous *Heaven's Gate*.

Montana has served as a snow-covered no-man's-land in Clint Eastwood's *Firefox* and supplied a large building blown to smithereens in Charles Bronson's spy thriller *Telefon*. Sometimes Montana is naturally Montana: Kootenai Falls, the largest undammed falls in Montana, served as the setting for the 1994 film *River Wild* starring Meryl Streep, a thriller about a family on a rafting vacation that is tormented by some ruffians and rough water. *The River Wild* was filmed on two of Montana's whitewater rivers: the Kootenai River (and Kootenai Falls) near Libby, and the Middle Fork of the Flathead River. Testament to Montana's treacherous nature: a rafting sequence in *The River Wild* almost killed Meryl Streep one August afternoon.

Going-to-the-Sun Road, the 52-mile scenic road that crosses the Glacier National Park from St. Mary on the east side to Apgar Village on the west, overtakes the opening shots of Stanley Kubrick's *The Shining*. The true Hi-Line, that ribbon of remote land from Fort Peck to Shelby, served as a metaphor for the soul searching done by the main character in the independent film, *The Hi-Line*.

The state has provided scenery for Hollywood successes (*The Revenant, Forrest Gump*) and some of its most notorious flops (*Heaven's Gate, The Missouri Breaks*). Oscar winners (Sean Connery in *The Untouchables*) and future presidents (Ronald Reagan in *Cattle Queen of Montana*) have read their lines in the state. Montana productions boasts a high rate of Oscar glory, including *Thunderbolt and Lightfoot* (Jeff Bridges was nominated for Best Actor in a Supporting Role) and *Runaway Train*, in which Jon Voight (Best Actor in a Leading Role) and Eric Roberts (Best Actor in a Supporting Role) earned nominations for their stunning performances in this story about two convicts who escape into the icy Northwest wilderness aboard an out-of-control freight train.

"It's a beautiful state with so much variety that it's impossible for exteriors not to look good. Because of the landscape and the latitude, the magic hour in the summer is consistently spectacular and long-lasting," said cinematographer Mikael Salomon, who filmed parts of both *Always* and *Far and Away* in Montana.

"We obviously have the Western atmosphere. We obviously have mountains and snow," said Garry Wunderwald, Montana Film Commissioner from 1974 to 1990. (By 1974, as interest in Montana mounted and more studios were going on location, the Montana Film Office in Helena was organized to woo the filmmakers. Wunderwald ran a one-man show to attract Hollywood to Montana.)

"But we also have wide open spaces, such as Eastern Montana. And we have locations that lend themselves to scenes other than strictly Western. We're trying to overcome the stereotype images and show people that there is more here than cowboys and snow-covered peaks." Wunderwald spent more than a decade convincing production directors in places such as California and the East that Montana isn't too isolated to reach or too cold to work in.

Montana continually allures filmmakers "for the beautiful locations and the Western mystique," said Sten Iversen, one-time Montana Film Commissioner. "People think of Montana when they think of the West. They don't think Idaho or the Dakotas. We have something special, and the film business knows it." It's partly the name, Montana, Spanish for mountain, he said, noting, "It has a nice, rhythmic quality. It's a wonderful handle."

And the films have, in turn, attracted more folks to Montana. Farmers, ranchers and teenagers answered a casting call for parts in director Robert Redford's 1992 movie about fly-fishing and family *A River Runs Through It*. Norman Maclean's ruminative recollection of his Montana youth is a meditation on fly-fishing, religion, art and family. A skilled, careful adaptation of a much-admired story, *A River Runs Through It* is a convincing trip back in time to a virtually vanished American West, as well as a nicely observed family study. The film undoubtedly enticed more visitors to the state's trout streams, leaving locals even more irked than they already were at the vacation styles of the rich and famous.

State government has been involved in recruiting movie *business* only since 1974. But long before that, Montana locations, authors, and stars have had a place in the film industry almost since the first motion pictures were made. Our state has inspired not only filmmakers but a host of directors, writers and actors, including the Helena-born Gary Cooper (1901-1961), who starred in many Westerns—roughly projected at 141 titles—though not a single one of them rolled film in Montana. "Not unless there was an obscure one nobody knows about," said Iversen. "We've tried to log them all." The son of a Montana state supreme court justice, Cooper graduated from Grinnell College, then served as a guide in Yellowstone National Park. He moved to Los Angeles and found work in films as an extra because of his ability to ride a horse. Cooper's most famous role was probably the 1952 picture, *High Noon*, directed by Stanley Kramer for which Cooper won an Oscar for his performance as Marshal Will Kane. Cooper's unique, patriotic screen persona earned him five Oscar nods and two wins (he took home his first Oscar for his role as World War I hero Alvin York in the 1941 Howard Hawks film *Sergeant York*).

On June 28, 1961, Helena's Marlow Theater hosted the world premiere of Gary Cooper's final film, *The Naked Edge*. "This showing of 'The Naked Edge' will not only be the first anywhere in the world but will be nearly three weeks in advance of the film's official release for audiences everywhere," wrote Helena's *Independent Record*.

Hollywood's *BoxOffice* newspaper says that movie "world premiered at the Marlow." Helena's Marlow Theater, a movie palace that opened in 1918, was demolished in 1972. However, the highly esteemed International Movie Database Web site, IMDB, records Helena as the American premiere, but lists the United Kingdom as playing the movie one month before Helena. But other publications credit Helena with the "world premiere." Cooper, who was born in Helena in 1901, had died on May 13, 1961, about a month before the premiere.

Montana's "First Lady of Film" was born Myrna Williams, on August 2, 1905, in Radersburg, Montana, 40 miles southeast of Helena. She took the name Loy as a stage name in 1925. Loy's witty portrayal of Nora Charles in *The Thin Man* films of the 1930s and 1940s transformed her into an enduring screen legend. She created one of the most loved and timelessly entertaining characters in film history. In 1936, a poll of 20 million fans voted her "Queen of the Movies" and Clark Gable "King," and the two were subsequently teamed in a number of films.

Lane Chandler (1899-1972), Hollywood character actor, was born in Culbertson and made a career in low-budget Republic westerns during the 1930s and 1940s. Butte-born Jean Parker (1912-2005) became a leading lady in MGM productions from 1932 until the mid-1940s. Actress and singer Martha Raye (1916-1994) was born in a charity ward of a hospital in Butte where her parents, traveling vaudeville performers, found themselves stranded. Raye, who appeared in several patriotic musical comedies from the mid-1930s to the late 1940s, received a special Oscar from the motion picture academy in 1969 for her dedication to the nation. Butte's scandalous Mary MacLane's *Men Who Have Made Love to Me* book was transferred to the screen in 1917. The controversial author and feminist starred in the movie version but the full-length feature failed to generate much interest, and unfortunately, no copies are known to exist. Whitefish author Dorothy Johnson wrote *The Man Who Shot Liberty Valance*, John Ford's last great Western. It starred James Stewart as an Easterner who heads west to build a law practice. John Wayne is the veteran cowboy, and Lee Marvin is memorable as the ill-fated title character. Montana novelist A.B. Guthrie Jr. wrote the screenplay for *Shane*, considered a classic western.

A statue of William S. Hart, a silent film-era star—the "John Wayne of his day"—sits east of the Yellowstone County Museum, near the Billings Logan International Airport. Hart had come through Billings in 1926 for the 50th anniversary of the Battle of the Little Bighorn. He was very impressed with the city of Billings, liked the people and the view, and he commissioned and paid for the life-size statue of himself standing next to his favorite horse. It was dedicated July 4, 1926, during a three-day celebration.

Motion picture producer Jerry Molen, a close associate of Steven Spielberg, whose production credits include *The Color Purple* and *Schindler's List*, was born in Great Falls. Film director David Lynch, who achieved cult status with the lurid, voyeuristic *Blue Velvet*, was born in Missoula.

Other Montana-made movie connections include George Montgomery, Ian MacDonald, Patrick Duffy, Dirk Benedict, and Steve Reeves. Though he did not possess a Herculean acting capacity, Glasgow-born bodybuilder Steve Reeves (1926-2000) and his enviable Herculean physique were massive box-office draws in Italian gladiator films decades before anyone ever heard the name Arnold Schwarzenegger. Movie comedian Dana Carvey, famous for the 1992 hit film *Wayne's World*, was born in Missoula. In 2015, J.K. Simmons became the first University of Montana alumnus to win an Academy Award for acting. The 1978 music graduate won best supporting actor for his role in *Whiplash*.

Montana stakes a claim to the development of Native cinema, including the seminal *Powwow Highway*, a comic road movie about two Northern Cheyenne Indians who follow a vision of their spiritual heritage. When activist Buddy Red Bow's estranged sister is framed and jailed in New Mexico, the two men take his buddy Philbert Bono's rust-wrecked '64 Buick "war pony" on a road trip that makes some very unexpected stops along the way.

And, of course, the stars can't get enough of the Big Sky State. The glamorous have been flocking to it in droves since the late 1980s. Ted Turner and Jane Fonda once frolicked with the buffalo on his 127,000-acre spread near Bozeman; Jeff Bridges met his wife at Chico Hot Spring in the mid-1970s during filming of *Rancho Deluxe* and has been a resident for 40 years. When Bridges once exhibited his paintings in Livingston's Danforth Gallery, people drove as far as 125 miles to attend the opening. The curious crowd jammed the sweltering gallery, standing elbow-to-elbow, everywhere except within six feet of Bridges.

Two longtime Paradise Valley residents included Dennis Quaid (who filmed *Everything That Rises* there in 1989) and his then-wife, Meg Ryan, who cheered the pig wrestlers at the Park County Fair; Glenn Close, who first came to Montana for a part in *The Stone Boy*, rode around on a mule at her modest farmhouse outside Bozeman; and Michael Keaton still fly-fishes on the Boulder River, a Blue-Ribbon recreational trout fishery just a few steps from his door.

Montana is avant-garde because it is so decidedly behind the times in so many ways. What makes it different from the majority of celebrity hotspots is unassuming living, anonymity, and our residents' low susceptibility to trends and fads. "In Aspen, there are 100-odd restaurants. We have about three four-star restaurants, and they're miles apart. There's no social scene, no designer boutiques," said longtime resident Becky Fonda in 1991.

"It's a long way from the trade lanes and booming coasts, but it's wonderful place to live and work. Trouble is, everybody wants to claim it all at once," said author Thomas McGuane (*The Missouri Breaks, Rancho Deluxe*), who anticipated the trend by moving to the state in 1968.

Patrick Markey, producer of *A River Runs Through It* and *The Horse Whisperer*, and Livingston area resident, elaborated on the state's beauty. "There are places in the Rockies that are more postcard-beautiful," said Markey. "When you see them, it's very apparent why people would go there. Montana presents itself in a different way. Its beauty is actually deeper than that. There is such ruggedness to it and a humbling power to its beauty. You just have to be in it for a bit to understand." James Woods, a veteran of three made-in-Montana films, referred to Montana "as one of the most beautiful places on earth." Aerial coordinator Al Gerbino, who worked on *The Untouchables, Beethoven's 2nd*, and *Broken Arrow*, viewed Montanans as "caretakers of some of the most beautiful country in the world." Repeat business is nothing new in Montana—Charles B. Pierce chose Montana instead of his home state of Arkansas when he shot three pictures in a row here in the 1970s—*Winterhawk, Winds of Autumn*, and *Grayeagle*.

Montana's relationship with film has been sublime, serious and even outright silly. *Damnation Alley*, a picture about a machine called the "Landmaster" that moves across the United States after a nuclear war, among large cockroaches and scorpions, was shot on Flathead Lake in 1976. *Evel Knievel* retells the life story of Butte's famous motor cycle daredevil, with George Hamilton playing the role of Knievel. Steven Seagal's *The Patriot*—about a respected doctor who must race against time to find a cure for a lethal virus unleashed by a paramilitary militia leader—received threats from purported militia members. *Heaven's Gate*, filmed in and around Kalispell in the late 1970s, was a critical flop, yet at the same time it was a real boon to the community. Montana film commissioner Garry Wunderwald found it a mind-boggling experience to watch director Michael Cimino squander money—and the film company left approximately $19 million in Montana. But, ultimately, the experiences of the cast, the crew, the production teams, and the local communities have been overwhelming positive.

"But what I really like about [moviemaking] is that it hits every sector of the economy," said former Montana Film Commissioner Lonie Stimac, who took over as director of the Montana Film Office in 1990 after Garry Wunderwald's retirement and filled the position for 10 years. "The companies, they hire locksmiths, they need sanitation people to come out to their sites and clean up, they rent heavy equipment, they rent motel rooms and buildings. And it doesn't leave any damage or pollution it its wake. It's very environmentally friendly."

As testament to Montana's enduring presence, personality and power on screen, 2016 saw *The Revenant* secure a number of major film awards. In *The Revenant*, Leonardo DiCaprio's character, trapper Hugh Glass, endures a harsh winter in the pursuit of vengeance and redemption, and the frigid scene shot at Kootenai Falls sets the stage for the drama that unfolds.

Josh Cooke (left) and Jamie King film a scene east of Livingston for the dark comedy-crime caper *A Fork in the Road*.

A Fork in the Road

CAST
Jaime King, Josh Cooke

DIRECTOR
Jim Kouf

LOCATION
Laurel, Bozeman, and Livingston areas

2008

Director Jim Kouf, who lives in the Bitterroot Valley, co-wrote the script for this dark caper-comedy. Co-written by Kouf and Alan DiFiore, the tale touches on the many forks in the road of life and the consequences of selecting a path. In *A Fork in the Road*, an escaped convict and a young woman beset with relationship troubles try to run from their problems and bounce from one mishap to the next, while always intending to do the right thing. The duo meets several nasty characters along the way, yet manages to elude disaster. While *A Fork in the Road* is an enjoyable but formulaic action comedy, the Montana scenery was undeniably gorgeous.

"I think the movie came to market just as the economy tanked," said Jim Kouf recently. "It was as bad of a time to come to market as you could imagine. That's the risk you take. But the film still has a life of its own."

Bobby Brooks of Laurel was the special effects supervisor on the movie. Brooks exploded a vehicle as part of a staged car accident near Silesia. He wired the car that was placed at the bottom of the cliff with a couple of firecrackers made with black powder and fast-burning flash powder to explode the car's gas tank.

"On a low budget film like this project, you get just one chance," said Brooks. "One car. One explosion. One take. There is no second take." He speculated that a similar explosion would cost $20,000 to $30,000 in Hollywood. "We did it for hard costs of about $1,200 for the car and the explosives, plus my day rate, as special effects supervisor."

The film was shot entirely in Montana, primarily in Bozeman, Laurel, and the Paradise Valley.

"We shot it in about 19 days. [For] *Disorganized Crime* (which Kouf wrote, directed and filmed in the Bitterroot Valley years earlier) we had about a 50-day shoot."

Produced for $1.4 million, *A Fork in the Road* looks like a mature Hollywood production. Kouf and cinematographer Claudio Rocha stretched their tiny budget so that the production looks big, effectively camouflaging its small cost. Dennis Virkler, a twice–Oscar-nominated editor, cut the film for the screen.

The story finds a convict escaping from custody and setting off on foot to hide in Paradise Valley. He teams up with a lady who just might have killed somebody, and the two of them try to keep one step ahead of the cops. The story is played for broad laughs, more than for drama. A two-timing husband and a sleazy businessman provide many chuckles—as does the odd-couple relationship between Will and April.

Jaime King is memorable as April, an unhappy wife with an abusive husband. King provides the pathos that keeps us caring about the tale. *A Fork in the Road* is a very simple, clean, funny film, designed to entertain a general audience without special effects, bad language or bedroom trysts.

"They don't make films like this anymore," said Kouf. "All of the film is character-driven, and it's hard to do character stuff in a big outdoor setting on that kind of budget. The scenery is beautiful. We were out shooting cliffs out in Laurel and at a beautiful ranch in Paradise Valley. The movie was designed around the seven main cast members, with very few outside parts."

Several local non-actors found parts, including Helena National Guard officer Captain Tony Lecce, who was cast in the role of a highway patrolman in the film.

A Fork in the Road failed to earn a theatrical run and headed straight to DVD. At the film's world premiere at the Myrna Loy Center in Helena, Governor Brian Sch-

weitzer introduced the film, which had been encouraged and supported by the Montana Film Office. Writer/director Jim Kouf thanked everyone for the opportunity to make a film in Montana. "It was a pleasure to work in Montana," he said. "We plan to do more, if we can. Even if you don't like the story, we know you'll like the scenery."

Featuring Henry Winkler, *A Plumm Summer* was the fictionalized tale of a real "kidnapping" that took place in Billings: the victim was a TV puppet named Froggy Doo.

A Plumm Summer

Cast
Jeff Daniels, William Baldwin, Henry Winkler, Chris Massoglia

Director
Caroline Zelder

Location
Bozeman and Livingston areas

2007

The screenplay, written by Montana native Caroline Zelder, is based on a real-life children's television show broadcast from Billings in the 1960s. Based on a true story, this adventure drama follows Elliot Plumm (Chris Massoglia), a teenage boy neglected by his alcoholic, amateur-boxing champ father (William Baldwin), who, along with his girlfriend and younger brother, tracks down a marionette stolen from a popular local children's television show.

A Plumm Summer is the fictionalized tale of a real "kidnapping" that took place in Billings: the victim was a TV puppet named Froggy Doo on *The Happy Herb and Froggy Doo Show*, a popular regional children's TV show that premiered on the small screen in Great Falls (KFBB-TV) in 1955 and moved to Billings (KULR-TV) in 1963. The actual 'frog-napping' case took place in Billings in 1966.

Henry Winkler, who gained fame as Arthur Fonzarelli (the "Fonz") on television's *Happy Days* in the 1970s, played the role of "Happy Herb" McAllister (and the froggy voice of Froggy Doo) in the film. The independently financed film, a production of Fairplay Movies of Beverly Hills, had a small budget of $4.2 million, but Winkler predicted that the appeal would be large when the movie hit the big screen in 2007. (He was off the mark; the film grossed approximately $53,000 and was shelved after a meager opening weekend.)

Winkler said that after being approached to play the part of Happy Herb, and watching a DVD of the original show, "I realized that this was going to be a great character to play, and a wonderfully delightful project." The movie tells the story of two young brothers on the hunt for Froggy Doo after his kidnapping. The marionette was stolen from the television studio, and the thieves, who were never caught, actually demanded $150 for Froggy Doo's return via a ransom note, which caused the FBI to investigate the case. The decapitated body of Froggy Doo was found hanging on a fencepost two days after his kidnapping, and his head was recovered a month later. Though the brothers and their search in *A Plumm Summer* is fictional, two children did see Froggy Doo's head in the back of a car, which led to its recovery.

"It is certainly not the way it went down in real life," said Winkler of the movie script, "but it was inspired by the real facts…I think it is a funny, emotional, compelling family film. It's got some bite to it." Winkler also said he was impressed with the cast and crew.

"Our director [Caroline Zelder] is a first-time director…she had done a short [film] before, but this is her first feature film, and you would never know it," he said. "She knows exactly what she wants, which is very important if you're going to direct a film…she is really good with her actors, and wonderful with the crew. As an actor, I feel very well taken care of."

Happy Herb's relationship with his wife "is torn apart by Happy Herb's devotion to Froggy Doo," said Winkler. The production of *A Plumm Summer* occurred in southwest Montana (including Bozeman and Livingston). Livingston is surrounded by three mountain ranges, and the Yellowstone River—world famous for its blue-ribbon trout fishing—borders its southern city limits. Yellowstone National Park is only 56 miles away.

Bozeman casting director Tina Buckingham said that Montanans made up about 60 percent of the crew, with Big Sky talent representing about 40 percent of the cast. She said that approximately 650 people took part in the production. "These people [the producers and directors] are so nice, with such kindness, integrity and love of film in Montana," Buckingham said. "They really want to help the state get on board for better [film production] incentives."

Winker recalled that at the time of filming several movies with a Montana setting had shifted north to Canada and that the Montana legislature had been slow to pass a competitive film tax incentive package. Though Winkler said he was ambivalent when it came to turning Montana into a thriving film base, saying that "in a way I hope it doesn't, in a way I hope it does.

"It is so gentle and still here…so comfortable," said Winkler, who has been coming to Montana to enjoy his favorite pastime, fly-fishing, since the mid-1990s. "Fly-fishing is like a washing machine for your brain."

During the filming, Winkler took time out to visit with local children. Winkler, who is dyslexic, collaborates on children's books and decided to spend an afternoon sharing his latest work with children at the Bozeman Barnes & Noble.

Director Caroline Zelder said that Montana's scenery, weather and crew base were hard to beat. When the Derby Fire, which burned more than 208,000 acres in south-central and southwest Montana, left dozens of families homeless, Zelder and producer Frank Antonelli donated approximately $5,000 worth of clothes and toys to those impacted and displaced.

"For every shot you see on film, 4 feet away from there are 90 people who have been working 16 hours for days," said Antonelli.

"It has an epic look to it at times," said Zelder of the landscape captured on film. "No one's going to believe this movie was made for what it was made for because it looks so big with the big sky. I wanted to capture the freedom of childhood, which today is really difficult in the cities."

Governor Brian Schweitzer made his silver screen debut playing the role of Sheriff Strunk. "*A Plumm Summer* is a priceless Montana story," said Schweitzer. "I'm honored to be a part of this production and extremely excited to have this film open in theatres across the state."

Despite its dismal showing at the box office and icy reception among critics and audiences, Winkler later said he still has no doubt *A Plumm Summer* belonged on the big screen. "The movie is beautiful and tender and relatable—a wonderful adventure—it's just great characters and a great story and the story is true."

A River Runs Through It

CAST
Brad Pitt, Craig Sheffer, Tom Skerritt

DIRECTOR
Robert Redford

LOCATION
Livingston, Paradise Valley,
Bozeman area–Gallatin Canyon

1992

Movies are usually conceived over a four-figure lunch in Beverly Hills or in the chrome-and-glass boardroom of some multinational corporation. *A River Runs Through It*, Robert Redford's film adaptation of Norman Maclean's novella, was hatched during an argument somewhere near Livingston, Montana, in the early 1980s.

Writer and rancher Tom McGuane was engaged in a game of one-upmanship with Redford. The subject of their verbal joust: the West and the writers who best represent it. "I accused Tom of being a carpetbagger," said Redford to the *Chicago Tribune* in 1992. "I said he was really a Michigan writer who spent time in Florida, fell in love with Hemingway, and then moved to Montana. A.B. Guthrie, Wallace Stegner—I consider them western writers. And I told McGuane I don't think much of Hemingway."

McGuane recalled first introducing Redford to the novel. "It was an accident," he said. "Redford was visiting me and we were talking about western books we liked. He hadn't heard of Norman Maclean's book, which I considered to be the best book ever written about the West, so I gave him a copy and the rest is history."

Norman Maclean was 73 when he sat down to write his first book, a memoir of his family in Montana in the 1920s. He had taught at the University of Chicago from 1928 until 1973, retiring as the William Rainey Harper Professor of English. In 1976 *A River Runs Through It and Other Stories* won the Pulitzer Prize for best fiction.

The book is a deeply personal but fictionalized story about Maclean's father, a Scottish Presbyterian minister, and Maclean's brother, an incomparably strong and graceful fisherman who was drawn to gambling, drink, and violence. What's most memorable is that the brothers share a love of fly fishing. A river, the sound of water flowing over rocks, an old man's hands tying a fly to his line, and the movie's evocative narration changed Montana forever.

Richard Friedenberg adapted the novella to the screen. Friedenberg said that one of the problems with writing a screenplay from the essentially autobiographical story was that of the 104 pages, 52 were written about fly fishing. "Norman wrote a short story very beautifully," said Friedenberg. "The odds against [making a movie] were tremendous, but Bob [Redford] wanted to do it."

Redford was aware that many people considered the book a classic—one perhaps best left untouched by Hollywood. And there were people in the film industry who derisively called the project "Redford's fly-fishing movie."

Redford said he was no judge of what audiences want to see and was motivated solely by what interested him on a personal level. He mitigated the gamble by promising his backers to keep the budget under $10 million,

Director Robert Redford explains a scene to stars Brad Pitt (left) and Craig Sheffer (center). *A River Runs Through It* became an iconic image of Montana.

low compared to most budgets then averaging double that figure.

The challenge in adapting *A River Runs Through It* was its lack of plot. The novella is a series of memories, and, in the words of one reviewer, an "uncanny blending of fly fishing with the affections of the heart." Most of all, it is a tribute to a dead brother, and a lament—five decades after the fact—that no one in the family could help him. In the early morning hours of May 3, 1938, Maclean's brother Paul was found beaten to death in an alley, the bones in his right hand—his punching hand—fractured, his skull crushed by a gun butt. In making his film, Redford said he avoided dwelling on the story's violent aspects.

"The book was a love poem to Norman's family," said Redford in the *New York Times*. "They were a deeply loving family, but the members didn't understand each other. Their lives went into that dark area when the questions become: How does one ask for help? How does one give help? What part of oneself does one give? All these questions are rolled into the big question of love and helping and understanding one another. Those are the questions that interested me."

Redford believed he had found a way to crack the narrative puzzle of translating *A River Runs Through It* into a movie. Screenwriter Friedenberg said he compressed the story into a shorter time period to expose the dark side of Paul that "led him astray and was ultimately very deadly." Through interviews with Maclean, and by reading letters the author wrote 60 years ago to the woman he married, Redford added details from the Macleans' lives that are not in the book. Redford also used narration to keep the author's voice—an integral ingredient—in the film.

The story's similarity with his own Scots-Irish heritage also attracted Redford. "My father, while full of good humor, could be strict and stern, uncompromising and stubborn. If you did the wrong thing, silence was often your punishment," Redford said. "This book was a part of my life before I even read it. Lots of its elements were

In *A River Runs Through It*, Brad Pitt played Paul Maclean, a hard-living newspaperman and a superb fly fisherman. When clients ask fly-fishing guides to take them where the film was made, the guides take them past "Brad Pitt Rock" on the Gallatin River from which the actor made a memorable cast.

of interest to me: time, memory, love, understanding, bonding, the role of nature and how it shapes our lives."

Actor Tom Skerritt, Maclean's Presbyterian minister father in the film, saw his own father in the part, a man who loved his children but could never show them that love openly and freely. The reverend had to look to Montana's fishing holes to find the words he was unable to express, hidden beneath the rocks of the moving waters. Years later Skerritt said his father, like the one he played in the movie, "was from Canada and was from about the same generation. And he had that same Anglo-Saxon stiffness and unwillingness to display affection. I cannot remember my father ever being affectionate except for giving me a half dollar once and patting me on the knee when we were driving in the car. But he never gave me a hug and I never heard him say, 'I love you.' But I knew he loved me."

Redford told the *Denver Post* he also made *A River Runs Through It* for what it had to say about the van-

ishing, pristine West, a subject on Redford's political agenda. "It's not the essential reason, but there's a connection," he said. (For 20 years, Redford had waged war with Utah Department of Transportation over its plans to widen and straighten the road through Provo Canyon near his Sundance home, ski resort and film center.) Redford said he did not make the film as an overt political or environmental statement but hoped it would provide audiences a glimpse of, and an appreciation for, Montana's rivers before they were muddied by development and clear-cut logging. The Blackfoot River, for example, the river revered by Maclean in his book, was rejected to portray itself in the movie in part because of pollution and surrounding development.

The first obstacle in making the film was Maclean, a man skeptical of Hollywood and actors. He had already rejected William Hurt when the Oscar-winning actor arranged to meet Maclean for a day of fishing and showed up with an entourage but no fishing license. "He was a short, wiry, tough, cantankerous old man," Redford said of the author to the *Washington Post*. "He was reminiscent of some of the people I first met when I came to Utah. Some of the sheepherders I met up here were the same way: wily and wise; they threw out a bit of a bluff, a screen of bull…and provinciality. The only thing he asked is that I not screw up his story."

Redford visited Maclean several times to build a relationship of trust. Redford and Maclean went fishing together and exchanged letters. "To tell you the truth, I'm scared to death of Redford," said Maclean at age 84, shortly before his death in 1990. "Nobody ever changed a story as much as he did in *The Natural*. It's a travesty of the quest for the Holy Grail, as [Bernard] Malamud wrote it. The Holy Grail is nowhere and so are our dreams."

"I respected his ambivalence [about making the film] because after all, it took Norman 40 years to write it and he wanted the last say," Redford said, so he set about constructing a relationship with the old Montanan. The two talked about Montana in those halcyon days, and the people who lived them. "He told me wonderful anecdotes about going to Dartmouth College and how that proved to him that the world was full of bastards the farther you got away from Missoula. He had a real Western, frontier attitude, and didn't have much use for uppity Easterners, people with their noses perched too high."

At the end of their talks, Maclean was still leery. "He'd say, 'Hollywood is nothing but the old grease and weasel. The grease is when someone is shaking your hand, making an agreement. The weasel is when they weasel out of it.'" Redford recalled what Maclean said next: "There are two reasons I agreed to talk to you, *Jeremiah Johnson*, which tells me you know something about the West, and *Ordinary People*, which tells me you know something about families. Frankly, that's your big leg up with me, but no guarantees."

The director and the writer eventually cut a deal: Redford would commission a script and Maclean could reject it. But if Maclean approved it, he was to step aside and let Redford make his movie with no interference. Maclean watched the first process of the draft being made and once he was satisfied with Redford's vision, he stepped aside.

"Redford made two promises to Norman," said Joel Snyder, Maclean's son-in-law. "One was to be true to fly fishing, and the other was that he would not take liberties

Robert Redford poses with Colorado octogenarian Everett Rohrer (right), who supplied the 1907 Baldwin locomotive for the scene of young Norman Maclean departing for college. The same locomotive has been used in more than 30 films, including Montana productions *Heaven's Gate* and *Far and Away*.

with the portrayal of his brother. He would not degrade him and would not display his death."

"This film was not trying to be a Montana picture book," said Oscar-winning cinematographer and director of photography for the picture Philippe Rousselot. "Not because we don't like it. But because it has been done before. It is a much more intimate story between two brothers. The goal of this film is not to bring more tourists to the rivers of Montana, and it's not telling people you should fish. But it's telling something about the relationship between brothers and members of the same family."

Rousselot did find "the quality of light in Montana is wonderful. The geography seems to be alive and constantly changing its rhythm as the sun reaches across the big sky. *A River Runs Through It* is about beauty and grace and I found the right spirit to create the atmosphere I needed in this beautiful part of the United States."

Redford scouted Missoula for a few days in mid-March 1990, once turning up at Worden's Market for lunch. "We wanted Missoula to play Missoula," said production manager Allen Alsobrook, "but, unfortunately, it's gotten so modern it would've been an impossible task to make it 1911."

"Missoula's been through cyclical booms, which are great for the economy but murder on filmmakers," said Patrick Markey. "To rebuild a downtown for a period piece is very expensive. Livingston hasn't been through those cycles, and we had the Gallatin, Yellowstone and Boulder rivers to choose from for the fishing scenes."

Shots of the Upper Yellowstone and Gallatin rivers were used for many river scenes. The trout used in the film were pond-raised in Montana and, according to the movie company's official press release, "were kept in a specially aerated and cooled tank truck until their big moment in front of the camera." No hooks were used, and no blood was drawn. A line was tied to each fish's lower jaw "under the careful observance of the Montana Humane Society."

None of the actors had ever fly fished before making the movie. Filmmakers announced that anybody who had anything to offer in terms of improving their fly-fishing knowledge or skills should come on over. The fly-fishing company Orvis sent a truckload of gear for casting practice. A man from Hamilton drove to the set to lend the crew a mechanical fish that could jump out of water and look like a real fish fighting a line.

The production crew also asked John Bailey, proprietor of the famous Dan Bailey's Fly Shop in Livingston, to serve as its fly-fishing consultant. Bailey spent 10 days fishing with Brad Pitt and Craig Sheffer, who played the brother Norman in the movie. He also stood by during filming to make sure the fly fishing looked authentic and correct. At one point after seeing the outcome of the day's fly-fishing shots, Bailey said he and a friend decided they would have to take their names off the film because "the fly fishing looked horrible." Afterward Redford walked up to Bailey and said, "That was awful." They reshot all the scenes.

Markey knew they needed to make the fly-fishing scenes look authentic or the film would immediately lose its audience. Once the scenes looked good enough, he could begin to establish the human characters. "Most people think this is a movie about fly fishing," he said. "But it's not. It's a movie about family."

At one point the filmmakers held a tryout for local fly-fishing doubles. Dozens of people turned out. None got a part except for an old man who played the elderly Norman at the beginning and end of the movie. "He came out of nowhere," Markey said. "That guy had done it all. He had a heartbreaking face." He had just the elegance needed for the movie.

Livingston was transformed into a town of fake storefronts constructed over Callender Street. Paved roads were covered with gravel. Horses and buggies replaced vehicles. Livingston mothers with day jobs dressed up as 1920s prostitutes and solicited customers while leaning over a balcony. Livingston's Vann Gravage, age 6, landed a speaking part in the film as the young Paul Maclean. He said every kid in town tried out for the part.

Inside the Livingston Civic Center, a set was constructed to be a replica of the inside of a house in the Bridger Canyon area north of Bozeman. To allow for more flexibility, the house interior scenes were shot at the Civic Center while the real house was used for outdoor scenes.

There were four "period" costume changes needed, for the years 1912, 1919, 1927, and 1938. Craig Sheffer had about 55 costume changes, and Pitt had about 30. Five of Sheffer's 55 changes included four sets of identical costumes to ensure dry clothes were available after wet fishing scenes. About 100 costumes were used for the picnic scene, 50 for the train scene, and another 50 for the church scene. Since the church was filmed in all four periods, 50 costumes for each period were needed.

"The pavilion scene is the dance where young Norman Maclean meets Jessie—the woman who is going to become his wife," said production designer Jon Hutman. "And for me, in his memory, that would really be the most beautiful and magical thing in the movie. Very pure. Very beautiful. Those simple, open air pavilions existed all over the country in this period of time. I think they are incredibly evocative of that time.

"The design of the pavilion [in the movie] is based on one from an amusement park that existed in Butte until 1972. I had a guy come up to me at the set who was one of the firefighters there or something like that, and he said, 'Yeah, I grew up in Anaconda. How did you think of this [the pavilion]?' I said, 'It's loosely based on Columbia Gardens.' He said, 'I knew it. I went there and did dances at that pavilion as a kid. You know, you've struck a chord.'"

Carpenters and prop people used false store fronts to remake one of Livingston's streets into a replica of 1920s Missoula. A bookstore, a hardware store, and a tobacco store were stocked with magazines, antique fishing creels, pots and pans, and tobacco tins. Wooden sidewalks were laid and antique light standards put up. Striped awnings shaded the sidewalk. Antique autos were parked on the street. Behind the false fronts, though, life in the 1990s went on as usual. Inside a sign shop was the Fireball Athletic Club. Behind the 1920s bookstore façade Maverick Realty sold homes and land. A hazardous waste firm looked like it peddled hardware out front. The Mint Bar's card room was switched over to general merchandise. Women hired as extras were dressed in the lace and linen finery worn by bawdy house girls of the day. Earlyn Sherwood of Emigrant recalled being wrapped up in a saucy robe, bloomers, and a tightly-laced corset. "Fun but sweaty," remembered Sherwood. "I got claustrophobia."

Christine Schuman, who worked as an off-set tailor and seamstress in a shop in downtown Livingston recalled a memorable exchange with Australian actress Brenda Blethlyn, who played Mrs. Maclean. "She came in and sat down and she asked me to talk about anything, because she wanted to get the Montana accent down," said Schuman. "She said I was the only person in the office or group who spoke like a Montanan, and I guess she got her accent from listening to me talk. She came in two or three different times to get the accent down and to ask me about different things."

Tracy Mayfield, of Red Lodge, met Redford in a lunch line, chatted with him momentarily and was called back to be a stand-in. "Redford rewrote a scene during lunch and they needed more people in a bar scene," said Mayfield. "I was picked to play a bouncer in a doorway during a poker game. My six words were 'Paul'—I nod at Paul—'not a good idea, Paul.' I spent the rest of the afternoon in a fight scene getting pushed into the wall. I got paid $448 for those six words."

Another Montana actor who landed a speaking part was the Reverend Bob Holmes of Helena who, at the time, was semi-retired but still active as a chaplain for the Lewis and Clark County Sheriff's Department and the Helena Police Department. Holmes played a Helena newspaper editor. "I have a lot of respect for Redford and his films," said the sixth-generation Methodist preacher. "They tend to be about values."

Colorado octogenarian Everett Rohrer supplied the 1907 Baldwin locomotive used in the movie. Rohrer and his son-in-law John Pickar moved the train a couple of hundred feet several times as the film crew repeatedly shot a scene of young Maclean departing for college while his brother saw him off. (The old Northern Pacific depot in Bozeman was adorned with signs renaming it the Missoula Northern Pacific station.) In another scene, Rohrer's locomotive chugged up Bozeman Pass. The train engineer supplied the same locomotive for more than 30 other films, including Montana productions *Heaven's Gate* and *Far and Away*.

The human saga plus the fly fishing produced what Montana film commissioner Sten Iversen called "a stunning love affair with the state. It had an almost lyrical quality as it showed the real West in its natural beauty. People wanted a piece of it. That picture made us almost iconic."

A River Runs Through It earned an Academy Award for best cinematography, and the beauty of the film has attracted visitors to the state from all over the world. A 2006 University of Montana study found state tourism exploded from 2 million visitors in 1988 to 10 million in 2005.

Justin King, owner of Montana Troutfitters in Bozeman, described how the film changed the area: "From a retail shop point of view, it was a great thing for business. From the viewpoint of being a local kid that grew up on the river, it went from being able to find anyplace to fish by yourself to having to get up early and get out there before everyone else." When customers ask to fish where the film was made, guides take them past "Brad Pitt Rock" on the Gallatin River, from which the actor cast in the movie.

Perhaps most importantly, the film drew attention to the state's blighted rivers. "Norman's fishery [the Blackfoot River] had gone through tough times," said Markey. "Now it's a viable fishery again. The film was maybe the impetus to get that done."

Some opine that the film contributed to a crowding of Montana's remote and special rivers and an influx of "outsiders." "Some people say we had a hand in ruining Montana," Markey said. "Growth scares everyone. It's good for many, though."

Maclean passed away in 1990 without seeing the film. He probably would've been ambivalent, daughter Jean Maclean Snyder said. Jean, an attorney, described the movie as masterful and appreciated Redford's work. "A lot of what I liked was the very artful job they did of casting people and of the way in which the country was used. It looked so beautiful," she said.

Son John Maclean, an author and fly fisherman, said *A River Runs Through It* "was the most enticing fly-fishing movie ever made. In the first year after it came out, the fly-fishing industry grew by 60 percent, and the following year by another 60 percent." He said that, among anglers, "the book is the Bible and the movie is what did it."

Still, Redford told *Newsweek* in 2012 that he was ambivalent that Maclean didn't live to see it. "Part of me is sorry he couldn't have the experience, the satisfaction, assuming I did a good job," said Redford. "On the other hand, it might never be a good job as far as he's concerned. You seldom satisfy a writer who has given up a book for a film. There are things he wrote that aren't there. There's going to be a different face on a character. It drives writers crazy, because they see the book being taken away from them."

All the Young Men

CAST
Alan Ladd, Sidney Poitier, Mort Sahl

DIRECTOR
Hall Bartlett

LOCATION
Glacier National Park

1960

Glacier National Park substituted for Korea in *All the Young Men*, a drama about racism set in the Korean War.

"Racial integration in the United States Marines is sluggishly celebrated in a variation on a well-used Western plot in the picture that opened at the Forum yesterday," began the review of Hall Bartlett's *All the Young Men* in the *Denver Post*.

Filmed in and around Glacier National Park and Fort Hood, Oregon, the meagerly plotted film follows the career of Sidney Poitier, a black sergeant put in command of a small detachment of Marines caught in an exposed position during the fighting in Korea in 1951. The war story depicts 13 young Marines cut off from their unit and holding a road until the main body of troops can come up.

Filming got off to an inauspicious start: Because of a lodging shortage at Glacier National Park, director Hall Bartlett had as many of the "Marines" as possible killed in the first scenes and sent back to Hollywood.

From there, all the clichés are worked into the story by Bartlett, who wrote, directed and produced it. The sergeant is at first nervous and indecisive. He is subject to the sneers and obstructions of a busted "topkick" played by Alan Ladd. He is also the temporary victim of a Southern bigot. Other fellows in the outfit are reflective of various standard attitudes. There's the mild, sentimental youngster who likes everybody, white or black. There's the good-natured Swede (world heavyweight boxing champion Ingemar Johansson, making his debut as a Swedish soldier whose ship has been sunk) who loves the United States as the land of the free. There's the American Indian who sympathizes with the sergeant as a member of a subordinated race. And there's the guy from the city streets who makes the wisecracks. Ethnic accuracy was not part of the attention to detail. Bartlett cast his wife, Ana. St. Clair, as a Korean woman, Mario Alcalde as an American Indian, and Blackfeet Indians as North Korean soldiers.

There are also several others representing a familiar range of musty war movie clichés: apple pie, sweethearts, death, communism and longing for home. Inevitably, they all stand tough together through a couple of perilous nights and days, yammering, fighting off enemy attacks, and giggling at night-club routines. Ultimately, Ladd is wounded and requires a quick transfusion of blood. Poitier supplies the transfusion and everyone is perfectly bonded.

The potpourri of actors, jokers (comedian Mort Sahl made his motion picture debut), boxers, and crooners assembled in Hollywood in early October 1959. By mid-month, they descended upon Glacier National Park in northwestern Montana. The bone-chilling location, near Canada and 6,000 feet above sea level, marked Bartlett's attempt to replicate the American invasion into mountainous North Korea. Clad in parkas and heavy boots, they moved from one arctic locale to another, ending up in Timberline, Oregon. Other than the Swede Johansson, they all hated the cold. During one scene, as the unit ran across an icy expanse, Sahl fainted. Weather on Logan Pass frustrated the film crew, which lost several days due to fog, snow and biting wind. "We need a good snow and then clear skies," Columbia's publicity agent Bob Fender told the Kalispell *Daily Inter Lake*. "Snow alone can't help us because we can't shoot unless we have the clear weather to go with it." War correspondent Quentin Reynolds was at St. Mary's writing a trailer for the movie. The author suffered from a virus during his visit, but still said he found Glacier "fascinating." Shelby mayor Dr. Stephen Adaskavich presented boxing champion Johansson with a copper key to the city of Shelby in St. Mary's on Tuesday, October 20, 1959. As the daily work progressed on filming the movie, films of each day's shootings, called "dailies" or "rushes" were sent to Hollywood. A driver took the film to Great Falls where it was put aboard an airplane. When it arrived in Hollywood the film was developed and critiqued, enabling the crew to get a report every day on the quality of the film they'd shot.

Ultimately, neither Ladd nor Poitier could have saved a script of "war film banalities and stale racial melodrama." A reviewer for the *Los Angeles Times* neatly summed up the thin, egalitarian plot: "Through it all, Mr. Poitier struggles with commendable patience and dignity, bearing the black man's burden of well-intended but specious patronage. Finally, reinforcements break through and racial integration is saved. We don't think anyone in the audience can welcome it more than does Mr. Poitier."

Columbia Pictures created two separate advertising campaigns: one for whites, one for blacks. The poster for black theaters touted Poitier's rejection of white authority as the main theme. It pictured Poitier seizing Ladd by the collar. "Spit out what's on your filthy little mind," it read, assigning Poitier a line that does not exist in the film, "and then take your orders from me!"

Almost Heroes

DIRECTOR
Christopher Guest

CAST
Chris Farley, Matthew Perry

LOCATION
Missouri River

1996

In 2003, comedian Chris Farley died from a drug overdose at age 33. Boisterous on the big screen, notoriously wild away from it, he left behind a legacy of both comedy and crisis. Farley's routine—repeated in five seasons of *Saturday Night Live* and three No. 1 films was as straightforward as it was stereotypical. He was presented to the world as overweight, obnoxious, obtuse, sweaty, and wasted. These tragicomic depictions are forever enshrined in the colorful annals of American television and film comedy.

Farley's seemingly one-dimensional life was in reality an inordinately complex pathology. Farley's family and friends struggled with his self-destructive vices: they were unsuccessful when it came to stopping the drug habit and reckless lifestyle that sent him to an early grave. Farley came from an affluent, Irish-Catholic upbringing in the village of Maple Bluff, Wisconsin, and his improvisational routines and comedic stints in Chicago and five years on *Saturday Night Live* led to his ascent as a film star. *Almost Heroes* is notable as a swan song to Chris Farley. While several of the film's comedic attempts are memorable, others, as one reviewer commented "only fall flat as insipidly inane and gross."

Almost Heroes pairs Farley with Matthew Perry (then on TV's *Friends*) as Bartholomew Hunt and Leslie Edwards, two would-be explorers trying to beat the Lewis and Clark expedition through the uncharted American West. In this silly twist of revisionism, Lewis and Clark were not the first to reach the Pacific Ocean—it was Hunt and Edwards.

The pair are the classic Laurel and Hardy combination. Edwards is a serious, cultured, foppish socialite

A spoof of the Lewis and Clark Expedition, *Almost Heroes* is notable as the final film for comedian Chris Farley, who died of a drug overdose at age 33.

looking for success; Hunt is a rugged, wizened, light-hearted alcoholic who knows his way around the back country. Throughout the film, one of them comes to the rescue of the other. In one instance, Hunt attempts to retrieve an egg from the nest of a psychotic eagle to save Edwards' life. Even though these heroic acts do not always go smoothly, Edwards and Hunt ultimately realize that they make a great team.

Along the Missouri River, they pick up a rag-tag bunch of recruits to help them in their quest to overtake Lewis and Clark's entourage. Among them is Guy Fontenot (Eugene Levy), a Frenchman with a penchant for biting off people's ears, and the one-named Bidwell (David Packer), a hard-luck fellow who loses a leg to a savage bear and an ear to Fontenot's razor-sharp teeth.

As crazy as this seems, *Almost Heroes* actually manages to push the limits of comedy even further. As noted in the *Denver Post*: "Some of the gags are laden with bath-room and sexual humor that isn't appropriate in this particular movie. For example, one of the adventurers tells a story about how he had eaten two pieces of sheep dung in his stew. Postcolonial America may not strike the history student as very comical and entertaining, but *Almost Heroes* almost pulls off this feat, especially for the benefit of Chris Farley fans."

Another review said, "Given his reputation for making almost nothing but dumbbell, Z-grade comedies, it would have been a lovely gesture to say something nice about the late comedian's final starring role. Unfortunately, that would require the majority of film critics around the country to either say nothing about it or lie. In fact, this laughless farce could be the absolute nadir of Farley's career."

Neither Farley nor any of the other actors actually set foot in Montana.

"*Almost Heroes* was a second unit Montana film," said Sten Iversen. "Second units do not include actors and use fake plate shots. *Almost Heroes* was different from *Forest Gump*, which was a full-on movie set. *Almost Heroes* had no set or crew, very minor. The second unit flew to the Missouri River to use it as a backdrop. The white cliffs of the Missouri River are not very accessible and are really remote, accessible [only] by boat. So they shot the Missouri River backdrop aerially, and used low-production green screen or CGI [Computer-Generated Imagery]."

Always

CAST
Richard Dreyfuss, Holly Hunter, John Goodman

DIRECTOR
Steven Spielberg

LOCATION
Libby area

1989

The Libby airport was transformed into a base for forest-fire retardant bombers and their crews in *Always*.

Montana Film Commissioner Garry Wunderwald received a call from Steven Spielberg. He needed an airport. "Out of 300 airports, Spielberg picked a Montana one," said Wunderwald. The Libby airport, which offered a spacious 5,000-foot runway surrounded by the Cabinet Mountains, was the one Spielberg chose. Libby's 2,000-foot elevation and the scenic background convinced him it fit the movie's needs. He visited Libby and examined the airport as well as Bull Lake, where other scenes would be filmed.

The man who gave audiences *E.T.* and *Close Encounters of the Third Kind* and numerous other big-screen extravaganzas started work on *Always*, a story about forest fires, a pilot and his girlfriend, in Libby in late May 1989. The film is a loosely updated version of a WWII movie entitled *A Guy Named Joe*, with the story line changed to focus on aerial firefighting pilots instead of bomber pilots. (The 1944 film starred Van Johnson, Spencer Tracy and Irene Dunn.) Richard Dreyfuss stars as Pete Sandich, a daredevil aerial firefighter pilot who loses his

life after taking one risk too many. With the assistance of spiritual guide Hap (Audrey Hepburn in her final screen appearance), Pete becomes a guardian angel to novice pilot Ted Baker. At the same time, Pete must also help the girl he left behind, Dorinda (Holly Hunter), move past her grief.

Spielberg, however, didn't like to refer to *Always* as a remake. "I think the film owes a great inspiration to...*A Guy Named Joe*," said Spielberg in a 1989 interview. "But it's not really a remake. It was the basis for a new story." In fact, *A Guy Named Joe* had been one of Spielberg's favorite movies since he was a child. He often publicly remarked that *Joe* was one of only two films that had actually moved him to tears (the other was *Bambi* in 1942). As a boy, Spielberg related to Pete's presence as an invisible force while he watched powerlessly as his parents' marriage fell apart. Spielberg had flirted with the idea of a remake for years.

The first draft of the *Always* script was written in 1980. "I had a lot of false starts," said Spielberg in 1989,

Montana governor Stan Stephens listens to *Always* director Steven
Spielberg on the set near Libby.

life after we depart. That we have a chance to come back
and help other people not to make the same mistakes we
made. To express themselves when they couldn't; to say
the things they're always afraid to say."

The Libby airport featured large sets re-creating a fire-
dispatch center, a control tower and the like. "Once they
liked the airport, that was a big plus," said Wunderwald.
"They scouted the Lincoln airport but the roadway wasn't
long enough to take planes." Libby was chosen over Lincoln and Benchmark, a ranger station on the east side
of the Bob Marshall Wilderness, because of its altitude.
Always needed a paved runway surrounded by trees. All
three fit the bill, but repeated landings and take-offs in
summer conditions would be safest in low-lying Libby.
"It also helped that Libby doesn't have much commercial
flight service," said Peg Crist, who worked with Idaho's
commerce department in Boise. "That was another key
factor in their decision, an airport that didn't give them
schedule problems to work around."

A crew of approximately 180 descended on the town
May 22, 1989, and the shooting finished in early July.
The remake had a budget of $20 million. Some of the
townsfolk had the opportunity to take part in the movie. "We needed 175 local extras, all dressed as firemen,"
said location manager Patricia Fay. "That was probably
the most unusual part of the shooting. We had to get
all these guys dirty—I mean really dirty, because we all
know what firefighters look like. But we had a great turn-
out, and our extras were really great. A lot of them had
really fought fires at some time."

The crew—300 strong—filmed for three weeks in

Libby, then headed to Ephrata, Washington, for some
scenes before returning to Libby for more shooting.
"First we shot all the groundwork scenes at a firebase
set we built at the Libby Airport," said Fay. "The crew
built most of the sets, actually—the firebase, the control
tower, the cabins, everything." *Always* also shot in the
nearby town of Dry Fork, an hour's drive from Libby.
"Dry Fork is a little town in the mountains that burned a
year before shooting. So we re-created some burn scenes
there. We were using everything around Libby—the forests, the lakes. Lots of times, we had to go an hour and a
half out of town to find the look we wanted."

Libby Airport turned into a regular smoke jumper
base, with a dispatch control tower and a weathered-
looking Quonset hut and fake pumps. Off the edge of
the airport, a fire camp with tents and other structures
and a meandering dirt road were created.

The dramatic forest fires captured on film for *Always*
were a combination of real footage and special effects.
Spielberg had started sending out crews more than two
years earlier with the permission of the Forest Service in
order to capture aerial footage of actual fires burning in
the Yellowstone National Park area. In 1988 alone, a total of 248 fires sprang up in the Greater Yellowstone area
during a particularly dry summer. Spielberg sent a Lear
jet to Jackson Hole that summer after winning permission to fly over flaming Yellowstone National Park. For
additional forest fire footage, Spielberg re-created fires
by re-burning areas of Yellowstone that had already been
under flames. In order to control the new fires safely, the
special effects team, with the supervision of coordinator
Mike Wood, rigged the pre-burned trees to ignite on cue.

While some fire conditions would be simulated, a little foresight netted the filmmakers very realistic footage.
"Because of the fires they were able to get this wonderful
footage for the film," said Wunderwald. "They would
have never been able to simulate that."

Spielberg initially debated about making *Always* a period piece and keeping the World War II backdrop. He
had always been drawn to the World War II era in history, evidenced by its presence in many of Spielberg's previous films such as *1941* (1979), *Raiders of the Lost Ark*
(1981) and *Empire of the Sun* (1987). "I like the period
because it was naive and it was somewhat innocent," he
explained in 1989, "and it represented the growing pains
of the 20th century. And it's a very fertile time for movie
stories." In the end, Spielberg chose to update *Always* to

contemporary times in the American West, though the film retains a recognized old-fashioned quality reminiscent of films from the 1940s. In a nod to its predecessor, the pilots in *Always* fly modified vintage World War II bombers, and 1940s slang is sprinkled throughout the dialogue. "I wanted the story to be somewhat timeless," said Spielberg. "A lot of the old World War II bomber pilots have kept their old airplanes, or at least restored, bought and used parts and turned them into firefighting equipment. I thought that would give a timeless feeling."

When it came time for casting, Spielberg was adamant about using "believable actors" in the parts. "I didn't want to make this movie with glamour queens or the icons of stardom of the 1990s. I wanted real people that we could relate to," he said. Names like Paul Newman and Robert Redford were considered for Pete, but the role ultimately went to Spielberg friend, Richard Dreyfuss.

According to Spielberg, while shooting *Jaws*, he and Dreyfuss discovered their mutual affection for *A Guy Named Joe*, discussing it at length during breaks on the set. Dreyfuss tried to get Spielberg to promise him the part of Pete if he ever did the remake. But, according to Spielberg's own account, the director wasn't sold on the idea of his friend as a romantic leading man at the time. A decade later, however, Spielberg changed his mind after observing Dreyfuss' acting range. Audrey Hepburn came out of her acting retirement to play Hap. "I loved it, and I wouldn't mind if [Spielberg] asked me again, like next summer," said Hepburn in 1989. "I had really one of the best times of my life." *Always* would be Hepburn's final film appearance before her death in 1993.

Cinematographer Mikael Salomon's beautiful photography throughout *Always* provides one of the film's greatest strengths. His crisp images capture the dramatic visuals of the raging forest fires and the exciting flying sequences, neatly choreographed by veteran aerial coordinator and pilot James Gavin. Longtime Spielberg composer John Williams created the musical score.

More than 150 local extras were recruited from the Libby area to portray the base workers. The basic Forest Service maintenance buildings were really hollow fiberglass shells and the cameras and camera operators could be found on portable scaffolding. Filming took place on a circular path of daisy-covered greenery in the middle of an area burned out by the Kootenai National Fork's Dry Fork fire that had struck in 1988. "For some scenes it took over an hour to 'green,' or put brush around artificial trees on the set for just one take, while for other scenes—mostly night shots—up to seven takes were needed," said land specialist Mike Fantasia. In fact, during one shooting in July, the fire crew members, including Fantasia, had to lather up a mucous-like "fire gel" over their faces and hands to help them withstand great amounts of heat. The staged forest fire set included shrubs, other plant materials, and 30 ceramic snags—or standing dead trees—through which liquid propane was pumped and ignited. "We were already hotter than hell and then I heard Steven Spielberg yell at his assistant director that 'That's a wimpy looking fire!'"

Actor John Goodman told the *Boston Herald* this anecdote about working with Spielberg in Montana: "Steven is in the eye of the storm, with planes flying and the crew and commotion, and he comes over and says, 'God! I love making movies!'"

When veteran Billings pilot Denny Lynch dove in to attack a controlled burn during the filming of *Always*, the director Spielberg yelled, "Where are you going?" "The camera's what's important here, not fighting the fire," he was told. "I had to keep remembering this was a love story, not a B-26 story or a firefighting story," said Lynch. Lynch, who ran Lynch Flying Service, said he's still not sure why he got the call from Hollywood to pilot slurry bombers for the Spielberg film, although he had something of a national reputation in flying circles for piloting vintage aircraft. Lynch, whose dad started the company in 1931, had been flying since age 16. Lynch said he recommended Libby for filming because it offered "an airstrip that could accommodate the firefighting planes, against a spectacular backdrop including the Cabinet Wilderness." He said his suggestion at first fell on deaf ears and that he was sent to check other airstrips in Colorado and California before finally getting one of the photographers to look at Libby. He ended up with lead man Dreyfuss sitting on his lap during one runway cockpit scene (Lynch was under a blanket and could still see the gauges and work the controls), and he wore a wig in another sequence when leading lady Hunter was supposedly flying the plane. For the film, he made four retardant drops over an actual forest fire. The cameraman wanted the drops done from 600 feet above the ground. Pilots fighting real fires usually fly within 100 feet above the treetops, since dropping the retardant from higher altitudes is less effective. Lynch fought against his inclination to fly lower. "I had to remember I'm taking pictures, I wasn't putting fires out," said Lynch. Spielberg, he recalled, was a stickler for precision. "With Spielberg, you don't do anything once. You do it about four times."

Lynch said he flew 150 hours, burned up two airplane engines and had a dramatic brush with disaster when a front landing gear broke, all for 11 minutes of flying on the screen. The landing gear broke while Lynch was bouncing the plane off the runway to simulate a rough landing. "I think I've got a problem," Lynch recalled saying after realizing what had happened. He flew to Spokane where firefighting equipment was available for a crash landing, but he was able to land safely after doing a vertical climb and a quick dive that snapped the disabled landing gear into locking position. Later, Lynch said the cast presented him a cake inscribed, "I think I've got a problem," and they gave him the first piece—between the eyes. But he said Spielberg and the cast were a pleasure to work with. Now a member of the Screen Actors Guild, Lynch joked: "I'm hoping that 'Always II' will come along."

Taleena Ottwell, of Kalispell, served as Holly Hunter's stand-in, a person who walks through the star's part so that lighting and camera angles can be set up before scenes are actually shot. At 5 feet 2 inches, Ottwell was Hunter's size, and she was willing to color her hair to match Hunter's medium-brown. She looked enough like the actress, in fact, that other extras on the set sometimes asked for her autograph. "I signed my own name and 'Holly's double,'" said Ottwell. "I didn't want them to think Holly wasn't friendly." Ottwell also was photographed as Hunter's double in several long-range shots. Libby high school student Cameron Carmicheal landed an assignment as a production assistant. For one day's shoot, Carmicheal had to round up 50 extras to act as patrons of a tavern. His duties occasionally included bringing lead actor Richard Dreyfuss his breakfast.

According to the film's production manager, Gary Daigler, the people of Libby were extremely cooperative and welcomed the production "with open arms." They may have welcomed the film a bit too much though. "The city of Libby is so small," said Daigler, "that after our location manager was there for a few weeks everybody would know if she had a glass of wine with dinner, or where she had her hair fixed, or what she was doing each night. She became, to a degree, a local celebrity!"

Montana governor Stan Stephens praised Spielberg's directing and the film's special effects. "This has to help

Montana," said Stephens, at a screening preview in Helena that had to be personally arranged by the director. "It's just a 'win' situation to have this label on our state." Wunderwald arranged for the governor and Mrs. Stephens to observe the filming of one scene involving actress Holly Hunter at Bull Lake, and to have dinner with Spielberg afterward. "What we hope is this gets an Academy Award and reference is made to the scenes in Montana." Stephens said before the preview. "It was a real coup to get him in Montana," Stephens said of Spielberg, adding, "As far as I'm concerned, [*Always* is] already picture of the year."

Variety said that *Always* "has a predominately goofy, adolescent tone," yet still found it an entertaining fantasy. The *Daily Herald* explained that the "corny, sentimental film" worked so well because "the locations at remote airstrips in Montana and Washington State are gorgeous and the forest fires are truly intimidating."

Years later, the Spielberg thriller *Jurassic Park* passed over Montana when it came to the movie itself. Montana paleontologist Jack Horner, famous for his discovery of dinosaur breeding grounds in northern Montana, worked as a consultant on the film. Lonie Stimac, director of the Montana film office, said parts of the dinosaur movie were to be filmed in Montana, but filmmakers instead decided to stay in California to save money. The Montana landscape was simulated in California. The Montana Film Office rounded up memorabilia to lend authenticity to dinosaur-dig scenes, shipping baseball caps and T-shirts from the University of Montana and Montana State University and posters of Montana scenes, including one of a rodeo, to the movie. Montanans' contributions to the movie weren't all behind the scenes. Special-effects artist Andy Shoneberg, a former Billings resident who had worked on Hollywood films for several years, helped build the *Brachiosaurus* used in the movie.

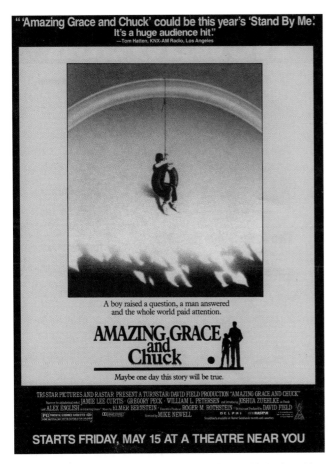

"'Amazing Grace and Chuck' could be this year's 'Stand By Me.' It's a huge audience hit."
—Tom Hatten, KNX-AM Radio, Los Angeles

A boy raised a question, a man answered and the whole world paid attention.

AMAZING GRACE and Chuck

Maybe one day this story will be true.

STARTS FRIDAY, MAY 15 AT A THEATRE NEAR YOU

Amazing Grace and Chuck tells the story of an unlikely friendship between a 12-year-old Little League pitcher and the star of the Boston Celtics basketball team, who unite to oppose nuclear weapons.

Amazing Grace and Chuck

CAST
Jamie Lee Curtis, Gregory Peck, William Petersen

DIRECTOR
Mike Newell

LOCATION
Bozeman, Livingston, Helena

1987

Amazing Grace and Chuck tells the story of a friendship between a 12-year-old Little League pitcher and a star of the Boston Celtics professional basketball team.

Chuck Murdock (Joshua Zuehlke) is a Little Leaguer in small-town Montana who is so profoundly affected by the sight of an intercontinental ballistic missile while on a field trip that he decides to make an important gesture: he will not play another game of baseball until the issue of nuclear disarmament is addressed.

News of his unlikely strike reaches Amazing Grace, the moniker by which a star Boston Celtic is known. He too agrees to renounce his favorite game in support of Chuck, not to mention moving to the same small town. More peace-minded athletes follow, much to the chagrin of Chuck's father and ultimately the movement grows, until Chuck has the ear of the U.S. President, played by Gregory Peck.

Amazing Grace and Chuck is another early film from director Michael Newell (*Four Weddings and a Funeral*, *Donnie Brasco*, and *Harry Potter and the Goblet of Fire*.) Filming began in the Bozeman, Livingston and Great Falls areas in July 1986, and continued throughout the summer. Other portions of the film were shot on location in Boston. "The absence of smog, the friendliness and generosity of the people in the Livingston and Bozeman areas and the cooperation the production company received from the state and local government, that really means a lot," said Gregory Peck to *Premiere*.

Montana was one of three states competing for the picture. "There was a lot of pressure from Utah and Colorado to host the movie," said Montana film commissioner Garry Wunderwald. "They were wining and dining the movie people pretty hard." The wooing began in February, 1986, when Wunderwald attended the Los Angeles Expo sponsored by the Association of Film Commissioners. Wunderwald got a nibble from Turnstar, but "I really had to plead to get them to come back [to Montana] for a second look. They needed a place which would serve as a White House for the presidential scenes, so I showed them the old governor's mansion in Helena." The film people did return for a closer look and decided to shoot the movie in Montana. Ironically, Wunderwald said the company then made plans to shoot the presidential scenes in Washington, D.C. "They finally gave up on that idea as well, and the presidential scenes were shot on a set in Montana."

Amazing Grace and Chuck provided part- or full-time employment for hundreds of Montana residents. Producers filled a number of roles with Montana residents. Auditions were conducted May 16-19 in Missoula, Boz-

Actor Gregory Peck played the U.S. President in *Amazing Grace and Chuck*. He praised "the absence of smog" and "the friendliness and generosity of the people in the Livingston and Bozeman areas."

eman and Great Falls. Dozens of people lined up at the Ramada Inn in Great Falls on May 20, 1986, for a chance at roles in *Amazing Grace and Chuck*, venturing from as far away as Miles City, Boulder, and Cut Bank. Director Newell and casting director Lynn Stalmaster were hoping to fill many of the roles with area people, but were still looking for the black actor to play the title role. "He should be between 26 and 32, with charm and integrity, but he's street smart, too," said Stalmaster. Will he come from Billings? "Possibly, if he connects with us," said Stalmaster. Ultimately, the role went to basketball player Alex English. There were 13 speaking parts for extras available in *Amazing Grace and Chuck*, all filled by Montanans. Big Timber resident Gwen Petersen said she wanted a part so badly that she made her husband, whom she was driving to the hospital for treatment of a back injury, wait in the lobby where auditions were being held, while she tried out. She appeared as "the mean school teacher."

When the owner of one Great Falls motel was watching the casting, a crew member noticed his good voice and presence. Despite his concern that he'd never had an acting lesson, the casting crew insisted he read for a part. He got it, played the principal of the school, picked up $1,100 in two days and "had a ball doing it," remembered Wunderwald. Camera stores, sports shops, restaurants and hotels reaped financial benefits. The handful of actors and actresses lucky enough to land speaking parts were paid $361 per day.

Turnstar Productions also paid the city of Bozeman $15 an hour for the use of off-duty uniformed police of-

ficers. Minnesota youngster Josh Zuehlke—who plays Chuck, the boy the film revolves around—and his cohorts also racked up 20 horseback rides at $14 apiece. The Universal Athletics sport shop also benefited from the production. "It's a sports-oriented movie, so we've silk-screened a lot of team names onto Little League uniforms," said salesman Steve Weil. Most of the uniforms were donated to the movie. "Manufacturers like to see their stuff in movies," said Weil. "It's no accident that you see athletes wearing Nike or Adidas shoes." The toughest order was getting warm-up sweatsuits for English, a forward for the Denver Nuggets. "He was something like 6-foot-8 inches tall with a 32-inch waist," said Weil. "We had to have four sets custom-tailored at the factory." The movie company rented out the basement of Langford Hall.

Wunderwald said that in 1986 making movies on location was in vogue "because shooting in California always looked the same in them days. There was not much to shoot that hadn't already been seen." Montana, by contrast, was still rather unknown and therefore ideal. "They needed a real long look for their shots, something without a lot of man-made objects. That's something I could offer them." Another prime asset, said Wunderwald, was "Montanans' kindness and good attitude. That's something I could offer them."

Wunderwald recalled a string of successful stories about how much money a movie company spends on location, like the one about the photo store owners in Bozeman whose cash receipts increased by $200 per day while *Amazing Grace and Chuck* was being made; drycleaners "who just couldn't believe" the volume of work they were taking in as entire movie wardrobes arrived for cleaning and pressing. "The carpenter that built the set for a White House scene they needed, told me he made $13,000 in three months," said Wunderwald. If people think they won't be affected by a production company in their town, "look at the car rentals, motels, travel agencies, airlines and restaurants that movie people use," said Wunderwald. "You can't believe how fast that adds up. And people who just volunteer to do some work so they can be around a movie set end up working full-time." Jamie Lee Curtis purchased a Pathfinder in Bozeman.

Montana State University's film department and its two major studios were utilized. *Amazing Grace and Chuck* used one of the studios to film a sequence that required a television commentator announcing national news. The film shot each day was sped to California, processed immediately and returned for viewing "rushes" right on campus. "I always show interested film companies the performing arts building at the University of Montana and the excellent facilities on the Bozeman campus," said Wunderwald. Film and television students at Montana State University gained camera experience "they could never have gotten in L.A. without working up in the field," said Wunderwald.

Shooting began on July 7 and ended August 26. "I've seen feature films in Montana spend anywhere from $1 million to $20 million," Wonderwald said. "The money goes into areas you don't even think of a movie company spending on…things like dry-cleaning bills and cowboy boots." Mary Jane McGinley, owner of the house at 610 S. Willson Avenue, where much of the Bozeman action was filmed, agreed that the movie money sometimes took an unusual route to the economy. Turnstar Productions rented her house for the film, but the real bonus was that they re-decorated the place. "They did all the painting and wallpapering and they tore out the old carpets," said McGinley. "They refinished the wood floors when they were finished." Unlike Wunderwald, McGinley said she didn't have to lobby very hard to get the movie makers interested in her house. "They were just driving past and liked the look of it," she said, "so they stopped, knocked on the door and asked to rent it."

English, who delivers a solid performance as Amazing Grace, retired after the 1991 NBA season. When legendary Boston coach Red Auerbach, who appeared in the film as himself, was informed that English would be playing a Celtic, he said, "I only wish I could keep him."

The film—made on a modest $5.4-million budget—was released in about 50 theaters nationwide and was never advertised. It died quietly

"The studio said, 'If we give this a national release, we're throwing money down the drain,'" said producer/ writer David Field. "For those of us who made it—the actors who worked for scale, the director who worked for scale—that was hard to take. But we knew we were rolling the dice. The film has always been controversial.

"The people who hated it were offended by what they took to be a grotesque simplicity. They invested so much in saying 'This couldn't happen,' and it angered them when I said, 'Yes, it could.'"

Beethoven's 2nd

Cast
Charles Grodin, Bonnie Hunt

Director
Rod Daniel

Location
Apgar Village-Glacier National Park

1993

In the summer of 1993, the makers of *Beethoven's 2nd* descended on the village of Apgar at the southwest end of Lake McDonald in Glacier National Park. Beethoven is the name given to a lovable but horrendously messy Saint Bernard who escapes dognappers to become adopted by the Newtons, much to the chagrin of the fussy head of the family, George Newton (Charles Grodin). The original children's movie *Beethoven* grossed nearly $150 million worldwide.

The sequel followed the light-hearted adventures of Beethoven and his human family, including a western vacation. The film's vacation portion was filmed in Montana. The scene was a panorama of rugged peaks, Lake McDonald's green water, a 175-member cast and crew from Universal Pictures and a pack of St. Bernards.

The continuing adventures of the huge, lovable screen star and his human family were filmed in and around the Flathead Valley, Glacier National Park and the Flathead National Forest. Part of the movie is set in "Glen Mountain," a mountain village where the Newtons go on vacation. They spend their vacation helping Beethoven rescue Missy, another St. Bernard with four puppies. The film's entire budget was $25 million.

More than 50 park employees, working on their own time, worked crowd control and helped supervise the filming at Apgar and several other locations in the park. The park's bill was approximately $45,000, plus $300-a-day filming permit fees. "It's not the kind of wildlife we were looking for," commented a woman visiting from New Orleans. The Park Service was concerned that tourists' opportunity to visit the park wasn't hampered by the film making or that the land wasn't harmed. "It's gone

The original *Beethoven* was a smash hit. This sequel did nearly as well. Much of it was filmed at Lake McDonald in Glacier National Park, as seen in the background of this promotional photograph.

really well," said West Lakes District Ranger Charlie Logan, in charge of overseeing the movie makers. Logan said that there wasn't so much as a swear word said on the movie set loud enough for tourists to hear. Before the filming began, the crew was warned by a boss that "you screw up once and you're out of here," said Logan.

Co-producer Gordon Webb noted that all of the St. Bernards used in the filming had to be kept on leashes at all times, which required some of the movie to be shot outside the park. Likewise, second unit establishing shots on helicopters were accomplished outside Glacier—over Flathead Lake—because aircraft are not allowed to fly below 5,000 feet in Glacier.

Universal brought 100 people to the Flathead, with another 100 or so local extras and stand-ins employed. Universal Pictures was estimated to have pumped about $1.2 million into area businesses. Locals Terry and Rhonda Fields and their three children (Travis, 14, Terra 11, and Tavia 4) were used as extras. Pay was $5 an hour. Travis, a Columbia Falls High School sophomore, was

also in a fishing scene on Lake McDonald, and went for a horseback ride with some of the cast. Terry, a potman at the aluminum plant, worked 12-hour shifts and had one week a month off. He made good use of the week. Two-plus days involved filming inside Eddie's Store, an Apgar landmark owned by Jerry and Donna Larson. "*Beethoven's 2nd* filming was great," said Donna. "They are super people, wonderful to work with, and most considerate of park visitors." The cast and crew stayed in Kalispell, Columbia Falls, and Whitefish.

Although snow-packed and in the dead cold of winter, director Rod Daniel said when he saw pictures of Glacier National Park, "it was a done deal." Daniel said he was looking for a location with mountains, a lake and a resort village. After searching in northern California and the Pacific Northwest, they found Apgar. Daniels said it's in character for Grodin's uptight persona, Newton, to pick a place like Apgar to vacation in the *Beethoven's 2nd*. Not a posh resort, he said. Along with all the other accouterments of a film production, about 80 St. Bernard puppies played the roles of the four puppies in the movie. St. Bernard puppies grow so fast they're only good for about one week of shooting, said co-producer Joe Medjuck. Breeders and kennels from around the country helped supply the puppies. All arrivals were made up to have markings that matched the movie puppies. The puppies were part of the story line, which included a love affair between Beethoven and the female St. Bernard, Missy.

Behind the screen a lot of attention was given to the canine stars. When Universal Studios packed up two DC-9 airplanes and flew into Glacier Park International Airport, it was the St. Bernards that went first class, not the actors. This upstaging occurred so that enough room for the dogs would be provided by removing the first class seats. The dogs were exercised every hour and fed three times a day. While the typical adult dog eats about eight cups of dog food a day, these pooches ate a whopping 12 cups. It took three trucks accompanying this troupe of canine actors to accommodate all their dog paraphernalia.

The entire thrust of the first film was to show George's exceedingly reluctant but nonetheless growing affection for the super-smart Beethoven, whose alertness saves the Newtons from disasters large and small. Since George had ended the first film loving Beethoven as much as did his wife Alice and three kids, the challenge facing the sequel's writer Len Blum was where to take George and Beethoven next. Blum's answer was to have Beethoven fall in love. It's one thing for George to come to accept Beethoven but another for him to accept a second dog— and of course, the inevitability of puppies.

Reviews were surprisingly agreeable. The *San Francisco Chronicle* said *Beethoven's 2nd* "has been made with care" and the "sunny glow" cinematographer Bill Butler brings to the film is "precisely right for a family film," and director Rod Daniel, "ever adroit with comedy, makes everything work beautifully." Another reviewer added, "*Beethoven's 2nd* gets away with its fantastic moments because its story has been painstakingly grounded in the realities of everyday family life."

Big Eden, a gay romantic drama and love story which debuted in theatres in 2000, unfolded against the massive backdrop of Glacier National Park.

Big Eden

CAST
Arye Gross, Eric Schweig

DIRECTOR
Thomas Bezucha

LOCATION
Flathead and West Glacier areas

2000

Big Eden, a romantic drama and, well, ultramodern love story, unfolds against the massive backdrop of Glacier National Park. Henry Hart, a successful, lonely New York artist, returns to "Big Eden," his northwestern hometown, to care for his sick grandfather. Two of Hart's former Flathead High School classmates are also in town. A myriad of old feelings and high school recollections are brought to the surface as the three friends are the object of the townspeople's matchmaking endeavors.

Henry finds he must come to grips with his relationship to a man named Dean Stewart, his best friend from high school, and the object of his unrequited love. Henry's feelings for Dean, which caused him to flee Big Eden nearly twenty years ago, appear to have grown stronger over the years. Henry's reappearance sparks a transformation in Pike Dexter, the shy Native American owner of the town's general store. Pike is surprised when he finds himself falling in love with Henry.

As this undeclared triangle unfolds under the scrutiny of Big Eden's community, practically everyone in town develops a stake in its outcome.

Big Eden is a contemporary twist on the fables of home and family. Starring Arye Gross and Eric Schweig, as well as Oscar-winner Louise Fletcher, *One Flew over the Cuckoo's Nest* (1977), nearly all of *Big Eden* was filmed in Montana, including Apgar Village, Glacier National Park, Kalispell, Somers, Swan Lake, and Whitefish.

"*Big Eden* was a fun project," said Sten Iversen, who had a small role as a party guest and bachelor. "I found all of their locations and I worked extensively with the production team. We had to interact with the National Park Service at Apgar and we shot at a park service cabin on the east end of Lake McDonald and shot scenes in Lakeside. We shot at a school at West Yellowstone, where the park service employees go to school.

"We found a church [Holy Nativity Episcopal Church in Whitefish] and had to find a general store, and we cndcd up using the Swan Lake Mercantile and repainted the exterior. The church was difficult, because the film has a gay storyline, and we had a long discussion about approaching the church. There was a church outside of Whitefish that was open to let them film. We had a lot of discussion. Some of the producers said it was none of their business, and wanted to give them the part of the script that omitted the gay context, but we decided to go with full disclosure."

Released five years before the Northwestern-set *Broke-*

back Mountain and two years after the Wyoming murder of Matthew Shepard, the film earned awards at LGBT film festivals as well as being nominated for a GLAAD Media Award.

"I had these fantasies of moving out West," said director Thomas Bezucha, "chucking it all in and going to teach art in some elementary school in Montana. I would express that fantasy and all my friends would freak out and say, 'Are you crazy? You can't do that, you're gay, do you know what they do to gay people out there?' I sort of got into this idea of—it was amazing how prejudiced people in an urban setting were about rural people—the preconception about the mindset out there, and I thought, 'Well, what if that weren't the case?' all my friends were saying, "You're nuts. You can't do that," and so *Big Eden* was a little bit of a "What if?" What if you could, what if people weren't homophobic, what if they were great, what if, what if? And so that was a way of spinning out that fantasy."

Bezucha, who first became entranced with Montana after reading Norman McLean's *Young Men and Fire*, said that *Big Eden* wasn't autobiographical. "Not really. I was living in New York and I worked for Ralph Lauren, designing stores. I did that for about 10 years. I had always wanted to be involved in film and at that moment in time I was thinking, "Oh, if I could get into production design… and so I decided that the best way to do that—I'm not terribly bright—was to write a script; that would be the shortest path. I wanted to change my life and get involved with film. I wasn't quite happy with my life and, aside from the film, there was just a general fantasy of changing my life and a couple of things all happened within a year that led me to *Big Eden*. I discovered the music of Dwight Yoakam. I read a book by Ian Fraser called *The Great Plains* and went on a business trip to Cody, Wyoming, for a cowboy auction and just fell in love with the West. So if there's a germ, it started there."

"*Big Eden* is definitely a stretch for Montana—it's a gay romance fantasy," said Allison Whitmer, who served as a member of the film's art department. One of the main locations—the old man's house—is the former summer vacation home of an old Montana gasoline company, Heccoline, based out of Havre. It was the summer home of the gasoline people and ended up with new owners or heirs. There is a guy who makes cedar strip canoes in Summers or Bigfork and we used one of his canoes. It's different. There is a gay Native American as a lead, George Koe (who plays Sam Heart, Henry's brother). We didn't tell a lot of people about the plot. Kalispell may not exactly be the best place to talk about a gay romance—and with a Native American and another guy from New York, no less."

Iversen said that *Big Eden,* shot in 24 days, was an example of the changing landscape of Montana-based films in the early 2000s. "*Big Eden* came at a time of CGI (computer generated imagery) and at a time when bigger films needed more and more incentives. There was more room for small budget pictures to be made in Montana. We re-focused and changed our marketing strategy and looked to smaller independents because we couldn't keep up with the incentives. *Big Eden* is a small film—well under a million dollar budget. But Bezucha went on to do *Family Stone,* (a 2005 American comedy-drama film starring Dermot Mulroney and Sarah Jessica Parker) which had a big cast and was a pretty major film."

Nonetheless, anyone who has spent time in Whitefish, Glacier National Park or Swan Lake will note the familiar sites, ranging from Apgar Village to beautiful McDonald Falls. With a snow-capped McDonald Peak towering in the background, an all-out Fourth of July picnic got under way again and again and again in Glacier National Park. The picnic was complete with flying flags, a band on stage and frolicking kids. Between takes, about 75 extras wearing summer attire put on coats and blankets to warm up in the October chill. Despite the cold, the extras enjoyed the experience. "I thought it would be fun, because I've never done it before," said Shari Johnson, a Columbia Falls Junior High School guidance counselor. Johnson's part involved dishing up marshmallows, watermelon and Black Star beer at the picnic. Several students from West Glacier School missed classes to appear in the picnic scene. "This is kind of fun," said Dwight Bergeron, a Kalispell resident and square dancer in the movie's Fourth of July picnic scene. "I like doing 27 'takes.' You get to hug the same person, who you don't know, 13 times." Actor O'Neal Compton likened the weeks of filming to "camping out."

"Here we are all staying at the 'Village Inn' right on the lake, with no phones," said Compton. "We play guitar at night and look at the mountains when we wake up in the morning. What could be better?"

Actor Arye Gross spoke of seeing "glorious solar events" each night as the sun sunk below the mountains.

"I wish I could work here all the time, but that means there would be too many movie people here."

Variety magazine said that the "story of how and why painter Henry Hart makes the shift from go-go Gotham lifestyle to a satisfying life in Montana is far from convincing, however, raising serious questions about motivation and intent at almost every juncture." Another review said that the movie's "excessively sober approach finally becomes a problem," since it is "depicting as unreal a West as *Northern Exposure,* but without that series' deliberate exaggerations." And yet another review questioned the authenticity of film. "Circumstances also stack the deck in favor of Montana, and the view of the idyllic town set on a glassy lake bordering Glacier National Park makes one wonder why Henry left in the first place. Indeed, the folks of Big Eden are uniformly kind, mannerly, hospitable, if not a bit pushy…and seem unanimously happy to see Henry back."

Bright Angel

CAST
Dermot Mulroney, Lili Taylor, Sam Shepard,
Bill Pullman, Benjamin Bratt

DIRECTOR
Michael Fields

LOCATION
Billings

1991

Economically and geographically, Billings was the sensible choice. Following a competitive selection process, *Bright Angel,* based on a story by Montana author Richard Ford, picked Billings rather than Great Falls or Casper, Wyoming. Helmdale Films decided that shooting the film in Billings was less costly than shooting in Great Falls for four weeks and then moving to Casper for three weeks.

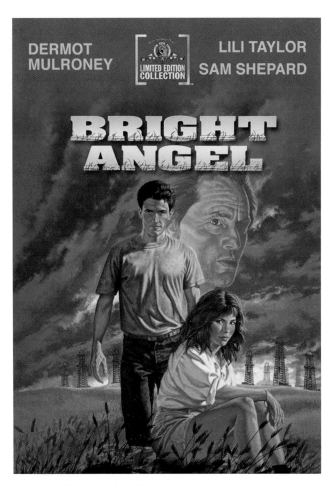

Bright Angel was based on two stories by Montana novelist Richard Ford. It was filmed entirely in and around Billings.

Billings was chosen because its oil refineries give the appearance of Casper and it had a good strip, a street of neon signs, taverns and fast-food joints. Filmed entirely in and around Billings, *Bright Angel* locations include the Livestock Commission, Lazy K-T motel, Spur Bar, Hide-A-Way Bowling Alley, and the Rimrocks' geology.

The Billings Livestock Commission Company in Lockwood, east of Billings, served as Casper's bus station. The film's art department converted the Livestock Commission into the Casper bus depot, adding details such as printed bus schedules lining walls. Signs on doors and windows were changed, notices added on bulletin boards, and ticket agents stood behind counters. Extras filled the café across the hall, and a few moved around, carrying suitcases through the hall and into the depot. Not all the buildings used by the crew went through such dramatic transformations, but the Yellowstone County Sheriff's office got a new paint job when the color didn't jibe with what was needed.

The film marked a repeat visit for Hemdale Productions, as the production company was in Montana in 1987 shooting *War Party*. *Bright Angel*, which tells the story of a woman traveling through parts of Montana and Wyoming to raise bail money for her jailed husband, began filming in the Billings area July 10, 1990, and finished August 30. Shot on a budget of nearly $4 million, *Bright Angel* is a film about turning points, moments that scar and change you forever. It's a coming-of-age story of unusual bleakness and empathy, and it has real verbal style. The characters speak an odd, poetic, homiletic lingo, and their words tend to resonate in the vast, empty landscapes around them: the Montana plains slashed by highways that stretch endlessly toward far horizons and occasional towns.

In the opening sequence, as dusk smothers the placid blue waters of a Montana pond, as shimmering lamplight illuminates all that is beautiful and dangerous out in the open…there is gunfire. Almost every man in *Bright Angel* carries a weapon, without which he is incapable of communicating. Screenwriter Richard Ford, who adapted the movie from two short stories in his 1987 collection *Rock Springs*, is something of a literary populist and he's set his tale among common people in these towns: characters that, for all their surface strength or bravado, operate under a terrifying vulnerability.

"*Bright Angel* was a very real breakthrough with Richard Ford's material," said actor Bill Pullman. "It has an authentic feel and it's kind of the New West that affects Montana, and of which Montana has some aspects. It's not the old Big Sky Country and there are a lot of new pressures—politically, socially—and there is the pressure on the lifestyle of the loner cowboy. Director Michael Fields helped give a new take on the western theme in *Bright Angel*, and the truck driving, oil-drilling quality of the eastern part of the state. It felt great to be part of that of storytelling."

Ford's protagonist, George (Dermot Mulroney), sees his family split apart when his father (Sam Shepard) catches his mother with a lover. He fights with his best friend, Claude (Benjamin Bratt), over a runaway, Lucy, who is passing through on her way from Canada to the oil fields. Throwing in with Lucy, he winds up trapped in an outlaw world, a dangerous subculture from which there may be no exit.

As *American Cinematographer* keenly noted: "Richard Ford and director Michael Fields conduct an inverse

In addition to the principal stars Dermot Mulroney and Lilli Taylor, *Bright Angel* featured (clockwise from top left) Benjamin Bratt, Valerie Perrine, Sam Shepard, Burt Young, Mary Kay Place, and Bill Pulman. (Hemdale Film Corporation)

journey through the hallowed archetypes of the American Dream. Hunting, friendship, and sexual initiation, life on the road, good vs. evil, the Big Fight, and the Big Break. They're all there, but somehow, they've gone dark, sad, off-key."

"Along the way, they're forced to grow up," said creative producer Paige Simpson. "It's a serious play, but not black. It's realistic. Richard doesn't like to call it a coming-of-age film. Rather, it expresses that at the end of the day all you have is yourself."

Film News singled out *Bright Angel* as one of the year's smarter, slicker productions: "Movies are often smashingly filmed—photographed, edited and dressed to the nines—but few of them, by contrast, are really written. That's what sets *Bright Angel* apart, even though, in adapting his stories ["Great Falls" and "Children"], Ford comes up with something of a patchwork. Both tales, originally set in 1961, only carry through the first part of the film. The movie, by contrast, is post-Vietnam—

George's car is a battered '72 Impala—and the latter section, far more melodramatic, with juicy psychopathic star turns for heavies Bill Pullman and Burt Young, actually feels more like a movie script. Yet, Ford's writing survives the spottier structure."

Other critics agreed that even if *Bright Angel* wasn't completely successful, it still caught and preserved a mood, a sense of place.

Bright Angel wasn't without its own controversy. Mike Connolly, an organizer for Teamsters Local 399 in Los Angeles, rode into the Magic City in late July 1989 and claimed that workers on the movie were being underpaid. "It really is a shame," said Connolly. "They're [Hemdale Films] just running over these people." If Hemdale Films was unwilling to raise wages, Connolly said he would seek the help of local unions to picket production of the film. Darrell Holzer, president of the Yellowstone Central Labor Council, pledged its support to the Teamsters Local 399 effort. Holzer said the decision arose from a disparity between what drivers for *Bright Angel* were earning and salaries being paid to drivers on the set of Steven Spielberg's production of *Always*.

Union drivers on the latter were getting up to $2,000 per week, compared with $500-$600 per week for the Billings movie. Connolly said drivers for the Spielberg film were being paid $16.61 per hour and received time-and-half after eight hours for workdays that typically ran 16 to 18 hours. He claimed that some *Bright Angel* workers were getting "as little as $35 per day for working 16 to 18 hours." He said those wages seemed to violate Montana law. The film company maintained that it was a low-budget movie that couldn't afford to pay as much as the Spielberg production.

Pickets arrived one morning at 6 A.M. at the Spur Bar, where the company was filming a boxing scene. Two union supporters were arrested by Billings police and jailed for disorderly conduct. Crew members said someone had damaged equipment, disconnected cables, thrown electrical equipment on the roofs of buildings and dumped sewage out of a truck containing rest rooms for crew members.

A half-dozen local workers rebutted the claim that they were being underpaid. "I feel we're being treated very well," said Rene Rosell Yarborough, assistant location manager for the Hemdale Films production. Besides their salaries, workers received benefits such as catered meals and insurance. "It's certainly more money than I'd be making not doing anything." Dennis Sprankel, a cable puller, said he had worked on the crew for about a month. "I quit a job that I had been working at for six years," said Sprankel. "Opportunity came knocking at my door. I don't appreciate people screwing around with it."

Sharon Hemsing said she earned $400 per week as a craft-services employee who brought out soda, snacks and rolls. "Everyone enjoys each other. I'm real happy," Hemsing said of conditions on the *Bright Angel* set.

Picketers went to the movie set at the Spur Bar for a demonstration but eventually lost enthusiasm for efforts that soon petered out.

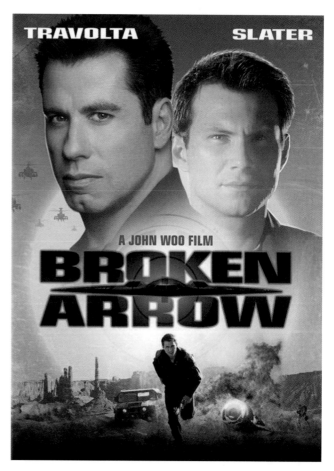

Broken Arrow was a box-office hit starring John Travolta and Christian Slater and directed by action filmmaker John Woo.

Broken Arrow

CAST
John Travolta, Christian Slater

DIRECTOR
John Woo

LOCATION
Lewistown area

1996

Burlington Northern shut down and abandoned its Lewistown-Denton-Geraldine railroad line that it had purchased in the early-1980s from the Milwaukee Road. Central Montana Railroad (CMR) rebuilt and reopened

The thrilling train scenes in *Broken Arrow* were filmed along 40 miles of railroad tracks near Lewistown. Here Samantha Mathis clings to a boxcar as the train speeds past the Montana countryside.

the line that runs from Spring Creek Junction on the edge of Lewiston to Denton, which had weeds growing between rotting railroad ties.

In the summer of 1995, the film *Broken Arrow* spent six weeks shooting action train sequences along 40 miles of the railroad's tracks—northeast of Lewistown on Hanover Road. "Broken arrow" is a military term used to describe a nuclear device that is unaccounted for and, in the movie *Broken Arrow,* two Stealth bomber pilots go from friends to enemies when one of them steals a nuclear weapon and plans to hold it for ransom. The Twentieth Century Fox feature was directed by John Woo and scripted by Graham Yost, a pedigree that ensured *Broken Arrow* would be painted with an action-oriented brush.

Montana Film Commissioner Lonie Stimac said that Bill Badalato, executive producer of *Broken Arrow,* flew into Great Falls and raved about it as "an oasis in the middle of the plains" that would work well as a setting for either a midwestern or western movie. Or, in this case, an action movie.

Badalato said the site was selected because "We could do our work uninterrupted. It's difficult working with trains. You can't stop business. Our goal was to dig in and work and not have to worry."

They could do this because the Central Montana Railroad is little used in the summer for hauling wheat or barley, but springs to life after the fall harvest.

"We actually added many sequences to fit with the track," said Badalato. "We created our own train and prepped it with explosives in California, so it could be specially rigged. We used Central Montana Rail engines." Twentieth Century Fox selected Montana over an Arizona site that had been chosen earlier.

"The attraction was that we could use 40 miles of privately owned railroad, and also be able to do aerial shots of the train," said Ann Riley, Twentieth Century Fox publicist. "We could put the trains back and forth without having to worry about locals coming onto the set and not having to switch trains on the track." Riley noted that longer daylight hours were an added factor in the movie company's decision to go to Lewistown.

Broken Arrow is a duel between two military pilots, played by John Travolta and Christian Slater, who are assigned to a top-secret low-altitude training mission with a Stealth bomber. Turns out Travolta is a bad-seed traitor who plans to kill Slater, steal the bombs, and sell them to a syndicate that will blackmail the government.

At the beginning, Vic Deakins (Travolta) takes a test ride in a B-3 stealth bomber armed with twin nuclear warheads. After punching out his young copilot, Riley Hale (Christian Slater), he crashes the plane, absconds with the weapons, and threatens to detonate them unless the Pentagon meets his extravagant financial demands.

The climax to the action-filled movie portrays several stunning escapades aboard a train. A number of elaborate train cars were shipped to Montana, including several custom-built cars used in the filming of the final sequence. The 150-person crew for *Broken Arrow* spent all six weeks near Lewistown to film the train sequences. It was a closed set and no extras or locals were needed. Some of the more dangerous scenes were filmed along the tracks, including helicopter action shots, gunfire, high falls, and special effects.

"CMR was privately owned and they were willing to let us film…on rail lines is a nice commodity," said scout Bill Kuney. "With the big rail lines, film shoots are usually out of the question. This line was small, basically a co-op, run by the CMR grain farms to the Burlington Northern Line. I believe the line ran twice a week and the railroad was able to be controlled and the film company was allowed to lease the tracks.

"Christian Slater used to walk his dog in Lewistown. I believe the actors liked it, because they didn't really have to hide from the paparazzi and the normal scene. Lewistown was the kind of place where you could be out walking your dog through town."

The rail company furnished locomotives, cars and engineers 12 to 18 hours a day, six days a week, from late June through early August 1995. A couple of helicopters exploded on or near the train, and people riddled with bullets fell out of box cars, but most of the flames were studio special effects. None of the railroad's property was damaged. One day, stuntman Dan Wynands fell 250 feet from the Sage Creek Trestle. The next week, another stuntman fell from the moving train in flames wearing a $5,000 face mask and three pairs of fireproof clothes. That fall was one of the biggest stunts in the film, a "full-body burn," said assistant producer Bill Badalato. "That involves putting a stunt player in special wardrobe to protect them from the burn and a special mask to make them look like the actor." The stunt fully engulfed Myke Schwartz, the stuntman portraying the villainous character Brandt. It was one of the film's most dangerous stunts to accomplish. Because there would be no retakes, the scene was filmed with seven cameras, which were also protected from fire.

Director John Woo, who was born in Hong Kong, said the actors were happier to be in Central Montana than they were with filming in Arizona. "Every day when you wake up you see green, smell the fresh air, and its keeps you relaxed." Woo brought his wife and three children. "This lets them see something they haven't seen before, the beautiful land, the deer, all of the animals. It helps to make their minds more open. In Hong Kong, they hardly ever see this much green. There's too much pollution and noise. It's nice to come to a place like this."

An autographed photo of Travolta and co-star Howie Long hangs in the CMR office, located in the shadow of the Denton grain elevator. Long, a former NFL star, said he was surprised when he received the call to audition for *Broken Arrow*. Long said that the original script by Graham Yost (who made his feature film debut with the critical and box office hit, *Speed*), didn't care for his character, who was killed about one-third of the way into the movie. Long declined the role. After a rewrite that eliminated several characters and expanded the role of Kelly, Travolta's bad-guy pal, Long met with director John Woo and later read for the part. Long enjoyed working with Woo, known for martial-arts action films such as *The Killer* and *Hard Boiled*. Long said that doing the stunts in *Broken Arrow* was even more physical than playing bone-crunching professional football: "Running across a train going 35 miles per hour, jumping from box car to box car."

Then there was the challenge of one of his co-stars: "Christian was lobbying really hard to beat me up [in one of scene]. They told him he wasn't that good of an actor." Long didn't do his own big stunts. "I've been operated on a whole bunch. I've broken everything there is to break. But I think my athleticism is something that will serve me well, if it works out." He said that he has fond memories of the film and is appreciative of the opportunity. "I'm not a jet-setter. I have a nice car, but I have a truck. I have a home that's paid for and I have a place in Montana. I have three kids and they go to a good school. And I don't want for anything. I have all the socks and underwear I need."

Christian Slater was seen in a hat and very dark sunglasses at the Sport Center. He was surrounded by bodyguards who purchased fishing equipment for him, but he never spoke. Slater ate at the Denton Café and tried to bring his Rottweiler into a local restaurant; Travolta, who entertained the set with dances from *Grease* and *Saturday Night Fever*, was seen hanging out at the Golden Spike Lounge. High school kids guarded the explosives for $6 an hour. Several Lewistown residents' names made the extended credits, including set production assistants Tim Hoffer and Tom Rapkoch.

Broken Arrow shot to the No. 1 spot in its opening three days, with an estimated $15.4 million in box office grosses. While audiences decided it needed no fixing, critics hardly embrace it. *The Hollywood Reporter* called it "pretty indistinguishable from countless other overblown action films."

"It's a big, loud, defiantly schlocky action bash that keeps blowing things up because it doesn't know what else to do," wrote *Entertainment Weekly*. "The movie is, in essence, a drably low-tech chase thriller brimming over with visual clichés (a chopper chasing after our hero, thugs blasting away with machine guns," wrote the *Village Voice*.

As Roger Ebert noted, "A lot of stuff gets blowed up real good in *Broken Arrow*, including a train, four helicopters and a mountain, but these brief flashes of special effects don't do much to speed up a slow, talky action thriller…"

In a nod to the Montana action sequences, the *New York Times* took note of how "Mr. Woo orchestrates his giddy, daring stunts on a newly spectacular level" and "things crash or explode here at regular intervals, with virtually nonstop acrobatics in between."

The Montana scenes retain a brightness and beauty, even if the movie isn't of the type commonly associated with the state.

"*Broken Arrow* was filmed in the month of August and the crew stayed in Lewistown," said Maribeth Goodrich, assistant to the Montana Film Office. "The owners of the CMR were film-friendly and worked with us cooperatively. The only thing about the film was that it wasn't billed as Montana. The thing I remember most was that for some reason it was the wettest summer in Montana for years and years, there were only five, six days without measurable precipitation. Instead of Lewiston looking like a brown, dried place, it was gorgeous, lush, and green. Those train scenes and trestle scenes in August take your breath away."

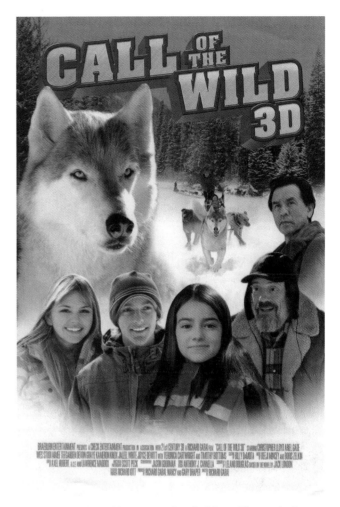

The "red-carpet" world premiere of *Call of the Wild 3D* took place on June 10, 2009, at Helena's Cinemark 8 theaters.

Call of the Wild 3D

CAST
Christoper Lloyd, Timothy Bottoms, Wes Studi

DIRECTOR
Richard Gabai

LOCATION
Lincoln, Philipsburg

2009

Call of the Wild 3D is a modern adaptation of Jack London's short novel about a sled dog, *Call of the Wild*.

Christopher Lloyd, who played the eccentric Doc Brown in the *Back to the Future* movies, plays a grandpa in the film.

"If you're familiar with the original text, at the end of the "*Call of the Wild*, when Buck becomes leader of the pack, he had many descendants," said director Richard Gabai. "At the beginning of our story, a girl visits her grandfather out in the country and she runs into a wounded descendant of Buck." The granddaughter, Ryann, played by 10-year-old Ariel Gade, nurses the dog back to health, and he becomes part of a sled dog team.

"It's just a wonderful script, and the role I was asked to play—the grandpa—I really liked," said Lloyd, who lived in Darby in the 1980s. "He's kind of lonely, his wife recently died and he's excited to have his granddaughter come visit and have another voice in the house."

The granddaughter is unhappy to leave her big-city life and luxuries in Boston to spend time in the snowy mountains of Montana with her grandfather. "She arrives with a lot of superficial pursuits and feelings—she's very much involved with status and keeping up with the Joneses," said Lloyd. Ryann has a change of heart when she finds an injured wolf dog, which she nurses back to health and fights to keep from a villain who claims to be the dog's owner. All the while, the grandfather reads London's story to Ryann.

Crews filmed the restart (which follows the ceremonial start that is held at a more public location) of the Race to the Sky dog sled race near Lincoln. "It's a very low budget film, but it's got a big heart and a big scope," said Gabai. "We had the state of Montana behind us, the community of Lincoln and the community of Philipsburg."

"Our kitchen was the computer room," said Lincoln resident Maureen Fisher, "all four bedrooms were for the stars, the sewing room was the costume department and the big family room upstairs became the dining room with tables and couches and a TV. They were using our bedroom for filming so I slept on the couch."

Other cast members include Timothy Bottoms, Veronica Cartwright, Wes Studi, Jaleel White, and Joyce DeWitt, who played alongside Suzanne Sommers and John Ritter in the television sitcom *Three's Company*.

Philipsburg's Sweet Palace candy store appears in the film. "Richard was filming a scene in front of the Sapphire Gallery jewelry store and needed a gun," said Shirley Beck, owner of Sweet Palace. "So he turned to our staff and asked if anybody had a gun, preferably a long rifle. You can image what happens when somebody says that in Montana. Within seconds everybody ran out the back door and came back with a half-dozen long rifles. And these were mostly women."

The crew was in Montana for several weeks in March 2008. Shooting finished in the spring, with a release date in the winter of 2009. The "red-carpet" world premiere event, which includes an invitation-only screening of the movie, took place June 10, 2009, at Helena's Cinemark 8 theaters.

"This was the first all-live action, dramatic, digital 3D film," said Gabai. "We were a small company making a big film on a small budget. We could never even attempted this without the support of the community."

The film only grossed $28,024. Word-of-mouth reviews such as Utah's *Deseret News*, which called the movie "clunky" and "a real mess," put a very thick nail in its coffin.

Cattle Queen of Montana

CAST
Barbara Stanwyck, Ronald Reagan

DIRECTOR
Allen Dwan

LOCATION
Blackfeet Reservation, East Glacier area

1954

Shot in July 1954, *Cattle Queen of Montana* is an 1880s story with Indians, friendly and unfriendly, a greedy white man, a party of settlers arriving from Texas with their cattle herd to "pre-empt," or take over an inhabited homestead claim.

Barbara Stanwyck and future U.S. president Ronald Reagan co-star in the romantic action story of the men and women who pioneered the West when, according to

Barbara Stanwyck pulls a gun on Ronald Reagan in *Cattle Queen of Montana*. Much of the film was made around Glacier National Park, where this picture appears to have been taken.

publicity materials, "the greedy and godless made Montana territory a name of shame."

The film provided the two stars with offbeat roles and some of the most magnificent scenery ever presented in Technicolor.

Barbara Stanwyck portrays Sierra Jones, who "fights like a tigress" to help break the grip of the avaricious, to defy hired killers and to win the love of Ronald Reagan (government officer Farrell), as she refuses to be run off the land for which her father has given his life. Jones receives a violent welcome to Montana from a band of Indians who murder her father, and she is subsequently forced to rise up against neighboring ranchers who wish to wrongfully appropriate her family land. RKO Radio Pictures noted in its promotional material, "Reagan has one of his most rugged roles since he switched from sports announcing to acting 49 films ago." As the stranger who hires out as a gunman so he can discover the source of guns for the "unfriendly Indians" helping

land-grabber Gene Evans to become the ruthless dictator of the rich Buffalo Valley, Reagan proved that he could ride and handle a gun with the best of western stars. The cast also included Lance Puller, Tony Caruso, Jack Elam and Yvette Dugay in featured roles.

While most of the film was shot at the Iverson Ranch, in Chatsworth, California, *Cattle Queen of Montana* was partially filmed in the St. Mary area in and near Glacier National Park. Leading lady Stanwyck reportedly so impressed the Blackfeet Indians (she did most of her own stunts) that they made her a tribal princess.

There were 94 crew who flew in from Hollywood to Cut Bank. Headquarters was Hugh Black's motel and the new lodge. Cast included local rangers and Blackfeet Indians. The title is derived from Mrs. Nat Collins, a Montana woman who was known as "Cattle Queen." She was an early prospector in what is now Glacier National Park, and had a mining claim on Mineral Creek, tributary of McDonald Creek. There is a Cattle Queen

Several over-the-top movie posters were made for *Cattle Queen of Montana*.

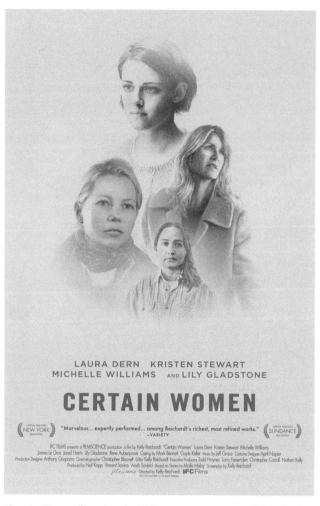

Certain Women, filmed in the Livingston area, was an official selection at the 2016 Sundance Film Festival.

Creek, named for her, which flows into Mineral. Dr. George C. Ruhle, the park's first chief naturalist, referred to Mrs. Collins: "Next to Calamity Jane the best known of the women of Montana pioneer days."

The New York Times concluded its review with this critique of the film and nod to Montana: "Although the scenic beauties of the Montana countryside are a good reason for Miss Stanwyck to make the trek from Texas, it is a generally unprofitable trip, considering the plot with which she is forced to tangle."

The Fox theater in Billings hosted the Montana premiere of the RKO-Technicolor picture.

On January 14, 1989, President Ronald Reagan and his wife, Nancy, watched the film at Camp David. It was the final film that Reagan watched before the conclusion of his presidency six days later.

Certain Women

CAST
Kristen Stewart, Michelle Williams, Laura Dern

DIRECTOR
Kelly Reichardt

LOCATION
Livingston area

2016

Certain Women was among the selection of 15 feature films at the 2016 Sundance Film Festival. *Certain Women* is the sixth feature from independent filmmaker-director Kelly Reichardt (*Meek's Cutoff, Night Moves, Wendy and Lucy*) and produced by Independent Spirit Producer's Award winners Neil Kopp and Anish Savjani of the film production company Film Science.

Set in Montana, the film is based on stories by award-winning, *New York Times* bestselling author and Helena native Maile Meloy. The film's narrative follows the lives of a lawyer, a cowboy and a married couple intersected in the "New West," where the men are struggling to get their lives straight in the face of aging, injury and bad luck—and the women are imperfectly carving out an identity.

The cast includes Laura Dern (*Wild, Jurassic Park*), Michelle Williams (*Dawson's Creek, My Week with Marilyn*), Kristen Stewart (*Twilight* saga), Jared Harris (*Sherlock Holmes: A Game of Shadows*) and Rosanna Arquette (*Pulp Fiction*). Also starring in the film is Blackfeet actress Lily Gladstone, who was cast in a supporting role opposite Kristen Stewart.

Certain Women shot for 30 days in March and April 2015, hiring a primarily Montana-based crew and spending over $1.4 million in state. The film has a tentative release date of late 2016.

Cold Feet

CAST
Keith Carradine, Sally Kirkland, Tom Waits,
Bill Pullman

DIRECTOR
Robert Dornhelm

LOCATION
Livingston area, Paradise Valley

1989

Though it is set in Montana, and the scenes are full of horses and mountains and cowboy hats, *Cold Feet* is the sort of film where Tom Waits, as a comically inept hit man, walks into a western clothing business and asks for some "cowpoke stuff." The film does not send up the old West so much as it looks at the modern West from an indifferent, even ironic, point of view.

Written by the novelists Tom McGuane and Jim Harrison in the 1970s and revised by McGuane a dozen years later, this wry comedy follows three anti-heroic outlaws adrift in a half-baked, contemporary West. Ratcheting up the cynicism is one of McGuane's timeworn tricks and this film revels in its anti-establishment 1970s roots.

"I have to credit Robert Dornhelm, who ferreted the script out of some musty closet, liked it and wanted to do it," said McGuane. "Cassian Elwes was the original producer on this thing, and somehow or another it went to Avenue. So its long shelf life (of 12 years) is sort of an accident.

"I'm almost prepared to think that what the American movies want to be about is [sex] and shooting, and that you're simply fighting city hall to write about anything else."

Keith Carradine is Monte Latham, a small-time thief and marginally the brightest member of the trio. He wants to keep his bachelor status, though his girlfriend, Maureen, has feet as blistering hot as Monte's are frozen. Sally Kirkland's Maureen has a vast wardrobe of bright dresses and an intense desire to marry a "charming, dishonest'" man such as Monte. Maureen is a silly lampoon of every macho cowboy's dream and nightmare united; she is oversexed and determined to wed.

Keith Carradine and Sally Kirkland starred in *Cold Feet*, a crime caper filmed around Livingston.

After the trio of smalltime crooks—Carradine, Kirkland and Waits (as Kenny)—smuggle some emeralds into the United States from Mexico, hidden in the leg of a champion stallion named "Infidelity," Monte steals the horse and escapes to his brother's failing ranch in Montana. Kenny and Maureen get a camper and trail him across the West. They stop at Monte's daughter's school, where the kids dress in combat fatigues and are taught survival skills ("Prepare for the big one" reads a sign on the school grounds), only to find that she has gone on to her Uncle Buck's ranch. Bill Pullman plays the down-home Buck.

Cold Feet unwinds as "a series of witty, delightfully underacted scenes strung on a flimsy plot," according to one critic, a meandering story whose humor is based on mismatched personalities and crackpot dialogue.

It "has both the sense of humor of Thomas McGuane and Jim Harrison, and all the things that amused them and shared their interest a little bit," said actor Bill Pullman, who worked as a summer performer in Montana's Shakespeare in the Parks traveling company, and as a professor at MSU before embarking on a successful career as a professional actor. "Their characters get caught up in their own emotional struggles, and it's said that they worked together on it and did it in 11 days. They must have had a good time laying it out and getting it down. I believe the director (Romanian-born Robert Dornhelm) added his own tweaks. At the time, Eastern European cinema was interested in the Americana subject, and you see the torque between the two."

The film, as one critic jeeringly noted, "takes on the quality of an in-joke" when Kenny and Maureen walk into a bar and the man tending it turns out to be Jeff Bridges, in an uncredited appearance. Kenny instantly insults a group of locals, and as they walk out, one of them—in fact, it's McGuane—looks Kenny in the eye and asks, "Anybody home?"

Casting director Tina Buckingham said that the scene with Bridges and McGuane was one of the movie's most memorable elements.

"That is the number one thing that jumps out and that is Bridges' cameo and casting him as the bartender and McGuane as a bar patron in the bar scene," said Buckingham. "That was so much fun. Nobody knows that that is McGuane sitting across in the bar. Jeff Bridges' wife, Susan, was an associate producer on the film.

"Everybody on that set was great fun. Tom Waits was fun and he'd drift into a bar and play, and he was such an idol of mine. Sally Kirkland was a trip and a half. The director was from Europe and I kept bringing him Polaroids of unusual faces and locals to cast. We ended up going to the group home and bringing mentally challenged adults, who had a fabulous day on the movie set. As casting director, the joy is giving people their 15 minutes of fame, and they are in heaven."

Buckingham's own career as a casting director started in a local salad bar because she wanted to meet Jeff Bridges. In 1974 she was standing in the lettuce line at the Overland Express when she overheard two men talking about what was taking place on the set of *Rancho Deluxe*. She asked them how she could meet Bridges. They told her where they were filming and invited her out.

When she arrived the next day, she was hired as an extra. "I got to gawk at Jeff," said Buckingham. In 1988 she walked into the office of Avenue Productions, which was producing *Cold Feet*, and asked for a job. An employee was needed for extras casting. Buckingham was hired. "I had no idea what to do," she said. "I spent the weekend following Renee Haynes, the casting director, around. On Monday I showed up for work on *Cold Feet* and I knew what to do."

Filmed in Livingston, *Cold Feet* presented an initial challenge that film commissioner Garry Wunderwald had yet to encounter. Wunderwald had to find a hydraulic table for a horse operation. "It was hard to find that. If we couldn't find one, they were going to move the film." In the summer of 1987, film crews decamped to the Gallatin National Forest halfway between Butte and Billings. While the finished product was a disastrous dud, Waits' character Kenny was generally singled out and liked.

As tedious as the filmmaking process was to the musician, Waits relished the chance to spend time with his family in the wilds of Montana. "This is the best summer I've had in a long, long time," he told *Variety*, describing the afternoon he'd just enjoyed in a nearby swimming hole. He said he'd been out collecting rocks with his

daughter, Kellesimone, who told him that pretty stones were good people who had died, whereas "all the little ones you're not interested in are bad people." He said the mountains and "wide open spaces" were so beautiful "it takes the top of your head off."

Deseret News typified the acrimonious response from reviewers and audiences: "Some movies are quirky and charming, some are bizarre but endearing, and then some simply try too hard to have quirky charm and wind up being forced and annoying…'Cold Feet' falls into the latter category."

Continental Divide

CAST
John Belushi, Blair Brown

DIRECTOR
Michael Apted

LOCATION
Glacier National Park

1981

This lighthearted 1981 film stars John Belushi as Chicago writer Ernie Souchak, who takes to the Colorado Rockies to study eagle researcher Nell (Blair Brown). Belushi is a well-known, street-smart Chicago newspaper columnist, and he isn't anything like the facetious wise guys Belushi usually played. Belushi is funny and believable on his first, unexpected trip to the mountains, where his friends have sent him to hide from a tough Chicago politician of whom he has run afoul. "Am I pleased or frightened?" Belushi asks, on one of his early glimpses of the wild, and it takes him an authentically long time to make up his mind. A decisive factor in his coming to like, or put up with, the outdoors is Brown, a dedicated ornithologist living alone in the Rocky Mountains. They meet. They fall in love. Later, he becomes more accustomed to a naturalist's life, going so far as to ask insouciantly—after Nell comes home and finds Ernie's had a run-in with a cougar—"How was your day?'"

Most of *Continental Divide* was filmed in Colorado. Wilderness scenes were shot in Glacier National Park of Montana as well as Washington and Colorado. *Continental Divide* includes shots of the eagles that migrate each fall to Glacier Park. Most of the scenes were filmed in Colorado. Scenes of Ernie and Nell camping in a tent were filmed near the Summit House at Crystal Mountain Ski Area east of Mount Rainier—and Rainier is noticeably visible in the background of the shot. The final scene of the film takes place in "Victory, Wyoming" but is in reality the former Cedar Falls train depot on Rattlesnake Lake near North Bend, Washington.

One reviewer from the *San Francisco Chronicle* lauded the "spectacular Rocky Mountain scenery" that is somehow rivaled by the equal glamour he finds in the movie's Chicago scenes. The *Los Angeles Times* noted that "the first half takes place in the wilderness, with the comic banter interspersed with stunning footage of bald eagles" and with a remarkable sequence in which Brown uses rope and ice to fashion a sled.

Audiences, not impressed with Belushi's departure from the crude, naughty slapstick that earned him such acclaim, stayed away from the romantic movie. Critics reacted mostly favorably. Gene Shalit applauded director Apted for the film's unfailing "humor and inventiveness." The *Chicago Sun-Times* commented, "Mr. Apted has made this a sweet, engaging movie that audiences will very much want to see end well." Sadly, it would be John Belushi's second to last film; the comedian died of a drug overdose in 1982.

The 1930 railroad thriller *Danger Lights* was filmed partly at Miles City.

Danger Lights

CAST
Louis Wolheim, Robert Armstrong, Jean Arthur

DIRECTOR
George B. Seitz

LOCATION
Bozeman area, Miles City

1930

This adventure-drama features steam locomotives and is a must-see for railroad fans. Immortalizing the unswerving faith and courage of all American railroad men, Radio Pictures' *Danger Lights* was the first great railroad melodrama of the talkies when it debuted in December 1930. It was advertised as a "stirring tribute to the stout hearts who keep the wheels moving." With Louis Wolheim as the two-fisted, hard-swearing, roaring division boss whose indomitable strength holds the rails fast; Robert Armstrong as the ace engineer whose love for the railroad transcends his selfishness; and Jean Arthur as the railroad-bred beauty whose charm fires these iron men to death grips. *Danger Lights* is truly the song of the rails romanticized.

Railroad men will appreciate the countless authentic touches of *Danger Lights*: roundhouse operations; emergency clearings of landslides and washouts; long freights plunging off mountain passes; the headlong stride of the limited expresses with their deluxe coaches; all the stirring glory of railroading in novels now appear in sound and light.

Danger Lights was filmed over the-right-of way of the Chicago, Milwaukee, St. Paul and Pacific road. The railway yard in Miles City was a main setting, while rural scenes were filmed along the line through Sixteen Mile Canyon, east of Maudlow. The film opens with a landslide across the tracks in Montana, with a repair crew dispatched to clear the line.

Every facility of the Milwaukee Road was made available to the Hollywood technicians in order that the picture be technically correct, with sufficient equipment to depict the sweeping immensity of operations of a railroad such as the Milwaukee. There were times during the filming when as many as four trains were used to obtain one shot. During production between Butte and Chicago, the company lived most of the time aboard their special train. Many additional trains and locomotives were brought in as needed.

Danger Lights features rare footage of a "tug of war" between two steam locomotives, documentary footage of the activities in the Miles City yard, and what is believed to be "the only motion picture footage of a dynamometer car from the steam railroad era in the country." (Railroad buffs say the Milwaukee Road's new dynamometer car shown in the film was actually on its first work assignment. Such cars, manned up to 24 hours a day, measured and recorded data for analyzing many aspects of their pulling locomotives' functions, as well as some track-load conditions. The first such car in the U.S., simpler than the 1930 model, began service in 1874.)

In the film, a landslide on the Chicago, Milwaukee,

Danger Lights featured newcomer Jean Arthur, who went on to a long Hollywood career.

St. Paul & Pacific Railroad ties up traffic and throws employees into confusion until Dan Thorn, division superintendent, sets about clearing the debris. Enlisting a group of hoboes from a boxcar for the work, Dan spots Larry Doyle, previously an engineer but discharged for insubordination, and succeeds in putting him to work as a fireman. Larry meets Mary Ryan, engaged to Thorn, and they fall in love; he plans to marry her when he is given a vacation; but on the night he is to announce their plans, there is a washout on the line. Notified of the lovers' elopement, Dan saves Larry from an oncoming express when his foot is caught in an electric switch, but Dan suffers a brain injury. Larry drives a fast train to Chicago, where an operation saves Dan; and upon his recovery, he gives his blessing to Mary and Larry.

The October 1930 issue of *Milwaukee Magazine* called the film "an epic of the railroad, a picture that is faithful in its portrayal of one of the greatest institutions, one of the greatest factors in the economic life of America." The Milwaukee Railroad abandoned its line in 1980.

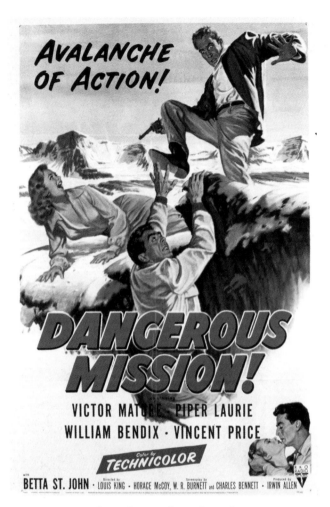

Dangerous Mission featured top Hollywood stars, but many reviewers felt Glacier National Park, the actual setting in the script and where much of the movie was filmed, stole the show.

Dangerous Mission

CAST
Victor Mature, Piper Laurie

DIRECTOR
Louis King

LOCATION
Glacier National Park.

1954

Dangerous Mission was a low-budget programmer for RKO Radio Pictures that squeezed in a number of well executed scenes of avalanches, forest fires, steep glacier cliffs, and sparking electrical wires. First known as *The Glacier Story*, its Glacier National Park portion was filmed from July 20, 1953, into August with a crew of 67. It included a forest fire, though not filmed in Glacier, and a rugged cliff sequence with a nasty fall filmed in part near Sun Point.

Technicolor and 3-D filming made Glacier's mountains seem even higher and more colorfully beautiful than they are. Producer Irwin Allen and Director Louis King had something to work with at St. Mary Lake, which provided about 90 percent of the outdoor setting.

Starring were Victor Mature, William Bendix, Piper Laurie and Vincent Price. Mature plays the special agent hunting a dangerous murder suspect while Bendix has the role of the Chief Ranger at the park. Laurie plays a woman believed to have been a key witness to the murder. She had fled to the park to hide and taken a job as a cashier in a restaurant. Both the law and the suspect then head there to try to track her down. Betta St. John plays an Indian girl in the film. A secondary story involves the life and work of the national park rangers.

The movie opens in sleek style with the after-hours gangland shooting of a man playing *One for My Baby* on the piano in an empty New York nightclub. Unfortunately for the killer, a woman has witnessed the shooting—she screams and flees the scene. Following this opening, we are introduced to Matt Hallett (Mature), who drives into Glacier National Park in Montana. He checks into a large resort hotel and meets a variety of hotel workers and other guests. Among them are photographer Paul Adams (Price), and cashier Louise Graham (Laurie). Park Ranger Joe Parker (Bendix) keeps watch as the main characters sort out each other's true motives and identities. Ultimately the assassin sent to silence the witness-in-hiding sparks a chase, which leads to treacherous cliffs in the glaciers of the park.

Dangerous Mission was filmed in 3-D, and many of the effects shots lose something when viewed "flat." In one scene, Mature brazenly subdues a live wire that has been severed during an avalanche. The wire wriggles about shooting sparks as Mature vaults over it and climbs a pole to disable it; while the scene plays well, it was probably doubly exciting to those seeing it on the big screen while wearing Polaroid glasses. The film also features several

Arch-villain Vincent Price forces a park worker across a glacier at gunpoint. This sound-stage set featured a fairly accurate painting of Glacier's mountains.

wonderful Technicolor location shots, especially towards the final act as the principal characters are approaching the glacier setting. Shot in the bright outdoors with an eye toward layered compositions, these sequences undoubtedly must have been impressive when witnessed in stereo.

In an interview with *Film Magazine*, supporting player Walter Reed discussed working on location at Glacier National Park, and having "a whole lot of fun doing it." The company stayed in park cabins; Reed shared a room with Dennis Weaver, who also played a park ranger. Reed said, "Victor [Mature] was in the next room, but he didn't have a shower or bath tub. I told him I'd leave the door unlocked from our side, and when he wanted to take a shower he could go in there. Well, soon he was not only showering, he was using my razor and other things.

I said, 'Victor, when you get to my toothbrush I'm going to close the door and lock it!'"

Time wrote that "*Dangerous Mission* is a misguided tour of Glacier National Park in which the public inspects such unnatural phenomena as a studio glacier, a special-effects forest fire, an avalanche in miniature and Victor Mature."

The review emphasizes a blooper in which Laurie takes a bad fall off a cliff.

"Bouncy little Piper bounces back, only to take another tumble into a crevasse where Price lies dying interminably in shaved ice. As she shivers on a frigid shelf above the killer, the audience shivers in sympathy. But Piper, as the camera reveals when Victor hauls her out on a hawser, needs no sympathy to keep her warm. She is wearing snuggies."

Dangerous Mission was the eighth film for young actress Piper Laurie, and the first that she made away from her home studio, Universal. Laurie had been under contract with Universal since the age of 17; her film debut was *Louisa* (1950), starring Ronald Reagan. *Dangerous Mission* at RKO was an early dramatic role for the actress. Irwin Allen's only film prior to this one was the Groucho Marx/William Bendix comedy *A Girl in Every Port* (1952). One of Allen's most noted works, *The Poseidon Adventure* (1972), continued his penchant for putting a variety of familiar faces in constant peril.

Not all of the press related to *Dangerous Mission* was negative. One review of *Dangerous Mission* mentioned the good sequence with Blackfeet Indians, and the Hollywood idea of what sells theatre tickets: an avalanche, forest fire, falling off a cliff, some romance and "real Indians." Another review in 1954 said that the whole package of "Dangerous Mission" didn't rank as an outstanding movie. Yet it would bring worldwide audiences a combination of first ranked stars such as Victor Mature with fresh, spectacular settings. *Screenplay* wrote, "This picture is a million dollars worth of publicity for northwestern Montana."

Damnation Alley

CAST
Jan-Michael Vincent, George Peppard

DIRECTOR
Jack Smight

LOCATION
Lakeside, Bigfork

1977

In the summer of 1976, Flathead Lake was the site of sun, swimming, and something called the "Landmaster," an enormous 12-foot-long all-terrain personnel carrier designed to withstand anything. Twentieth Century Fox,

Damnation Alley, starring Jan-Michael Vincent (center) and George Peppard (right), remains a sketch of 1970s nihilism, offering something a little zany for everyone, including an enormous all-terrain personnel carrier named "Landmaster" that swam across Flathead Lake.

the studio behind this adaptation of Roger Zelazny's novel, assumed that a film about ex-military operatives rolling across a bug-infested, post-apocalyptic landscape would satisfy the public's appetite for disaster and buddy pictures. Indeed, *Damnation Alley* remains a sketch of 1970s noxious nihilism, offering a little zany something for everyone: crazed survivalists; mysterious radio transmissions; giant tidal waves; the Earth shifting on its axis. The Landmaster and the surviving souls are saved when they emerge onto the calm shore of New York. Montana fills the part of New York, as shot along the banks of the Flathead near Lakeside. The Landmaster looked a lot like the world's largest Tonka toy, a 22,000-pound machine, which cost between $250,000 to $300,000 to construct—the mechanical star of the science fiction film which is based on the world's destruction resulting from World War III.

The Landmaster's beginning started in Houston, Texas, with a basic frame and a 391 Ford Allison truck engine. From there it was transferred to Hollywood, where Dean Jeffries, a noted auto customizer, began the job of working from blue prints to finish the new Twentieth Century Fox star. "I worked 24 hours every day for two months to construct, cut, weld and fit every section of the machine," said Jeffries. As time passed, it grew from a frame on the floor to a shell and finally to the silver machine adorned with space age equipment to fit the theme of its assignment in *Damnation Alley*. It could reach a top speed of 55 miles per hour over weeds, rocks, and sand. Moviemakers did their magic by inserting space age camouflage in parts of the machine. The film had a $7.2 million production budget, including the Landmaster.

"When we first got the machine, it wouldn't float," said Jim Kohler, production controller for the film. "We were finally able to rig it so that it would float."

Though the movie is dated, it precedes some of the other more memorable post-apocalyptic giants such as *Dawn of the Dead* and *Mad Max*. The cast and crew of *Damnation Alley* lodged at the Outlaw Inn in Kalispell. Bill Kuney was the owner at the time and he recalled an exchange he had with actor George Peppard, who plays an ex-military operative who rolls with the Landmaster across the barren landscape.

"The Outlaw Inn was the kind of place where people from construction and loggers and all kind of others, they all congregated together and was one of the most popular places in the area. I think the hotel was one of the best operating in the Northwest. George Peppard didn't think so, because he commented that the bathroom facilities was one the worst public restrooms and men's rooms he had ever been in. I visualized someone must have thrown up and had problems. But it wasn't bad. There were used paper towels someone hadn't thrown in the garbage can and soil and grease spots along the basin. Nothing I'd get too concerned about. I guess he was used to the restrooms with an attendant, with hot towels. Nice guy, but that changed my mind a little bit. Jan Michael-Vincent had an older model car that he drove in with, and he didn't want to be recognized."

Kuney recalled that the presence of the Landmaster sparked much curiosity. "They parked it by the hotel parking lot. It had three wheels on each side and the wheels rotated. It caused a lot of attention."

Other parts of the movie were filmed at the Valley of the Fire in Nevada, the Bonneville Salt Flats and Salt Lake City in Utah, Marble Canyon in Utah, and at the meteor crater near Flagstaff, Arizona. While the movie barely seems relevant to today's high-cost, high-flying, high-budget science fiction films, its quaint blend of Montana as Manhattan and cartoonish caricatures makes it worth the viewing.

A zombie apocalypse movie needs plenty of body parts, as shown by the fake arms and legs on the set of *Dead 7*, filmed in Butte.

Dead 7

Cast
Joey Fatone, Nick Carter, A.J. McLean, Jeff Timmons

Director
Nick Carter

Location
Butte

2016

SyFy's movie *Dead 7* is a futuristic zombie Western with one big twist: the cast is composed mostly of Nineties and early millennium boy-band stars. In the summer of 2015, members of 'NSync, O'Town and the Backstreet Boys came to Butte to film. "This has been a dream of mine for quite some time," said actor and *Dead 7* writer Nick Carter, of the Backstreet Boys. "I wrote this script seven years ago and it finally came to fruition. It's just been a great experience having all my friends and people who are from the same generation and do music and have a musician-based cast."

Much of the movie was filmed at the Anselmo Mine in historic Uptown Butte (now part of the World Museum of Mining). The cast filmed in several other locations, including the showcase brothel at the Montana 1800s Ranch near Anaconda and the Dumas Brothel at 45 E. Mercury in Butte. Old rusted buildings transformed into set locales, with tents used as dressing rooms for the actors. Special effects makeup artist Jonny Bullard explained the skill in turning someone into the walking dead. "We actually start with a plan," said Bullard. "We start putting on certain prosthetics and as we go, we see what works with that character, and sometimes it just speaks to us and we'll change the character's looks to what is starting to develop, so just kind of go with the flow."

Approximately 250 local residents were contracted as background actors. "I love this city so much," said actress Carrie Keagan. "Everybody has been so accommodating, and the locals have been so wonderful to us," added Carter.

Carter said that Butte's unique environmental feng shui was hard to match. "There's just a lot of really rich-looking sets that you just couldn't pay for in Los Angeles or anywhere else, and it really fit the script as well," said Carter.

The film was released in April 2016.

Devil's Pond

CAST
Tara Reid, Kip Pardue, Meredith Baxter

DIRECTOR
Joel Viertel

LOCATION
Libby area

2003

Devil's Pond stars Tara Reid and Kip Pardue in an R-rated thriller about a young Connecticut couple honeymooning at a remote lake in upstate New York. This smorgasbord of inflated horror genre clichés clearly wants to evoke comparisons to earlier, much better classics. The film is so note-for-note similar that it's easy to visualize a split-screen YouTube comparison video, if you can imagine such a horror.

Reid had already built up a decent resume in television and smaller-budget movies. But it was her role as the sexy Bunny in the Ethan and Joel Coen–directed hit *The Big Lebowski* (1998), starring Jeff Bridges, which significantly raised her profile. Her biggest role to date came in 1999 with the popular raunchy teen comedy *American Pie*, a coming-of-age flick that surprised critics with its tremendous success at the box office. At the time of *Devil's Pond*, Reid's celebrity was tethered to her reputation as a dubious paparazzi party girl and bikini-clad lush.

In the film, Reid plays a country club–raised princess who has fallen for a ruggedly attractive outdoorsy type, and he's planned for them to spend two weeks on an island in the middle of a lake. He doesn't tell his non-swimming sweetheart that it's a shotgun shack perched on a tiny island in the middle of a gigantic swimming hole, and that he's a psychopath who has no intention of ever letting her leave.

When director Joel Viertel called Montana Film Commissioner Sten Iversen about potential shooting locations in Big Sky Country, Iversen stepped—or in this case, dove—into action.

"*Devil's Pond* was looking at places in New Zealand to film and looking really all over the place," recalled Iversen. "The main requirement was a cabin on an island in the middle of a lake—or an island to build a set cabin on. I thought we had about four viable options in the state of Montana. But to find an island that was the right size, the right fit for this film, the best option was [Horseshoe Lake] in northwestern Montana.

"The director liked the photos I sent him from the shore. But he wanted to see photos from the island—how it would look from there. I had to do my part and I put my camera in a dry bag and swam across the island to take pictures. I guess it was a natural scout of some kind."

The Epworth United Methodist Church on Second Avenue East in downtown Kalispell serves as the wedding scene, standing in as Connecticut. Producers were looking for "an old-fashioned church for a ritzy wedding." Local extras lined the pews in this scene, hoping for a split-second of eternity on the silver screen. "We're just here to fill space," said Jeremy Bashus of Kalispell, who acted as a wedding guest.

Apart from the church scenes and a short montage of driving scenes, the film takes place at the island in Thompson Chain of Lakes, between Kalispell and Libby. Reid spends most of the movie attempting to escape from the island and the smothering love of her deranged husband. Except for a brief cameo by *Family Ties'* Meredith Baxter (as Reid's mother), the action involves the couple or Reid staring despondently into the water.

Production staff built a set cabin on the lake, and, excluding the sparking an inadvertent forest fire on the shore of the lake, which burned approximately an acre and a half, the production arrived and left without a trace. The fire broke out on a peninsula near a dock that was being used by the film crew. The fire was contained to the peninsula with some help from a Forest Service helicopter that dropped buckets of water on the blaze. "We thought we were in a…load of trouble," said production manager Bruce Gillies. "There's a lot of firewood out there."

The film company, which paid the state $300 a day for use of the lake, removed some stumps but no live trees. Crews planted additional trees when they left.

The film has its fair share of gaffes—at one point, a director's chair is visible in the background—and the most impressive thing about *Devil's Pond* is that it somehow manages to be both predictable and incoherent at the same time. Paltry and forgettable, the woman-in-danger histrionics ended up going direct to DVD.

"The film starts off as a romantic honeymoon but soon turns into a nightmare," said scout John Ansotegui. "Some may argue that the real star of the film was the location. As first-time director Joe Viertel was able to squeeze more drama from this isolated mountain lake than from either of his two leads combined. *Devil's Pond* was not a huge success, but Tara Reid was able to parlay her talent into a number of successful television roles."

Reid told the press that she enjoyed the serenity of the area. "It's so beautiful here—a lot different than what we're used to."

Diggstown

CAST
James Woods, Louis Gossett Jr., Bruce Dern

DIRECTOR
Michael Ritchie

LOCATION
Deer Lodge

1992

Producer Robert Schaffel found himself struck by the originality of Leonard Wise's novel, *The Diggstown Ringers*, and assumed that the book was a real contender for a good movie. He optioned the book and brought in screenwriter Steven McKay of *Hard To Kill* (1990) to punch up the story. *Diggstown* drew the talents of actors James Woods, Academy Award-winner Louis Gossett Jr., and Oscar-nominee Bruce Dern. "The fun of playing a con man is that you're not just playing a character, you're the character your character is pretending to be," explained James Woods. "The challenge was deciding just how far to turn the screws without breaking the screwdriver."

Diggstown opens to scenes that were filmed at the Old Montana Prison, featuring Woods as Gabriel Caine, a con artist who has just been released from the penitentiary. Based on a tip by his cellmate, Caine heads for Diggstown, Georgia, a small town run by the ruthless boxing fanatic John Gillon (Dern). Arriving there, Caine sets his sights on the ultimate con game. Conning Gillon into believing that he's the one being scammed, Caine makes a bet with him. Caine will supply a fighter he's convinced will beat any 10 men whom Diggstown has to offer over the course of one day. The palooka, "Honey" Roy Palmer (Gossett), a 48-year-old ex-heavyweight, must be coaxed out of retirement in order for Caine to exact his plan. As the fights begin and the double crosses begin to spiral out of control, Palmer must reach inside himself to recapture the glory of his youth and ensure victory for Caine.

Woods delivers one of his best performances as the conniving scoundrel Caine. Gossett and Dern deliver

Diggstown's opening scenes were filmed at the Old Montana Prison in Deer Lodge, shown here with lunch tables set up for the film crew.

fine supporting turns, as do former heavyweight boxer Randall "Tex" Cobb, Oliver Platt, Orestes Matacena, and Heather Graham. World champion kick boxer Benny "The Jet" Urquidez taught Gossett and his challengers boxing techniques, and fight coordinators James Nickerson and Bobby Bass choreographed all the ring action. Several professional athletes, including heavyweight fighter Alex Garcia and Kansas City Chiefs' Willie Green exchanged punches with Gossett, a former athlete himself who, at one time, turned down a tryout with the New York Knicks to pursue his acting career. "To be over 50 and get a clean bill of health from a doctor and improve on that is indeed a miracle for me," said Gossett. "My heart rate is down. My blood pressure is the blood pressure of a pro athlete. It all extends my life."

Eight residents of the Butte Pre-Release Center were cast as extras in October 1991. Three played the part of inmates in the movie, while five enjoyed the ultimate role reversal—they portrayed prison guards. "It was fun," said Tony Burt, who was in custody a second time for violat-

ing parole on an initial sentence for robbery, who played an inmate. "I knew once I was done I could walk out." Burt had been moved to the pre-release center only a few weeks before the deadly prison riot at the new prison in Deer Lodge in late September 1991. "It made me realize where I had just come from, that I got a better life out here. You don't realize what you miss."

Ed Salle, who portrayed a prison guard in the movie, may have had a double sense of déjà vu. He had worked for a time as a correctional officer at the prison, but at the time of filming was serving time for negligent homicide resulting from a fatal 1990 car crash in Anaconda. "It's nice seeing the other side of the fence," he said. "I got to play my old role."

Both Woods and Gossett were on hand during the two-day shoot, and meeting the actors was a highlight for the pre-release residents. "They were wonderful guys," said Ross McCord, who had been paroled after serving out his sentence for mail fraud and now played a guard. "They were really a nice bunch of people." "I wanted to see Mr. Woods," said Salle. "He was really kind. They didn't treat us like inmates. It was pretty good." Other pre-release residents taking part in the filming of *Diggstown* were Jack Pennington, Norm Kettleson, David Kimble, John Lucero and Dan Castello.

The inmates-turned-actors discovered movie-making can provide interesting situations. For one, the setting of the film is Georgia in the summer. The inmates did their best to act hot in a cool Montana October. "It was cold," said Burt, who acted his part in a tank top. The inmates also were sprayed continually with water bottles "to make it look like they're sweating," said Salle. "We were all shaking." Some were involved in a semi-nude shower scene, but they weren't in the raw very long. "They only had enough hot water for one shot," said McCord, who wasn't in the scene. "It was a one-shot deal."

Though inmates said the film-making experience was enjoyable, it wasn't exactly action-packed. "It was boring, really," said McCord of the shoot. "There was a lot of sitting around." The benefits, however, outweighed the boredom. "Boy did they feed us," said McCord. "Anything we wanted." The pre-release residents earned over $100 for their efforts, and the paycheck was most appreciated. "Now with winter here things are really getting tight," said McCord. "We probably would have done it even if the whole movie was a nude scene." McCord said he wondered at first about "the public image" of inmates acting in a prison movie so soon after the riot in the new prison. But, he said in November 1991, "the movie won't really be out for another year," allowing possible tensions to wear off. He said he was grateful to the pre-release center, which was responsible for the movie experience in the first place and which provided transportation for the residents throughout the weekend of filming. "They bent over backwards for us," said McCord.

Mike Thatcher, director of the pre-release center, said he was contacted by the film's casting department about hiring movie extras, and said he "invited a guy to the center that evening." Casting people interviewed, took pictures and, later, returned the names of the eight residents selected for the movie. The movie provided needed job opportunities for the inmates, who were required to pay rent at the center. Thatcher said work had been harder to come by at the time of filming and speculated that the riot may have hindered some businesses and citizens from hiring pre-release inmates. Bill Peterson, a counselor at the center, said he'd heard "good feedback" from

residents about their movie experience. "It seemed like it was good for them. It got 'em out of the center…[they] got to be productive."

Disorganized Crime

Cast
Fred Gwynne, Corbin Bernsen, Ed O'Neill, Hoyt Axton, Lou Diamond Phillips

Director
Jim Kouf

Location
Hamilton area

1989

Disorganized Crime is, as one critic described, "one of those movies with a funny concept, one or two big laughs and lots of dry spots." At the outset the camera focuses on a trio of crooks (Fred Gwynne, Ruben Blades, William Russ) who don't know each other but who all get off the train in a small Montana town simultaneously. The story has them being summoned by Corbin Bernsen, a New Jersey bank robber who wants to knock off this small town's bank. Why he's in Montana is never explained, except that he's on the run.

The three crooks are ex-cons, all experts in various aspects of the game, joined by a fourth (Lou Diamond Phillips) who picks them up and drives them to Bernsen's dilapidated lodging high in the hills. What none of them know is that Bernsen has been arrested by two bumbling New Jersey cops (Ed O'Neill, Dan Roebuck). It isn't long before Bernsen escapes, however, and tries to make his way back to his house—getting lost in the woods along the way. Meanwhile, Bernsen's four friends, all squabbling among themselves, plan the bank robbery by themselves, hoping to run into Bernsen along the way. Meanwhile, the Jersey cops stumble along trying to track down Bernsen, ultimately enlisting the aid of the local

The cast of *Disorganized Crime* posed for a publicity photo aboard the back of a train car owned by business mogul Dennis Washington. From left to right: Corbin Bernsen, Lou Diamond Phillips, Ruben Blades, Fred Gwynne, and William Russ. (Photo by Steve Slocomb)

sheriff (Hoyt Axton), but wholly oblivious of the other four crooks or the impending bank robbery.

Variety magazine summed up *Disorganization Crime's* unevenness: "There are some amusing moments here and there, and some of the actors—particularly Blades, O'Neill and Russ—try hard to invest humor into their characterizations, and Gwynne gives the script more dignity than it deserves, but there are an awful lot of deadly dull draggy scenes, and Bernsen is way over the top in his role as city mouse in the country…This is the kind of movie that thinks it's funnier than it is but just keeps on going anyway."

One scene of *Disorganized Crime* (originally titled *Waiting for Salazar*) was shot in Missoula, but the majority of the action took place in the Bitterroot Valley. Interior bank shots were filmed in the former Evans Furniture Store Annex and Bitterroot Stock Farm office in Hamilton. Jim Kouf, who wrote the screenplay, lives south of Hamilton in the Bitterroot Valley. He and his wife, Kim, and their production company were allowed to use

almost all of Victorian Mall and turned it into a movie-making command post with numerous telephones, computers, walls full of maps, location snapshots, blueprints and drafting desks. The exterior of Citizens State Bank was used for the robbery attempt scenes (the brick façade of the bank turned into simulated marble). Plenty of action takes place around the Ravalli County Sheriff's office. A key scene occurs in the Angler's Roost. Scenes in Hamilton were shot at the A and W, C and D Cleaners, The Brass Rail, The Coffee Cup, the Ravalli County Courthouse, Bitterroot Drug, Mountain Outfitters, and on Main Street. Some scenes were shot at Honey Hardware and Chadal Tires in Darby. The only Missoula scene that remained involved the Northern Pacific depot, where the characters played by Gwynne, Russ and Blades arrive on a train. Millionaire businessman Dennis Washington permitted the inclusion of his private rail car for $1,500, a paltry sum compared to what Amtrak requested. "I just tried to take advantage of everything around me," said Jim Kouf. "There's nothing I would change on this one. I like what we did. This one I'm really happy with. You really give up a certain amount of yourself when you give up your script."

A century-old house, built for copper baron Marcus Daly's racehorse jockeys, ended its days posing as a hideout in *Disorganized Crime*. The ramshackle home, known locally as the old Crawford place, was dismantled for reassembly at a site in the Darby area. The entire house was rebuilt, sagging porch and all, as were all the elements from the surrounding yard—an old dog house, telephone poles and a rail fence. It was destroyed after filming.

"To me, even watching it all these years later, it's all about the guys and the casting that's most interesting," said Kouf recently. "We wanted Edward James Olmos (as head robber Salazar), but Corbin Bernsen just did a movie for Disney, and Bernsen was on Disney's radar. Many times, the studio gets involved in the casting. We wanted Christopher Lloyd, a neighbor of mine in Montana. We got Fred Gwynne and Lou Diamond Phillips, who had just come off *La Bamba*. We got Ed O'Neill, who I think just started doing *Married With Children*. I wrote the movie and the script for the town of Hamilton and the area and I'm glad that Jeffrey Katzenberg let me make the movie here. We had no money for the screenplay and none to direct it. Parts of it were shot at my ranch, like the hideout, the scene in which Corbin is lost in the woods. I watch it these days and I say, 'There's the bank, there's the real estate office, there's the post office.'

"It was nice because the crew got to walk to work. Fred Gywnne was floating the river and fly-fishing and O'Neill and (Daniel) Roebuck stayed at Angler's Roost, in those log cabins bunched together. I was born in Hollywood, raised in Burbank, and I had relatives in Baker, Montana. Growing up in California, I was always a skier, a rafter and a backpacker—and in California, when you go backpacking, you have to make a reservation, because there are so many people. I knew that in Montana you could go to the mountains and drink the water out of the river. We moved to the Bitterroot Valley in 1985, and one of my daughters was born in Hamilton during filming."

"*Disorganized Crime* holds so many special memories," said producer Lynn Kouf. "Main Street in Hamilton was our back lot. We shot at the Coffee Cup café and we shot all along the river. For us, we were lucky because the locations were free. We show it to the kids and to

new people a lot. The mountains don't change. We still love watching it and showing it to new people."

Singer, songwriter, and actor Hoyt Axton moved to Victor in the Bitterroot Valley after he filmed *Disorganized Crime*. Axton was known for writing songs such as *Joy to the World* ("Jeremiah was a Bullfrog"), which was a smash hit for Three Dog Night in 1971, and for his television and movie appearances, including *The Black Stallion* and *Gremlins*.

The initial cut of the movie ran about three hours and Kouf trimmed the film down to 100 minutes. The Roxy Theater in Hamilton hosted the world premiere of *Disorganized Crime* on April 10, 1989, attended by most of the cast and crew. More than 300 people crammed in for an invitation-only showing and afterward jammed into the Elks Lodge for a reception.

Don't Come Knocking

CAST
Sam Shepard, Jessica Lange, Tim Roth

DIRECTOR
Wim Wenders

LOCATION
Butte

2005

More than two decades after director Wim Wenders and writer Sam Shepard spun their moody, meandering road trip of family reclamation with *Paris, Texas*, they attempted a lighter vein in *Don't Come Knocking*. The German director had fallen in love with Butte on a road trip several years earlier and returned a number of times. He scouted his own locations, and his love of Butte shines through in the 2005 comedy-drama.

In 1978, Wenders came to Butte because he wanted to direct a film version of Dashiell Hammett's novel *Red Harvest*, which was set in Butte. Wenders couldn't secure

Don't Come Knocking was filmed primarily in Butte, including the tragicomic scene in which the main character played by Sam Shepard slept overnight on a couch in an empty city street.

the movie rights to the book, but the character and history of the town left an impression on him. His first day in town, Wenders witnessed and photographed the fire—as chronicled in his book *Once*—that destroyed the Silver Bow Block, located across Granite Street from the *Montana Standard* offices. "Since then I've always wanted to make a movie here," said Wenders.

"Wim Wenders came to Bozeman and shot a commercial for a German clothing company and I was the casting director," recalled Tina Buckingham. "At the end of day one, I asked him, 'Why are you in Montana to shoot a commercial?' He said, 'I am scouting crew for a movie that I want to bring here.'…For five years he and Sam Shepard came to Montana and scouted the entire state looking for locations. They ended up in Butte—a movie set waiting to happen."

Sam Shepard stars as a fading Western movie star, who abruptly runs off from his latest film to reconnect with his mom and an old flame (Jessica Lange) and ac-

quaint himself with newly discovered kin. Shepard's character, Howard Spence, has ditched a Utah movie set, leaving the production he's starring in high and dry. A quick glimpse into his trailer—liquor bottles, smears of cocaine, slinky groupies—tells us most of what we need to know about Howard's lifestyle. A little later, he flips through a scrapbook of infamy: affairs, fights, drug and alcohol busts splashed over the years of headlines.

Butte's grand and gritty locations are front and center. A magnificent ruin: that's how the American West is pictured, a surreal epic-manqué. That description also applied to the visually majestic but dramatically inert movie, and to the ravaged but still-handsome face of its 60-something writer and star. Shepard had physically aged into a symbol of the stubborn, cranky individualist who had been a constant presence in his plays and films.

The first leg of Howard's odyssey takes him from the desert movie set to the Elko, Nevada, home of his mother, whom he hasn't visited in 30 years. When she jolts him with the news that a woman from Butte once contacted her saying she had borne him a son, he impulsively decides to drive to Montana. In Butte, "depicted as a shabby former boomtown whose streets are nearly empty," as described by one film critic, Howard meets a former casual lover, Doreen, who owns and operates a local bar—actually the iconic M&M. He also encounters the grownup son he knew nothing about until a day or two earlier. That son, Earl, is an angry musician who is so unsettled by his father's sudden entrance into his life that he goes ballistic and tosses all his own possessions out the window.

Howard also meets a second child, Sky, his daughter by an unidentified woman whose ashes Sky carries around with her in an urn. According to *Film Review*, from that point *Don't Come Knocking* "tantalizes us with ghosts and mysteries and the promise of psychic adventure until Howard reaches Butte, whereupon the movie grinds to a halt, mired in the mud of unsettled family business. From there it hems and haws, spinning its wheels trying to work up enough momentum to go somewhere, but it never budges."

Many of the film's images had been brewing in Wenders' head for 25 years. Wender made great use of the certain scenes that can only be found in Butte. One of the last scenes filmed in Butte was set on the north rim of the Berkeley Pit, a place generally closed to the public. In addition to the M&M, the movie also filmed at the Irish Times pub at 2 East Galena Street, an apartment on West Copper Street, and numerous other locations, mostly in the Uptown. The M&M's owner said he couldn't have been happier with the work that the *Don't Come Knocking* crew put into Butte's landmark bar and restaurant. For the first time in recent memory, the neon in the big M&M sign out front worked.

Indeed, Butte's pervasive flavor is the movie's most redeeming charm. Buckingham cast 400 people in the movie, "and quite a few got a one-liner here or there." She also brought in "authentic people, who'd actually worked at the M&M, as extras. "It is the most amazing city in America," said director Wenders.

"There was a bus driver named Leonard, who owned one of the bars in Butte, and he took me all over Butte," recalled casting director Tina Buckingham. "He was third-generation and he gave me my Butte education, and he continued to be a wealth of info for that movie. Butte has a lot of great faces. Leonard was really involved

with Butte theatre and he introduced me to a lot of actors. He was one of the bartenders. We shot in a few different bars. Actor Gabriel Mann, his band played in one of the bars and Leonard was in that scene. Katie Goodman, the comedian from Bozeman, I tapped…as a waitress next to Jessica Lange."

Other actors included Tim Roth, Sarah Polley, Fairuza Balk and Eva Marie Saint, who played Sam Shepard's mother. In a movie-within-a-movie scene, George Kennedy played a director, and Tim Matheson and Julia Sweeney played producers. (In 2004, Kennedy, a native of Eagle, Idaho, attended a free screening of *Cool Hand Luke* at the Mother Lode Theatre in Butte.)

The film flopped, having been budgeted for $11 million but earning less than $1 million in its first year. Yet there is much to admire in *Don't Come Knocking*. Reviewers rightfully singled out Wenders and the cinematographer, Franz Lustig, who fill the screen with pictures of "shimmering, mirage-like intensity" and "haunting visual panoramas." Such powerful images make *Don't Come Knocking* well worth contemplating. Roger Ebert gave it a "thumbs up," writing that "there are scenes that don't even pretend to work. And others that have a sweetness and visual beauty that stops time." The film manages to capture a semblance of what Butte has become in the twenty-first century, which perplexed Ebert: "These people move in intersecting orbits through Butte, a city that seems to have essentially no traffic, and no residents not in the movie except for a few tavern extras and restaurant customers. Consider a scene where the enraged Earl throws all of his possessions out the window of his second-story apartment and into the street. His stuff remains there, undisturbed, for days. No complaints from the neighbors. No cops. Howard Spence spends a night on the sofa, sleeping, thinking and smoking. It's a lovely scene."

Gabriel Mann, who played Shepard's long-lost son, noted how the cast spent a few days in Butte before shooting to get a feel for the town. "If you can imagine living in a city like that, it's bound to affect your performance," said Mann. Because most of the population of Butte has vanished, Sam Shepard noted, "We didn't have to do any crowd control or set up any roadblocks."

George Hamilton played Butte's own Evel Knievel in the 1971 movie of the same name. Sue Lyon, on the back of the motorcycle, played his wife, Linda. The movie premiered at the Fox Theater in Butte, with Hamilton attending.

Evel Knievel

CAST
George Hamilton, Sue Lyon

DIRECTOR
Marvin J. Chomsky

LOCATION
Butte

1971

On December 13, 1969, Robert Knievel, known throughout Butte as "Bob" before he adopted the Evel tag, had been recuperating in a Burbank hospital room from several bone fractures sustained in a crash while trying to vault his motorcycle over the fountains of Caesar's

Palace. Anyone who is worth his weight in copper has seen the newsreel footage of the real Knievel taking that horrible spill and rolling over and over, tangled in his bike, for dozens of yards.

Nursing his injuries was an afterthought. Knievel was more concerned about being ready to handle the jumps as the stunt man in his life story. Movie star George Hamilton paid a call on Knievel while he was recuperating and they discussed a film project in which Hamilton was to play the part of Knievel. West Coast papers, including the film and stage daily *Variety*, announced that week that Evel Knievel's life story would be filmed, just as the Butte-born motorcyclist had been maintaining all along. The picture, by Ash Productions, rolled in the spring of 1970 in and around Butte, in Las Vegas, Nevada, and Santa Fe, New Mexico. The film was produced by Fanfare Corporation. Around 40 Hollywood actors and technicians came to Butte the first part of April 1971. Among them were Hamilton and Sue Lyon, who played Evel's wife, Linda. Hamilton discussed the movie with a reporter from *Life*:

"In America we've long had a theory that all men have an equal right to become everything they want. But there's a new theory being pushed on us—that every man has to be something whether he wants to or not. That's what the theory of Evel Knievel is about. He's an individual who doesn't care about establishment or hippie, both have their phony sides. I'm not sure why Evel does what he does on a motorcycle. But I do know that by the time the picture is finished I'll be able to say it in one sentence."

Evel Knievel premiered in Butte on Wednesday, July 21, 1971, at the Fox Theater. The show played for a week and then moved on to the Motor Vu Drive-in. Butte fans surely recognized much Mining City terrain in the film. Around 130 local people were employed by film makers. Scenes were shot at Homestake Lake, the Montana Bar, Judd's Hardware, First National Bank, Butte High, Ramada Inn and City Hall. The film features some vintage shots of Butte circa 1970, including some footage of the East Ridge and the upper reaches of the Butte Hill, including Walkerville. One sequence early in the film was shot in the M&M bar.

Evel, who had painfully earned the right to be billed as America's king of the stunt men, served as advisor on the film and joined the company during its stay in Butte. One of the things he "advised" producer Joe Solomen was to blow up Butte's City Hall, rather than a mock-up, for one of the film scenes. In the film, Knievel is preparing to perform at the Ontario Motor Speedway. The scene jumps to his boyhood days in Butte, his teenage years courting his wife in a most unorthodox manner, and on to his youth involved in good natured ruckuses with the law in the person of the Butte sheriff, played by Hal Baylor.

Depicted are his encounters with Turquoise Smith, the promoter who gave him his first opportunity to perform stunts as a professional. Hamilton portrays Evel in most scenes but it's the daredevil himself who's shown in the film jumping cars and canyons. Besides his 50-yard leap over the fountains at Caesar's Palace in Las Vegas where he broke his back, footage includes a similar 50-yard jump over 19 Dodge autos at Ontario Motor Speedway in California. The film ends with shots of Hamilton alongside the Grand Canyon, which Evel once hoped to jump, but where permission was denied. At the time of filming, Knievel had purchased land bordering the Snake River Canyon and intended to try that stunt on Labor Day, 1972.

The movie is set in the 1950s, which presented the problem of rounding up older model cars, dressing actors in fashions of that era, and getting rid of long hair and beards. Local people in the film with cast parts included Howard Larsen, a miner; Ben Bentley, bar patron; Roger Edington, bartender; Ted Henningsen, man in bar; Ski Kidwell, miner; Barbara Parsons, girl near the pond; Mary Peters, Marge; Ralph Schmidt; plumber, Pat Setzer; little cowboy; and Fred Henningsen, who plays the part of Evel at age 7. Carolyn Larsen and John Breshnahan served as local liaison personnel.

Film reviewer Roger Ebert sensed that there was something much too self-congratulatory about the project, too diluted. He panned director Marvin Chomsky's "slice-of-life approach," with shots of the young Evel trying to outrun police cars, charging up the stairs of his girl's dorm on a cycle, making his first stunt jumps with a rodeo, etc.: "To me, the life of Evel Knievel contains the same seeds of self-doom as Dostoevski character's. That's what I miss in the current George Hamilton movie version, despite its generally interesting texture and its flicks of black humor. Evel Knievel is a man who, for unknown and probably terrifying personal reasons, has set out to methodically punish himself in a spectacular public way. "I was talking about this characteristic of Evel's once

with Joe Solomon, whose Fanfare Films produced *Evel Knievel*, and Joe said he thought maybe Evel's mother had something to do with it. When Evel tried to jump the fountain at Caesar's Palace in Las Vegas and broke about a dozen bones, Solomon said, Evel's mother was inside the hotel—and didn't even come out to look!"

Ebert did appreciate the irony of the movie depicting Evel as some sort of hypochondriac, afraid of being X-rayed, terrified of polluted water, convinced that his fans will tear him apart ("A 14-year-old girl almost killed Elvis once.") and afraid, indeed, of almost everything in his life except his jumps. The movie failed to ignite at the box office and quickly disappeared, though Knievel received a flat rate of $25,000 for his rights and consulting fee. More than a bit dated, the film is a droll, cartoonish throwback to the 1970s, when Evel Knievel, the father of extreme sports, was a ubiquitous figure in entertainment-oriented pop culture, death-defying TV appearances, a line of toys, and advertisements on the back covers of comic books. Knievel was a unique entrepreneur with a blessed gift for hucksterism, a circus act writ large, and this cinematic tribute retains its suitably campy charm.

Everything That Rises

CAST
Dennis Quaid, Mare Winningham, Meatloaf

DIRECTOR
Dennis Quaid

LOCATION
Livingston area

1998

Director and star Dennis Quaid captures Montana's scenic grandeur in this film, shot in the lush Paradise Valley near Livingston. Quaid made his directorial debut with this TV movie, a contemporary western with Quaid also credited as executive producer.

Dennis Quaid directed and starred in this contemporary family drama that was filmed on his Livingston ranch.

Tough, unemotional ranch owner Jim Clay (Quaid) and his faithful wife Kyle (Mare Winningham) have a teenage son, Nathan (Ryan Merriman), who hopes to enter the rodeo big leagues, just like his dad. Instead, an auto accident leaves Nathan a paraplegic who must use a wheelchair. Jim's devastation is compounded by feelings of guilt and blame. The situation brings father and son closer as the family attempts to deal with the tragedy.

Bozeman doctor John Vallin served as medical consultant on the movie, advising Quaid on what words he would use to describe the spinal cord injury his son in the film had suffered. "I thought it was a lot of fun, more enjoyable to be a technical adviser than treating a spinal cord injury," said Vallin.

As a subplot, Quaid and his family try to hold onto his family's land in the face of development. The singer Meatloaf plays Quaid's sidekick. Bozeman fishing guide Bob Coppock served as the photo double for Meatloaf, meeting two requirements: He came close to Meatloaf's hefty measurements (shirt size of 17-34 and pant size of 42-31) and he was comfortable on a horse. Erin O'Neill

of Bozeman was chosen as Quaid's double, a perfect match in height, weight, and coloring.

The film premiered July 12, 1998, on TNT, when Quaid still lived in Livingston. "I've been coming here for over 20 years," Quaid told *Entertainment Weekly*. "I have a place around here. I'm still called a frequent visitor in all the newspapers. They'll never call me a resident because I've never spent 20 winters up here."

The story in the original script by Mark Spragg of Cody, Wyoming, took place in the 1960s, but Quaid said it worked well in the 1990s. "We're reflecting on what's going on here in our story," said Quaid. "We're not trying to comment on it, saying it's bad, it's just the way things are. They're not making any more land."

"This whole story is close to my heart," said Quaid in 1998 to *Parade Magazine*. "All guys have father-son issues."

Quaid learned to rope for the movie. "It's very hard. I knew how to fall off a horse really well. I wouldn't call myself a great horseman.

"I'm not too keen on owning horses. They need to be ridden, to have a relationship with you, and we're not out there enough [at the time Quaid, his wife, Meg Ryan, and their 6-year-old son, Jack, had a home of 300 acres in the Livingston-area]. There are lots of horses in *Everything*."

"Dennis Quaid was responsible for bringing that film here," recalled casting director Tina Buckingham. "It's the only movie he ever directed and he wanted it to be in his backyard. On the very first day, before first shot, Quaid told everyone, 'I don't know if I can do this or not. But I'll give it a shot.' Quaid really treated himself like a local and people treated him the same way. For the whole time that Quaid lived in Livingston, he was treated as a normal guy, because he acted like it."

Daily Variety stated "*Everything That Rises* is beautifully filmed by Jack Conroy and his team." The *Hollywood Reporter* chimed in, "The photography and sets add a strong sense of realism," before haranguing against "a predictable story line" and story characters who "seem more stereotypical than they need to be."

The land-race scene was "awesome," according to most participants. "It made the ground shake." A few extras suffered broken bones.

Far and Away

CAST
Tom Cruise, Nicole Kidman

DIRECTOR
Ron Howard

LOCATION
Billings area

1992

Director Ron Howard remembers seeing Ireland for the first time at age four. His plane stopped at Shannon Airport for refueling en route to Austria, and the verdant greens of the Emerald Isle were instilled into his memory. Howard also remembers being on the set of *The Music Man* (1962), shot in the wide-screen Technorama format. "I recall huge, oversized cameras that took five or six people to lug around, and all day to set up."

And Howard recalls visiting his great-grandmother in Kansas and being shown a yellowish newspaper clipping, with a hazy photo of Oklahoma Territory's Cherokee Strip Land race—a late-19th-century lottery offering deeds to land—taken as a cannon was fired to start the run.

"It was an incredible picture. All these horses and wagons," recounted Howard. Pointing to a blur in the lead, his 96-year-old great-grandmother said, "That was your great-grandpa Tomlin," who was an Irish emigrant.

Three of Howard's great-grandfathers rode in the race. None got any land.

All these experiences separately influenced Howard's 1992 production, *Far and Away*, a Universal Pictures release starring Tom Cruise as a 19th-century Irish tenant farmer named Joseph Donnelly, who finds love and land in America.

The climactic scene in *Far and Away* depicted the 1893 Cherokee Strip Land Race in Oklahoma. Here the 200 wagons, 400 horses, and 800 extras assemble on the movie "set" that was more than a quarter-mile long, on a ranch near Billings.

Far and Away was sold as a big, old-fashioned movie event, an epic shot on giant-sized 70-millimeter film, sweeping across two continents. Large formats have come and gone through the years, going all the way back to the silent era. Though never challenging 35 mm as the industry standard, the various wide film formats enhanced event pictures. Since the 1970s, 70 mm release prints (65 mm is the camera negative size, prints are 70 mm to accommodate sound) have actually been blowups from 35 mm negative film. The use of 65 mm production had been largely dormant since the 1960s, save for select non-theatrical, amusement park presentations and some visual effects. Howard credited Mikael Salomon with the idea of originating in 65 mm for *Far and Away*.

"I wouldn't have thought of this one myself," said Howard. "I hadn't seen the tests." And then he had the memory of those daunting cameras used for *The Music Man*. "I like to operate with a fair degree of momentum. I like all the shortcuts that camera packages have provided over the last 10 to 15 years, and I'd hate to give those things up."

Far and Away has three distinct looks: pastoral Ireland, the congested Boston of the industrial revolution, and the wide-open American Midwest. Late-19th-century Boston exteriors were re-created on the streets of Dublin, while the interiors were shot in Ireland on Ardmore Studio's stages, with a Montana warehouse used as *Far and Away*'s cover set.

Joseph (Tom Cruise) falls in love with Shannon Christie (Nicole Kidman), a wealthy landowner's daughter, and they masquerade as brother and sister. The couple travel from their rural homeland to Boston and to the western plains in search of land and freedom. In the climactic final scene, set in the Oklahoma Territory in 1893, the pair face off against hundreds of other settlers—and each other—in a tumultuous land race. They hope to stake a claim to a small share of the millions of acres that the U.S. government is giving away.

Production of the Montana portion of *Far and Away* began in Billings on May 28, 1991. In July 1991, after months of careful planning, the rush was re-created on a ranch outside the city.

Director Howard, anxious about the safety of his cast and crew, had trouble getting to sleep the night before shooting began. Fortunately, his fears turned out to be groundless—almost. "We had some broken bones," said producer Brian Grazer. "But nothing horribly serious. No deaths."

Though Paramount's own official numbers vary, approximately 800 riders and extras, 900 horses, mule and oxen, and 200 wagons were filmed on a quarter-mile-wide set. Horses were wrangled, ruts were smoothed over, and a self-contained city (called Tent City) was built. Swarms of people lined up in covered wagons, buggies, hay carts, on horses and mules and on foot for the race.

For the culminating free-for-all action sequence, riders and extras were given little more than these simple instructions: "Get on those horses and just go in that direction. Don't hit anybody and don't get hit. And go as fast as you can."

"There were so many different cameras running for that scene," recalled Dillon resident Stan Smith, a member of the core stunt crew. "It was all going at 35 miles per hour and one wagon rolled over and sent some extras to the hospital with some broken ribs. My job was to stay with Tom Cruise and the 20 extras on the first camera. Cruise was the center of my attention and I stayed with him. It's one of the most detailed singular shots ever filmed on 70 millimeter."

Ten cameras were set up to film the maneuvers, including the two new Panaflex 65 sync-sound cameras, two new Arriflex 765 cameras, three hand-held Panavision 65 mm cameras, two Eyemos (35 mm with anamorphic lens) on the ground, and a VistaVision camera for one helicopter.

Two helicopters with cameras, plus four cameras on a car carrying Howard and several others, cruised in front

Under Montana's Big Sky, film crews shoot the starting tower for the Oklahoma land race.

of the horse-mounted Tom Cruise. "The scene was awesome," said J.P Gabriel, video assist operator, owner of Filmlites of Montana, a company that provided equipment—lights, generators, ladders, even director's chairs and dust pans—to the production of *Far and Away*. "When the race started, the ground shook. That was a great job."

The surge in popularity of films set in western locales had spurred interest in Montana. One cast member said that *Far and Away* "rode the wave of *Dances With Wolves*." (As far as *Dances with Wolves*, Kevin Costner traveled to Montana and he wanted to film the movie in the town of Big Sky. But several facts stymied it: Costner couldn't locate a buffalo herd of 12,000 necessary for production, and smaller herds couldn't be combined due to the risk of potential cross-contamination diseases; another possible option, the National Bison Range, nixed the idea of any location shoot on its land.)

Production designer Jack Collis discussed how he helped construct Tent City, a town of shanties and tents, which complemented the *Far and Away* land rush.

"The director of photography, Mikael Salomon, wanted to shoot the race in back light, which became a major consideration in determining the exact location of the town. I felt it was important, once the line of the race was established, that Tent City should be visible in the background to give a visual continuity to the sequence. As for the town itself, the research of the period showed the temporary nature of these structures, and I used a variety of buildings and tents to create a town that would meet the requirements of the script, and one which we would call Tent City."

Far and Away has a number of crowd scenes and wide shots of scenery. In several scenes, Montana picturesquely duplicates the lush green landscape of Ireland. "My assignment on *Far and Away*," recalled scout and Helena resident Bill Kuney, "was to locate settings that duplicated the greenery of Ireland and the flat rolling hill look of Oklahoma, in areas generally void of civilization and power lines. And, believe it or not, find an abandoned railroad tunnel and a railway roadbed without rails."

Much of the movie is a buildup to the land rush scene,

The night before filming the big land-rush scene, director Ron Howard (right) was so anxious about the safety of his cast and crew that he had trouble getting to sleep. He later said the Montana filming was the best location experience he ever had.

as noted agitatedly in the *Denver Post*, which found Howard's story contrived: "Ron Howard, who directed 'Far and Away' and conceived the story with its screenwriter, Bob Dolman, is faithful to every cliché lurking beneath Joseph's promise. The camera rises over the dead man's body as his soul escapes, then swoops across the green hills and out to sea, trying to look grand for no particular purpose…Shannon plucks chickens, Joseph becomes a boxer, they chastely share a room in a whorehouse and consort with stock characters like the ward boss. They are a likable enough pair, but their predictable adventures are a snooze. Of course nothing will stop them from their dream of Oklahoma, not even a mawkish Christmas scene that ends with blood on the blatantly fake snow and that causes their temporary separation."

Moments before the land rush scene, Joseph receives advice from the apparition of his dead father, whose voice reminds him, "Without land a man is nothing." Film critic Gene Shalit opined that the transition between certain scenes was sloppy and disjointed, and that the land rush was too little, too late to salvage a "protracted dud" of a film.

"With an ease only movie heroes can manage, he [Cruise] jumps off a train in the middle of nowhere and is suddenly in Oklahoma. Scores of covered wagons and horses race across the land, toppling over one another, creating the kind of visual excitement the film desperately needs. But by then, in the last half-hour of this 2-hour-18-minute film, the real race is toward the story's suspenseless end."

The *Los Angeles Times* enjoyed the land rush scene—and apparently not too much else: "Joseph and Shannon's episodic journey from Ireland to Boston to Oklahoma offers fewer surprises than a mediocre mini-series. And though the film turns into a rousing western during its Oklahoma scenes, it feels so familiar that Pa and Hoss and Little Joe might come galloping into sight any minute. Despite the movie's ambitious scope, there are small-sized imaginations at work here."

Tom Cruise's fight scene for *Far and Away* was filmed at the Billings Depot. The movie included some local residents as extras. Another scene moviegoers are sure to remember was shot in Montana during the golden hour, at the tail end of daylight, when the air itself is painted with a reddish-golden hue. The scene was impossible to shoot in one day and had to be pieced together from matched footage shot over a number of days.

Cruise and Kidman stayed in a home on the West End during filming. Howard also stayed in Billings. "Ron Howard was so good with the historical detail of the film," recalled Dillon's Stan Smith. "He made sure all the right details were put into the set that stood as the town, which was constructed outside of Roundup. There was nothing out there, no electricity. Yet, they made a little town out there for the movie. And it was a very family-oriented set. Howard had his family there."

And despite unflattering reviews, *Far and Away* did big business, grossing approximately $58 million.

"And we made Ron Howard so happy that he's sending his friends this way," said Jim Abel, chairman of the Billings Film Commission. Abel, a writer, producer and director with his own company, started the all-volunteer commission in the late 1980s. "Montana is hot and getting hotter," said Abel optimistically in 1989. "We're right in the center of it, and not just for the classic Western, but lots of crossover pictures with contemporary themes, shot in the West."

Billings business owners attested that the movie business provided a substantial shot in the arm for the local economy. DeeDee Juffila, owner of Home-Style Laundry, said *Far and Away* had been a welcome boost for the business that she and her husband started earlier that year. Billings Construction Supply provided the film crew everything from portable toilets to tables and chairs. "We're always busy during the summer, but the movie has been good for our business," vice president Tim Compton. "I can't imagine anybody who doesn't like having them here," said an employee for H&H Lumber Co., which provided some of the building materials for movie sets.

Chiropractor Paul Valenzuela prospered, treating between 40 and 50 people. "People get stiff and sore from doing stunts, and the production people sometimes need treatment, too." Valenzuela had treated people working on *Son of the Morning Star* the previous summer. "Because of that, I was on the state's contact list. The first people from *Far and Away* to come to Billings contacted me," said Valenzuela.

"We came there [to Montana] because the script dictated it," said Larry DeWaay, co-producer of *Far and Away*. DeWaay said the movie company spent between $6 million and $6.5 million while on location for two months in Billings. "Montana is the easiest and most comfortable place to make a movie that I've ever worked," said Mike Malone, location manager for *Far and Away*, who previously worked on *War Party* and *Amazing Grace and Chuck* in the state. "The people are open and happy to see you in Montana, and those in the public service sector look at the film industry as a very positive plus for the state. They do whatever they can to accommodate us."

For the most part, he said, prices charged by local vendors were fair, and government officials were cooperative. "We affect just about every area of the community," said DeWaay, noting that the film company rented more than 100 vehicles during its Billings stay. Local people had also been reliable and extended hospitality to the crew members. "When I ask for 330 extras to show up on a certain day, that's how many show up," said DeWaay.

Overall, the Billings experience was reasonably free of hassles. "Ron [Howard] once said that it had been the best location experience that he's had," said DeWaay.

Fast Walking

CAST
James Woods, Kay Lenz

DIRECTOR
James B. Harris

LOCATION
Deer Lodge

1982

For a while in July 1980 it almost looked like the old Montana State Prison in Deer Lodge was open for business. Guards dressed in blue uniforms, heavy shotguns resting in their arms, paced back and forth along the walkways above the dark granite walls. But it was all an illusion, concocted by a film crew from California for *Fast Walking*, a film about a guard, his inmate cousin, and assorted criminals and con artists, all tied up in a plot of intrigue, murder and racial confrontation. Based on the book *The Rap* by an ex-guard at San Quentin prison, it was adapted for the screen by James Harris, producer and director. Filming was budgeted at $4 million.

During a break in shooting, James Woods, who starred as the prison guard nicknamed "Fast Walking," said he was "ecstatic" when he heard the movie was going to be filmed in Montana. "I love this country up here," he told Butte's *Montana Standard*. "The people are great. They're just so friendly."

One factor that added to the authenticity of the film was that among the 180 extras in the movie were correction officers from Deer Lodge who had worked at the old prison. Milt Fadness, who was a guard at the prison 1964-1972, said the film crew made the prison look "pretty much the same as it used to be. That's a pretty nice job they done in there." Bill Nimmo, a guard 1959-1978, also was hired as an extra. He said: "These actors seem like real nice people, every one of them." Jim Blodgett, assistant warden at the new prison just outside town, provided help, lending guns to be used as props or providing expertise on the facility's renovation.

Blodgett, as head of the Powell County Museum and Arts Foundation, said at the time that he hoped to make the old prison into a museum and landmark—which came to pass. He told the *Montana Standard* that the effort would be much easier after *Fast Walking* was filmed there, and that remodeling would make the prison an obvious choice for future movies.

Shooting *Fast Walking* provided Garry Wunderwald with a unique challenge of locating "50 black extras willing to come to Old Montana State Prison." Wunderwald called on an acquaintance to help, who rounded up extras from the Billings and Missoula areas. "There [were] only 1,200 black people in the entire state," said Wunderwald. "So it was no easy task."

Wunderwald, a Great Falls native, graduated from Montana State University with degrees in history and sociology. He began working for the state as a lab technician with the Highway Department in 1965. He became a photographer for the agency a year later and in 1971 he joined the state tourism office as a photographer and writer. He took over the film office in 1977.

One of the things he tried to emphasize during his tenure was that the benefits of films go beyond what a film company spends. For example, during production of *Fast Walking*, Lorimar Pictures put a new roof on the prison ($50,000), replaced broken windows, and repainted. "After they left, the prison was in good enough shape to open for tours," said Wunderwald. "And in a very short time they made enough money to pay the heating bills for the winter."

Ultimately, *Fast Walking,* a surprisingly sleazy tale about a corrupt prison guard involved in a plot to murder a black revolutionary serving time in his prison, walked briskly in and out of theatres, barely earning enough to pay for its cost.

Clint Eastwood produced, directed, and starred in *Firefox*, with many scenes shot on the prairie north of Glasgow.

Firefox

CAST
Clint Eastwood, Freddie Jones

DIRECTOR
Clint Eastwood

LOCATION
Glasgow, Cut Bank

1982

Imagine the conning tower of a nuclear submarine pushing its way up through the middle of a wheat field near Glasgow, Montana. Farfetched? Crazy? Impossible? No. Nothing is impossible in the movies. How do you turn a wheat field into an Arctic ice field where a submarine will surface? Build a fake conning tower, add styrofoam blocks of ice and then wait for snow.

That's what happened in 1982 during the filming of the movie *Firefox*, produced, directed and starred in by Clint Eastwood. Many scenes were shot on the prairie north of Glasgow, which was doubling as an Arctic ice pack. The landscape of St. Maries/abandoned Glasgow Air Force base became quarters in the frozen Arctic. The abandoned B-52 air force base, which included a bowling alley, hospital, quarters, hangars with 67-foot-high doors, and a 13,500-foot-long runway, had been well-maintained.

Firefox is about an American pilot sneaking into Russia and stealing the Soviet's new top-secret, thought-controlled jet fighter. The script called for Eastwood to land the aircraft on the Arctic ice and refuel from a waiting American submarine. "They were looking for a place that had snow and was flat and bare so they could create the look and atmosphere of the Arctic ice pack," said Montana Film Commissioner Gary Wunderwald. Eastwood called Wunderwald and then flew to Montana to look at possible sites. In addition to the "look" of the site, Eastwood also wanted an airport nearby and a hanger or other building large enough to hold the 60-foot, 28,000-pound plywood mockup of the Firefox aircraft.

Filming was to begin by early fall (October 1981), and Wunderwald immediately thought of the Beartooth Pass for early snow. That was before he found out the size of the plane (the Firefox was trucked up from California). When Eastwood flew into Bozeman, "we started talking and I learned that the plane to be used in the movie was wooden and weighed 28,000 pounds and would be trucked up to Montana on a 60-foot trailer." The size and awkward nature of the cargo made the steep, winding Beartooth Highway location impractical and dangerous. And the plane's wood construction required that it be stored when not in use.

Wunderwald decided to look at Cut Bank and Big Timber, both of which possessed large hangars left over from World War II. Eastwood chose Cut Bank for its glacial view to the west and its open plains to the east that could, when snowbound and ice-encased, pass for the North Pole.

One day, the hangar was visited by a pair of suspicious-looking men whose appearance may have held international implications. "There were two men in a black car hanging around, acting strangely," said Wunderwald. "It is quite possible that they were Russian agents who heard about it on the news and decided to check it out. Perhaps they were looking at what they thought was a secret site and cased the place out."

Eastwood and company tried to film the Arctic scenes near Cut Bank: A plywood mockup of the conning tower was erected in a wheat field, and Styrofoam blocks of "ice" were placed around the conning tower to make it appear the submarine had just broken its way up through the ice. Before they could film, however, high winds whipped

How do you turn a Montana wheat field into an Arctic ice pack where an American submarine surfaces in *Firefox*? Build a fake submarine conning tower, add Styrofoam blocks of "ice," and wait for snow.

the snow from the wheat field. "And then it began snowing and blowing…and snowing and blowing…and snowing and blowing," said Wunderwald.

So the film crew flew back to California and they waited…and waited.

"The conditions just weren't right," said Wunderwald. "It got to be March. We were afraid we were going to lose them—that they would have to pull out of the state." Finally, the Glasgow area received a heavy snowfall and Wunderwald suggested they move the site. They did. The scene was set up in a field near the end of the airport and filmed.

"They didn't mess around," said Wunderwald. "When conditions were right, they flew the actors and camera crew in from California, shot the scene in just five days and were gone." Wunderwald estimated that at least $100,000 was spent in Montana to film the Firefox plane sequence.

Clint Eastwood attracted much attention in Glasgow, especially around dinnertime. He spent a couple of nights having dinner at Sam's Supper Club, which raised eyebrows. "The hotel wouldn't let anyone near him," recalled co-owner Lee Erickson. "He signed the ceiling of the club. As soon as he finished his dinner, people scooped up everything at his table, empty beer bottles, napkins, you name it."

Glasgow Chamber of Commerce president Becky Erickson presented Eastwood with an honorary key to the city.

Two scenes for *Forrest Gump* were shot at Glacier National Park. In both, Jim Hanks doubled for his actor brother Tom. The stone bridge was at the St. Mary Entrance. Top, the scene with "Forrest" (far right) on the Going-to-the-Sun Road didn't end up in the movie.

Forrest Gump

CAST
Tom Hanks, Gary Sinese

DIRECTOR
Chris Woods

LOCATIONS
Glacier National Park, Blackfeet Reservation

1994

Frozen in Fear

CAST
Eric Roberts, Rod Steiger

DIRECTOR
Robin P. Murray

LOCATION
Darby and Hamilton areas

2001

Forrest Gump jogged through Montana on his journey across the United States and back. Two scenes appearing in the movie were shot in and near Glacier National Park. For this film Tom Hanks snagged his second Best Actor Academy Award.

In one of the film's most iconic scenes, Forrest Gump runs—and runs. From coast to coast, from tiny bridges to harbors and lighthouses, he runs some more. Jim Hanks, Tom Hanks' brother, doubled as Forrest Gump for the scenes shot in Montana. The golden wheat fields that appear briefly on screen are near Cut Bank, Montana. In another scene, Forrest runs across a stone bridge with jagged snow-covered mountain peaks in the background. This scene was filmed at the St. Mary Entrance to Glacier National Park. Additional footage, shot along the Going-to-the-Sun Road, ended up on the cutting room floor. In the blink of an eye he's jogging through the wheat fields.

"Forrest Gump's second units originally shot in a grain field on the east side of Glacier Park," said Garry Wunderwald. "It was intended for the scene with Forrest running over the bridge, but they realized it needed to be shot at a higher elevation. The one scene was on the east side of the pass of Going-to-the-Sun along a bad curve, the worst corner on the whole road, and we had to stop traffic. The park was good about it. The camera truck actually shot out over the drop, several hundred feet down to get him coming around the corner and down the road. I believe they shot another scene, one farther down the highway, in front of a tunnel, and another in the middle of a grain field. I don't believe they ever did use the grain field scene. But they did use the scene of Forrest running across the bridge just inside the park. It was a difficult setting to set up."

Stevensville, Montana, director Robin P. Murray filmed two movies in Montana, both of which ended up heading straight to video. The first, *Season of Change* (1992), ended in a class action lawsuit against him. The second, *Frozen in Fear*, which stars Eric Roberts as a mentally disturbed sociopath and artist, is also known as *The Flying Dutchman*. The premise of *Frozen in Fear* revolves around a beautiful West Coast art dealer (Catherine Oxenberg), who purchases a painting from an isolated, sleepy logging town in Montana. The painting sells at her gallery for a large premium. So the dealer and her assistant, excited about their discovery of a promising new talent, decide to visit the artist. Slowly, the two women become ensnared in the artist's shadowy and twisted family history, and his dangerous obsession. The movie features the scenic splendor of the Bitterroot Valley as the artist's fictitious hometown – a crucial bolt of beauty in all that psychological darkness. The cast and crew of the film—shot in the winter of 2000—included a host of Montana residents.

Missoula artist Melanie Catlin's paintings, characterized as the work of a psychotic, became the central focus in *Frozen in Fear*. Approximately 25 of Catlin's disturbing works are featured in the movie. She did all the paintings in the late 1980s, while attending an art school in New York. "I love the idea" that the paintings are the work of a psychotic, said Catlin. "When I did the paintings, my teachers said the [human] figure is dead, and that you had to do abstracts. The fact that I was painting huge figures and body parts drove them crazy. I wasn't going out chopping bodies up or anything. But they're violent, passionate-type paintings. It goes with the character of the man in the film."

Filming *Frozen in Fear* in the Bitterroot Valley worked out positively, said Murray. "It was fantastic," he said. "We were on budget and on time. And all the people from Montana were great. They came from all over the state. It was a great crew. We knew we had some problems because we had an extremely small budget and only 17 days to shoot it. It was very, very tight. But everyone hung in there and got the work done on time." According to Murray, *Frozen in Fear* received a strong response in Europe, though it didn't see a theater release in this country because it didn't "have the star power to attract major audiences," he said. "It's extremely difficult to get a theatrical release. It's so expensive for marketing. It costs $3 million right off the bat. And a decent theater release is a minimum of $5 million."

Several students of the University of Montana dance school appeared in the movie, including Gillian Todd, who plays a featured role as hippie girl who falls prey to Roberts' deranged character. Catlin also gets a cameo appearance in the movie. The production crew spent all of its time in the Bitterroot, renting properties, designing "ice cavern" set pieces inside the Darby VFW hall and finally rolling film. Some of the scenes were shot around two cabins at the edge of Lake Como, at that time of year a solid sheet of snow-dusted ice. One of the two cabins was built in 1935 by the Hamilton Hikers' Club as a destination and meeting place for their newly-formed group of hiking, skiing and camping enthusiasts. For the duration of the Lake Como shooting, it served as the mess hall for the roughly 45-person crew.

Missing women. Deranged killers. Predictable plotlines. *Frozen Fear* ended up heading to straight to video and serves as nothing more than an insignificant blight on the résumés of Eric Roberts and Rod Steiger or anyone else involved in this mess. "*Frozen in Fear* is kind of a terrible flop," said Allison Whitmer, assistant costume designer. "The story goes that the guy that directed it, well, his wife's father was a Hollywood guy and I guess she got all of his unpublished scripts –and *Frozen in Fear* was one of them."

"Two things that stand out," added Whitmer. "One of them is that Eric Roberts is one of the most professional, giving actors I've ever worked with, despite his [negative] reputation. Two is that it is one of Rod Steiger's last movies. He wore the same costume the whole movie, even though the movie took place in separate periods. He wouldn't change his shirt. With most actors,

they take off the shirt and you wash it for the next time it's worn. But Steiger, he wore the same costume and he stunk by the end of it. But he told great Hollywood stories and was a sweet man. There is a scene filmed in the Daly Mansion with Steiger mumbling to himself and chasing people around. That tells you what kind of movie it was."

Whitmer recalled that Rod Steiger's body double in one sex scene was a local Bitterroot resident who had little clue as to what the job description entailed. "There is a sequence when a character comes upon Rod Steiger making love and he didn't want his ass shown, so we hired a body double and he didn't know what a body double did. So I had to explain to him, you take off your pants and you hop on the bed and they will film your ass. [Film income] was a nice boost to the local economy."

"Rod Steiger was a major treat for me," said director Robin P. Murray. "He was always ready and could get in character at the drop of a hat. It was great to spend time with him and hear his stories about *On the Waterfront*, *Doctor Zhivago*, *The Pawnbroker*, etc. Real pro, the crew loved him, quite the comedian on set.

"Eric Roberts, another super actor. The first two days on the set we clashed quite often. I attribute that to just sizing things up, but after that he was super to work with and plays a great bad guy, as everybody knows."

Several years earlier, Murray had generated a firestorm of bad publicity for the entire film industry when he made a movie in Montana called *Season of Change—* see page 125.

Veteran character actors Ben Johnson (left) and Iron Eyes Cody are filmed on the set of *Grayeagle*.

Grayeagle

CAST
Ben Johnson, Iron Eyes Cody

DIRECTOR
Charles B. Pierce

LOCATION
Helena area

1977

In *Grayeagle*, Academy Award winner Ben Johnson (for *The Last Picture Show*) plays a widowed mountain man and trapper named John Colter whose "half-breed daughter," Beth, is kidnapped by Grayeagle, a supposed super-warrior with a mission. As the Indian heads for the hills with the girl, Johnson lights out after them, running into every conceivable cliché of melodramatic complication. Johnson is joined by his proverbial trusty Indian sidekick, Standing Bear (Iron Eyes Cody), and the two embark on a series of epic rescue missions.

This movie was shot in the Gates of the Mountains, 15 miles north of Helena, near Interstate 15. The gates, sheer cliffs which rise to 1,200 feet above the Missouri River, were named by Captain Meriwether Lewis of the Lewis and Clark Expedition in 1805.

Grayeagle, one of several Charles Pierce–helmed Westerns with a Native American theme, falls on, according to one reviewer, the "hilariously inept" end of the spectrum.

The *Albuquerque Journal* chastised Pierce, saying "the man's lack of taste, talent or financial commitment have produced several eminently forgettable films in the past; *Grayeagle*, on many accounts, is inexcusable."

The *Kansas City Star* skewered it as "a shameless copy

An Indian camp for *Grayeagle* was set up at Gates of the Mountains north of Helena.

ing idiotically whenever she's not forming goofy facial expressions." On the technical front, cinematographer and editor James W. Roberson did receive some accolades for "generating attractive shots of the film's Montana locations" and *American Film* complimented Pierce for "lending texture to Montana with his usual eye for physical detail."

of John Ford's classic *The Searchers* [1956]," only with a more sympathetic point of view on the Indian psyche. "*Grayeagle* is dull, melodramatic, silly, and turgid," trashed *Film Monthly* magazine. For instance, "Pierce awkwardly attempts to generate operatic levels of emotion," so whenever he lingers in slow motion on a "significant" event, the picture "slips into self-parody." It doesn't help, of course, that two of the film's most crucial performances, noted one reviewer, "are outrageously awful." Grayeagle is presented as a noble warrior and Beth develops affection for her captor. Eventually, all the plot strands converge in a mawkish twist-ending that transforms the action saga to a tearjerker.

Johnson's sidekick, Iron Eyes Cody, the veteran "Native American" actor and humanitarian, owned a Hollywood career which stretched back to the earliest big-screen westerns, but he achieved perhaps his greatest success in a famous anti-pollution ad on the small screen. In a public service commercial, Cody paddled a canoe past a belching smokestack and along a polluted stream before arriving at a busy highway. As he surveyed the urbanized landscape, garbage thrown from a passing car landed at his feet, drawing a single, bitter tear from his lined face. The camera stayed on Cody's face while the announcer said, "People start pollution; people can stop it." It turned out that the most famous Native American actor harbored an unspoken secret: he was born Espera DeCorti to Sicilian immigrants in Louisiana.

Critics took aim at everything—and everyone—in the picture, criticizing "miscast and terrible" actors, especially Cord, as well actress Lane Wood for "scream-

Heartland

Cast
Rip Torn, Conchata Ferrell

Director
Richard Pearce

Location
Harlowton area

1979

Heartland, a story about a family that settles in the American West, is a portrayal of pioneer ranch life. There are two very different ways of recalling the lives of the pioneers and one is to remember the terrible physical hardships that also affected the settlers' psychological dislocations and disorders. By far the more popular method is to recall the pluck and perseverance that overcame all obstacles and made America great. There's nothing wrong with this method, though it does tend to be sentimental, prompting us to grieve for an innocence that probably never was. What better place to document the growing pains of a young nation than on the high plains of central Montana, where the land and even the buildings hadn't changed since these pioneer scenes were originally played out a hundred years ago. Montana was a natural setting for *Heartland*, made by the cooperative efforts of Montana's Motion Picture Location Office. "We had the script and the actors and a vision of the set, but it was the State's Motion Picture Office that led us to the abandoned homestead area," said executive producer Annick

The achingly realistic *Heartland* was filmed near Harlowton and White Sulphur Springs.

Smith. "Garry Wunderwald of that office assisted us in countless ways. Garry made us feel welcome in the near-by town of Harlowton, and introduced us to cowboys and ranchers without whom we could not have made the film."

The stark, rugged saga of frontier life was shot in the area of Harlowton (north of Billings), White Sulphur Springs, and Garneill. Location scenes included storms over the prairie and local cattle brandings. It wanted, as did other movies shot in Montana, seasonal change, with the last of winter and then spring.

The screenplay, based on the real-life story of Elinore Randall Stewart (played by Conchata Ferrell), is about an impoverished Denver widow who, in 1910, moves from the comparative ease of the city to the wilds of Burntfork, Wyoming, to become the housekeeper for a taciturn Scottish rancher named Stewart (Rip Torn). With her small daughter from her first marriage, and with Stewart, whom she eventually married, Mrs. Stewart survived just about everything the frontier could throw at her.

"There was a big hole in the media and we had to por-tray women's lives as they were," said Annick Smith. "One of the main ideas was to make a film depicting the pioneer experience of women in the West. Up to that time, in the 1970s, mostly what you saw was pretty pioneer wives who stood by the sides of their husbands and cooked dinner. We knew there was more. It's based on a real historical woman, Elinore Stewart. So many of the pioneers arrived, and mostly came on the railroads, calling the Western plains 'Garden of Eden.' Many people felt fooled when they got to the West. Poor people could claim land as long as they farmed—and many were disappointed.

"It was hard life for a woman. You had to make your own soap, your own clothes, do your own wash. You'd do backbreaking work and have child after child. There were severe, unexpected emergencies. There were people who went crazy. Elinore was a survivor, in an isolated situation and a climate like Montana. We had great method actors and serious actors. Rip Torn was there day after day roping fences to practice roping. Barry Pri-mus (who played Jack) visited local ranches to learn the experience."

Though Pearce has made documentaries and features for television and was the cameraman for Peter Davis's Oscar-winning *Hearts and Minds*, this was his first theatrical feature as a director. "Once we began, we were all committed to making a film that could be shown to those Montana ranchers without them laughing us out of the theater," said Pearce. "It wasn't a remake of Western mythology, it treated people with care, it had respect for place and time—a film about people, to be sure, but also a film where the environment was a real character."

It is also Beth Ferris's first theatrical screen credit as a writer. *Heartland* was shot entirely in Montana under difficult circumstances and it has the benefit of three remarkable performances—by Rip Torn as the dour rancher, a man whose humor, though buried, is as real as his courage; by Conchata Ferrell as the no-nonsense housekeeper, a big, hearty woman who is strong without being tough; and by young Megan Folsom, as her small daughter.

"Both Annick and I had experience in the wilderness and we both felt that Western women were not really represented," said Ferris, the main writer and co-producer of the film. "Elinore Stewart planted the potatoes and she worked behind the horses, which is how she eventually died. The domestic work was like a funnel. Rip Torn and Barry Primus went to great extent to learn. Neither were horse people and neither had worked around cattle. We used neighboring homesteaders as consultants. At the time of the film, cowboys were still branding in the mountains and still rounding them up. Rip and Barry worked alongside the cowboys."

Casting, budgeting and scouting for locations began early in 1979 and by March the location had been found, a hilltop in the Snowy Mountains of north-central Montana, a hilltop about 50 miles from each of three small towns, Harlowton, Judith Gap and Two Dot. And atop that hilltop was an abandoned homestead which was refurbished with planking, fabrics, props and clothing, all of it purchased from people in nearby towns. "The ranchers became our consultants," said Smith. "They felt, they told us, that the film was about themselves, about their lives."

Because the seasons are as important as anything that happens in them, the photography by Fred Murphy is much a part of the film's success. Murphy seems to have achieved his effects with high color contrasts that are never too bright and that have the texture of early black-and-white photography. The film was shot at the center of the state, where if you look one way you see the beauty of mountains, and the other the barren high plains landscape. Cinematography captures arresting images of homesteads twisted by the wind on the drive from Harlowton to Judith Gap.

The film was shot during a period of five weeks in April and May 1979. During the shooting, the 25-member crew commuted each day from rented quarters in Judith Gap to the hilltop homestead, and to keep warm between scenes they huddled around the wood-burning stove in the basement root cellar of the house. "That was all we had, except for a shed out back and two trailers for the cast," said Smith.

"We shot on the plains and wanted the barrenness, the openness," said Smith. "We wanted to emphasize the space and distance and keep away from anything that looked like a ski resort. We looked a long time for the proper setting, looking in Wyoming and Utah, but we chose not to film in Utah because it was so remote, a long way to Salt Lake City and, if we stayed in Montana, we wouldn't have to rebuild. In Montana, we found a great huge open prairie. A film like *Shane* concentrated on the beauty of the mountains in the Tetons. But we were doing an anti-mythical story."

Heartland doesn't entirely avoid the clichés of the genre. It may be time to declare a moratorium on the slaughter of pigs on camera to indicate the fundamental laws that rule the farm. Also, there must be ways to celebrate the so-called miracle of life without forcing us to endure both human and animal births.

"There is the scene of testicles being eaten over the fire by the cowboys," said Smith. "From the branding to a castrating, people thought it was a little tough. But if you eat meat, that's how it happens. The people in the community at first viewed us with suspicion. But we respected them and they saw that. And we were spending money in very depressed communities. There was one scene in which Conchata Farrell and Lilia Skala did not want us to kill the pig, and there was a constant battle going on around when we were shooting the pig-killing scene. [After it was killed on film:] We used the pig and that pig fed us."

"We were more about showing it as it really was," said Ferris. "PETA [People for the Ethical Treatment of Animals] picketed the film. In the branding scenes, we showed actual people and their cows, and scene after scene, there are locals from Harlowton. We couldn't have done it without them. They were incredibly interested, some even invited actors to their houses."

"The hotels in Harlowton and Judith Gap were filled and so was the main location at the Wolf Ranch," said film commissioner Garry Wunderwald. "Michael Housman, the producer, bought the ranch and the property after the film over. Though he lived in New York, he brought his son back for his birthday every April. In Judith Gap there is a gazebo there that he had built as kind of a thank you to the town."

Reviews of *Heartland* ranged from guardedly enthusiastic to full endorsement, with most settling some place in the center, including this praise from the *Chicago Sun-Times*: "The nicest thing about *Heartland*, a new low-budget, uncommonly beautiful film written by Beth Ferris and directed by Richard Pearce, is that even though it celebrates the people of the American frontier, with emphasis on the women, it largely avoids sentimentality."

Accomplished television and film actor Barry Primus, who has starred in more than 60 films, said that he has a soft spot for *Heartland*: "*Heartland* is really one of my favorite films. It was written by the people who really knew that world and being on the real location in Montana inspired everyone to find real behavior and to get away from any cliché cowboy ideas. Richard Pierce is a wonderful director, who won the Berlin Film Festival."

Heaven's Gate

Cast
Sam Waterston, Kris Kristofferson, Christopher Walken, John Hurt, Jeff Bridges, Joseph Cotten, Mickey Rourke

Director
Michael Cimino

Location
Butte, Glacier National Park, Kalispell

1980

Michael Cimino directed two movies in Montana: *Thunderbolt and Lightfoot* and *Heaven's Gate*. In between, he directed the Academy Award-winning *The Deer Hunter*.

Michael Cimino had been an advertising wiz who moved into film industry with the Clint Eastwood/Jeff Bridges crime caper, *Thunderbolt & Lightfoot*, in 1974. His follow-up was an elegiac Vietnam drama, *The Deer Hunter*, a critical smash that went on to win five Oscars, including best picture, in 1979. Cimino demanded absolute creative freedom to make his third film, *Heaven's Gate*. Six days into filming, he was five days behind schedule and had spent $900,000 on a minute-and-a-half of usable footage. Two weeks into filming, the studio calculated that, at the rate he was going, *Heaven's Gate* was going to cost them $1 million per minute of running time.

The screenplay, originally titled, *The Johnson County War*, was one of the first screenplays Cimino ever wrote. The story is based on fact: a struggle in the early 1890s between Wyoming cattle owners and immigrant settlers that led to a bloody conflict between the hard-pressed settlers and the mercenaries hired by the cattle owners.

Cimino demanded absolute creative freedom to make *Heaven's Gate*. Six days into filming at Glacier National Park, he was five days behind schedule and had spent nearly a million dollars on only 90 seconds of footage. The film destroyed Cimino's career and United Artists studio, yet it may be the most gloriously scenic and meticulously detailed Western ever made.

Starring Kris Kristofferson, *Heaven's Gate* was filmed at five different sites in Glacier National Park as well as several areas adjacent to the park, with a few scenes done in Idaho and Colorado.

United Artists was required to post bonds of $50,000 and $100,000 for damage and liability before the permit to film in the park in the summer of 1979 was granted. An entire frontier town was built on the shores of Two Medicine Lake in the park.

Cimino went about making what is still the most gloriously scenic and meticulously detailed Western ever seen. A relentless perfectionist, he kept a grueling pace on the set but drove himself harder than anybody. Every ingredient had to be impeccable, even if that meant building a Wild West town, piling the roads with thousands of tons of earth, transporting a vintage steam train from a museum in Montana at a cost of $150,000, and signing up 1200 extras, all of whom were dressed in authentic period costumes, and many of whom were sent to daily

sessions where they were taught everything from horse-riding and shooting to roller-skating and cock-fighting.

Montana film commissioner Garry Wunderwald recalled his experiences with Cimino and *Heaven's Gate*: "Six months before filming, I received the call from Michael Cimino, who was coming off the success of *The Deer Hunter*. They needed a place to build a town, and I took Cimino and [executive producer] Charles Okun scouting. When I showed Cimino Two Medicine in East Glacier, he asked, 'Can we film here?' Well, it turned out that they were digging or replacing an area at the hotel, and they said that if Cimino could meet the requirements, then he could use that site. They started the filming in February or so and with the success of the *Deer Hunter*, I guess he thought he should have carte blanche, and you could see what was going on with some of the attitudes. They built the town in a parking lot at Two Medicine and he flew back and forth from where he was staying in Kalispell every day."

The set of *Heaven's Gate* was completely closed, leaving observers disappointed. Wunderwald found it mindboggling to watch Cimino spend approximately $19 million in Montana, $100,000 on helicopter rental alone. "The helicopter was very important to Cimino for scouting," said Wunderwald. "I believe he was renting the helicopter for something around $500 an hour and he used it for around 120 hours. He should as well have bought the helicopter. The folks who rented him the helicopter, they gave him a pin at an honor[ing] banquet. I'm sure they loved him for it. [The film company] rented about 70 vehicles for the full eight months they were there. They built an entire skating rink and a chapel. Then Cimino tore part of the rink down and enlarged it.

"They asked me to help locate an old pot-bellied wood-burning stove for the skating rink," said Wunderwald. "I found an antique one and they paid $3,500 for it. When Cimino told somebody to go get something, he expected them to come back with it. He never blinked an eye at what something cost. They had a cast of 600 people on hand at times. They rented a huge building normally used to store Christmas trees just to house the wardrobe. And I think they bought every bit of canvas in the state to make a tent city.

"When Cimino came to town, he decided he'd need a four-wheel drive jeep to get around. He asked me to go to the dealer [Stanley Chevrolet] with him and help pick something out. The dealer asked Cimino what he wanted. Cimino looked at me. So I just started listing everything I thought he'd need—roll bars, a winch, and the works. I didn't pick the color, though. Cimino did that. I never would have picked black."

Before a frame of film was shot, the cast had to go on some extensive training courses, what Jeff Bridges later called "Camp Cimino." Lessons ranged from shooting to horse riding, cock fighting, and bullwhipping lessons, to Yugoslavian dialect coaching. Isabelle Huppert, who plays an immigrant prostitute, spent three days in a Wallace, Idaho, bordello. A former Green Beret specialist gave instructions in firing handguns, an exercise, according to Cimino, that "sensitized the actors in the use and handling of weapons, and in how to use them not as props, but as lethal aids."

One early scene would see several prominent cast members dancing on skates, which required actors Kris Kristofferson, Jeff Bridges and Brad Dourif to spend hour after hour in training. "They had to skate for a couple of hours a day," said prop master Robert Visciglia, "for maybe a week or two weeks." Brad Dourif puts the length of time spent training at a much longer six weeks—enough time for the cast to become adept at waltzing around on skates for Cimino's lengthy scenes. Ironically, the roller skate waltzing scene was one of many, many sequences that ended up on the cutting room floor for the 149-minute *Heaven's Gate*.

"The movie started in April in Glacier and the routine was that you would report at three in the morning to wardrobe in a huge warehouse, 300 to 500 people at a time, file out and on to a bus and get props," recalled Tina Buckingham of Bozeman, who worked as an extra. "You would get on a bus and drive an hour and a half around the bottom perimeter of the park to Two Medicine, to a dug up parking lot. The town was set in a private area and there was a church on the lake and the rolling skating rink and period costumes. We'd eat breakfast in the dark because Cimino wanted to be on the set so he could get these dawn shots. He and Christopher Walken had won Academy Awards on a Saturday night and started production on *Heaven's Gate* on a Monday."

Cimino's mania for realism went beyond the location shooting. "Every article of clothing, every structure, every sign," he told a reporter, "is based on a photograph of the period." Cimino, affectionately nicknamed "the Ayatollah" by the crew, was tireless in his demands for authenticity: "Even when detail is there but not seen, I still feel it contributes something to the overall texture of the completed film. It's a necessity for me to feel the presence of that detail in order to work properly on a set, or on a location. It even helps the crew. It affects in intangible ways. The more unity you can create, the better the result. Also, encountering a real place changes the performances of actors in subtle ways and changes the spiritual texture of the film."

Cimino's hours planning and creating every single shot, as he chose each individual extra—from a line-up of dozens—and arranged them around the set depending on their look and height. "He would actually paint by selecting extras and putting them in the right place," recalled Vilmos Zsigmond, Cimino's cinematographer. "Pretty much like a painter would paint. He'd paint by picking people up and dropping them into place." This process was made more laborious because of the sheer scale of the film—some scenes required 50 or more extras, all personally selected by Cimino. "It took time,"

Visciglia remembered. "Maybe a couple of hours to pick 50 people."

"Certainly one of the most difficult problems was assembling enough craftsmen in each of the production categories," said Cimino. "For example, I believe that at one time we had four construction crews working—two in Montana [one on the east side of the Continental Divide, the other on the west side, both in mountainous terrain], another crew in Denver [rebuilding the train that ultimately was shipped to Montana and Idaho], and a fourth and largest crew in Wallace, Idaho, building the largest set, the city of Casper. In addition there were the wranglers, which at our peak, numbered 80 or 90, and 40-odd stunt people, plus the regular production crew. I think the total numbered approximately 400."

Cimino demanded 52 re-takes of a single scene involving Kristofferson drunkenly cracking a bullwhip in a hotel room. The shot in the finished film is over in a matter of seconds. "I'm not used to doing 57 takes, I'm really not," said actor Brad Dourif. "I'm not used to doing a minimum of 32 takes. It was like workshopping on film—we did the happy version, we did the crying version, we did the furious version." One day, a crowd of those extras sat around for hours while Cimino waited for the light to change, and when an assistant director suggested, mid-afternoon, that it might be time for a lunch break, Cimino snapped, "Lunch? This is bigger than lunch."

Outlaw Inn owner Bill Kuney remembers the film's producer, Joann Carelli, often appeared anxious. "She seemed troubled, to say the least," recalled Kuney. "You could tell that something was amiss. The producer was getting instructions from United Artists, and they put the responsibility on her shoulders to control [Cimino] and she couldn't do it. You could see she was distressed."

Kuney also recalled that the Outlaw Inn knocked out a wall to give Cimino more space to operate. "Cimino had one of the largest executive rooms in the hotel, but there was no adjoining or connecting room," said Kuney. "Cimino had to have more space, so we had to cut a door to give him two rooms—and we charged him.

"As a director, he was on top the heap then and all of a sudden after the movie, he just disappeared. We thought that they would go into the summer, but we were booked full with conventions, and we realized that they weren't even close to completing the project, so we had to figure out how to keep everyone happy. They were still filming into the late fall and early winter, with that many people on the payroll for that long."

Kristofferson would jam with his band in the hotel's lounge when he wasn't rehearsing scenes. Some of the Outlaw Inn staff were apparently caught sneaking peeks of a rehearsal session, and that didn't bode well with Kristofferson, according to Kuney. "Kris Kristofferson got upset with us once, he and Isabelle Huppert had to learn how to dance on roller skates and we had some banquet rooms on the second floor and one had a slip glass window by the door to look, and they practiced at night. Our employees found out what they were doing and started peeking in and watching. Kristofferson saw that and got a little upset about it."

Heaven's Gate's grandest set piece was its battle sequence between settlers and mercenaries. Requiring dozens of horses, extras, wooden wagons, and explosions, it took weeks of planning and around a month of arduous filming. Just to make things even more difficult, Cimino had chosen for his battle location a field located some three hours' drive from his base of production in Kalispell. Cast and crew were bundled into vans at 3:30 each morning, clutching pillows to catch more sleep as they were ferried. Each day's filming was long and potentially even dangerous, as Cimino whipped up a combination of dust, wagons, and gunfire.

"I don't know how long we shot those battle scenes," said Jeff Bridges, "but it was frightening, some of it. Each time I'd pray to God that none of us got hurt. We'd just keep doing it over and over."

"We would ride around in a circle for three or four minutes at a gallop," recalled extra Eric Wood. "You've got wagons in the mix. Dust so you can hardly see." Some of the crew members, however, didn't seem to mind. "Hell, this picture can go on forever as much as I care," said one of the horse wranglers in the summer of 1979 to the Associated Press. "My boys and I have never been paid like this. I love Montana!"

The footage Cimino reluctantly shared with UA looked spectacular, which caused the producers to back off. Despite concerns that Cimino was hemorrhaging money, UA were still convinced they could have a hit on their hands.

It was when UA execs David Field and Steven Bach visited the set of *Heaven's Gate* that red flags swirled. The climactic battle sequence was costing a fortune in talent [from a local tribe of Native Americans, according to producer Joann Carelli], and costing a fortune to irrigate. Cimino had decided that his battlefield had to be covered in lush, green grass. This meant that the land had to be cleared of rocks and an irrigation system had to be installed to encourage the grass to grow—meaning yet more expense.

"He's talking about hundreds of people and horses and wagons and explosives," Bach later explained. "Who the hell is going to see grass?" When Bach suggested to Cimino that the grass was unnecessary or the scene could be shot someplace else easier to access, Cimino rebuked him, insisting that his luxuriant vision was "part of the poetry of America."

Most of the filming was done in Montana, except for a scene at a train depot in Idaho, another expensive diversion. "Cimino did not like the train depot in Kalispell," said Wunderwald. "There were just too many people in Kalispell, and I thought we were going to lose the movie because of it. He didn't like the train depots we looked at, and he wanted to head to Idaho. The problem was that I couldn't drive the rental car in Idaho, so we had to stop at the border and change cars. He ended up liking the Wallace depot."

"Gosh, the cost of Cimino having all of these buildings constructed and built in Kalispell and then having them dismantled and then hauled over to East Glacier," said Kuney. "Then, add the big roller skating rink and the church, all built in Kalispell. In Glacier, you are not allowed to build on a paved parking lot and he hauled truckloads of dirt to cover the paving. But the dirt came in from outside of the park. He spent a lot of money on the North Fork of the Flathead. He bought property and a small landing strip. I'm sure the company paid for all of that."

Cimino outstayed his Montana welcome. The filming of the exorbitantly expensive box office dud left a lot of people with a bad taste in their mouths. Mostly it was the antics of the cast and crew, destroying hotel and rooms and "carrying on," noted a Park Service official. "There were a couple of incidents," said Wunderwald. "One… involved a crew member who sprayed plants with some kind of chemical—a no-no—and they also brought a load of soil to the filming from another area. Also, back then, there was drugs and alcohol on the set." Park officials informed Cimino on the final day of scheduled filming that he would not be permitted to film beyond the agreed time. "I received a call at around one in the morn-

Montana governor Tom Judge talks with actor Kris Kristofferson on the set of *Heaven's Gate.*

ing from Cimino, he had just gotten word that he would have to leave the park, and he called me everything in the book," said Wunderwald. "He had heard that they were going to cancel his permit."

The critics pronounced *Heaven's Gate* an "unqualified disaster," and the viewing public agreed. Ever since, *Heaven's Gate* has been a synonym for Hollywood folly. The budget grew from a proposed $7.5 million to an agreed $11.6 million to a total of $44 million. The film made a paltry $3.5 million at the U.S. box office—and the humiliation continued. When the film premiered in New York on November 18, 1980, at nearly four hours long, actor Jeff Bridges remembered the audience's befuddled silence. "After all that work…Ugh, it was terrible." Cimino's reputation plummeted. Transamerica sold off United Artists, effectively killing the studio.

"Cimino genuinely believed that he was acting responsibly and that he was going to make a great film and that the studio would get its money back," said documentary filmmaker Michael Epstein. That didn't happen, and even to this day, added Epstein, "It's seen as an epic failure. It still scares every executive in Hollywood."

Cimino's pride and joy had become a carnival. And while the flop might have irretrievably hurt his career, it did not rub off on Montana as a location, for one critic noted that "Montana came out the star."

Thanks to Cimino's perfectionism, *Heaven's Gate* is feted by some as a masterpiece. The film was ranked at number 98 in BBC Culture's poll of the 100 greatest American films. At least one cast member, Bridges, said that Cimino has gotten a bad rap for the film.

"Michael Cimino received a lot of bad attention for

Heaven's Gate, and undeservedly so, I think," said Bridges years later. "I consider it a classic, because it really puts you back into what the times must have been like (in 1890s Wyoming). The movie is leisurely paced, it's quite slow, but the filmmaking has a rhythm, and I've ended up enjoying it more and more over the years. It's a beautiful film and set at an amazing time in our nation's history—hiring gunmen to kill European gunmen—those kinds of things."

When the filming ended, Bridges ended up with a log house that functioned in the picture as a brothel. He dismantled it and had it re-located to Livingston, near the Absaroka-Beartooth Wilderness. "Toward the end of the movie, there is a whorehouse in *Heaven's Gate* and Michael Cimino said, 'Does anyone want this cabin?' He said that the owner or whoever was going to burn it down. I numbered the logs and took them four hundred miles south to Livingston. To this day, I'm living in the *Heaven's Gate* whorehouse," Bridges said.

Hidalgo

CAST
Viggo Mortensen, Omar Sharif,
Zuleikha Robinson, J.K. Simmons

DIRECTOR
Joe Johnston

LOCATION
Blackfeet Reservation, St. Mary-area

2004

Hidalgo is a western action film starring Viggo Mortensen (Aragorn in *Lord of the Rings*), loosely based on the exploits of an American cowboy who was once advertised as the world's greatest long-distance rider; in the film's stunning conclusion, 570 Blackfeet Reservation horses run uninhibited in the largest uncontrolled horse stampede ever successfully captured on film.

Mortensen plays a half-Lakota cowboy named Frank T. Hopkins (1865-1951), a former Buffalo Bill Wild West show performer and successful endurance rider, who accepts an offer from an Arabian sheik to run the 3,000-mile Oceans of Fire race across the Arabian desert for its $100,000 purse.

"Endurance racing was all the rage in the 1880s," said *Hidalgo* scriptwriter John Fusco. "It was sort of like our extreme sports today and it was very popular. Big sponsors would put up cash prizes in races across the country. Frank Hopkins had entered a race in 1886 and it was a race from Galveston, Texas, to Rutland, Vermont. Hopkins and Hidalgo did the race in 30 days and second place came in 14 days later. That's how they became so well known. Hopkins was approached for a whole different animal. The Super Bowl of which was a 3,000-mile endurance race across the Arabian desert."

"It's the story of a South Dakota cowboy who races his horse against a Moroccan prince," said Sten Iversen, manager of the Montana Film Office. The Walt Disney picture, Iversen predicted, was "going to be a big blockbuster." And, with a budget of more than $100 million, he believed the tale of personal redemption stacked up nicely as a major Oscar contender.

Most of the scenes in the movie were filmed in South Dakota, Nevada, and Morocco. Even though *Hidalgo* recounts Hopkins' racing his horse in Arabia in 1891 against Bedouins riding pure-blooded Arabian horses, the movie—directed by Joe Johnston—journeyed across the sublime terrain of Big Sky Country. After Frank and Hidalgo travel to Arabia and win the Ocean of Fire race, Frank uses his winnings to buy a herd of Plains horses destined for government slaughter. We see the massive horse stampede as Frank Hopkins releases his herd into the wild along with his faithful horse. Hopkins wanted the stock—portraying turn-of-the-century mustangs planned for extermination by the U.S. government—to run free across the prairie.

The cast and crew for *Hidalgo* landed on the Blackfeet Reservation for 21 days in August 2003. The reservation made an ideal location for the stampede scene. Divide Mountain rises like a behemoth in the background of Hidalgo's final sequence. "They scouted extensively all over Montana, Wyoming and South Dakota," said Iversen. The location clincher, though, was the availability of livestock. The filmmakers first expected to use "dude horses" or "slaughter stock" in the stampede. They ended up with mostly unbroken horses, some as unruly at heart as the mustangs they portrayed. Director Joe Johnston hired local wranglers and brothers Dutch Lunak and Scottie Augare to round up the 570 reservation horses, corral them and train them to stampede across the prairie. Augare, who had multiple non-speaking roles in the movie, estimated there were a couple of thousand horses on the reservation. Augare and Lunak, a stunt man and wrangler for movies including *Dances with Wolves* and *Last of the Mohicans*, had only to call their friends and relatives to gather the horses. "Almost everybody here on the reservation owns a horse," said Browning rancher Sam Lane. "That's just the way Indian people are." Augare and Lunak trained the horses to recognize an electric fence. They also branded the horse's hooves "to prevent ownership quarrels when the shoot was done." One job they delegated to the less instructed was "trapping gophers" and filling hundreds of their holes so the horses wouldn't tumble when they raced across the prairie. "These horses know this country; they won't turn over," said Lane.

Despite ample planning, the scene was unmistakably hazardous. Director Johnston first requested 1,500 horses. But the scene as Johnston envisioned it would be an impossible feat. The makers of *Lonesome Dove* tried a 350-horse stampede and couldn't control the herd. In the 1969 John Wayne movie *Undefeated* (1969), they attempted a stampede of 750 horses and lost them, too.

"I was like, OK guys, let's get real," said Rex Peterson, southern California horse trainer who coordinated all the equine scenes for *Hidalgo*. Peterson had worked with enough horses in the movie business to understand that 1,500 stampeding horses would be "wholly unmanageable." Instead, Peterson said he used helicopters and a large team of wranglers, including many locals, "to pull off the scene in 12 takes." But the treasured other details he has kept secret. "Everybody in the movie business wants to know how we done it, and I ain't going to tell them," said Peterson, who worked on *The Horse Whisperer*, *All the Pretty Horses* and *Black Knight*, among others. Some of the scene's success may be credited to genuine Hollywood trickery. "The horse "Hidalgo" is actually played by five different American paint horses," said Ansotegui, "four of which actually had to be painted to match the lead horse, J.J."

In the other key scene from *Hidalgo* filmed on the Blackfeet Reservation, Peterson protested when the stu-

In the climactic ending of the horse and cowboy adventure *Hidalgo* starring Viggo Mortensen (shown here), hundreds of wild horses run free across the Montana prairie.

dio insisted on auditioning 300 Hollywood-area actors for a scene requiring 20 Native American riders on bareback. He wasn't surprised when they only found two who could stay on a running horse with no saddle. Peterson finally made a call to Browning and hired the rest of the riders for the scene, which portrays a Buffalo Bill's Wild West show Indian raid. Many of the Blackfeet actors also dressed as Arabians for other scenes. "They eventually hired a crew of locals who could gallop bareback," said Ansotegui. "In fact, unlike most spaghetti westerns that hired everyone but Natives to play Natives, Touchstone Pictures hired a large crew of Blackfeet to ride as Indians in Buffalo Bill's Wild West Show and act as Arabians."

"When they were filming, we had no idea it was going to be such a big movie," said Brandie Lane, daughter of Sam Lane, who stabled three of the five "Hidalgo" horses while they were on location. During filming, the Lanes had a chance to visit with Mortensen, who autographed Brandie's copy of *Lord of the Rings*. "He's just a common-type guy," Sam Lane said. "He really liked being here," Brandie added. "He liked horses, he liked the country.... At first I didn't think he'd be able to ride, but he could." At one point Mortensen "confided" that he "envied" the Lanes' lifestyle and said he'd "be willing to trade." "I told him I'd rather be in movies traveling around the world," said Brandie.

"Ironically, as *Hidalgo* was being shot, the close relationship between Hopkins and 'Hidalgo' is mirrored between J.J. and Mortensen," said Ansotegui. "So much so that when production wrapped, Mortensen purchased J.J. as his own."

The Lanes said that they had trouble comprehending how a film company could spend three weeks and a quarter million dollars on four minutes of movie. "All the work that went into just a couple minutes of movie, it's just amazing," said Brandie. They also were awed by the caliber of the catered meals the filmmakers ate. "They had lobster and everything," Brandie recalled. "But they seemed more into home-cooked stuff." Sam Lane said it took him a month's work after filming concluded to remove the horse corral and reclaim his land. But he was happy to do the work. The film crew was good to work with and the money was good. "A guy could use one of them every two or three years," he said.

"There was a reason we traveled from California to Montana," said unit publicist Dave Fulton. "The natural beauty of Montana is fantastic and the work we did there was great."

One other notable note includes the performance of J.K. Simmons as Buffalo Bill Cody. In 2015 alone, Simmons' film credits included nine movie roles, including his critically acclaimed and award-winning performance in *Whiplash*. He garnered a whopping total of 40 acting awards in 2014, including a Golden Globe and Screen Actors Guild Award. As he told ABC News, "I began with no real training as an actor. It was just because I could sing and they needed somebody to be the lead in a musical at the Bigfork Summer Playhouse up by Flathead Lake, Montana." The possibility of acting beyond Bigfork presented itself and after Simmons graduated from UM in 1978 he moved to Seattle in search of larger stage roles. While trying to establish a career in theater, he stayed connected to Bigfork and returned for six seasons at the Playhouse, which he described as "formative."

With a budget of more than $100 million, pundits believed *Hidalgo*'s tale of personal redemption stacked up nicely as a major Oscar contender and box office smash (it grossed approximately $108 million in the US, but no Oscar nods).

Hidalgo, which employed about 100 Blackfeet tribal members, ended in a minor controversy when members of the Blackfeet Indian Reservation learned that only a few landowners profited from the filming production instead of the many. "The production staff of *Hidalgo* found two or three people, who owned the land in the final stampede scene, and they paid them something like $2,300 apiece," said a staff member who worked on *Hidalgo*. "Well, then others came out and sued for $300,000 to $400,000 and they went forward on litigation. I guess there were several fractional interests and it seemed like every other Indian owned a piece of it—or claimed to. It settled out of court. Not for much." And that wasn't the only controversy as multiple historians attacked the film for its historical inaccuracy, including one Native American who called *Hidalgo* "a monstrous fraud" and Hopkins, the man, as a "liar" who fabricated his ancestry and his origins.

Holy Matrimony

CAST
Patricia Arquette, Joseph Gordon-Levitt

DIRECTOR
Leonard Nimoy

LOCATION
Great Falls area

1994

The production designer of *Holy Matrimony* had the challenge of recreating an entire Hutterite communal religious settlement. Shot mostly on a ranch near Great Falls, the film-set colony consisted of six buildings and were sold to an actual Hutterite colony when filming was complete. The Hutterite set constructed at the Prairie Nest Ranch near Belt accounted for almost half the money spent on filming, costing $270,000 for materials and $180,000 on labor. The gray, blue-roofed buildings included housing, a church-community hall and schoolhouse. A steel granary sported a sign reading "Hutterian Brethren Jerusalem Colony of Alberta, Canada."

"We built the Hutterite colony during a cycle of torrential rainstorms and thunderstorms," said producer David Madden. "The crew had to continue to build through the downpour and mud because we could not delay the film."

Holy Matrimony is a romantic comedy featuring actress Patricia Arquette and directed by actor-director Leonard Nimoy. Colony Productions opened an office in Great Falls in the summer of 1993. Forty-two days of filming included two weeks of filming at the facsimile Hutterite colony. When work at the ranch concluded, shooting continued the last three days at Montana State Fair, capturing carnival and crowd scenes.

The movie featured stars Arquette and Joseph Gordon-Levitt fighting FBI man John Schuck following a $200,000 robbery of the fair. Gordon-Levitt, 12, was dressed in Hutterite garb. He had recently appeared in *A River Runs Through It* and was accompanied by his mother, Jane Gordon of Los Angeles. "Joey likes acting," she said. "We're very proud of him." The actor went on to play Tommy Solomon in the TV series *3rd Rock from the Sun* and whistleblower Edward Snowden in Oliver Stone's political thriller biopic *Snowden*.

Filming in Great Falls followed the State Fair shooting. The film, which operated on a budget of $10 million, cast Montanans for 30 small speaking roles. Including extras, the total crew was approximately 80 people.

"Basically it's the story of a young boy who has led a protected life in a Hutterite colony and a 25-year-old girl who has led a hard life in her search to rise to stardom," said co-executive producer Dan Heffner. Nimoy told *Parade* magazine: "A girl coming from a chaotic background with a lot of fantasy life and wishful thinking that gets her in trouble encounters a young boy with a Hutterite background with strong roots and spirituality. He's more adult than she is. It's a comedy of bonding."

Patricia Arquette recalls her experiences on *Holy Matrimony*. "I was working a lot," she said recently. "I didn't have a chance to see much nature. The movie was a whole different genre for me. I didn't quite understand it all. It was very elusive."

The Shrine Parade in early August was rerouted to accommodate movie shooting. Malmstrom Air Force Base slightly altered the flight path of its refueling planes and helicopters so the noise wouldn't disrupt filming. The film company asked if the Air Force could avoid flying over an undisclosed ranch where the replica Hutterite colony would be filmed. Malmstrom officials initially denied the request, but told the filmmakers they would advise when training flights would be heaviest. But after the filmmakers said the noise from routine KC-135R training missiles was creating problems for their sensitive recording equipment, Malmstrom reconsidered. Safety

Leonard Nimoy (pointing)—*Star Trek's* Spock—directed the romantic comedy *Holy Matrimony* in the Great Falls area with stars Patricia Arquette (center) and young Joseph Gordon-Levitt, who was fresh off his role in *A River Runs Through It*.

wasn't affected by the minor flight adjustments, and filming at the ranch wrapped in fewer than 10 days.

"We were in Great Falls because it was the best place to make the movie we wanted," said producer Heffner. "We didn't have many alternatives without spending months and months. We needed a state fair, wheat country, a colony."

"For *Holy Matrimony*, the location manager and I scouted for more than a week," recalled former Montana Film Commissioner Garry Wunderwald. "The first place I took them was a wheat farm. I tried to get a Hutterite colony that would let them film on it, but the Hutterite colonies, some of them didn't even allow television or film. I took him to several communities and we were driving to these Hutterite colonies. Word got around that we were looking for locations on colonies. We started asking for cabbage, just to get to talk to them. I found one big wheat farm outside of Great Falls, and it had a cluster of buildings and grain elevators, probably the ideal spot.

"The location manager liked that we were six or eight miles from Great Falls and they could save some expenses for supplies. Great Falls had a large fairground and they shot some of the final scenes during the fair. We flew, we traveled on highways, and we went to a dozen or more ranches and farms, and ultimately they decided to do it on the first farm we looked at. They built three or four dormitory-style buildings on this place, and it worked out fine."

Tony and Harriet Heinert, owners of 3-D Furniture Refinishing in Vaughn, bid successfully on a project to refinish 20 pieces of furniture for use in *Holy Matrimony*.

Many of the items were in serious need of repair; many had layers of paint to be removed. The order included chairs, dressers, tables, cupboards, a wardrobe, wash stand, cabinet, and a roll-top desk.

Greg Mackenstadt, of Great Falls, repaired and reconditioned 25 of the film's cars and trucks, including two dissimilar 1974 Chevrolet pickups that he stripped of chrome and trim and repainted blue to resemble identical "plain Jane" Hutterite trucks.

Stinar's Trustworthy Hardware in Belt doubled as the United States Border Inspection Station, complete with traffic barricades and Customs officials. The front of the store was partitioned to make it appear like the inspector's office. "You are entering Canada. Please stop and report to customs officials," read a nearby sign. Others like "Tax-Free Duty Shop" had been erected on nearby buildings. Leonard Rossmiller, whose land northwest of Great Falls was used for the dramatic car blow-up, was pleasantly surprised. "I thought they did a great job. It took them a couple of days to roll that car. It only took a couple of seconds on the screen."

Holy Matrimony was directed by Leonard Nimoy, best known for playing the character Spock in the *Star Trek* television shows and films. Nimoy died in 2015 at age 83.

"After it was decided that the location could work, Leonard Nimoy came in and we spent three or four days together," recalled Wunderwald. "He was a nice guy. I took him to one colony east of Lewistown, and the colonies, they had varying degrees of strictness. This one was known to be more liberal than most of them. The hotel that we were staying at in Lewistown, the owner was good friends with the boss man of the colony. The boss man was in town on business the day we were there. We explained what we were doing and he invited us to the colony.

"Nimoy wanted an idea as to how the colony operated and wanted to be inside the buildings. The colony head said he'd be happy to do it. The only building off-limits was the building that the pigs were in. At the schools the kids have to learn German and they had a school teacher who was not a Hutterite. Nimoy was happier than hell that he had all this info. One of our biggest problems in the Hutterite community was alcoholism. They drank a lot of wine and booze."

The sonorous, gaunt-faced Nimoy had won a worshipful global following as Mr. Spock.

"Nimoy and I went to the Dairy Queen in Lewistown after dinner to get ice cream and three or four kids, they recognized him and it looked like they were getting ready for autographs, and he slipped out of that place so fast. He really didn't want to be recognized by anybody. All of sudden they were befuddled. Too bad, it would have made their day and their month and their week and year."

Stan Smith, of Dillon, Montana, who worked as a Hutterite extra, recalled a much looser Nimoy. "Nimoy was a great joke teller," said Smith. "On the day I was there it was windy, and there was nothing out there to catch the wind. It was Patricia Arquette's final day before she had to leave for another project. I drank a lot of coffee and listened to Nimoy tell stores and jokes, dressed up as a Hutterite." Jim Redeau, owner of Tracy's Restaurant, which appears in the film, said Nimoy impressed him during his first visit to the all-night restaurant on Central Avenue and Second Street. "I asked Nimoy if Tracy's was going to work, and he said, 'Yeah,' and he smiled at me," said Redeau. "He said he liked the town, and he liked the people. You don't have to be nervous around him. He was a real casual kind of guy."

Nimoy spoke glowingly to *Rolling Stone* about his experience in Montana while filming *Holy Matrimony*. "The panorama, like I've never seen before, unobstructed, miles and miles in every direction. And the people have been really remarkable for us. We have tremendous help, tremendous warmth and support here."

In the end, *Holy Matrimony* is an exhausting exercise, a near-miss of a project that's more admirable as a premise than effective as a product. It burned badly at the box office and was yanked from theaters after a dismal opening weekend.

Daily Variety found it "innocuous but problematical."

Location manager Mark Zetler of Dillon takes a minute to preserve a memory in the making of *Iron Will*, which used southwestern Montana's wintry landscape to accentuate the drama of a 1917 sled-dog race.

Iron Will

Cast
Mackenzie Astin, Kevin Spacey

Director
Charles Haid

Location
West Yellowstone area

1994

Iron Will, which tells the story of a famous sled-dog race in 1917, used southwestern Montana's wintry landscape and mountainous terrain to accentuate the drama of the race. Duluth, Minnesota, served as the film's primary shooting location, but Montana provided the winter wilderness.

Bill Kuney, the state's film location coordinator, said Disney officials "couldn't find the open look they needed in Minnesota. While they scouted statewide, the southern end of the Madison Valley offered them the wilderness look they wanted," said Kuney. The "more dramatic, eerie shots" that were necessary for portions of the racing sequences were found around Quake Lake—near the west entrance to Yellowstone Park.

Iron Will was directed by Charlie Haid, best known onscreen for playing Ranko on the television series *Hill Street Blues*. *Iron Will* is based on a 522-mile sled-dog race, the Red River–St. Paul Sports Carnival Derby, which took place in 1917 from Winnipeg, Manitoba, to St. Paul, Minnesota. The real-life young man on whom fictional Will Stoneman is based was Fred Hartman, 26, who entered the race with a team of five dogs. Hartman, a native of Troy, New York, attended the University of Saskatchewan. He moved to Manitoba to make his fortune in the booming gold-mining region.

After that didn't pan out, Hartman entered the sled-dog race promoted by Louis W. Hill Jr., whose father was president of the Winter Carnival and whose grandfather was railway magnate James J. Hill. Louis Hill utilized the many railway lines (built to transport the Iron Range's rich production of ore, taconite, and timber to Lake Superior ports) to publicize the race. Newspaper and movie studio cameramen stood atop Hill's railroad flatcars to record the race.

The 10-day race began January 24, 1917. Unlike the fictional Stoneman, however, Hartman had especially bad luck. His dogs began fighting and his lead dog was killed. Hartman had to lead the team himself.

Disney shot most of the film in the "Land of 10,000 Lakes" of Minnesota and neighboring Wisconsin from January 9 to April 1, 1993, for 12 weeks while temperatures plummeted to minus-40 degrees Fahrenheit. Much of the shooting on location in the flat lands of Minnesota, primarily along the Lake Superior shoreline, as well as in Iron Range cities such as Floodwood. Although the race takes place between Winnipeg and Saint Paul, neither city actually appears in the film. However, fictional racer

Will's mountainous terrain was filmed south of Ennis.

During the filming, the crews drove on roads going up to 8,000-foot elevations on granite peaks. Snowcats were used to get into some places with cliffs and crevices, and then the snow plows would go in. An army of production assistants on snowshoes were used several times to pack down the snow on the trails. *Daily Variety* noted "it's obvious that the filmmakers didn't fake [Astin's] dashing and tumbling through the snow."

"*Iron Will* was different for a couple of reasons," said location manager Mark Zetler. "One of them was because they brought [sled-dog] teams, about eight to ten different teams, there had to be 80 to 100 [animals] all together. Wolves always fight, because it's part of the pecking order—and there was fighting. The other thing was that the snow around Yellowstone and Quake Lake was so deep that the dogs couldn't function. So we sent the production assistants out on snowshoes a day or two before the shoot and they tromped…in three, four feet of snow, to make a trail. I think they are the best shots in the movie. We had to make those trails, which were four feet deep in snow up to your neck."

"We are extremely pleased that another quality film company like Disney has come to Montana," said then-governor Marc Racicot. "This is a great opportunity to show off what our state has to offer to people all around the world."

The movie, which grossed a paltry (at least by Disney standards) $21 million, met largely unfriendly reviews, including this lambasting in the *Chicago Sun-Times,* which found the film lacking freshness:

"'Iron Will' is an Identikit plot, put together out of standard pieces. Even the scenery looks generic; there's none of the majesty of Disney's genuinely inspired dog movie, 'White Fang.' Accuracy in journalism requires me to report that the movie has been efficiently assembled and will probably be quite entertaining for people who like movies about plucky youths in dogsled races."

Jimmy P: Psychotherapy of a Plains Indian

CAST
Benicio Del Toro, Mathieu Amalric

DIRECTOR
Arnaud Desplechin

LOCATION
Browning, Glacier-area

2014

Jimmy P: Psychotherapy of a Plains Indian is set in late-1940s Kansas, the story of a gifted analyst (Mathieu Amalric) who takes the case of a Native American war veteran named Jimmy Picard (Benicio Del Toro) whose blackouts and blinding headaches appear to have no physical cause.

Del Toro's amorphous physical features allowed him to naturally blend into the role of a Blackfeet Indian. His eyes could be Asian. His skin pigmentation Italian or French. His nose possibly Slavic. Shady circles under his eyes and a deep, raspy voice render him ethnically indistinct. Put together, a little unsystematically, the disparate features merge into the arresting face that has made him a raw international screen presence.

"I got lucky I guess as far as the look," said Del Toro, the Puerto-Rican born, Pennsylvania-raised star of *Traffic, The Usual Suspects, Fear and Loathing in Las Vegas* and *Savages.* "I can use it to my favor. You have to have a thick skin when it comes to your looks, and never doubt or fear it. I should thank my dad and my mom, really."

In the past he has played a British werewolf; a stressed to the bone Mexican police officer; a mentally disturbed Native American; a gangster called Frankie Four Fingers; and the Argentine revolutionary Ernesto "Che" Guevara. In *Jimmy P,: The Psychotherapy of a Plains Indian*, Del Toro's leathery amorphousness reveals itself in the face of Jimmy Picard, a Blackfeet World War II veteran.

"I do have a real responsibility when representing different groups of people and taking on groups of people that, at first, I don't know that well," said Del Toro. "It's a gift. And I'm lucky that way. I'm lucky that way because I have the opportunity to explore culture. As a

Jimmy P: Psychotherapy of a Plains Indian stars Benicio Del Toro (left) as a troubled Native American war veteran helped by a gifted analyst (Mathieu Amalric, right). The opening scenes were shot in Browning and East Glacier.

Puerto Rican, here I am playing a Native American, and that's a leap of history."

Jimmy Picard suffers from extreme headaches and bouts of dizziness perhaps related to a skull fracture he sustained during his service. Oblivious, barely responsive, and seemingly indifferent to life, Jimmy shows symptoms of post-traumatic stress disorder. At first taken to a To-peka, Kansas, military hospital, Picard is soon transferred to the nearby Menninger Clinic, where he bewilders the staff by exhibiting standard brain activity.

The film draws its inspiration from "Reality and Dream: Psychotherapy of a Plains Indian," a case study by the ethnologist and psychoanalyst Georges Devereux about his treatment of a Blackfeet Indian whom De-vereux encountered at the actual Menninger Clinic in 1948.

Directed by Frenchman Arnaud Desplechin, the film chronicles Jimmy's advances and relapses and the emer-gent bond between scholar and patient. The opening scenes of *Jimmy P.* were shot in Browning and East Gla-cier in July 2012. The year is 1948, and World War II has been over for nearly three years. The setting is a ranch in Montana, where the former Army Corporal Picard lives with his older sister, Gayle.

"With the movie *Jimmy P.* much of the Montana filming was shot in and around the town of Browning," said location manager John Ansotegui. "Although the story takes place post-World War II, the locations used in Browning were used as flashback and dream sequenc-es, so they all needed to have a weathered, pre-1940s feel. They used a street and buildings in Browning for those scenes.

"Production crews for *Jimmy P.* first contacted the State Film Commission in February of 2012, and, by that summer, they were shooting in Browning. That's a fast turnaround for a feature film. Many films spend years in pre-production before a single frame is shot, and other projects never even make it to production. I had some connections on the Blackfeet Reservation who showed me around some of the properties. With any script, there are specifics and you make a big list. With *Jimmy P.*, there is the shot of the mountains and the plains, and as the location manager you are trying to find that special place. As far as the buildings, in Browning, they were easy to find, simply because nothing has been updated."

One-hundred-twenty enrolled members or descendants of the Blackfeet tribe were used in the production and several University of Montana professors were among the locals cast. The round house in Heart Butte served as a key scene in the Montana location.

"Historically, a round house is a religious and social gathering place for Native Americans," said Ansotegui. "Part of the location scout's job is to gain access to buildings and places that have often been vacant for years. It took months before we were able to track down the one person who had access to the building. It turned out to be well worth it because the locations were used in the production for a number of key scenes. The round house was a nightmare—it involved getting a hold of a priest in Heart Butte—and he was near impossible to get a hold of."

Ansotegui said that part of his job as location manager is to assuage skepticism and make sure that the production leaves a property in no worse shape than before.

"People are generally skeptical when someone is poking around looking for locations for a movie," said Ansotegui. "They are either real enthusiastic or they don't want to talk to you. On "Jimmy P.," with the case of the round house, they allowed to let me to look at a sacred place that had not been used in a long time. We replaced the wood, the door, and the floor. The roof had been leaking for years. We really fixed the building to their benefit."

Del Toro said he spent approximately 10 or 11 days on location in Montana. To understand the Blackfeet people and to cultivate the characteristics of "Jimmy P.," Del Toro says that he leaned on Blackfeet educator Marvin Weatherwax.

"I met Marvin and I spoke at length with him," Del Toro said. "I met other people. And even though most of the picture was shot in the Detroit area, Montana is important to it. I got a lot of help for sign language and the history of the culture, all of it, even one of the religious ceremonies. I spent time in Browning and I hung out with Marvin, and one thing that struck me was that there were no movie theaters in Browning. They are said to have had one 15, 20 years ago. But there's no movie theater today, and that's a little bit of a sad note."

The globe-trotting Del Toro said that Montana's beauty immediately distinguished it from the majority of the other places he has visited.

"First thing I thought was, 'Wow, that is a lot of space,'" said Del Toro. "The first time I arrived, and I flew in and then we drove in a Winnebago. I saw the beautiful sky, the beautiful horizons. I stayed at the Super 8 in Cut Bank, and one of the impressions, the first impressions, was walking into the bedroom of the motel, and seeing the beautiful skyline, and the train tracks, and a bridge. It was like something out of a John Ford movie, from another era.

"I looked out the window, out of the Super 8, and I took some pictures. The sky. The high-rolling train. It was like a painting. If John Steinbeck was a painter, he would paint that. Something about that, it hits the soul and plugs it up, and makes it speak in stereo. God, or call it whatever you call it, was there."

Del Toro said he held no misconceptions about the troubles and hardships of the modern Blackfeet in Browning. "There has been change, a recent change of the leadership, from what I know," said Del Toro. "And the people I met were happy about that change. But there is still very little for the youth—not a bowling alley, or a movie theater, or a boys' club, nothing there. The people need something to pay attention to. With all the space, being a kid with all the space, you can see as far and high as you can look. It's a place for dreamers, but it would be nice to give Browning a place to work on that dream."

Between pictures and on the set, Del Toro—noted for his rigorous self-examination of the material—enjoyed whatever down time he could set aside. "One of the things you do to relax is music," said Del Toro. "It allows you to relax and it motivates you to get up. Music gets you through and allows you to wind down, and music is a good motivator. I read a little bit, maybe watch other movies. When in Spain, I will go to a museum. In Montana, you just open the window."

Del Toro said that he when he takes his next trip to Montana it will most likely involve leisure. And, he said, the very first thing on his agenda when he returns will be an appointment with a fly-rod and tackle box. "I'll tell you, one of the things I want to do is to do some fly-fishing to relax," said Del Toro. "I've never done it. I here that's a good way of letting go. I guess that we city folks don't have that connection. You have it in Montana—constantly. I gravitate toward that connection as I get older."

Montana's Lily Gladstone played Sunshine First Raise in *Jimmy P.* and also had a significant role in *Certain Women*. PHOTO COURTESY OF LILY GLADSTONE.

Born and raised in Browning, actress Lily Gladstone returned in 2012 for the film. "That was incredibly surreal," said Gladstone. "To be able to work on *Jimmy P.,* with such a strong script and a renowned director, and someone like Del Toro, that was amazing." One of the opening scenes of *Jimmy P.* utilized the Browning train station. As Gladstone stood on the platform, preparing for her role as Sunshine First Raise, Del Toro coolly sauntered around the corner. Up to that point, the actor's rough-hewn face and saggy eyes had been the stuff of videos.

"I will never forget the moment filming at the Browning train station," said Gladstone. "I remembered traveling out of there as a kid. And there I am getting the microphone put on, and my skirt was up. Embarrassing, right? Those hazel green eyes floored me. He said, 'I'm Benicio.' I said, 'I know'."

As Del Toro gazed out at the mountainous geography, Gladstone identified the tips and summits in the distance. She pointed out Red Crow Mountain in the Lewis and Clark Range—outlined like a horse saddle—and shared a family legend about Red Crow, her third-great grandfather. She is of Native American/First Nations heritage, from the Amskapi Pikuni (Blackfeet), Kainaiwa (Blood) and Niimipoo (Nez Perce) nations.

"It is named after one of my ancestors," said Gladstone. "I told him about that. I told him that I grew up looking at that mountain. You can see it on film—over his left shoulder. That mountain was a bit of a focal point my whole life."

After their conversation ended, Del Toro hugged Gladstone and said, "You are good, keep doing it." "I said, 'I hope to see you again.' He nodded and smiled, and said, 'you will.'"

Jimmy P.: Psychotherapy of a Plains Indian drew generally favorable reviews—the *Village Voice* called it "superb" and "engrossing"—and earned selection in several international film festivals, including Festival De Cannes and New York Film Festival. The film was nominated for the Palme d'Or at Cannes Film Festival in 2013 and three César Awards.

"I thought that the final cut of 'Jimmy P.' that was sent to Cannes, was way too much of a love story," said Ansotegui. "I think the shots we shot in Montana were amazing, the hand games, and the Indians as extras in period costumes. It has hasn't changed much in 100 years and we got the last round house that hasn't been burned down. It's a tough place to shoot, a tough place to put a crew. But you go in with the right attitude and after all is said and done the people who were involved with it really liked it."

Josh and S.A.M.

CAST
Jacob Tierney, Noah Fleiss, Martha Plimpton

DIRECTOR
Billy Weber

LOCATION
Billings area

1992

Josh and S.A.M. is a sappy film about the confusing transitions of adolescents dealing with divorced parents. Two young brothers escape their crazy, quirky family and embark on an adventure across the country. The production company required an area that could look like seven different states, and the greater Billings area was chosen. Principal photography was shot there, while Castle Rock Entertainment spent three months there during the summer of 1991.

A pastiche of contemporary youth traumas and road movies, *Josh and S.A.M.* rambles along good-naturedly, if rather aimlessly. It twists and turns along the route, too often using gimmickry and jettisoning its reality base. However, by the time it reaches its destination, the film has actually scored enough points for viewers to forgive much of its dopiness and its emphasis on the corny.

After their parents' divorce, brothers Josh (Jacob Tierney) and Sam (Noah Fleiss) decide to go on an underage road trip. Sick of being ferried between their distant mother and remarried father, Josh and his brother steal a car and set out for Canada. In the movie, the brothers travel from Dallas to Calgary, and see everything from wheat fields to bright city lights. The production company required an area that could resemble the different states—among them Texas and Florida. "There are all these scenes—everything from wheat fields to downtown Calgary—and most of that we're faking here [in the Billings area]," said executive producer Arne Schmidt. "We're going to be all over Billings. It's a road movie, and we have over 90 locations to film in 69 days, so you'll see us around."

When the production required a store-lined street that would pass for a Dallas thoroughfare, it took five minutes of closing the northbound lanes on 24th Street West from Lampman Drive to Grand Avenue.

The film, while gorgeously shot, is schematic and wholly implausible. Locations throughout Montana, Utah, and Canada were used. Much of the action takes place on the road in specially constructed vehicles to accommodate a stunt driver hidden behind the two young boys. In addition to Billings, Columbus was the site of several scenes, including the New Atlas Bar, the Branding Iron Café, and the Senior Citizens Center, which was transposed into the inside of a bus station (the outside of the Harris Agency was facelifted for the outside of the station). Parts of Laurel that are identifiable in a scene on East Main Street near Hazel Avenue focused on the two child actors talking, and a set and exterior shots of the Boise Cascade building. At Bob's Interstate Service and the Purple Cow Restaurant in Hardin, the crew filmed a scene in which 12-year-old Josh cuts his forehead and doctors himself with mini-pads and Scotch tape.

Roger Ebert picked apart the film's myriad weaknesses: "The movie's basic problem is one of credibility. I know it's only a story. I know I'm supposed to play along with it. But scene after scene is beyond belief. Take, for example, a sequence where little Sam is driving the car at top speed through a fruit orchard. There'd be no way he could avoid hitting trees except through the heavy use of special effects. What am I supposed to do? Think, 'Gee, this is exciting—he's barely missing those trees?' I'm too old for that, and I have been since I was in junior high school."

Other outlets found the S.A.M. subplot way too contrived, too easy, too manipulated, including the *Los Angeles Times*: "The gimmick is that Sam believes everything Josh tells him, even after Josh tries to explain he was always kidding. Sam comes to believe he's nothing but a robot, and so one of the big wrenching emotional climaxes comes as Josh convinces the kid he's a real little boy after all. Give me a break."

The Castle Rock production opened August 27, 1993, via Columbia Pictures at some 1,000 theaters and expanded Labor Day weekend. The film failed to generate a buzz or solid word-of-mouth and quickly sank, which Castle Rock's co-founder blamed in part to the film's PG-13 rating.

"In all the focus [sessions] we had, there really were no parents who felt it was inappropriate for 8- or 9-year-olds," said Martin Shafer. What accounted for the rating? "The 8-year old kid driving a car; them getting money from a cash machine on a credit card one of the kids stole; and a scene when they're running near a train and one of the kids goes under a train."

Despite an improbable plot and a production low on thrills and high on character development, the *Hollywood Reporter* commended Frank Deese's script for exploring "commonplace problems in fresh and inventive ways" and Don Burgess' "first-rate cinematography."

Keep the Change

CAST
William Peterson, Rachel Ticotin

DIRECTOR
Andy Tennant

LOCATION
Livingston area–Paradise Valley

1992

Keep the Change was based on a novel by Thomas McGuane of Livingston, where the movie was filmed. In this scene, adversaries Jack Palance (left) and William Peterson ride along the Yellowstone River.

"I'm so broke, I can't pay attention," mumbles Joe Starling, the jesting, angst-addled painter who is the ferociously alive antihero of *Keep the Change*. As played by William Petersen, Starling has the artist's version of writer's block: he stares at a blank canvas and can think only of the bare palette of his own life. Part of Starling's problem, he realizes at the start of the film, is that he's whiling away his life in sunny California with a girlfriend about whom he is permanently ambivalent. So he steals her car and heads back home, to Deadrock, Montana. He has a vague notion that if he straightens out his past, he'll be able to move on with his future.

Starling flees to Montana for several reasons: to feel sorry for himself in the vast openness of the Starling family cattle spread; to brood over the troubled relationship he had with his late father; and to seek out his one true love, Ellen (Lolita Davidovich), now married to his former best friend.

Keep the Change is based on the 1989 novel of the same name by Thomas McGuane—a writer who has spent his career describing simple-minded Montana screw-ups like Starling, guys whose relationships with women amount to, as he once described, "love-'em-and-leave-'em, yet who draw women like flies because they're so handsome, so tragic, so alluringly self-pitying."

Starling could easily have been an insufferable oddball, but Petersen, who also produced this movie, turns him into a yearning charmer, a sympathetic slacker with noble intentions. With its affably aimless pace, low-key acting, and an insistence on the redemptive silliness of love, *Keep the Change* is similar to other movie adaptations of McGuane's work, feature films like *92 in the*

Shade and *Rancho Deluxe*. But this is the first McGuane-inspired movie to capture the dry wit of the novelist's prose, to keep the meandering tempo of the story from wandering into tedium. "I saw one of your paintings in a magazine once," says Ellen to Starling of the artist's abstract works. "It looked like custard next to a house."

For *Keep the Change*, Starling's sardonic voice-over narrates the story, so we hear Starling make murmuring declarations like, "I am consumed with temporary insanity."

The tease is that the narrative here barely exists: Starling goes home, sidles up to Ellen, brawls with her husband, and helps to save his family land from a neighboring rich, greedy landowner. (He's played by Jack Palance on what looks like his day off from *City Slickers*—same sort of character, same mean, sly attitude, same clothes). Oscar winner Palance is amusing as Starling's arch-enemy.

"He's in great shape," said William Petersen. "The one-arm push-up [scene in *City Slickers*] didn't surprise me a bit." Stan Smith, of Dillon, worked on *Keep the Change* as an extra, and he recalled Palance as being warm and humorous. "He was great to work with," said Smith. "Great story teller and somewhat of a joker. Because he knew I ran a movie theatre [in Dillon] he thoughtfully gifted me with a small bag of 'fartless' popcorn seed so he would have an excuse to come see me at my theatre. He loved popcorn, but it didn't like him, so he thought this was a funny gift. He did show out of the blue and joined me for coffee and talked about everything under the sun but film."

Also appearing opposite Petersen in *Keep the Change* is Buck Henry as his boozy uncle (who wants to become Montana's first shrimp wrangler).

There are times when *Keep the Change* is inane and pretentious, but Petersen's straightforward, unmannered performance keeps the film intriguing.

Petersen said he enjoyed playing the intense, moody artist-turned-cowboy in *Keep the Change*. Petersen didn't have to kill to get the part—he just had to buy the book's movie rights, commission the script and produce the film.

"McGuane's characters are always a little quirky," said Petersen. "But they're so rich, so expressive. There isn't an actor around who wouldn't kill to play one of them. I'd been trying for a long time to get the rights to one of his books. When I switched agents, it turned out my new agent also represents Tom. He set up a deal. It's a small, quirky story that we could never do as a feature, so we took it to Ted Turner's TNT. I always loved Tom's stuff. I read all of his work when we were making *Amazing Grace and Chuck*. (Petersen played the father of the title character Chuck in that movie, filmed in 1986.)

Petersen said that when he opens a Thomas McGuane book he feels as if he is looking into a mirror. "I relate very much to all of Thomas McGuane's male characters," said Petersen. "His conflicts are not dissimilar to my conflicts in my life. In this story Joe Starling is unsure of the future and decides to deal with his past to avoid facing his future. It's a symptom of the midlife crisis."

Keep the Change was described as "a zippy little romantic comedy" by *TV Guide,* which also concluded it was "easily the best and quirkiest TV movie cable's TNT has yet presented."

The *Atlanta Journal-Constitution* didn't much care for the film, though it did enjoy the scenery, which included a stampede scene at Turner's ranch, interesting bar interiors, and an upscale ranch house that fit a masculine modern-day cattle baron: "We lose a few grace notes in the translation from novel into TV movie of Tom McGuane's *Keep the Change*, but what's left is more than enough to make us believe that we, too, might re-invent ourselves, after a dose of the past and Montana. Lolita

Davidovich and Montana's big skies help a failed artist re-invent himself….There's also lots of Montana on which to project these emotional weathers, and director Andy Tennant does so lovingly."

The Hollywood Reporter conceded that "*Keep The Change* has been crisply photographed. In fact, this is a most noteworthy attribute of the movie." *Parade* said *Keep the Change* "benefits greatly from the brisk pace and beautiful Montana scenery provided by director Andy Tennant."

Layover

CAST
Stacey Miller, Daniel Rhyder

DIRECTOR
April Wright

LOCATION
Bozeman

2008

Layover is a small-budget film shot entirely on location at the Bozeman Yellowstone International Airport. "It's a neat film for several reasons," said scout John Ansotegui. "It is a neat film because we marketed it to Sundance. We met the director [April Wright] at a Sundance reception in January and come March the production was here working on the movie. It's very unusual to get that type of turnaround that fast on a film. Secondly, it's all shot inside the airport. It's about two people getting snowed in and we happened to have the Bozeman airport with snow in March, and it looked wintry."

Ansotegui credited the Bozeman Yellowstone International Airport and the Bozeman Chamber of Commerce and representatives of the City of Bozeman for assisting in the production. "It was amazing to have the willingness of the town and all the local businesses who see the filming of a movie as a positive impact," said Ansotegui, who played a bartender in the film. "We were able to get them the Bozeman Airport for free if we filmed it in the middle of the night. As far as the bartender role, I just cleaned a glass and looked as if I was doing something."

Director April Wright said that the openness and accessibility of the airport sealed her decision to film in Bozeman. "Places obviously provided different access," said Wright. "You'd have different access issues in Los Angeles and it was easier to film in more remote places like Montana. The entire state only has one area code—so it wasn't the bureaucracy. Since the script revolves around two people stuck while changing planes it was smart to have at least one 737 there. I guess you could just CGI (computer-generated imagery) one in today, but in 2007, we actually shot at an airport and see an actual airplane. The airport has a lot of character and color, and that made it really interesting.

"We shot for two weeks, six days a week, and we shot in the public areas, generally starting in late afternoon to early in morning. At one point we shot behind security on the jet way, and the workers had a shorter shift to recertify after we left the area. But we wanted to have bad weather. It got there it was hot—80 degrees—but everyone kept saying, 'don't worry, it will cool down.' For the opening scenes we got a big blizzard came in on the day we needed it. We used a lot of students from the film school at Bozeman for different crew positions. We flew in the actors, me, producer, the DP (cinematographer), and his camera. All the rest of the local crew or film crew was from Bozeman."

Wright said that Bozeman's isolated beauty helped the actors get into—and stay focused—in the parts, and that the nightlife was equally memorable.

"It was great," said Wright. "We would be shooting in the morning and then go to the bars at 7 A.M. I'm a night owl. I loved it. It was perfect for me. But to have the actors more isolated and going home each day and night in Bozeman, I knew it would be different for them. Living in Bozeman helped the flavor and feel of their performances."

Bozeman is an attractive city for people looking to find peace and quiet and a plethora of outdoor activities. It's also been home to a number of famous people, from musicians to award-winning actors to astronauts.

"During the filming, Peter Fonda walked through the airport," said Wright. "But he didn't end up in a shot. He just came through, I guess, on his way home."

Layover was a small budget film shot entirely on location at the Bozeman Yellowstone International Airport. Photo courtesy April Wright

The highly acclaimed *Little Big Man* was shot in eastern Montana. It starred Dustin Hoffman (left) in the title role and was directed by Author Penn, who later returned to Montana to film *The Missouri Breaks.*

Little Big Man

CAST
Dustin Hoffman, Faye Dunaway

DIRECTOR
Arthur Penn

LOCATION
Virginia City, Billings

1970

Roughly one-third of the movies made in Montana are westerns or have had a western theme. They range from *The Devil's Horse* in 1920 to *Little Big Man* 50 years later. Framed by the reminiscences of a 121-year-old survivor

of the Battle of Little Big Horn—Jack Crabb (Dustin Hoffman)—director Arthur Penn's tale was filmed on the actual site of that 1876 battle. In this western comedy/drama, Crabb recounts stories of being captured by Indians, becoming a gun fighter, and acting as a scout for General Custer at the Battle of the Little Bighorn.

Penn brought on-location realism to *Little Big Man*, intending to de-Hollywoodize the western. As the film opens, a history graduate student has come to a veterans hospital to interview Jack. "I am more interested in the primitive lifestyle of the Plains Indians" and their "way of life," he condescends. "The tall tale about Custer" or another Old West "adventure" story that Crabb is about to tell has no credence in history, the interviewer explains. Jack takes control of the interviewer's tape recorder, and the camera preps audiences to hear the truth. "You turn that thing on and shut up," he scolds and his story begins.

When Penn directed and Hoffman acted at the Little Bighorn Battlefield and at Crow Agency in Montana, it was the summer of 1969. At 5:30 A.M. Penn arose, sipped coffee, and left his Montana rental for the *Little Big Man* film set. There, cowboy and Indian extras tiptoed across "prickly pear cactus" and moved toward "mock villages" set up on the Crow Reservation and at a local ranch. Penn hoisted his tortoise-shell glasses off his head and yelled, "Cut. Let's do it again." The production crew tipped over covered wagons and positioned burnt tipis. Makeup artists prepared their actors and actresses for the retakes. Hoffman took breaks in his portable trailer, reading the *Village Voice* and *New Republic.* At the end of the day, Penn shipped the takes to Hollywood and awaited their return. Back at the screening room in Billings, some of the cast joined editor Dede Allen for a preview of earlier clips. After screenings Penn returned to his Montana home and sipped martinis while perusing the *New Yorker, Time, Newsweek,* and other eastern glossies.

Penn set up cameras in eight Montana locations. He was fixed emotionally on the victims of frontier history, not the victors. Shot on local ranches, on reservations, and in Montana towns, Penn's rendition represented the way the West was instead of the way it was imagined. At least, that was the idea behind the project—converting Thomas Berger's *Little Big Man,* published in 1964, into a manifesto for Indian empathy. For Penn, social activism, westerns, and Montana were a natural fit. Where better to stage this revision than the territory itself because, most likely, as the director said, "It just doesn't get any better. Montana is the real thing." Having just discovered Montana while vacationing there and listening to local rancher Earl Rosell and Billings mayor Willard Fraser talk about the "Treasure State's" magnificent scenery, Penn saw potential for a successful blend between story and scenery. Rosell and Fraser made trips to Hollywood on their own dime to tout Montana's pleasures and vistas.

Long before Montana established a film commission, Rosell believed the area perfect for filming. His day job was as insurance salesman, but he was an expert horseman and his love of westerns paralleled his passion for horses. Between 1969 and the mid-1980s, six feature films and many commercials were shot on the ET Ranch co-owned with his wife, Antoinette "Toni" Fraser Rosell. The ranch's first coup was *Little Big Man*. There followed *The Missouri Breaks*, *Son of the Morning Star*, *The Legend of Walks Far Woman* (television movie with Raquel Welch), *Far and Away* and *The Return to Lonesome Dove*.

Rosell's nephew Wally Kurth, an actor known for his roles in *General Hospital* and *Days of Our Lives*, said his uncle encouraged his career path. "He loved kids and our dreams," Kurth said. "He took us to sets—imagine watching Dustin Hoffman or Marlon Brando and Jack Nicholson. Earl said, 'Kids, they put their pants on one leg at a time. You can do it, too.'" He'd been wooing Hollywood since the 1950s.

Little Big Man left $16 million in the area during its nine-month shoot. "These film people are wonderful to work with and it's a good, clean industry that trickles down many streams," said Rosell in 1969. "The people all eat, drink and make merry. They buy jewelry and western souvenirs. They buy much material locally for the locations—cement, lumber, hardware. They hire local electricians and carpenters. It helps a wide range of people and business economically." He saw himself as a kind of P.T. Barnum of local movie trade. "If somebody wants 600 Indians in full ceremonial dress in front of the Northern Hotel at 6 A.M. tomorrow, I'm your man."

Rosell's Montana locations would enable director Penn to revise cinematic representations and help historically subordinated groups become agents in narratives on screen. Montana offered a real look for an updated image of Native Americans. Penn made a point out of shooting at "authentic Montana locations" because he wanted his film to "represent the West as it was, not as it was

imagined." Although, he admitted, he wasn't aiming for historical accuracy. "You use history and social situations for insight," he said, "and also to say, 'This is the way I understand the background and foreground of a given situation dramatically'."

Little Big Man shot east of Billings at the Rosell Ranch, in the Billings area, at Alder Gulch, the Crow Indian Reservation in Hardin and the Cheyenne Indian Reservation in Lame Deer. Parts of *Little Big Man* were shot on the site of Custer Battlefield National Monument on the Crow reservation; some pointed it out as ironic that some of the roles of the Cheyenne and Sioux were played by their hereditary enemies, the Crows, who had worked as scouts for Custer.

The period-authentic wooden buildings collected in Nevada City also served as a movie set, as it would for other Westerns such as *The Missouri Breaks* and *Return to Lonesome Dove*. The Bale of Hay Saloon in well-preserved ghost town Virginia City is where Hoffman's character met Wild Bill Hickok (Jeff Corey), when Crabb himself was considering becoming a gunslinger.

A part of *Little Big Man* was also shot in the Calgary, Canada, area. Oscar-winning actor Hoffman rented a house on Virginia Lane and moved in with his Labrador dogs, a cook and other staff. Hollywood master Dick Smith helped Hoffman age from teenager to 121-year-old. Hoffman, then just over 30 and fresh from his fame in *The Graduate*, had 35 makeup and costume changes in the film.

The Penn crew raised its cameras toward the Montana landscape in the context of multicultural debates in America. His film registered that social mix, beginning with the casting of a Canadian actor and longshoreman, Chief Dan George, in the supporting role of Old Lodge Skins, the Cheyenne patriarch. This role was personal for George. "I wanted to show that an Indian, if he had talent, could play an Indian better than a white," the chief said, "simply because he was playing his own nationality." To complete the picture of authenticity, Crow Indians filled in as extras.

Penn treated Custer (Richard Mulligan) as a megalomaniac by first casting Native Americans in positive roles opposite Custer and his military. Custer's negative portrayal represented the savage side of the American past and the wrongdoings of the federal government. When Penn placed a tribal leader in a leading role and filmed Native Americans in indigenous landscapes, the effect was nothing less than a sign of film's power to change attitudes and influence beliefs.

Charles Champlin of the *Los Angeles Times,* for example, noted that unlike "other recent films" about the tragedy of confrontation, Penn's was different. *Little Big Man* showed "the Indians as men and women and children…rather than as a Culture or a Historical Force," he said. The film "states the tragedy of the confrontation more eloquently and powerfully…and more effectively indeed than any film I can remember seeing."

Roger Ebert of the *Chicago Sun-Times* believed that: "It is the very folksiness of Penn's film that makes it, finally, such a perceptive and important statement about Indians, the West, and the American Dream."

When New York and Los Angeles viewers applauded *Little Big Man* at the respective openings in December 1970, they approved of new perspectives on American history. *New Yorker* film critic Judith Crist, for example, contended, "It strikes new ground in its concepts and new perceptions in its subtleties." She concluded, "its concern for humanity approaches universal truths that transcend skin color."

While many cheered Penn as a "ground-breaker," others accused Penn of pandering and confusing noble, corny sermonizing for art. There is "a cheapness in Penn's conception," complained a *Film Quarterly* critic, reflected in the ease with which "we identify with the Indians because they are nice."

The movie opened to critical acclaim at a gala premier in downtown Billings in December 1970, raising funds for the Yellowstone Art Museum and Rocky Mountain College's Center for Indian Studies. Hot fry bread, kick ball and Indian dances heralded the beginning of Little Big Man Day Wednesday, December 16, 1970, in Billings.

North Broadway between Second and Fourth streets was blocked off and entirely turned over to the Indian festivities. Four large Indian lodges poked skyward among the concrete buildings as Indian dancers from throughout Montana and neighboring states took part in an afternoon pow-wow. The dancers and celebration participants were outnumbered by the hundreds of viewers who lined the bordering. Christmas music played. "What's with the Christmas music," one Indian man chuckled, "this is supposed to be Indian day."

On hand were Richard Mulligan, his wife, Joan Hackett, and actress June Allyson. Don Nunley, properties manager for *Little Big Man*, was adopted into the Crow Tribe Warrior Society in the downtown area.

Attired in outfits ranging from pants suits to beaded buckskin dresses and from business suits to feathered headdresses, "1,400 plus Indians," according to the *Billings Gazette*, poured into the Fox Theater later that day for the premiere.

One of the biggest laughs came after the Cheyenne had attacked a cavalry unit and Dustin Hoffman's lead Jack Crabb, was unhorsed by a trooper after his scalp. Hoffman yelled and ducked over, under and around his horse before the trooper pinioned him and discovered Hoffman was a white man. The laugher ended during the scenes depicting the massacre of Indian villages by the cavalry and turned to shrieks when, in a chase scene, a stagecoach nearly turned over on an Indian clinging to its side. There was "scattered nervous laughter" when Hoffman's Indian wife, Sunshine, and her newly-born baby were shot to death by white cavalry raiding a village supposedly safely ensconced on a reservation. Several of the persons watching the movie took part in its filming. Floyd Real Bird, who owned Medicine Tail Coulee where the massacre scene was filmed, said he and his grandfather, in 1933, found the spine of one ill-fated seventh Cavalry trooper with an arrow embedded in it. The site of the find is noted in the Battlefield register.

Little Big Man grossed approximately $31 million.

Love Comes to the Executioner

CAST
Jonathon Tucker, Jeremy Renner

DIRECTOR
Kyle Bergersen

LOCATION
Butte, Deer Lodge

2006

Love Comes to the Executioner is a black comedy that is as quirky as the title implies. Written and directed by Kyle Bergersen, it stars Jonathan Tucker as a Latin scholar who takes the job as executioner at the same prison where his brother is on Death Row. He finds unconventional true love in his brother's incarcerated ex-girlfriend. This dark comedy takes place in a small, blue-collar community, occupied primarily by many European immigrants. Los Angeles line producer, Mark Dziak, said his southwest Montana roots helped put the Butte and Deer Lodge area into the spotlight.

Several of the scenes are filmed in Deer Lodge, one of the oldest towns in Montana. Located in a western mountain valley on the banks of the Clark Fork River, Deer Lodge was first a trapping and trading center and later an important stage stop between gold camps. Many of its buildings pre-date 1900. Montana Territory first established a penitentiary in Deer Lodge in 1871; the buildings now open to the public were begun in the 1890s. The castellated, three-story cell block of red brick was built in 1912. It contains 200 cells, each 6 by 7 feet. All the prison structures were built by forced convict labor—a practice later outlawed. After a violent prison riot highlighted the declining conditions at the old prison, a new facility was built in 1979.

Loves Comes to the Executioner was the fourth and most recent time Hollywood had selected Old Montana Prison as a filming location. The Old Montana Prison complex was most attractive to the production crew, since 40 percent of the film takes place inside a prison (they used the prison yard, the infirmary, the 1912 cell house and the convention center across the street). "When I read the script the first thing that came into my head was Anaconda and Butte," said line producer Mark Dziak, a Californian who as a kid made frequents trips to the Anaconda area to visit his grandparents. "The area really offered us everything. Photographically, there's a lot in Butte and Deer Lodge. It's locations that you can't get just anywhere, not in Los Angeles, certainly. We looked all over the country and also in Canada for prisons. The one we liked best was in Deer Lodge."

Other scenes from the film were shot on the streets of Deer Lodge, and in Butte at Cranky Hank's Corner Bar, Butte's Kiwanis Sunshine Camp, Ranchland Packing Company, and parts of the Bert Mooney Airport.

"I was quite involved with *Executioner*," recalled Montana Film Commissioner Sten Iversen. "The movie pro-

Butte and Deer Lodge, including the Old Territorial Prison, starred in *Love Comes to the Executioner*.

duction used the old prison and built these crazy sets in a warehouse in Butte. I drove hundreds of miles in a Suburban taking the director and production designer and coordinators around. It was great that they were allowed to make the prison the way they wanted it to look. The old prison is quite gritty as it is, it looked used, and not like a museum. One of the cool sets they built was in the old Safeway warehouse in Butte as an execution chamber. It was either octagonal or round, but it was the real deal, the real Hollywood set. It was neat being able to see inside this other world."

Stan Smith of Dillon, Montana, manager of the local movie theater, has worked in nearly 20 films, and received a small part as one of the inmates. After filming wrapped, Smith, who also works as the city's coroner, hopped in his car and drove southeast for home, where he encountered blizzard conditions and a stranded vehicle. "I got out of the car and it was a pair of two old ladies, who hit black ice or something," said Smith. "I get out—tear tattoos on the face and an off-blue prison uniform—and you could see the look on the old lady's face diving, just scrambling to lock the door. She's thinking, 'It's going to be the worst day of my life.' The highway patrolman got a laugh out of that one."

Me & Will

CAST
Sherrie Rose, Jason Hall, Patrick Dempsey

DIRECTORS
Melissa Behr, Sherrie Rose

LOCATION
Livingston, Wilsall

1997

Me & Will are two female drug addicts who are familiar faces on the Los Angeles club scene. They meet at drug rehab after Jane overdosed and Will crashed her motorcycle driving stoned. They hit it off immediately and escape the clinic to travel to Montana and find the bike from the movie *Easy Rider.* According to Will, "The *Easy Rider* bike was stolen or repoed when they shot the movie…and it's in my hometown of Wilsall, Montana." "How many miles to Montana?" asks Jane. "1,080," responds Will.

Me & Will is sordid, depressive film in which all of the women are white trash, tattooed, skanky, promiscuous, cuss-mouthed. The men are violent, controlling abusers or despicable cretins or incestuous sickos. Nearly everyone in the film has a substance abuse problem, which, in this case is a most euphemistic for being a pointless junkie. Former porn star Traci Lords has a bit part as an abused woman who gets beaten up and tossed out of a truck. Perhaps the most likeable character in the movie is a pit bull whose off-screen name was Chiva Knievel.

However, the screen time afforded to Montana halfway through the film is exceptional. In a scene in which Jane gets run off of her motorcycle by a motor home, the

backdrop is undeniably Montana. The Wilsall Hardware Company and the town of Wilsall find screen time. Another scene in which Will visits her pot-grower father, the backdrop is again most likely Montana. The film ends in 88 minutes in the same slimy, hopeless fashion as it began, though the final 30 seconds include, presumably, second unit flashes of Montana scenery. As far as the exact specifics of filming locations and filming dates, *Me & Will* is a mystery to Lonie Stimac, who served as the state film commissioner at the time.

"What very well could have happened is that they filmed in Montana and never contacted us," said Stimac. "Remember that the companies were not required to obtain a permit, so they could have come, used local contacts and wrapped a project without our knowing. Then what could have happened is that maybe crew members put Montana down on the list of location credits. It was probably second unit or only for a few days."

My Sister's Keeper

DIRECTOR
Nick Cassavetes

CAST
Cameron Diaz, Abigail Breslin

LOCATION
Glacier National Park, Blackfeet Reservation, St. Mary

2009

Glacier National Park is one of the most well-preserved ecosystems in the continental United States, with an estimated 175 mountains, 762 lakes, 563 streams, 200 waterfalls, 25 glaciers, and 745 miles of hiking trails. In addition to the geological wonders, the park is home to as many as 60 native species of mammals and 260 species of birds. According to geologists, Glacier National Park began millions of years ago when the "Lewis Overthrust moved a large section of sedimentary rock for about 50 miles." During the Ice Age, mammoth glaciers cut across this giant section of sedimentary rock, carving the breathtaking landscape that is Glacier National Park.

Movie crews have arrived in Glacier National Park several times, most recently to film a pivotal sequence in the heart-tugging drama *My Sister's Keeper*. Directed by Nick Cassavetes and based on the best-selling book by Jodi Picoult, *My Sister's Keeper* tells the story of a young girl (Abigail Breslin) conceived to be a bone marrow donor for her sister who seeks emancipation from her parents (Cameron Diaz and Alec Baldwin). Sixty crew members were involved in the seven day shooting schedule in September 2007, most hired from the Flathead Valley, the Blackfeet reservation, and the Bozeman area. Scenes were filmed at St. Mary and Two Medicine. The film's final scene and emotional climax is set against the backdrop of Upper Two Medicine.

"This film was mostly shot in Los Angeles." said scout John Ansotegui. "But for the final scenes they came to Montana to shoot right here. Normally, RV's are not allowed on the lakeshore, but we were able to work with the Park Service to allow production to build a bridge from the picnic area and to lay down slabs of plywood and crawl the RV to the spot.

"Overall, the Park Service was awesome, and they made something ridiculous happen easily. Hey, it's a weird request—planks of wood to crawl an RV in a national park. They are pretty strict with their rules. But it all worked. It's the little things that take a lot of discussion, like the propane tank in the scene that's emulating a fire, but that's not actually burning anything."

Former Montana Film Commissioner Sten Iversen further described the logistics of coordinating and shooting the final scene. "At Upper Two Medicine, we needed to get permission to have a motor home placed right on the shore of the lake for the final scene in the movie," said Iversen. "Obviously, camping is only allowed in designated camping spots and we had to develop a plan, and that plan involved many different people, from the key grip to the location manager. We had to convince the park that we wouldn't destroy vegetation and convince them that there would be no harm done. At first, we were heard things like, "We can't allow it because you would be hurting the botany or micro-botany.'

"Then, the idea became to build a bridge over the vegetation and to walk the motor home on plywood. The

The final scene of the heart-tugging drama *My Sister's Keeper* was filmed at Upper Two Medicine Lake in Glacier National Park.

Glacier Park botanist was called in to give her official opinion. She made it clear that she cared about the lichen and so forth. So, she gets down on her hands and knees, and she's examining the ground, and we are all holding our breath, and crossing our fingers. She gets up and says, 'No problem here!' That was an exciting day for us when that happened. It's the final scene in the movie—and a big deal."

Ansotegui said that the two actresses earned his respect for handling the howling winds and bitter cold with professional aplomb. "It came off as a beautiful shot and I give Breslin and Diaz props," said Ansotegui. "It was so [very] cold that day. I was bundled up like crazy. I thought it was pretty professional not seeming like they were as cold as they were. But it was brutal."

"The director wanted that final scene in a real location and saved money during the rest of filming to film in Montana for a couple of days," recalled film crew member Allison Whitmer. "It's a good example of having a good working relationship in film. There were park rangers all over the place, and it worked out just fine."

Academy Award-winning director Alexander Payne (right) was looking for authenticity when he filmed parts of *Nebraska* in Billings and Laurel. Here he talks with the film's stars Bruce Dern (center) and Will Forte (left) at the Billings bus station.

Nebraska

CAST
Bruce Dern

DIRECTOR
Alexander Payne

LOCATION
Billings, Laurel

2013

Academy Award winning director Alexander Payne (*Sideways*, *The Descendants*, *About Schmidt*) was looking for authenticity when he brought his crew to Billings and Laurel for a week in November 2012 to film parts of *Nebraska*.

Nebraska follows Woody T. Grant (Bruce Dern) of Billings, Montana, in his quest to collect a large sweepstakes prize he thinks a publishing house has awarded to him. In this sleek, stirring road trip comedy, the boundaries of art and life are probed with a knowing yet understated directness. (Bob Nelson wrote the screenplay and injected Billings into the script.)

Deny Staggs of the Montana Film Office asked Billings resident Anne Gauer to refer restaurants and hotels to the film crew before she even knew who it was for. Eventually, Staggs suggested to Paramount Pictures Executive Producer George Parra that he put Anne on board, and she began scouting for the film.

Her two-week stint as a location scout for "Woody and Kate's house" grew to a search for dilapidated hotels, hospital rooms, railroad tracks, cop cars and a law enforcement officer to act in the film.

"I was scouting police stations and photographing vehicles," said Gauer. "I checked out the [Montana] women's prison, Billings police station, Laurel police station and Montana Highway patrol office. I talked and met with different law enforcement agencies about locations and jurisdictions."

Gauer took a rubbing of the Yellowstone County Sheriff's Office emblem on the side of the patrol car, and took photos of the badges and uniforms, so they could be altered for the film.

While inside the Yellowstone County Detention Center on the search for old uniforms, she talked with Captain Dennis McCave, who, at that time, was nearing the conclusion of his 35th and final year in law enforcement, as commander of the county jail.

Gauer mentioned to McCave that there was a small part in the movie for a real-life Montana law enforcement officer. "They didn't want Hollywood to send a Montana law enforcement officer," said McCave. "I told Anne that, 'Well, if you need somebody, somebody to drive up in a patrol car and to approach him, and that's it, I'll do it.' I figured it was a bit thing and it would be no big deal. I had no idea."

"I knew that McCave had a personality that was outgoing enough to play this part," said Gauer. "A few weeks later, Casting Director John Jackson called and asked, 'Do you have any leads for the law enforcement officer?' I said, 'Well, I just happen to have a picture of someone.' Both Jackson and director Alexander Payne loved his look. He got the part."

McCave said that he saw the role as a positive community event for the city of Billings. While McCave and others did have concern that the officer's role would go over the edge into bumbling parody, that wasn't the case.

"I figured that if they wanted a real cop, I would give them a real cop. If they wanted a real police car, we would give them a real police car. I was humbled to be a part of it."

So, one chilly day, the Monday after Thanksgiving, Dennis McCave took the morning off from work to participate in a movie. McCave changed out his real uniform into his movie garb—regulations prohibited use of the exact insignia—drove to the 27th Street Interchange, and waited for the crew and trucks to start showing up.

It wasn't supposed to be a speaking role, but he would become the only Billings actor with a talking part.

It all unravels this way on film: Woody is a luckless, wild-haired, elderly fellow. He is alcohol-addled and stubborn, and determined to walk to Nebraska to pick up what he believes is a $1 million dollar sweepstakes prize.

Yellowstone County Sheriff's Office captain Dennis McCave took a morning off work to act in *Nebraska*. McCave wasn't supposed to have a speaking role, but his ad-lib asking Bruce Dern to step out of his car became the only talking part for any Billings extra. PHOTO BY ANNE GAUER

Before he gets very far, he is stopped by a local cop. There is a distinct mood set from the opening location, which feels like a paradise waiting to be loved and lost.

"Hey partner, where you heading?" the deputy asks. Woody doesn't answer. He just points to the highway—toward Nebraska. An old man burdened by the passage of time comforted by the duty of an officer.

"Dennis showed the style and the confidence to be able to play that role," says Gauer. "He was believable—the way he approached and related to Woody. He was the right choice."

Director Alexander Payne's instructions to McCave were simple. He essentially told McCave that it was better for McCave to be himself than try to be some version of what he thought that the director wanted.

As McCave recalled, "He didn't say things like 'stand here, or turn here, do this.' He didn't give exact directions or instructions. I know that he had in his mind precisely how he wanted to start. He wanted me to get out of the car, and to act as I would normally act. He didn't want to tell me how a cop would act in real life, or how I would act in that situation.

"Alexander gets there, and he says, 'Just be yourself.' He says, 'Just do it exactly the way you would act in a normal life situation. So I act how I normally act. I jump out and I start calling out. We did a couple of first takes, a second rehearsal, and then Alexander turns and says 'Mic him up.' So we do it over and over, and he says, 'That'll do it.'

"I took off the mic, and I went to sign some different papers. It was then that someone explained what was going on—that it was for the opening scene of the movie. I was done by noon, and I didn't even need to take a full day's vacation—just the morning."

McCave's impromptu exchange would make its way not only into the film's opening scene, but would later be used in the film's official trailer.

Ultimately, several scenes which Gauer had been scouting for when she met McCave were filmed in South Dakota and Nebraska—the police station, railroad tracks, hospital rooms, and old hotel.

"There is some unique local architecture in *Nebraska*," says Gauer. "We found the 1940s home in Laurel that was used as Woody's home. There is a shot of the Billings Bus Depot, and the scene along Montana Avenue with the statue of the little man on the LP Anderson Tire Factory. It's offbeat and unique."

On a day of filming in Laurel, neighbors of the home being used in a scene put up their bright, shiny Christmas decorations. Gauer had to ask them to remove the items so filming could begin.

"Those are the things you don't expect—like carrying away a lighted deer."

McCave, 62, actually has another screen credit to his name; he was an extra in the 1992 Tom Cruise adventure-romance *Far and Away*, also filmed in and near Billings.

"When I saw Captain McCave at the Yellowstone County Detention Center, I saw the picture of him on the set of *Far and Away* on the wall in the station," says Gauer. "So I knew he had the movie bug."

During that similar circumstance in the early 1990s, McCave had the chance to interact and socialize with some pretty famous folks, including Tom Cruise and Nicole Kidman. His wife had a friend in theatre, who suggested that Dennis and she bring their children to the casting call.

"Our friend said that I might as well fill out a card," says McCave. "I was put into the big fight scene down at the Depot. I got the call, and the kids didn't. There were seven days of filming all the different fight scenes. It was almost by accident."

Nebraska was nominated for six Oscars. Shot in glorious black and white, it was also nominated for five Golden Globe awards.

"I'm a little older than your average new person in films," said McCave. "But, hey, who knows where life goes from here."

Andrew "AJ" Marble was the manager of Billings Nursery & Landscaping whose quick-thinking preparedness was rewarded with a small part assisting in the production of *Nebraska*.

The film's opening scenes were filmed in and around Billings, and one morning around Thanksgiving 2012, crew members sauntered into his Billings Nursery & Landscaping, at 2147 Poly Drive.

"There were a couple of guys who came into the store looking for plants and pictures, and looking for oddities," Marble said. "I believe they bought the work of some local artists we had here at the time, to use for the movie or as a prop of some kind. And they bought a few house plants, too."

Soon, the conversation turned to the unusually warm weather in Billings that day and how the absence of real snow meant that mounds of it would have to be trucked in from elsewhere.

"The guys were saying, 'Hey, this is Montana, there should always be snow here,' and saying, 'Well, we didn't think that we needed to worry about snow in Montana.' But they didn't have the snow they needed," Marble said.

One of the men figured it would easiest haul snow in from Red Lodge. The others agreed. And then Marble spoke up.

"I told them that I thought Red Lodge would be a little more of a challenge," Marble said. "I also mentioned that my friend at the airport had at least six big piles of it. I knew that there were piles of snow on the runways. So they asked us if we had trucks, and asked us if we would be willing to haul it down to the set."

Before long, Marble was using a two-ton truck to deliver stockpiled snow to downtown Billings—including a load for one of the opening scenes outside the bus depot on First Avenue North.

"We then got another load and went out to Laurel to use it," Marble said. "But I guess it was creating too many puddles, and they didn't use that snow. I got to help with the artificial snow on the Laurel set."

Marble, born and raised in Billings, is a third-generation Montanan. Billings Nursery & Landscaping has been operated by his family since 1952. And this wasn't the nursery's first brush with Hollywood. "My father actually worked on the Tom Cruise film *Far and Away*, supplying plants," Marble said.

Northfork, filmed in the Great Falls and Augusta areas, portrayed a Montana community forced to make way for a dam. Part of the filming involved an ark that was constructed against the backdrop of the Rocky Mountain Front.

Local officials said the impact of having the crew—and its budget—around could be felt in Billings. "We really do recognize the economic and social benefits that it brings to residents of Billings," said Alex Tyson, executive director of the Billings Chamber of Commerce/Convention and Visitors Bureau. Late November, he said, "aside from holiday shopping, can be a little bit quiet. They've filled a hotel, and they're filling our streets, our stores and our restaurants, and having the ability to accommodate that is important to us."

"It's a proven fact that the impact of productions in the state is extreme," said Deny Staggs, location coordinator and co-manager of the Montana Film Office. "The trickle-down is really, really immense. Far more immense than people would think."

Money isn't the only thing a production brings. Locals still point to the Billings filming of the 1992 Ron Howard blockbuster *Far and Away* starring Tom Cruise and Nicole Kidman, a 1991 made-for-television movie about Lt. Col. George Custer called *Son of the Morning Star*, or even the lesser-known 1993 kid flick *Josh and S.A.M.* as points of pride.

"It's a moment in time for us," said Tyson. "It's fun on the social aspect of things and you take pride in your community when you can host folks like this."

Northfork

Cast
James Woods, Darryl Hannah, Nick Nolte, Anthony Edwards, Peter Coyote

Director
Mark Polish, Michael Polish

Location
Glasgow area, Fort Peck Dam, Augusta area, Great Falls

2003

Twin brothers Michael and Mark Polish produced *Northfork,* a visionary epic set in 1955 in a small Montana plains town about to be submerged by the opening of an immense dam.

They were 23 when they wrote *Northfork,* inspired by stories of their grandfather. Their paternal grandfather, an engineer and carpenter, helped build the Libby and the Hungry Horse dams. Their father, Del Polish, a pilot and builder, trekked them all around Montana during their childhoods. The family lived in Sacramento for many years, but always maintained its Montana connection.

James Wood, shown here on the set of *Northfork*, has made three films in Montana—*Fast Walking*, *Diggstown*, and *Northfork*.

"We consider ourselves born and bred Montanans," said Mark Polish. "We still have tons of family here, and we have a deep affection and appreciation for Montana."

"We knew it definitely was a Montana movie," said Michael Polish. "It was just a matter of when it would work." Michael directed the film and Mark portrayed James Woods' son.

Northfork was the third in a series of screenplays by Mark and Michael Polish, who spent part of their childhood in the Flathead Valley and would fly with their family from Washington state to see productions in the Fort Peck Theatre. "I love this state," said Polish.

About half of the cast and almost three-fourths of the crew were from Montana.

Michael Polish said he never knew that Fort Peck Dam existed until he started researching Montana dams for a movie location on the plains. "There it was in *Life* magazine," said Michael.

"I think that *Northfork* is an amazing film," said James Woods. "I guess you could say it is about transitions in life. Most people resist change and try not to acknowledge change or even understand what change is. Of course in our film we deal with the most fundamental of changes, the transition from life to death, the transition of understanding that that's part of the process of all of life. The part that Mark plays, my son Willis, and the part that I play, "Walter O'Brien," come together in our loss of my wife and his mom. There's a situation where a dam is being built that will wipe out an entire town and we are on the evacuation committee and evacuate all the people and we find a few who don't want to move, which is our challenge. And we also face the fact that my wife

and his mother are buried in the Northfork cemetery and this Northfork territory, and that's something that we both resist."

In May 2002, film crews descended on the Great Falls and Augusta areas. From the start, the directors were adamant about depicting a multilayered film portraying a Montana community forced to make way for a dam. The movie was filmed at Fort Peck Dam, a ranch outside Augusta, and the long-closed Russell Elementary School in Great Falls.

"It's a film about life and death and the inevitability of change," said Mark. "People seem to be touched by it because it's also a story of family and loyalty and loss and adjustment." The picture also has humor and hope. "We're not gloom-and-doom guys," said Mark. "I think we're typical of Montanans—resilient, tough, with a sense of humor. We tried to make our characters that way."

Ennis fourth-grader Duel Forest Farnes played a dying orphan who has strange hallucinations. From the start, Farnes didn't expect movie-making would be easy. "But I got the best crew to start out with," he said. It had been a big week for the 8-year-old; he lost a tooth, gone gopher hunting and spent an afternoon with Daryl Hannah. Was he fazed? Hardly. "When I grow up, I'm gonna be a bull rider," he said after finishing a solo swing set scene. "I already ride steers."

The short-haired cowboy had more experience riding animals than reading lines. In fact, his acting résumé could be summed up with one part in his school's play, *The Ugly Duckling*. The director and the other actors taught Farnes on the spot. Duel was picked from around 200 Montana boys. "He was cast because of his natural innocence and natural imaginative face," said Bozeman-based casting agent Tina Buckingham. "He's just a sweet little boy." The son of a truck driver and a waitress, Duel said he was having a pretty good time being a movie star. "I've jumped up and down, I've swinged and I've twisted up," he said. "It's fun."

"I first met Duel as a five year old, a mutton buster [rider of "unbroken" sheep, a western rodeo special event for youngsters], and he stole my heart," said Buckingham. "The guys from *Northfork* didn't want a Hollywood kid or a street savvy kid, but more of an oddball, you know, crooked teeth, a lisp, the less politically correct look. The first person I thought of was Duel. We were interviewing kids between the age of 6 to 13. At 13, they seemed too old, and even at six, some of them were too sophisticated. We ask kids what they liked to do. While most of them said they liked to play video games, Duel said he liked mutton busting. That stole Michael Polish's heart. Every actor took Duel under their wings and protected him."

The Farnes were not interested in exposing Duel or his three siblings to what mother Kristi Farnes called the "'Macauley Culkin life.' I'm from the Bitterroot Valley and his father's from Bozeman. We're pretty well grounded, and I still want him to be a little boy. It's very important to me to keep him grounded."

Michael Polish said that an innovative script enabled the brothers to lure big-name actors, such as Woods, Hannah, Nick Nolte, and Peter Coyote. "People will go far and wide and work really hard for good material," said Mark. "And you can't beat Montana, right? When Mother Nature's your art director, you can't go wrong."

Daryl Hannah, who plays a gypsy in *Northfork*, said that she took part because of the Polish brothers. "Michael and Mark are old friends of mine," said Hannah. "I've been up here once before, doing a documentary on predators in Glacier," said Hannah, referring to the 1998 TV movie *Wildlife Wars*. "It's beautiful," she said. "You never get to see antelope where I live."

One of the stars become a terrible source of stress when he told the brothers that he wasn't going to show up. Fortunately, the notoriously aloof Nick Nolte reconsidered.

"He wasn't on the call sheet," said Michael Polish. "Guys were thinking he wasn't go to show up."

"About the issue of having no backup for the role of Father Harlan," said Nick Nolte, "I don't think I've ever been in a situation where the filmmakers have had the guts to do something like that," said Nick Nolte. "Or is it a particularly sane idea? Because I was off doing *The Hulk* at the time. I didn't even honestly know if I could make it. And we were down to the last day that the directors had the two actors that I was to do the scene with. If I didn't show up that day, those actors were going to leave. That night I wasn't sure whether I could make it. I had just driven down from San Francisco, worked four days in a row at the end of *The Hulk*. I said to Mark Polish, going down, I don't think I am going to make it. I got to the house, and there was a party going on, and I said to Matt, "I think I can make it."

"I was doing the sermon and off camera, Mike said to me, 'Get the congregation to cry.' I had to ad lib. I could

see in this group certain people who had just lost somebody. That was just a feeling. So I just started talking about my mother's death, when I sat with her for four days. This whole dialogue. Never consciously realized that to be a witness for a friendship is really a major part of life. Not friends, not enemies. Just witnessing. When someone dies, we go out and we cry and say goodbye. The coming and the going and the witnessing of life, that's the purpose of life. It validates see each other's lives and existence—yes, I was here. Achievement does nothing because it vanishes. But the interaction of witnessing is highly emotional for me. That's literally what she had me do—my mother. She wanted me with her four days as she died. Not as a son, because if I was there as a son I would get into my own grief. She didn't want me to hold her hand and she wasn't afraid, she wanted someone by her side as a witness.

"I got to see how you die. It was quite easy. Up to that point, it was an abstract and fearful thing in my life. Something about the film, and I know people won't get it too much, by [Duel Farnes' character] Irwin's little journeys out into death and back. I thought [my mother] was dead, and another big breath would come. I got the distinct feeling that's what I was doing with Irwin, bathing him, being with him, knowing that he is leaving at a certain point. So much symbolism and so many parallels to life."

Montanan Christine Schuman, who started off in films working as a seamstress on *Far and Away*, recalled transporting a particularly gruff Nick Nolte from set to set. "Nick Nolte, I was driving him in a motor home from set to set, and he was mad at everybody and telling everybody to [get out]. [He said] 'I'm tired of this, let's go somewhere else!' I said, 'I have to take you to the next place.' He said, 'Let's go to Mexico!' 'How much gas do you have in the car?' I said, 'Are you serious? He said, 'I'm serious!' 'We can get straight across here and down to Mexico. This tank is full of gas.'

"I said, 'We can go to the next set and think about Mexico some other time.' I am sure he was wondering who is this cowboy with her cowboy boots, telling me I can't go to Mexico? He had his own stash of drink and did what he wanted. Although I let him know he couldn't smoke."

"Nolte was on something," said crew member Allison Whitmer. "We were busting our ass and he was yelling. James Woods was great, a real professional. But Nolte? A week later, they found him wondering around the highway out of his mind, [resulting in a well known] wild hair mug shot."

Nolte said that *Northfork* was his first visit to Big Sky Country. "Ted Turner invited me once, and I said I wouldn't go," said Nolte. "He's not really one of my favorite people." Nolte said he resents other stars who swoop into Montana and build multimillion-dollar homes. "I don't think it's fair to Montanans," said Nolte. "They come in and jack up property values, and then they don't ever come back." Nolte said he enjoyed talking with locals at Augusta's Buckhorn Bar and, while in Great Falls, he shopped for cowboy hats and boots, and visited several local hangouts, including Little's Lanes, Town Tavern, Tracy's, the Sip N' Dip, and City Bar. Nolte even spent hours at the Community Rec Center listening to the mostly punk, 21-and-under line-up. "It was great. I love to hear what the kids are singing about. They're the authentic voice of what young people in Montana are feeling."

James Woods discussed shooting at the Fort Peck Dam: "It holds back like 15 miles of water. And there's a little shot walking through the dam and I said, "Okay great, where do we go." And they said, 'Well, it's down in the dam. I said okay. Well, I thought there would be big elevators, you know. You go down this ladder…360 feet down into the dam. Straight down—and you get into a little place that's 600 yards long. It's that narrow, and there's no end to it. It takes about a half hour to climb down. And when you're down there, it's like you're in a long coffin, is what you're in.

"And you realize, 'I can't get out of here.' And it's holding back all this water, and it's leaking and there's electrical cables and stuff. One of the guys was really having a horrible time—and you think it's going to get better, but it doesn't, it gets worse.

"You keep thinking, 'Oh I'm gonna feel good—but you can't run out. It's like you're down here, and if something goes wrong, you got to climb for like 45 minutes to get out. And I'm telling you, I never thought I had claustrophobia ever, but you imagine like those guys, those miners in Pennsylvania."

The Polish Brothers' father, Del, who once built houses for a living, headed up the construction team that created the fictional town of Northfork, complete with its eccentric cemetery.

"Dad was sinking nails the whole way and special

thing about having Dad," said Mark Polish, "he knew the elements and could build in the elements. You've got ground as hard as cement and 70-mile-per-hour wind. We knew that having our dad not be a production designer was going to be a risk. There were not a lot of people who could do it. We were sitting in the kitchen. I said, 'Do you think you can build an ark?' He said, 'What size?' We talked for a couple of nights. Then we pulled the plug on the first production designer and I said, 'Dad, pack your [stuff], you are going to Montana.'"

"He built a church, a homestead house, a gravesite, an outhouse, and nothing ever fazed him. We have an inherent bond because he's my father. But there is also a man who sees no problem to build a 90-foot ark and the rest of what was needed in four weeks."

"*Northfork* was a movie that started movie on credit cards," said crew member David Storm. "Two-thirds through, the crew was not getting paid. The Teamsters shut down the set until they came up with the money. And it's still one of the coolest movies ever. Shades of white and black and gray and created muted tone sets. And then, Fort Peck Dam, the old cars and the guys in black suits."

The Polish brothers decided that the period story and poetic textures of *Northfork* called for 35 mm film. "We used a number of techniques to desaturate the image," said cinematographer M. David Mullen. "The most effective was to simply remove as much of the color from in front of the camera as possible. Luckily, the plains of Montana are already stark and monochromatic in the winter. Art direction and wardrobe were rendered almost entirely in shades of gray; locations were painted this way, and we even sewed together a black-and-white American flag and filled ketchup bottles in a diner scene with gray paint."

Mullen said *Northfork* provided the most satisfying moment on any project in his career. "Doing a crane shot in 35 mm anamorphic on the vast plains of Montana in the winter for *Northfork*. It was the closest I've felt to doing work in the spirit of John Ford and David Lean, despite the tiny budget."

While the cast and crew were in Great Falls, they helped draw further attention to the funky Sip 'n Dip bar in O'Haire Motor Inn. While relaxing between shoots, Darryl Hannah donned a mermaid costume and swam in the pool, recreating a scene from her 1987 hit movie *Splash*. Sip 'n Dip patrons said it was like "Splash 2002" with Hannah as a blue mermaid swimming and faking dead in the lounge's human aquarium on a Wednesday night. Hannah was among some famous people spotted in places such as Albertson's supermarket and Jaker's bar/restaurant.

Hannah was an excellent swimmer, said piano-bar performer and Sip 'n Dip icon Pat Sponheim, better known as 'Piano Pat," who sang Patsy Cline, Jimmy Buffett, and Frank Sinatra songs while the crew hung out. "She actually really performed," said Pat. "She was upside down with just her head showing. She was just doing things I didn't ever see."

Toney Wallace was sitting in the Sip 'n Dip drinking with friends, when "a young, attractive blond lady" came in with actor Anthony Edwards about 10:30 or 11 P.M. "And I said, wow, that woman looked like Daryl Hannah," said Wallace. "One of my buddies said that *is* Daryl Hannah. It was real cool." Bartender Vern Green said the crew was "awesome" and "lots of fun to serve." "Glad to see that even famous people can have fun at Sip 'n Dip," said Green. "She was partying right along," said Pat.

Hannah sipped on Moose Drool, while Edwards reportedly drank tonic water. In Hannah's first dip in the pool, she wore yellow trunks and a white tank top with the words, "My heroes have always killed cowboys." The lounge began to fill after word got out she was swimming there. "After that everybody just piled in," said Pat. "Before that it was pretty quiet. That perked it up." About 30 curious customers had all eyes on the glass window, as she and two men with the filming crew swam around the aquarium sporting mermaid-wear. It was déjà vu when Hannah would play dead. Afterward, "she shook hands with all of us," said Wallace. "She seemed real nice, real down to earth."

Before leaving the bar at closing time, Hannah wrote "Moose Drool" on the glass of the swimming pool behind the bar and signed her name leaving an "XO" mark. Hannah left wearing a "The Sip 'n Dip Lounge" T-shirt compliments of the lounge.

At one point, the Polish Brothers went bowling with Nolte and Woods. "Even while bowling, you could really see their individual natures as actors," said Mark Polish. "James bowled straight down the pipe while Nick was completely unconventional, yet they both had an equal amount of style."

The script supervisor, Betty Ann Conard, of Manhat-

tan, Montana, watched each scene with a hawk's eye, scrawling notes about who stood where and wore what. (Like most movies, *Northfork* was shot out of sequence.)

"I'm responsible for keeping track of everything that's filmed," said Conard. "I give notes and records to the editor so when he reassembles it, it makes sense." Conard also tracked details—which hand the actor held her bag in or which way she turned her head—to keep embarrassing mistakes from hitting the big screen. "You have to stay really focused," said Conard.

Bozeman grip Jason McKnight said Montanans shouldn't complain about movie stars taking a liking to the state. "They're not staying here," said McKnight. "They're coming in with a truckload of money, they're dumping it, and they're going home."

Brian Branton of Big Timber served as key grip. His responsibilities included working with the gaffer—the head electrician in charge of lighting—and the director of photography to make sure all the camera cranes and dollies were mounted and positioned properly. He also manipulated light for some scenes by blocking, diffusing and reflecting it. "Some films lack meaning and don't generate the positive energy that this one does," said Branton.

Producers allowed locals to take a peek at the process of making a movie, said Judi McTaggart, who owns Augusta's Western Bar with her husband. The McTaggarts watched filming of a flood scene in which a roof, a piano, a coffin and furniture were dumped into Willow Creek Reservoir.

Crew members stopped at the General Store in Augusta almost daily, buying items such as doughnuts, soft drinks and laundry detergent, said Cindy Atchison, an employee. "They always come in with a big smile, and they call me sweetheart," she said. "It gets depressing in this quiet town in the wintertime. It's really a pick-up to have them here." Crews rented office space and slept at hotels in Great Falls and Choteau. One week, they occupied 70 rooms in Glasgow's Cottonwood Inn while filming in the area of Fort Peck Lake.

Northfork producers employed several locals, including six construction workers from Augusta and Choteau, Showdown Ski Patrol director and EMT Chris Quinn, and Augusta resident Larry Atchison, a mechanic. James Zumbren, an electrician and bartender, said helping build sets was "way cool." One night after work, he noticed James Woods taking pictures of him and some other workers hanging out by a bonfire. "I thought, 'Hey wait—we're supposed to be taking pictures of you,'" Zumbren said.

Northfork recouped its $2 million cost at the box office. Most reviews were favorable. Critic Roger Ebert called it "a visionary epic" and the Polish twins "the real thing." The *New York Times* labeled the film "dreamy and entrancing" and the *Los Angeles Times* deemed it "a thoroughly original accomplishment of a high artistic order."

While one reviewer called the movie's visual acuity "constant and pure," others had a hard time keeping up with its hazy meditation of the vanishing American frontier. *USA Today* slammed it as "repetitious" and "too meandering," before concluding, "Northfork is the cinematic equivalent of an elaborate and poetically constructed non sequitur."

Indeed, to this day, people watch the gypsy angels and the animal with a giraffe's long legs and a dog's head and ask, "What was that about?"

"The film concerns itself with metaphors of transitions," said actor James Woods years later, "so obviously as the flood waters will rise when the dam is built and the people in the town will have to move to higher ground, and as we speak of bringing them to higher ground, we are of course talking about those transitions from life to death.

"And there is a young boy in it who is dying and he needs this group of people, they may be gypsies, they may be angels. There is a lot of angelic metaphors in the movie about being brought to heaven's gate and so on. A lot of it could be real or it could be fantasy. But it's very logically done so either one can work. It is one of the most metaphysically beautiful scripts I've ever read."

"It's bizarre but it's also extremely personal," said actor Anthony Edwards. "It emerges from the Polish Brothers' own original vision and the landscape and history that they come from. It's a film that, ultimately, you can't describe to another person. You just have to experience it for yourself. I think the importance will resonate differently for each person who sees it."

"It was so wonderful shooting a film there. It's home," said Michael Polish. "The landscape is awesome. It's a wonderful environment, and we love the wide-open look of the area up around Augusta."

Powder River was filmed in and around Glacier National Park.

Powder River

CAST
Rory Calhoun, Corinne Calvet

DIRECTOR
Louis King

LOCATION
East Glacier area

1953

Powder River is loosely based on the 1931 book *Wyatt Earp: Frontier Marshal* by Stuart N. Lake. However, the characters were changed for the film *Powder River* and only certain incidents from the original were used. The plot, an 1870s period piece about mining, concerns a reformed desperado named Chino Bullock, "woodenly interpreted" by actor Rory Calhoun, who as sher-

With St. Mary Lake in the background, *Powder River's* Rory Calhoun pledges his love to Corinne Calvet.

iff of Powder River plays watchdog to a schizophrenic young medico (played by Cameron Mitchell), trailed by Corinne Calvet, a curvaceous saloon owner, and Penny Edwards, a good woman. A sprinkling of gun forays suggests, fleetingly, that some sort of campaign is under way to rid Powder River of its varmints. *Powder River* was made in Glacier National Park and the North Fork of the Flathead River.

On July 6, 1952, movie makers cut a ferry in half on the North Fork to shoot their "loose" ferry scene without mishap. After the shooting the boat was shipped to the 20th Century-Fox studio in Hollywood. The boat was to be used there for additional closeup shots.

The capsized ferry boat was built in Kalispell by the Kalispell Cabinet Works and used to haul a horse team, stage, movie actors and gold shipment across the North Fork in the movie scenes. The cable holding the ferry was supposedly hacked free by outlaws, letting it float downstream but in reality it was still on the end of a long underwater cable attached to a log winch. The capsized ferry boat was hauled to the North Fork by the Kirkpatrick Brothers firm. They also erected the cable for it to

cross the river. The location of the rest of local filming was at the W. Smith farm, near Coram.

Powder River, filmed under the working title *Man From Powder River,* shot in the area for three weeks. At the close of filming, Lewis King, director, said he did not know which name was going to be used. No matter what it was called, it wouldn't have mattered, as critics lambasted the production.

Life magazine said: "An arch, half-hearted attempt at something different has been made in a little Western from Twentieth Century-Fox titled 'Powder River.' But the screen accompaniment to the Palace's new holiday stage program remains a tired, wet firecracker for any season. Rory Calhoun, Corinne Calvet and Cameron Mitchell are the hapless protagonists of this carelessly done offering in standard Technicolor, produced by Andre Hakim."

The *Boston Globe* said, "In fact, exactly what they are all getting at is anybody's guess, for the dull contrivances of the story extend to the acting in general, and the entire mess has been slung together under Louis King's direction with a smart-alecky indifference to conviction. Furthermore, the scenario that Geoffrey Homes has eked out of a story by Sam Hellman is as bad as it is baffling."

Powwow Highway

CAST
A Martinez, Gary Farmer

DIRECTOR
Jonathan Wacks

LOCATION
Crow Reservation, Hardin area,
Northern Cheyenne Reservation, Colstrip

1989

In this comedy-drama, two men with nothing in common but their Indian heritage leave their reservation and set off across the country.

Powwow Highway takes two Native Americans from Montana on a well-intended road trip to the southwest. The movie was praised as a "little zinger of a comedy with a rare backbone of intelligence."

Mainstream Hollywood generally employed ethnic characters for comic relief or as criminals; this left a vast, unexplored cultural terrain for independent productions such as *Powwow Highway*. In fact, it is one of the most commercially accessible movies ever made about Native Americans. There are fights, car crashes, love interests, and even a jail break.

For the Northern Cheyenne tribe of Lame Deer, Montana, the American Dream has taken a detour. Here Buddy Red Bow (A. Martinez) is a committed activist battling a suspicious land-grab. Sweet-natured, junk-food-eating Philbert Bono (Gary Farmer, in a performance Roger Ebert called "one of the most wholly convincing I've seen") is a serene spiritual warrior guided by sacred visions.

In *Powwow Highway*, it's harder for young people to find that spiritual path in the modern world than it

was in simpler times. Now the "war pony" is a junkyard Buick Wildcat, circa 1964, and the old wise ones, who could answer questions about the way of a warrior, are fed up with being sages and would rather let television play across their faces.

Taking off from their Montana reservation in Philbert's wreck of a car, they begin a roundabout odyssey that culminates in Santa Fe, New Mexico, where Red Bow's sister has been jailed on a trumped-up drug charge by villainous feds. The rusted Buick war pony, or "rez car," which Philbert has named "Protector," steals the opening scenes.

"I had to find a four-door hard-top 1967 Wildcat Buick for *Powwow Highway*," said film commissioner Garry Wunderwald. "I was out searching junk yards in Hardin and the Billings area. My dad was a Buick dealer at one point and I had a '61 Buick. The bad part is that I was still looking two weeks for another one after I found it. [By t]hat time in 1989, there wouldn't have been that many. Sometimes you just keep looking, as if you might find something better for them. I can't remember if that one satisfied them or not. I can't tell you if they picked mine or not [as the rez car]."

"The rez car is probably like a piece of luggage or something to other people," said Cheyenne/Arapaho film director and producer Chris Eyre. "And you kind of keep it together with tape and with string and I have all kinds of people tell me, 'Yeah I know that story about driving backwards [in *Powwow Highway*] because I actually did it' or that they had 'a rez car and the ignition didn't work so we had like a screwdriver in the ignition'—all sorts of stuff. Nobody's said to me to yet that they had a car with three wheels, but that would be a rez car."

As the film follows the careening path of a pair of buddies heading on a rescue mission with diametrically different ideas of how to get there—and how quickly—it's a pretty irresistible movie. But for innocent charm, it's given a run for its money by the young Canadian actor it presents, Gary Farmer, who delivers as the gentle, mammoth Philbert. But there is never a doubt that the 280-pound Philbert will make it to "warriorhood." Magnetic likability emanates from Farmer's Philbert—a kind of appeal that an audience reads at once.

Farmer's career took a dramatic turn in 1987 when Jonathan Wacks gave him the lead in *Powwow Highway*—a part Farmer says he got "because there aren't many Native American actors. We haven't had the opportunities most Americans have—most Native Americans lack the self-esteem required to pursue this work, and many Native Americans don't want to be a part of this industry. To go into the white man's world and have success goes against all kinds of beliefs." On the set of *Powwow Highway*, Farmer met Jean Stawarz, who co-wrote the film's script.

The *Los Angeles Times* praised Farmer's performance: "Very rarely, an actor's presence casts a shadow almost larger than the production that shelters him—or her. You saw it with Chief Dan George in 'Little Big Man.' With Louise Fletcher in 'One Flew Over the Cuckoo's Nest.' And you'll discover it again in 'Powwow Highway,' a little zinger of a comedy with a rare backbone of intelligence; unsurprising when you learn that the debuting director is 'Repo Man' co-producer, Jonathan Wacks."

Powwow Highway quietly camouflages its serious concerns about American Indians, letting us absorb them cumulatively during this wild odyssey.

Red Bow's estranged sister, Bonnie, apparently has been framed, then jailed with her two young daughters, for possession for marijuana. Red Bow and Philbert were at high school together, but Buddy's intense, though disillusioned political concerns and Philbert's lifelong simple style have kept their paths separate.

Wack's direction of the screenplay, by Janet Heaney and Jean Stawarz from the novel by David Seals, has a way of conveying hard facts obliquely but surely. As Toyomichi Kurita's eloquent camera sweeps the mean, littered face of the Northern Cheyenne reservation, even the dog seems to be limping. *Powwow Highway* is full of such snapshots and panoramas, mute instruction for those who will see.

The film's inspired comedy comes as Buddy's unvented fury collides with Philbert's quiet imperturbability. Philbert meanders, Buddy makes tracks; Philbert has spiritual stops to make on the way, Buddy may explode before he makes them all. One of Philbert's most important stops is the yearly powwow at Billings, Montana, an event Buddy sneers at. Indoors, in a gym, to him it's a joke: "As though a few lousy beads was a culture or something." Yet there's an exchange here with a damaged Indian Vietnam vet, and the pull of the dancing itself that begins to speak to Buddy.

But none of Buddy's feelings ever fully cultivate, and the characters generally play it safe and sound, as noted by *Deseret News*: "'Powwow Highway' is much more mainstream in style than the usual fare among experimental independents. But in the end that's what makes the film less successful than it might otherwise be. Halfway through it begins to look like dozens of other so-called road movies, and the ending is irritatingly hackneyed."

Newsweek stated that *Powwow Highway* "keeps you hooked into its energy, but it seems torn between wanting to explore its theme of politics and spirituality and wanting to follow commercial fashion."

Meanwhile, in Santa Fe, Bonnie's self-reliant girls have found a way out of their detention home at the same time a feisty, lifelong friend Rabbit Layton arrives to make bail for Bonnie. The boys arrive at about the same time, only to run up against the bossy belligerence of the Santa Fe policewomen. It's what makes Philbert's solution to all their problems—and his cherubic deadpan as he goes about it—all the more satisfactory.

In the end, it's the amiable mix of characters and the deeply satisfying action that fixes *Powwow Highway* permanently in our affections. The film won best director, best picture and best awards at the Native American Film Festival. "Powwow Highway is fashioned from the stuff of legends…It radiates good vibes," wrote *The Village Voice*. The online *All Movie Guide* called it "amusing and provocative…the first Native American road movie."

Pretty Ugly People

CAST
Missy Pyle, Melissa McCarthy

DIRECTOR
Tate Taylor

LOCATION
Missoula, Holland Lake, East Glacier area

2007

Missy Pyle hikes near Glacier National Park in *Pretty Ugly People*. PHOTO COURTESY BRUNSON GREEN

In September 2006, *Pretty Ugly People*, a dark comedy, began filming in northwest Montana. The premise revolves around a dying woman who wishes to bring six estranged friends together in the Montana wilderness. Upon arriving, the friends discover the situation isn't what they expected and the group of old high school friends end up on a wilderness trip to hell—not physical anguish, but emotional, as they give breath to all those unvoiced things they dislike about themselves or one another.

At its most basic level, *Pretty Ugly People* is a reunion movie about friendship and readjusting. After getting gastric-bypass surgery, Lucy (Missi Pyle) gets her college friends together for a long weekend so she can finally feel like "one of them." Lucy would like to gather them together "before her time is up." An ambiguous phone call with her friend, Becky, leads Becky to assume that Lucy is dying. Eventually, they all arrive at their Montana retreat to learn that Lucy has plans for them to go on a four-day hike through the wilderness, with no place to hide.

The old friends convene from all over the country to join Lucy's side: a culturally-conflicted black Congress-

man and his "ghetto-centric" wife (future Oscar winner Octavia Spencer), a male flight attendant, a reformed schoolteacher (Melissa McCarthy) and her frigid husband, a womanizing commodities trader, and a very successful, Grammy-winning hip-hop producer.

In one of the opening scenes, McCarthy's character shops at the Orange Street Food Farm, while several other characters arrive at the Missoula International Airport only to be met by a badly stereotyped hick played by William Sanderson. Allison Janney plays a bit role and during a conversation on an airplane she mentions "a ticket to Missoula."

Writer and director Tate Taylor scouted northwest Montana exclusively. The production company, Plump Pictures, opened a production office in Missoula on August 25, 2006. The film budgeted at less than $500,000.

"We got into the movie heavily in October 2006 and it was a blast," said producer Brunson Green. "There was just a kiss of snow on the ground and East Glacier was just shutting down and the leaves were changing. It's obviously a gorgeous, amazing place, and filming it was a lot of fun, like summer camp."

Scout Jon Ansotegui described the initial contact he

While on a hike in *Pretty Ugly People*, actor Josh Hopkins encounters a scene-stealing grizzly bear played by Brutus the Bear. (Photo courtesy Brunson Green)

had with the people connected with *Pretty Ugly People* and the general formula he follows in his work. "I will read the script and break it down and send them a package of logistics," said Ansotegui. "In many cases, the first place I go to is Bozeman, because it has a crew available. Productions don't want to spend money on hotels and transportation, and in Bozeman the local crew can stay in homes. It's during the initial scout where you are getting them comfortable with what is where. Then comes follow up calls and emails and then you get them more entrenched in the area.

"For *Pretty Ugly People*, they were looking at the Bitterroot Valley at first, but it was too overbuilt there. There are a lot of cases where people think they have an idea but when they see it, they change their mind. I showed them Looking Glass Pass and then they hired a location manager, Joe Young."

Hikers and backpackers will recognize some beautiful scenery around Holland Lake, and *Pretty Ugly People* spent time filming on the top of Looking Glass on the Blackfeet Reservation. The backdrop of Glacier National Park has lured more than one movie director to the Big Sky State. But only once has it served as the setting of a

nude sex scene. At Running Eagle Falls, minutes from Two Medicine Lake, one of the main characters is surprised by an old friend with a romantic picnic. After we see the lovely view of the picnic in the falls, they make love in several locations near the falls.

While the film received a tepid response from audiences and critics, it no doubt reveals the work of a cast and crew bursting at the seams with talent.

"One of the things we learned from *Pretty Ugly People* was the marketplace was changing as far as independent film," said producer Green. "Unfortunately, we finished it right as the economic collapse happened in 2008, so it was a long road to find a home for it. We did the festival route for over a year—I think 34 festivals.

"I still think it is a gorgeous, fun movie and the fact that Taylor developed a concept and wrote a script around Glacier National Park is interesting. We cast many of our friends who we've known for years, all of whom were super talented but had no opportunity to have leads in movies until then. Today, all of them are working actors and some are real movie stars."

Tate Taylor went on to direct *The Help*, a 2011 drama featuring an ensemble cast about a young white woman,

Eugenia "Skeeter" Phelan (Emma Stone), and her relationship with two black maids, Aibileen Clark (Viola Davis) and Minny Jackson (Octavia Spencer) during the Civil Rights era in 1960s America. *The Help* was nominated for four Oscars, including Best Picture, of which Spencer captured one for Best Performance by an Actress in a Supporting Role.

Melissa McCarthy, known for her high-wire comedic riffs and fresh ways to conjugate profanity, moved on to great success as an actress, comedian, writer, fashion designer, and producer.

Rancho Deluxe

CAST
Jeff Bridges, Sam Waterston, Elizabeth Ashley

DIRECTOR
Frank Perry

LOCATION
Livingston

1975

"The funniest stock-and-bull adventure ever to hit Livingston, Montana!" proclaims one of the *Rancho Deluxe* posters. "The kind of Western your old cowboy heroes (and their horses) wouldn't be caught dead in!"

"What happens when a team of pretty unlikely cattle rustlers meets a more unlikely pair of rustler-hunters?" says another. The studio marketing department evidently got on a roll with *Rancho Deluxe* and couldn't be stopped. Yet another poster says, "Oh give me a home with a low interest loan, a cowgirl and two pickup trucks. A color TV, all the beer should be free, and that, man, is Rancho Deluxe."

The comedy western was filmed primarily in Livingston. The sites include individual houses, businesses and ranches in the Paradise Valley south of the town.

It was directed by Frank Perry and released in 1975.

Jeff Bridges and Sam Waterston star as two cattle rustlers in then "modern-day Montana" who plague a wealthy ranch owner. Jimmy Buffett contributed the music and performed in a scene set in a then country-western bar, the Wrangler. Owner Bob Burns, who operated the bar with his wife, Mary Ann, and two daughters, placed a sign on the door—"Home of Rancho Deluxe"—and he enjoyed the general excitement in town arising from the movie. The bar, a hangout for "young longhairs and cowboys" said Burns, depicted in the movie true to life, cluttered with pool tables and arcade machines. The Wrangler also became the hangout for the crew.

Other local locations include Chico Hot Springs, the former Dan Bailey's fly-tying operation, and the Livingston railroad shops.

The anachronisms in *Rancho Deluxe*—cattle rustling with a pickup truck, riding the range in a helicopter—were humorous and movingly poignant because they emphasized the detachment between a romantic past and a motorized present that's lost all ideals, all purpose.

Bob Wetzel, who owned the Stockman Bar in Livingston at the time, found work on the set of *Rancho Deluxe*. One of Wetzel's jobs was "sharpshooter," as the movie shows Bridges killing a steer. Wetzel actually fired the shot that sent the animal crumpling to the ground. It was, obviously, before films carried any disclaimer about no animals being hurt or mistreated during filming.

Rancho Deluxe was written by Tom McGuane, who ran away from home at the age of 15 and went West intent on becoming a cowboy. He landed in Wyoming, at a ranch owned by the father of a girlfriend, in the 1950s. His travels brought him to the southern part of Montana, and "I knew this was where I wanted to live the first time I ever saw it."

Fifteen years later—after returning to Michigan to finish high school, flunking out of the University of Michigan, then studying playwriting at Yale and winning a Stegner Fellowship at Stanford—his novel *The Sporting Club* "made some money, enough to buy my first ranch," said McGuane. "And that was it. I never looked back."

He purchased 14 acres in the Paradise Valley south of Livingston with his first wife, Portia Rebecca Crockett. While continuing to write novels, McGuane ventured into screenwriting, first with *The Missouri Breaks*, which brought Nicholson and Marlon Brando into Montana for filming, then with *Rancho Deluxe*, his ode to Livingston.

In the over-the-top comedy western *Rancho Deluxe*, Jeff Bridges (left) and Sam Waterston (right) play slacker cattle rustlers in a contemporary Montana town. In the movie, an assortment of eccentric characters and looney situations prove the Old West is long dead. The script was written by Livingston resident Thomas McGuane and the movie was filmed there.

"*Rancho Deluxe* was a real culture shock for us," said Lynette Dodson, museum curator in Livingston, who was 14 when the movie cast and crew were in town. She can remember the excitement during filming, plus the reaction to the finished project.

Dodson says two of her girlfriends made $250 by drowning gophers, drying them out on towels in their kitchens, then selling them to the production company for $25 apiece for a scene in which a rancher shoots gophers.

Many local people appeared as extras in the movie, and lines were long when the movie finally opened at the Ellen Theatre. "It may have been the first time an R-rated film had played here; it certainly was the first R-rated film a lot of people here had ever seen," said Dodson. Jeff Bridges and a co-star have a fairly graphic—especially for

1975—outdoor sex scene not long into the film. Bridges wears a hound dog costume mask during the encounter. "You could see the lines of people waiting to get in," Dodson remembered, "and 20 minutes later, the lines of people streaming out."

There was still a bordello on the edge of Livingston in 1975, and wild times come 2 A.M., when the now defunct Long Branch and Wrangler bars, which sat next to each other on Park Street, disgorged their crowds. The Long Branch, said Dodson, was the cowboy bar, and the Wrangler the hangout for hippies and dopers. But that didn't make it any easier for townspeople to see their home, on the big screen, in a movie that featured drug use and a scene in a local whorehouse.

McGuane reportedly had an affair with *Rancho De-*

luxe co-star Elizabeth Ashley. Bridges met a waitress at nearby Chico Hot Springs during filming and shortly afterwards, in June 1977, they were married. At this writing, they are in their 33rd year together (though they've some way to go to eclipse Bridges' parents, whose union spanned six decades). So what's the secret to long-lasting nuptials? "The simple answer is love," said Bridges. "But of course understanding, communication and commitment certainly add to it."

Singer Jimmy Buffet wrote the music for and appeared as the lead singer of a bar's house band in *Rancho Deluxe*, performing "Livingston Saturday Night." ("Pickup's washed and you just got paid," go the lyrics. "With any luck at all you might even get…")

Buffet temporarily moved to the area. In 1977, Buffet's sister, Laurie, became McGuane's fourth wife. They held the wedding dinner at the local A&W Root Beer Stand. They're still married; he's moved to a 3,000-acre place south of Big Timber, which is 36 miles east of Livingston.

As far as the film, perhaps the *Boston Herald* best summed up the viewer's ambivalence: "*Rancho DeLuxe* is handsome, witty, apt and languid. It is so cool it is barely alive. First-rate ingredients and a finesse in assembling them do not quite make either a movie or a cake. At some point it is necessary to light the oven."

In the shooting script of *Rancho Deluxe*, there's a scene in which Harry Dean Stanton's character is weeding a garden. But in the film, he's vacuuming giant rugs on the ranch lawn—the famous "Hoovering-the-Navajos" scene. "There was a production problem—somebody got hurt or something," said McGuane. "That scene, which I love, I wrote about 20 minutes before they shot it. I had to write it that morning, but I can't remember exactly why. That's what's nice about those situations—in that air of necessity, you really get some great ideas."

Rancho Deluxe is a kind of parody Western, a genre barely younger than the Western itself. And as long as Frank Perry, the director, and McGuane, the writer, are being wry about ranch owners who ride around in helicopters and ranch hands whose chores include vacuuming the rancher's Navajo rugs, they do extremely well. All their characters are phonies, and this is fine. They are often very funny phonies. But the heroes—two fey and charming young rustlers who saw up other people's cows as an existential act—are infested with humorous self-pity. Through them the portentous message creeps in: the West is dead and inhabited by cretins.

Newsday noted that the message was straightforward, yet rambling and delivered without organization. "Nothing happens to the message; it doesn't go anywhere," noted *Newsday*. "It is used as décor." Still, *Newsday* said, "There is a great deal that this picture does well," including how it relates the ill-starred but decidedly non-tragic war between the two rustlers, Jack and Cecil, and the rancher, John Brown.

They begin by shooting a cow or two and sawing them up with a portable chainsaw. They go on to hold a prize bull for ransom—in a motel bedroom—and finally they attempt to steal a whole trailer-rig of cattle in partnership with Brown's ranch-hands. Jack, "played a bit too fatly and lovably by Jeff Bridges," according to one critic, "is a rich boy who has left his wife and bums around with Cecil, a literate and dopey Indian."

Both of them move through a perpetual haze of self-parody. As they drive their pickup truck from one cow-killing, one asks the other: "Do you believe in the tooth fairy?" When Jack makes love to one of two sisters who hang out with them, he slips on a comic dog mask at the crucial moment.

Cecil, acted by Sam Waterston, makes jokes about being an Indian. "Lets' burn and pillage," he suggests to Jack as the two sit around with nothing much to do.

They are blatantly inauthentic rustlers, and they know it. Their self-knowledge and their deliberate kookiness is their commentary—and the film's—on Western pretensions of retaining old values while in fact living off all the comforts and shortcuts of urban American life.

The film's other characters are just as inauthentic, but without self-consciousness, and this makes them much funnier. Brown, the rancher, wears lumberjack shirts and goes on about preserving "a West that's free." In fact he is a refugee from the hair-dressing business back east and wears his cattleman image as a child wears a soldier suit.

His wife puts in game appearances at cattle shows, tries to seduce the ranch hands with war cries of "how about a little desire under the elms?" and longs to go back east. Their lavish ranch house is airless, and its picture windows frame the spectacular mountain scenery as if it were, in fact, no more than pictures.

Brown's two ranch hands are just as phony. Their beautifully indirect seduction by Jack and Cecil into becoming their accomplices, played out in a bar, is the best scene in the movie.

As a decrepit and seemingly inept professional rustler-detective, hired by Brown, Slim Pickens for once has a strongly written comic role. He plays it with great effect, and Charlene Dallas, as his sluttish assistant, is almost as good.

Their earthy roles and acting styles do a lot to liven up a picture whose artfulness is marred by its own narcissistic excess.

Despite a preoccupation with puncturing the myths of the modern West, *Rancho Deluxe* operates most successfully as a slickly packaged youth movie. In keeping with the audience it is aimed at, the film is self-consciously cynical and insolent, and at the same time fundamentally romantic and seeking to be liked.

Roger Ebert described in great detail why he felt everything about *Rancho Deluxe* was "disastrously wrong": "Nobody in the movie sounds as if he comes from anywhere near Montana except for Slim Pickens, and he can only talk like Slim Pickens anyway. Everyone else speaks in strangely constructed sentences that sound written with little ear for human speech. Most of the words are pronounced with such painful completeness that dialog rhythms get lost and it's sometimes necessary to mentally repeat the words to figure out what was said…Tom McGuane's screenplay just doesn't have any laughs in it. Things get so desperate, he throws in old jokes where they don't belong, hoping they'll sound like dialog."

Rancho Deluxe was heavy on scenery and light on plot. There were some good-natured inside jokes. One guy, when asked what he was before he became a cowboy, replied that he did hot-comb commercials for a Butte television station. Despite this, Livingston residents objected to *Rancho Deluxe*. The producer was perplexed, but the reason was simple: "Livingston people don't like to be portrayed as a bunch of hicks and they didn't like the pornography," opined the *Bozeman Daily Chronicle* in 1975.

On March 14, 1975, a line of anxious people stretched from the front of the Empire Theater in Livingston, around the corner and nearly a full block down a side street. Bob Burns, owner of the Wrangler Bar where some of the scenes were shot, was one of the businessmen who peddled reserved tickets for the event. Burns was worried that some of the Livingston people would be shocked when they saw *Rancho Deluxe*. "I think the people are going to be a little surprised," he said. "It's as close to an X-rating as you can get." (The film is rated R.)

There was a moment of quiet applause when the late Richard Cavanaugh of Emigrant played his part as a ringmaster at a cattle show. The drama teacher had died of cancer several months before the film was released.

A sampling of the crowd reaction after the show indicated that the people "didn't think much of the finished product."

Pat Bauer, who worked with the movie company in her position with the Livingston Chamber of Commerce, had some reservations. "Monetarily, it was good for Livingston," she said. "But as far as the spectrum—looking at the community as a whole—it wasn't good for the community. It caused bad feelings, family problems and jealousies. It ran the whole football field." *Livingston Enterprise* editor John Sullivan disagreed. "Livingston is not really a totally unsophisticated town. The actors were a cast of characters in the true sense, but I don't think it did the community any harm to have them here. It opened a few people's eyes and their minds."

Rancho Deluxe was cited by some politicians as an example of why the Montana Senate shouldn't grant tax incentives to filmmakers. Sen. Larry Aber, R-Columbus, said he didn't like the types of pictures that were being made in the state. He said such movies as *Rancho Deluxe* made him ashamed to be a Montanan. Sen. Peter Story, R-Emigrant, said he wasn't proud of the picture either but believed the state economy needed the money generated by motion pictures. He said the makers of *Rancho Deluxe* dropped about $500,000 in the Livingston area.

"This is about our identity," curator Dodson said of *Rancho Deluxe*. "We were a railroad town, but we haven't been for a while. Who are we now? We've all felt and seen the impact movies and movie people have had on us. It's time to address it, to open the dialogue. I realize not all people here are happy with the impact."

Dodson said with *Rancho Deluxe*, McGuane held a mirror up to Livingston. "I grew up here, and we always thought this was a place where nothing ever happens," she said. "*Rancho Deluxe* was an end to innocence."

"*Rancho Deluxe* has special significance for me because I met my wife during the filming," said Bridges years afterward. "She was working her way through college and I couldn't take my eyes off the girl waiting tables with broken nose and two black eyes [from a car accident]. She said no. But she said that she might see me around town, though, being such a small town. We were married three years later. On one of our first dates we went along with a realtor."

According to Bridges, a *Rancho Deluxe* makeup artist mailed the couple a photograph 10 years after they married, showing the moment they met.

"The makeup man was going through his files and found some pictures of me asking Susan out," said Bridges. "There we are. I'm speaking our first words, and there she is answering no."

Red Skies of Montana

CAST
Richard Widmark, Constance Smith, Jeffrey Hunter

DIRECTOR
Joseph M. Newman

LOCATION
Missoula area

1952

Montana skies simmered and illuminated the screen in *Red Skies of Montana* to authentically portray the dangerous lifestyle of a smokejumper. Henry Kleiner's screenplay, based on a story by Art Cohn, centers around a paratroop crew chief who is the only survivor of an outfit that becomes trapped after jumping to battle a big blaze 400 miles northwest of Missoula. One victim is an old-timer (Joe Sawyer) whose only son (Jeffrey Hunter) is convinced that the crew met death because the crew chief (Richard Widmark) ran out on them. Widmark, delirious when rescued by helicopter, cannot remember details and secretly suspects himself of cowardice. When a subsequent fire is spotted in heavy timberland, jumpers led by Widmark fly to the scene and bail out to start a firebreak. Among reinforcements flown to Missoula is young Hunter, bent upon having a showdown with Widmark. During the fire fighting, Widmark displays great personal courage and heroism, saving all his men, and Hunter realizes that he has wrongly suspected him.

The movie is credited with exposing to the rest of the

Smokejumpers star in *Red Skies of Montana*.

world the dangers faced fighting forest fires. It's loosely based on the tragedy at Mann Gulch, north of Helena, where 13 members of a 16-man crew died in a fire in August 1949. As was the case at Mann Gulch, the crew chief of a deadly fire in *Red Skies* survives, although, in the movie, he's the only one who does. At Mann Gulch, foreman Wagner Dodge was one of three and faced an intense inquiry that resulted in an overhaul of the brand-new smokejumping program.

During the making of *Red Skies of Montana*, various Hollywood stars were severely injured: on a motorcycle, stung on the neck by a hornet, burned badly, missing eyebrows singed off unintentionally, and breaking two front teeth. Smokejumping was about a decade old when the filming got under way and, to those involved in that world, it was a big deal to have 20th Century Fox buy the rights to the story—and bring in box-office stars.

In August 1950, the film crew arrived in Missoula, including such stars as Victor Mature, John Lund and Jean Peters. Under the direction of Robert Webb, a photographic unit arrived months earlier to film background footage for the picture. But misfortune was to postpone much of the filming that year. Mature injured his knee in a motorcycle accident at the Ninemile camp. Lund was stung on the neck by a hornet during the shooting of a scene in the gym at Fort Missoula. By this time, the fire season was almost over and the filming was postponed until 1951. With the new film season, the cast had completely changed. Richard Widmark, Jeffery Hunter and Richard Boone arrived in Missoula in June 1951 to begin production.

Actor Richard Widmark (right) trains smokejumpers in the mountains near Missoula.

Filming was done at Camp Menard, Hale Field, the Federal Building in Missoula and at Hayes Creek near Missoula. There were no idle barbers in Missoula the first day the Hollywood contingent arrived. Director Joseph Newman ordered every actor in the troupe to get "the closest crew cut this side of a billiard ball." Operation Cue-Ball was necessary for the performers to authentically portray smokejumpers.

Missoulians will recognize a scene showing Widmark (playing Cliff Mason) being rushed by the press as he emerges from the Federal Building following a hearing into the fire tragedy. Most of the indoor scenes were shot in Hollywood. Two veteran Forest Service employees acted as official technical advisers on the picture. They were Fred I. Stillings, assistant chief of fire control for the Northern Region, and Fred Brauer, chief dispatcher whose distinguished record as a fire-fighting smokejumper included 57 leaps from airplanes. Both men spent five

weeks in Hollywood during production before returning to their Missoula headquarters.

The special effects were elaborate for the period. According to the director of publicity for Twentieth Century Fox Studios, 450 giant pine and cedar trees were trucked to Missoula from Big Bear, California, along with another 2,500 shrubs, bushes and flowers. The trunks of the trees were creosoted and set in concrete bases and the abundant shrubs, bushes and flowers were set out amid the towering trees to create an illusion. It was an exact replica of wooded mountain areas adjacent to Missoula.

Massive rocks made on location completed the scene. The "raging scorch-job" that followed, wrote the publicist, "was bigger than the burning of Atlanta for *Gone With the Wind*. The king-size conflagration, with 100-foot flames roaring across seven acres of man-made woods, cost 20th Century-Fox approximately $250,000 before the last embers finally faded away. "A motion picture of spectacular proportions, like this one, is Hollywood at its traditional best," declared Newman, who at 39 was regarded as one of the new bright young men of Hollywood. "It is the kind of entertainment that never can be duplicated, or even vaguely approached, by any other medium. And it is the forerunner of a definite new trend in the film industry."

Widmark described the screen assignment as "the toughest physical ordeal of my career," and that included the rigors of his role of a Navy Underwater Demolitions Team officer in *The Frogmen*. The star dropped 20 pounds during production and found himself on the brink of perpetual catastrophe. He suffered minor leg and hip burns when his trousers caught fire while he was running through blazing underbrush. Snappy action by firemen standing by with water hoses extinguished the ignited clothing. He was able to continue work after medical treatment for the painful burns. Another time the actor's eyebrows were burned off. And yet another, while on location he tripped and fell climbing from a helicopter and broke off two front teeth, necessitating temporary dental repairs.

Irish-born actress Constance Smith took the location trip to Missoula with 100 male members of the film troupe. All movie stars have stand-ins. When Smith was introduced to "an attractive resident of Montana" who had been hired to work as her stand-in on location, the two girls "let loose with more squeals than a porcupine stuck in a rail fence." The stand-in turned out to be Jean Tweedy Michaels, who had once worked as a stand-in for Smith in five British films.

Jeff Hunter, one of the "outstanding athletes in Hollywood," reportedly "astounded real smokejumpers" at their Montana training camp when, without previous instruction or practice, "he broke all existing records on the obstacle course," including rope climbing, sprints, mountain hikes with full pack, tower jumps and swimming.

Many of the scenes in the movie will still be familiar to those who know Missoula, including those at the courthouse and the dance hall at Lolo Hot Springs, as well as shots of the old Higgins Avenue Bridge and Hale Field, the region's first airport. Those who don't know Missoula might be more familiar with an actor who got his start in the picture, Charles Buchinski, later known as Charles Bronson. More than 500 residents of the community were hired as extras. Between scenes they "mobbed" Widmark, Smith and other members of the cast for autographs, until Director Newman had to issue a standing order of "No more autographs during working hours!"

Bill Brennan was a 20-year-old U.S. Forest Service smokejumper who made one jump in front of airborne cameras. He also helped burn hay and plant burnt snags up Lolo Creek to simulate the ash of wildfires for the close-up scenes. "They couldn't pay us, so they'd feed us, and they did a pretty good job of it."

George Feucht of St. Ignatius was in one of the film's most scenic moments. "I worked for the remount station at Ninemile at the time and they sent two strings of mules up to Blue Mountain to show it off," he said. "Somebody said I was in the very first part of it, riding a big sorrel." Feucht, now 88, was in charge of a mule string as it made its way up Hayes Creek. The Missoula Valley spread out behind them, though it was hidden by the opening credits. The mules behaved themselves while the cameras rolled. "They always did for me," said Feucht, who had experience handling the animals. "We'd shoe about 600 mules and horses in the spring to send out, mostly at Perma," where the Forest Service wintered the animals.

"The only incident was we stood around all day in the hot sun, and they had some outfit bring some meals over. But they didn't bring us any," Feucht said. Brennan remembers seeing *Red Skies* once, just after its release and not long after he was drafted into the Army. "I saw it at Camp Roberts and had a big laugh," he said. Firefighting "really wasn't like that at all. It just struck me as a little far-fetched."

Red Skies of Montana still holds a special place in both the annals of smokejumping and in the history of Missoula. The city hosted the world premiere of *Red Skies of Montana* in the winter of 1952.

Fox executives were nervous about *Red Skies of Montana*, a title more suggestive of a Roy Rogers–Dale Evans Western than the very respectable action-adventure yarn offered here. In some areas, they called it *Smoke Jumpers*, a no-nonsense title under which the *New York Times* ran its review: "Richard Widmark, Jeffrey Hunter, Constance Smith and a handful of Fox contract players are marking time—and how!—in a story by Art Cohn that has the two men feuding in a training station for firefighters. The others stand around and watch and a few random fires smolder, for the most part, in the distance (beyond the budget, we suspect)."

Return to Lonesome Dove

CAST
Jon Voight, Barbara Hershey, Rick Schroder

DIRECTOR
Mike Robe

LOCATION
Butte area, Virginia City, Billings area

1993

For *Return to Lonesome Dove*, crews built a $500,000 farm house, furnished it with thousands of dollars in antiques, and burned it to the ground.

In this sequel to 1989's *Lonesome Dove*, Woodrow Call heads back to his ranch in Montana. The sets went up at a fast pace the weekend of June 22, 1993. The crews, actors, equipment were all in Nevada City preparing the town for scenes. Sites in Nevada City had been altered to depict settings in Miles City, Montana; in Kansas; and in San Antonio, Texas.

Return to Lonesome Dove gives audiences a real indication as to how fastidious a professional film production has to be when dealing with the authentic. What did a doormat look like in 1879? How did people stack their firewood? How would people have hung harness back then? These are three of the dozens of questions that kept the art department of the movie crew of *Return to Lonesome Dove* busy. They had amassed a western history library many an historian might envy, looked through hundreds of photos at the Montana Historical Society, and toured an historic ranch to help them plan two ranch sets, one for cattle baron Gregor Dunnegan of Kenilworth and one for his rival Woodrow Call.

A tour of the set in Nevada City would have revealed a bewildering array of careful reproductions and artful deceptions, such as a building used as a lawyer's office in one scene then being covered with the façade of a hotel for a subsequent one. Sometimes the problem wasn't what was missing, but what should not have been there. A steam tractor and a railroad track visible from various angles in Nevada City had to be cleverly hidden behind fiberglass log walls.

Two buildings near the Kenilworth ranch set needed to be covered with military camouflage so that a view of the vast, "undeveloped" Kenilworth acres would really look undeveloped. One large false front was constructed next to the highway, about 20 inches from the sidewalks of town and down from the Nevada City Hotel. Other sets were put up inside the town off the back of its main street, plus different scenes were shot several places in surrounding Madison County, such as at Meadow Creek and near the town of Silver Star. Occasionally, in spite of their best efforts at authenticity, some concessions needed to be made.

A Montana town of the 1870s would have been virtually new, but the buildings of Nevada City have an undeniable aura of age. If the art department put up a new sign designating a livery stable, hotel or general store, it would have stood out conspicuously, so the artists aged new boards to a mellow gray, and treated the sign paint so that it had a well-weathered patina. Kenilworth's battle against the fencing of the open range required a scene in which cowboys string wire. But real barbed wire is heavy, hard to handle and prone to tear clothes and skin, so some of the wire would have to be non-violent rubber.

The costume department was busy making everything from canvas dusters for the cowboys to satin gowns for a "lady" who was not quite a lady. Still, it was not enough to simply make a duster of the proper style and material; it must then be soaked, dirtied, torn and crumpled. Even the horses don't escape the tricks of the movie trade, as a dusty, lathered-looking horse has to be covered in a careful coat of fuller's earth, the clay used as movie-set dust. The typical western-type street was built near an old barn south of Bridger. It didn't take film crews long to turn

Dillon resident and location manager Mark Zetler (center) goofs around on the set of *Return to Lonesome Dove* with actor Louis Gossett Jr. (left) and Gossett's bodyguard.

the lone barn into part of a street by building false front adobe buildings to the right.

A major project like the *Dove* miniseries meant big money for set construction. The company built a mansion in Ennis in the middle of a vacant field. The three-story home was built in detail, with everything but plumbing and foundation, and when the movie was over, it was sold for scrap.

And that was nothing compared to the Billings setting, explained Mark Zetler, location manager. That set, representing Clara's home in Nebraska, cost $500,000 to build. The ranch house, along with the outbuildings, was built in minute detail. The home itself was furnished with thousands of dollars in antiques. "We torched it… as part of the script," said Zetler, a graduate of Beaverhead County High School and Montana State University. The script, said Zetler, called for Clara to go through the ashes after the fire, recognizing individual pieces of furniture. "The fire got too hot and incinerated it all." Initially budgeted for $20 million, the mini-series wound up growing to $31 million.

Zetler was involved in coordinating everything that needed to be done in a specific location, including Environmental Assessment forms, reclamation of areas the movie might have disturbed, and cleanup. When the mansion was burned at the Billings site, it meant 15,000 nails had to be picked up. "We took out a foot of topsoil from the site and replaced it with new soil, then re-seeded it," said Zetler. The bill for cleaning up that one shot was $25,000. It meant removing miles of fences and power poles, building roads and arranging daily catering for up

to 200 people. And before any of it happened, Zetler had to find the site, deal with the owners and arrange insurance as well. It even meant getting the interstate highway shut down for five-minute intervals for key shots.

Several Hardin residents took part in the filming. Several of the final days of shooting took place on land between Roundup and Billings owned by Marian and Sandy Brown of Broadview. Typical Montana land of rocks, pine trees and dry, dusty dirt depicted Texas. Walt Secrest supplied the wagons, teams, and animals. Boasting a fleet of 16 wagons, including some authentic covered and ranch wagons, Secrest had grabbed hold of the ranch prop market for Western movies. Ranching and teaming had been in the Secrest family for generations. Surely, Secrest's ancestors never dreamed that at the end of the twentieth century their descendants would practice their old ways in front of movie cameras. "The wagons are just a hobby. They don't pay too big until you get on a movie," said Secrest.

Return to Lonesome Dove spent three months of filming in Billings and Whitehall. Secrest was a teamster in the movie and said he could see himself at a distance on TV. "Most of the big wagons on *Lonesome Dove* were my wagons," he boasted. The shooting of *Lonesome Dove* employed two filming crews which made it difficult for the extras to determine the plot. "They started at the back of that movie and moved forward. It didn't make sense, you didn't know what was going on." Tourists lined the streets, using their VCRs and cameras to film the numerous extras who milled around on the town's boardwalk.

Anyone who has visited the Moss Mansion in Billings will recognize its interiors. Parlors, the stairway, billiard room, dining room, library entryways and master bedroom were used, all part of the "Kenilworth Mansion," ranch headquarters for the opposing faction in the movie. Moss manager Ruth Towe declined to say how much the mansion made on the shoot, but confirmed that it was "in the thousands of dollars" and "very generous."

More than 100 camera and sound technicians, set decorators, carpenters and others began picketing on the sidewalks in front of Moss Mansion for higher wages while caterers and coffee vendors kept the striking forces supplied with espresso. The strike shut down production on the 160-crew first unit, which was filming at the mansion, and a 75-crew second unit, which was filming 21 miles out of town. "We've never been picketed before," said Towe, who came outside to take photos of the strikers. "This is kind of a historical event for us."

Truck drivers supported the strike by refusing to cross the picket line and many of the actors stayed away from the set. Actor Ricky Schroder, who stopped by briefly, joked with the striking workers and took photos of the picket line. Motorists on Division Street in support of the strikers honked as they drove by, including Billings firefighters who were deadlocked with the city over a new union contract, and city sanitation workers.

Strikers and management representative began negotiating shortly before 9 A.M., first on the sidewalks in front of the mansion and later, when crew members kept shuffling within hearing range, to the 18th floor of the Sheraton Hotel. The strike, which lasted until noon, "greatly" hurt the production, said Sandra England, a representative for the International Alliance of Theatrical Stage Employees and Moving Picture Machine Operators. "We've lost a half-day, but there's no such thing as a half-day in the film business," she said.

Laurel High School alumnus Pat Kukes played violin after auditioning for the part in Butte. He shared conversation with Oliver Reed and Jon Voight, and a chess game with Ricky Schroder. Kukes said that working on a film had changed the way he watches a movie. "Now I watch shows differently. Where are the cameras, and how many takes did they need to get that scene?" are questions he seeks to answer when he watches a movie. Kukes said he found his short visit to the land of the silver screen educational. "I thought the people would be more arrogant and temperamental. They weren't. They were very dedicated to the authenticity of the production."

Pay close attention to the horses and you'll see the work of Columbia Falls native Jane Leatherberry and her husband, Jim. The Leatherberrys worked as wranglers helping manage the 350 horses in the movie. The couple won the wrangling job while attending a horse clinic. Linda said they were "just goofing around" when they met a location scout from Hollywood looking for an area for horses to ford a river.

The couple traveled with the movie crew from May 15 through September 9. They were among a group of wranglers—sometimes 20, other times 50—who fed and cared for the horses and worked with actors riding the horses. "Everybody we worked with was really down-to-earth," said Jane. "They were all such neat people." Jane said most of the actors knew how to ride, although a few needed instruction. "You stay with them constantly," said Jane. "You don't want anything to happen to them. You are there to help them on and off. Even hanging on underneath the horse."

After two months in town, actor Lou Gossett Jr. said the only thing more impressive than the southwest Montana scenery was the hospitality. Gossett was serious enough about his sentiments to purchase a half-page ad in the newspaper thanking the many people he had befriended. Gossett lodged in Butte during filming and stayed several extra days after shooting was wrapped. Many of the crew members and actors rented homes in Butte for two or three months instead of staying in motels. Gossett, a lover of a variety of music, said he enjoyed the home of a local musician, who had been out of town for the summer, and the man's great stereo system. Visits to the Country Club, the YMCA, several restaurants, Copper Kings baseball games and bowling alleys kept Gossett in the Butte eye. Everywhere, he said, he was treated exceptionally well. "I want to come back," said Gossett. "That means it's not a short-term relationship."

Even with small delays caused by the wet weather, Gossett said the filming had gone well. "They're happy with it," said Gossett. "We're getting great footage. The scenery can't be matched. You can't paint those mountains…those snow-capped mountains." Gossett, then 56, joked that he had to bring some "bottled smog" from Los Angeles to avoid an overdose on clean air "so I could live."

Reese Witherspoon, her mother at her side, landed a small part as an extra. Voight's son, Jamie Jolie, landed a small part as one of Kenniworth extras, but "disappeared from the set" and was replaced. His sister, Angelina Jolie, was on the set watching her father and brother, but didn't have a part in the production.

Entertainment Weekly encapsulated the tepid response to the sequel of the Western classic: "Stick around for seven hours and you'll find that this is a perfectly decent Western; you might even shed a tear or two. But you'll also know that, when it's finished, a grand piece of TV mythmaking has been reduced to a horse opera."

The availability of the Butte, Anaconda and Pacific (RARUS) Railroad played a key role in filming Oscar-nominated *Runaway Train* in Montana.

Runaway Train

CAST

Jon Voight, Eric Roberts

DIRECTOR

Andrei Konchalovsky

LOCATION

Butte, Anaconda

1985

Garry Wunderwald, a staff of one during the 1970s and 1980s, despite a comparatively threadbare operating budget, scored some major triumphs in catching the eye of Hollywood's big boys. "Inquiries about Montana may come along two years or so before a company commits itself," said Wunderwald, at the time referred to as the Montana travel department's movie location coordinator. "I'd say I would get between 15 and 20 calls and written inquiries a week from companies wanting information."

The questions were diverse and numerous. What are the child labor laws in Montana? Are trucking permits required for hauling in equipment? How long does it take to get these permits? What about filming in national forests, national parks? Lodging, catering, costuming—and do you have cameramen, people with drama experience, carpenters with set-building knowledge, "grips" to handle equipment and security guards to protect it?

Special requests often meant 12- to 15-hour days for Wunderwald. For instance, when producers were undecided about whether to shoot *Runaway Train*, starring Jon Voigt, Eric Roberts and Rebecca DeMornay, in Montana, Wunderwald made special trips throughout the state to photograph various railroad tracks and stations, as well as terrain he knew was called for in the script. "Photos give them something they can touch and mark on," said Wunderwald.

Runaway Train had a curious journey to the screen. Akira Kurosawa, the highly acclaimed Japanese director of *Seven Samurai* and other classics, wrote the script years earlier but was never able to finance the film. Through his American friend Francis Ford Coppola, Kurosawa was introduced to director Andrei Konchalovsky, whose epic film *Siberiade* (1979) had impressed filmmakers in the Western world. The Russian had left the Soviet Union to make films in the United States, the first being *Maria's Lovers*. Konchalovsky decided that Kurosawa's script deserved big-screen treatment.

"They're going off the rails on a crazy train" (and other metaphors) in this film that stars Jon Voight and Eric Roberts as a pair of convicts who escape an Alaska prison and hop aboard a locomotive. Of course, they get trapped on the one train that somehow doesn't have an engineer. The out-of-control locomotive goes hurtling through the Alaskan tundra as those on board attempt to put on the brakes. Meanwhile, the two cons, along with a female love interest (the only railway worker left on the train), are being pursued by the prison's administrator. This all leads to an inevitable battle in the engine room between the movie's heroic prisoner on the run and the vindictive prison official. Despite its action-cliché premise, the two actors both received Academy Award nominations.

The availability of the Butte, Anaconda and Pacific (RARUS) Railroad played a key role with filming *Runaway Train* in Montana. Cannon Films, Inc., used the Butte-Anaconda area for three weeks in the winter of 1985 to film parts of *Runaway Train*. Anaconda's diesel train engines and railroad yards were used in the film. Competition for filming among Alaska, Wyoming, Utah and Montana was intense, said Wunderwald. Montana residents were invited to take part in the production, filling openings for about 20 bit parts and up to 200 extras for prison scenes.

"Cooperation from the private sector helped convince the producers that Montana was the perfect site for the film," said Wunderwald, citing John Green of the Butte-Anaconda Pacific Railroad and Ernie Hartley of the old territorial prison museum at Deer Lodge. The initial prison scene in *Runaway Train* was filmed at the Old Montana State Prison in Deer Lodge, featuring a massive red-brick cell house surrounded by 24-foot-high gray walls and towers, built with convict labor.

Veteran actor Don Pugsley recalled his first speaking role as a guard in the film: "*Runaway Train* was my first speaking role since I had just gotten my SAG (Screen Actor's Guild) card. I believe my line was, 'They came this way all right, no doubt about it.'"

While some of the close-in rail scenes were done at Anaconda, long shots down the valley were done in Alaska. Several scenes—some of which didn't make the final cut—were shot around the Anaconda railyard.

More than 30 years later, Eileen Briesch, a reporter for the local Anaconda paper at the time, recalled her experience watching the filming of *Runaway Train*: "I spent a whole day watching them film two scenes in the railyard in Anaconda, and the only thing that made it to the film was the stuntman as the old conductor having a heart attack falling off the train. So I know all that work can wind up on the cutting room floor."

Although Wunderwald was convinced the Deer Lodge Valley could have provided the long views filmmakers were looking for, Montana's lack of snow at that time caused the shift in plans. "And Burlington Northern wouldn't have allowed their tracks to be used anyway," said Wunderwald. In fact, none of the big railroads in the U.S. was willing to provide locations for the movie because of liabilities and the bad public image associated with a runaway train. (The state of Alaska owned its train system and was more flexible in this regard.)

Wunderwald recalled receiving a phone call from one of the producers at Golan-Globus frantic that the snubnose train—the actual "runaway train" in the film—had not been delivered from the Midwest. "The producer called and said that the train was late at least four or five days. It had been switching around across the country and it didn't come direct. The snubnose was more confined than the type of engine you'd see today. I was driving that day—pulling into Butte, I remember—and there it was. I was tremendously relieved to see it." Cannon hired 350 Montanans as extras, carpenters, electricians, teamsters, railroad engineers, and office workers.

Butte resident Marilyn Maney said the company bought 2.5 tons of potato flakes from area farmers to use as replacement snow because of a shortage of the natural stuff.

Mexican-American actor Danny Trejo's career began with *Runaway Train*. A former convict, Trejo had been feared by the worst of the worst. He operated protection rackets and fought his way to lightweight and welterweight boxing titles in every prison he did time in. After a 111-day stint in solitary and escaping a possible trip to the gas chamber on a technicality, he decided to change.

On release in 1969, he became a drug counselor and it was in this capacity he found himself on the set of *Runaway Train* in 1984. He was instantly given a part as a convict extra. Discovering he was pretty handy in the ring, Trejo was offered $320 per day to train actors for a boxing match. When warned some of their punches might accidentally connect, Trejo replied: "For $320 a day, give him a bat. I used to get beat up for free."

"I was asked if I could act like a convict. When I took my shirt off, this guy comes storming across the set. He said: 'You're Danny Trejo!' He recognized my tattoos. He'd seen me box in San Quentin, so they hired me to train Eric Roberts how to box. I learned how not to behave on a movie set from Eric Roberts. He was very demanding."

Trejo's mustachioed menace is now one of the most recognizable faces in Hollywood.

Season of Change was originally called *Nobody's Sweetheart*. An independent film without major studio backing, it was marred by allegations of fraud and financial wrongdoing by its director, Robin P. Murray.

Season of Change

CAST
Michael Madsen and Hoyt Axton

DIRECTOR
Robin P. Murray

LOCATION
Hamilton, Stevensville, Corvallis

1992

Season of Change is about a 12-year-old girl in post–World War II Stevensville. It was described by the production as a cross between *Anne of Green Gables* and *National Vel-*

vet. The family drama, which failed to attain a theatrical release, headed for video shelves starting May 23, 1995.

The film crew had found a Hamilton house and places in Stevensville for exterior and interior shots, as well as built a new front for scenes on Corvallis' Main Street. Problems festered as a trail of Murray's unpaid bills left a bad taste in the mouths of several local business owners. The film's negative sat in a postproduction house in Seattle and had a lien against it. Local business owners met with Montana Film Commissioner Lonnie Stimac and a Bitterroot Valley chamber representative who formed a class action suit. Several individuals and business were not reimbursed for props, work, or services during the filming.

Local resident Beth Robbins said she provided a family heirloom, a 1938 Dodge, to Murray's production house, Sterling Films, and what she got back was a car with two new dents, a stripped transmission and stripped window gears. She said Sterling Films had not paid her for the use of her car nor for repairs—and that she had to pony up her own money to get it out of a repair shop when the film company didn't come through.

"It wasn't just the unpaid bills," said Steve Slocomb of Hamilton, who served as director of photography on *Season.* "There had also been virtually no communication with people in the valley about what the status of the film was. People had given of themselves—their houses, family Bibles, other props."

In an interview with the Associated Press on February 24, 1995, Murray said he figured his Sterling Films still owed $40,000 to $45,000 to area merchants, ranging from $100 to a maximum of $7,000 or $8,000. "It is my intention to pay off all of them," he said. "I don't believe we dispute any of the bills to local merchants. It is our intention to settle up 100 percent."

Among those feeling the most frustrated was the production's biggest creditor, Andy Cannon, who was owed $12,000 of the $27,000 owed locally. Cannon was an employee of Sterling Films and his own company, Western Productions, was hired to provide costumes and props for the movie. "I feel like a victim and I've really been taking a lot of local heat," said Cannon. "I told [the producers] that this is not Hollywood and that they needed to make damn sure these bills were paid immediately."

The movie, which starred Michael Madsen and Hoyt Axton, was originally called *Nobody's Sweetheart.* An independent film without major studio backing, filmed in March 2000, in 17 days, it went over budget. Murray said the video release was the start of getting the film, which eventually cost $900,000 to make, into the black. "We just ran out of money," said Murray.

At least one Hamilton resident invested $20,000, a Cut Bank investor added another $20,000, and a Missoula investor put in $240,000 in a series of six payments to an escrow account at Farmers State Bank in Victor. The Montana State Auditor ended a four-year investigation with an order to Murray to stop selling securities in Montana.

Besides the bad taste it left in the mouths of the folks in the Bitterroot Valley, the only other interesting thing about *Season* was the involvement of Michael Madsen, whose long career spanned 25 years and more than 170 films. He has played memorable characters in myriad box office hits, including, Kill Bill, *Donnie Brasco*, and *Thelma & Louise*.

"Michael Madsen was great to work with, very professional," director Murray said recently. "He was always on time and ready to go. He is a very genuine guy that would go to great lengths to protect your back. Michael had one complaint on the project, the actress he played opposite was on one of these garlic diets, so her breath was awful. We had to have a breath spray on the set for all those scenes. He is a friend to this day."

Speaking of expenses, Murray said Hoyt Axton sang a sweet song for the burial of the child. "I asked Hoyt about the song rights, he said it was something he made up," Murray said. "Well, in postproduction, we found out that his mother wrote the song for Elvis, so it cost us a pretty penny to keep it in the film."

Murray insists that all parties have been recompensed, yet some claim that his debts are still outstanding. "Yes, there were some rumored financial issues stemming from the incompetence of the production manager Mr. Andy Cannon," said Murray recently. "The legitimate claims were resolved, but other baseless claims were dismissed in court. The most outstanding claim were the state and federal taxes that Mr. Cannon neglected to pay, of which I personally had to pay. I learned my lesson the hard way, so the next feature I did in Montana, 'The Flying Dutchman' starring Rod Steiger, Eric Roberts and Catherine Oxenberg in Darby, was under a completion bond."

"I have only one recommendation for people who are approached by a filmmaker or so-called filmmaker, and that's let the buyer beware," said Lonie Stimac, former Montana Film Commissioner. "You have to check and see if people are legitimate. That is one of the jobs of the film office, to scout out the people and to find out more about the last place they shot. Did they pay their bills? Were the location owners happy? Did they get paid? Were they happy? For people in the community, view it as a business deal and have contracts. [But] because it's Hollywood, there are dreams about those sort of things and people let their guard down. Because of the issue with the first movie Robin Murray was involved in, the state didn't take an active role in *Frozen in Fear*. We offered the help we could. But we had to pick a level of service."

Son of the Morning Star

CAST
Gary Cole, Rosanna Arquette

DIRECTOR
Mike Robe

LOCATION
Billings area

1991

On a Montana battlefield, 114 years after the death of George Armstrong Custer, after a long morning of warfare, Indian warriors and white soldiers paused for a hard-earned lunch. "I hope I didn't hurt you out there," a soldier said to a warrior. "Don't worry about it," the Indian answered. "Every cavalryman out there shot me at least 10 times."

Indian and cavalryman, producer and director, scriptwriter and wardrobe designer—all the people involved in the production of the four-hour television version of Evan S. Connell's 1984 book-length historical essay, *Son of the Morning Star* (apparently Custer liked to attack Indians at dawn), seemed united in their determination

Gary Cole (far right) played General George Armstrong Custer in *Son of the Morning Star*.

to do it right. They wanted to present, in the words of producer Preston Fischer, a "fair, balanced and accurate" version of the legendary event at the Little Bighorn on June 25, 1876.

Kimberly Morris, a Flathead Indian and recent Native American studies major at the University of California at Los Angeles, played the adult Kate Bighead, a Cheyenne woman who witnessed many key events of the Plains Wars. She said that she could understand Libbie Custer's point of view depicted in the film.

Rosanna Arquette, who played Libbie, lamented the "horrible" campaigns against the Indians, and appraised the love between George and Libbie as "romantic, because they were madly in love, and tragic, because he was such a jerk."

All the Indian parts were played by Indian actors. In one impressive scene T.C. Williams, a Navajo Indian and one of the make-up artists, matched the war paint of 39 warriors to their 39 horses.

A reporter from the *New York Daily News* wrote about the striking on and off camera cultural encounters. "During breaks in the battle, an Indian man arrayed for war drinks a Coke, eats a Snickers bar, and smokes a Marlboro; makeup people freshen war paint."

During filming, limbs, not lives, were at risk. One of the things that director Mike Robe learned filming the battle scenes was that problems can occur. The ground was pocked: a lot of horses were falling, puncture wounds and sprained ankles were common. There were several injuries, and over the entire shoot about 20 people were sent to a hospital, mostly from dealing with the cactus that fills the area. Lightly dressed, the Indians reported in with bad sunburns. "I asked one Indian man, 'Did you guys get sunburned like this 100 years ago?' recalled a paramedic of Arrow Medical Services. "He told me, 'I think it has something to do with the change in the ozone layer.'"

Director Mike Robe re-created the Battle of the Little Bighorn near the actual site of Custer's Last Stand, with a great deal of cooperation from the local Native Americans.

Many local Native Americans got parts in *Son of the Morning Star*, filmed on location in the Hardin area.

Robe in his own words: "We thought about filming at the actual site, about 55 minutes outside of Billings, Montana. However, that was impractical because it is now a national monument with gravestones and markers all over the terrain. But we were determined to simulate the topography as best we could, and not too far away we found Pryor Creek [as opposed to the Little Bighorn River], and staged the picture in those ravines and on a slope that duplicates the Battle of the Little Bighorn. We had Native American advisors who helped us throughout the picture. Many of the Indians in the show were from the Billings area and from the Crow Agency and South Dakota. They [Native Americans] ride beautifully, bareback at that. There's no way we could have done this without their cooperation."

Robe used more than 200 cavalry re-enactors in addition to stunt teams to re-create Custer's battles. Robe described using them in the production: "They're very knowledgeable about history, which lends a great deal of credibility to what you're trying to do. The re-enactors

bring their own horses and living quarters. They had their own camp at the Roselle Ranch, the private ranch where we shot a lot of the picture. It was fascinating to see them engage in mock warfare with the local Native Americans, and also to witness the conflict, resolution and camaraderie that developed between them."

The *Son of the Morning Star* production brought in experts from all over the country. Such details as Custer's buckskins were patterned exactly after those in the Smithsonian. The Native American specialists spent hours matching authentic makeup on the warriors and their horses. Bell Rock was one of 250 Indians employed in the production. A Crow, he played Custer's Crow scout Curly. His big moment came when he wailed his death song. The real Curly did the same thing, but he took off as the battle began and lived on for years. Tedious retakes, mud, mosquitoes, and sunburn were all in a day's work. "It pays some bills. It brings food to the table. It's a job," said Bell Rock, who returned to the local rodeo circuit when the filming was done. Extras received the minimum wage of $3.80 an hour, with double time after 10 hours.

Of its $12 million budget, Republic Pictures sprinkled about $4 million locally on everything from salaries to cellular phones to chateaubriand. For six weeks' worth of groceries, the caterers spent $65,000. Cast and crew left behind a further $1 million or so in personal spending. From a local pawnshop, prop master Scott A. Stephens bought two 1873 pistols at $290 apiece for his collection. Local businesses totaled up nice profits. In Billings, film people did early Christmas shopping at a boutique called Jumbles. Down at Jake's, where the cast hung out in the evening, the nightly take had swelled to the point where "they've turned a $300 bar into a $1,000 bar," said manager Christopher R. Lyon. When a snake was needed to slither across the set, local radio stations ran free announcement to find one. The owner would receive $50, a day's visit to the set, and the snake back. Three of the reptiles were volunteered. Attic Dreams Antiques rented a cruet set as a prop. After being used on Custer's dinner table, it was returned filled with salt, pepper, oil, and vinegar. Even with a hefty price tag of $175, co-owner Mildred A. Albert said "it's quite salable now, because it has a history."

Reviews of *Son of the Morning Star*, which aired during February sweep weeks, were generally unfavorable, though the scenery received thumbs up across the board. "Beautifully photographed near the authentic Montana locales," wrote *Knight-Ridder* newspapers. "For all its good intentions, it was one of TV's most confusing, dreary and uninvolving shows," stated one reviewer. "On screen, this didn't elucidate; it just aggravated," added another.

Knight-Ridder newspapers reserved special scorn for actor Gary Cole, who played Custer, "who seemed to be calling up expressions by the number and he looked like Nick Nolte dressed up as a prairie biker," and for Arquette, "suffocating under hairstyles fit for a charwoman and a wardrobe that might have come from a garage sale in Amish country." At more than three hours, "only insomniacs would have stuck around to see it all."

Megan Follows played a girl determined to keep her family's farm in *Stacking,* made in the Billings area.

Stacking

CAST
Megan Follows, Ray Baker, Peter Coyote

DIRECTOR
Martin Rosen

LOCATION
Billings area

1987

Stacking began shooting in and around Livingston, Harlowton, and Billings in June 1986. The low budget story concerns farm life in the mid-1950s and centers on one man's problems and triumphs. If the premise sounds a bit flimsy, that's because it is. One film critic from *Screen* pounced on the generic overview, comparing it to other "stories about regional Americana, often set on a farm, and more often set in the not-too-distant past…usually they're coming-of-age sagas in which an adolescent's sexual awakening threatens to disrupt the household but ultimately reaffirms family values."

The *Boston Globe* said the director compensated for the film's "relentless literariness and spectacular lack of cinematic quality by employing a good photographer who shoots brilliant sequences of sun rays warming the golden plain."

Another reviewer said that the film wasn't hateful or awful, but just inert. Set in Lavina, Montana, circa 1954, the film chronicles the coming-of-age of 14-year-old tomboy Anna Mae Morgan (Megan Follows). Anna Mae's papa got his arm swallowed by their hay-stacking machine, and he's laid up in the hospital. The neighbors want to buy the Morgan farm; Megan's mama (Christine Lahti) wants to sell it and move to California ("I've never seen the ocean," she sighs); but Anna Mae is determined to preserve her patrimony.

The film proceeds with a tractor's pace and delicacy. Apart from cinematographer Richard Bowen's panoramic sequences of the azure skies and sun-sparkled fields of Montana, there's not much to recommend this movie, which has all the narrative excitement of a mechanical arm turning a book page. Indeed, several reviews noted Montana's scenery as one of the film's high points, including the *Los Angeles Times*:

"Rosen has assembled and cast this project well and found some properly inspiring Montana locations: long stretches of land in mute, overcast colors, surrounded by sheltering banks of mountain, grain waving against the flat-looking sky. But he hasn't really illuminated the landscape or brought out the pulse of the material. The film lacks texture. The actors are good—but often they seem trapped in the frame, unable to breathe. The rhythm is oddly like that of Rosen's cartoon features—unspontaneous, metronomic, a little blocky."

"*Stacking* liked the western look," said film commissioner Garry Wunderwald. "There was an old hotel there in Harlowton and they loved that. I guess the film didn't do well. But as the film commissioner, even the lower-budget ones were worth taking care of too.

"The lighting here is very unusual—long evenings. If you see a film like *Heartland* you see the lighting and the land. *Stacking* shows off the land."

Sweetgrass had a cast of thousands of sheep. Filmed without commentary, narration or sound—except for the incessant bleating of the sheep—the film tells the story of the last journey of a family of Montana sheepherders into the Absaroka-Beartooth Mountains for summer grazing.

Sweetgrass

Cast
Thousands of Sheep

Director
Ilisa Barbash, Lucien Castaing-Taylor

Location
Absaroka-Beartooth Mountains

2009

Sweetgrass has a cast of thousands…thousands of sheep. Filmed without narration, interviews or music—except for the almost constant chorus of bleating animals—the film tells the story of the last journey of a family of Montana sheepherders up the Absaroka-Beartooth Mountains for summer grazing.

The family was once part of a large group of families that used federal permits to graze their sheep on public land. The sheep drive, a difficult journey of three months and 150 miles involving 3,000 animals and a handful of ranchers and hired hands from the Allested sheep ranch, is a practice that has been going on since the late 19th century. Tens of thousands of sheep once made the trip.

Husband-and-wife filmmakers Lucien Castaing-Taylor and Ilisa Barbash don't sentimentalize a dying way of life (overwhelmed by competition from factory farming).

In one scene, one of the cowboys complains to his mother about the long hours, incessant wind, ornery sheep and a bum knee. "I'd rather enjoy these mountains than hate 'em," he says.

The film is visually gifted, stacked with breathtaking shots: silently drifting snow, dense, shadowy clouds, and the lush mountainside.. Unsettling images exist, too: a bear attacks a sheep and some of the herders' famished dogs eat the remains.

A native of the UK, Castaing-Taylor spent three summers in the wilderness south of Big Timber. "It's not that easy to go in and out, it's such a long way," he said of the mountains. "Plus, the first year I was a greenhorn. I was clueless in the mountains."

"The first grizzly I saw charged me," he said. As Pat Connolly, one of the herders featured in the film, told it, Castaing-Taylor had been loaned a .357 magnum revolver. "It was useless," said Castaing-Taylor. They heard gun shots, Connolly said, and then on the radio one of the other herders reported seeing the bear running away. Then Castaing-Taylor came bursting through the bush, and "his eyes were big," Connolly recalled, "his nostrils were flarin', and he was packin' this pistol around."

"It's a good thing I'm such a bad shot and didn't hit the thing in six shots," said Castaing-Taylor.

Castaing-Taylor said that he wanted the audience to be "more involved" when viewing the film. In conventional documentaries, a narrator, he said, "talks down to the audience" by explaining everything and the film simply reinforces what the narrator said.

In *Sweetgrass*, Castaing-Taylor wanted the "pictures to stand for themselves and the audience to interpret it for themselves," recording the sights and sounds of everyday life in the mountains. Microphones and wireless transmitters with a half-mile range were attached to subjects.

"We spent more money on the sound than on the cameras. Occasionally, I would put a [mic] on a horse or a dog or a sheep, but they often broke them, and they are expensive. But people broke them occasionally, too. I wanted to be everywhere. I wanted to be with the sheep, with the packstring, with the camp. Everything had the potential to be interesting."

The 200 hours of film he recorded had been "whittled down to two hours" by him and Barbash into a movie that has been well received at film festivals internationally. Since then, it has been translated into five languages—French, Spanish, Russian, Polish, and German. At the selective New York Film Festival, it was considered one of the best films of the year.

Taking Chance

CAST
Kevin Bacon, Tom Wopat

DIRECTOR
Ross Katz

LOCATION
Bozeman, Ennis, Virginia City

2008

Taking Chance started production in Bozeman and Ennis in the summer of 2007 and debuted on HBO in 2008. Based on the first-person account of Lieutenant Colonel Michael Strobl (USMC), the film chronicles his poignant journey as the volunteer military escort officer who is assigned to accompany the body of 19-year-old Lance Corporal Chance Phelps (USMC), who was killed in action in Iraq, across America back to his hometown of Dubois, Wyoming, in spring 2004. Strobl was played by Kevin Bacon.

The military funeral scenes were filmed at Boot Hill Cemetery in Virginia City and on Ennis's Main Street. "Ultimately, we had more resources to offer and we had a better look, cinematically, for the film," recalled Montana Film Commissioner Sten Iversen. "The first half of the movie takes place back east. We double for Minneapolis at the Bozeman Airport [while] transferring the body."

"I am proud HBO Films has selected Montana to be the backdrop for this compelling story about a fallen hero's final journey home from Iraq," Governor Brian Schweitzer said in response to the news of filming. "This is an American tale that speaks deeply to many Montana families and it is an honor to participate."

Chance Phelps was killed April 9, 2004, by hostile fire

in Al Anbar Province, Iraq, and was posthumously award-ed the Bronze Star with Combat Distinguishing Device. He was assigned to the 3rd Battalion, 11th Marine Regiment, 1st Marine Division, and had been deployed to Iraq just one month prior to his death. More than 1,000 people attended his funeral in Dubois (population 960).

Bacon portrayed Lieutenant Colonel Strobl, a Desert Storm veteran who served 24 years in the U.S. Marine Corps. Strobl developed the original screenplay with the strong support of Phelps' parents, John Phelps and Gretchen Mack. Two-time Oscar-nominated producer Ross Katz made his directorial debut. *Taking Chance* was written by Strobl and Katz, based on Strobl's short story. Strobl enlisted in the Marine Corps in 1983 and served in all three active duty Marine divisions as a field artilleryman. He participated in operations Desert Shield and Desert Storm as part of the 1st Marine Division. He wrote the short story *Taking Chance* while serving with the Marine Corps Combat Development Command in Quantico, Virginia, in April 2004. He retired from the Marine Corps in 2007.

Seeing a casket carried into a funeral home is not an unusual sight—unless the casket is a prop and the pallbearers are film crew members. Such was the scene as *Taking Chance* began filming on Willson Avenue, Bozeman, outside Dokken-Nelson Funeral Service on the morning of August 17, 2007. Dokken-Nelson's manager, Chris Remely, was surprised by the amount of equipment and personnel needed to film even a small scene involving only three actors. "It is a production, my goodness," said Remely. The production, which had a budget of $10 million, took over much of the block immediately south of Babcock Street between Willson and Grant avenues. Other scenes were filmed at the Yellowstone Jet Center at the Gallatin Field Airport. Crews filmed inside an airplane mock-up.

The film's production design and art detail had to be meticulous. "This was a very difficult props movie," said director Katz, "because there are about a billion specific props that have to do with the military. We would go page by page through the script. I would describe a watch that someone was wearing. Our prop master, Rob Currie, would come to the set with seven options. He'd say, 'I know you said black, but Alar and I are worried about the reflection of this watch, so I've gotten these others, which I think are creatively what you want, but they're better for camera.'"

In *Taking Chance*, Kevin Bacon (left) accompanies the body of an American Marine back to his family in Wyoming, played by Montana.

"*Taking Chance* is a realistic film," said casting director Tina Buckingham "In the airplane scene, when they are taking the casket off of the airplane and people are paying their respects, people were crying. We had seven hundred people in downtown Ennis for the funeral scene and during the scene at Boot Hill for the burial, it was maybe June, all the lilac bushes were in bloom. They used artificial lilacs and wired them on the bushes. Kevin Bacon was present and nice. Some actors have edicts that you can't talk to them or take pictures. But he hung out and was present. It's funny, but at one point, I had all of these military guys—all actors—lined up in one spot and Bacon stopped by and thanked them for their service and their sacrifices. I had to whisper in his ear that they were actors." Locals Ben Trotter and Jordan Hildebrant had the chance to alternate as Bacon's stand-in, spending about 12 hours a day on the set, at approximately $120 per day.

The film crew spent about eight days in Montana, dividing its time among Bozeman, Virginia City, and Ennis. Collectively, the locations stood in for Phelps' Wyoming hometown.

Producer Lorie Douglas said about 80 people worked on the film in Bozeman, including around 40 local workers occupying positions from grips to production assistants to drivers. Several days would be spent in Ennis, filming the funeral procession scene and, along area roads, shooting some of the many driving scenes in the film. No one was allowed on the closed set inside the funeral home. Douglas said it was because of the nature of the scene. "This is the interior of the funeral home where our lead actor will first encounter Chance Phelps in his casket," said Douglas. "It's a very sensitive thing, especially when you're dealing with a true story."

"*Taking Chance* was a great production for Montana," said Iversen. "Wyoming tried to get it. But in order for the movie to take place in the real town in Wyoming, it just didn't work logistically. It was a remote town, no hotels, too far away, and they wanted a town like Bozeman that could support the main production. In *Taking Chance*, we doubled Ennis for Wyoming. There are great scenes at the Virginia City cemetery. It was a poignant movie and people were all very aware of the meaning behind it and story."

The *New York Daily News* lauded *Taking Chance*: "By all contemporary standards of filmmaking, 'Taking Chance' shouldn't work. It's a war movie with virtually no war action. It's a movie in which one main character is dead and the other main character hardly speaks. It bets against the odds, and it wins big. It's the most singular film you're apt to see this year, and very likely the most moving."

The film is touching, moving, caring and pays homage to the life and story of the individual who sadly ends up coming home in a flag-draped coffin. The film is an honest, non-politicized look at what war means in the context of a single person and all those who have been touched by him or her.

Iversen singled it out as one of most special productions he had the opportunity to be associated with. "That was the first film crew allowed at Dover Air Force Base and the permission went all the way to the Chief of Staff. Everything in it had to be very correct. We worked hard to get that correct. The entire town of Dubois, Wyoming, came and re-created their parts. It felt as if almost the whole town of Dubois was there. The effect on the town [of Phelps' death] was devastating. The film was opening them up to terrible memories. It was very poignant. There were a lot of quiet vibrations around it. *Taking Chance* won every single award it could win—Golden Globe, Emmy awards—and it was a privilege to work on a film of that caliber."

Telefon

CAST
Charles Bronson, Lee Remick

DIRECTOR
Don Siegel

LOCATION
Great Falls

1977

The year 1977 saw the release of *Telefon*, a bizarre spy thriller produced by James B. Harris in which Charles Bronson portrays Russian KGB agent Major Borzov, out to stop an unhinged Stalinist defector from unleashing a fury of sabotage across the United States. Nicolai Dalchimsky (Donald Pleasance) is a KGB records clerk and renegade Stalinist agent, upset by the cooling off of the Cold War between the Soviet Union and the United States. He steals a notebook of names of sleeping undercover KGB agents sent to the U.S. in the 1950s. Operatives received their assignments under hypnosis, triggering their missions upon hearing four lines from a Robert Frost poem.

Dalchimsky escapes to America and phones these agents, who perform acts of subversion against military targets. Bronson's task is to thwart a plot that could escalate to World War III. Crucial in the casting was Bronson as Borzov, a craggy, taciturn character that perfectly suited Bronson's bitter screen persona. Filming landed him in Finland—doubling as Russia—and there are several cameo appearances by Finnish movie stars. Helsinki pinch-hit for Moscow, with areas of the Finnish capital variously doubling for KGB headquarters, a Moscow apartment house and skating rink. The city skyline depicting Houston, Texas, is actually Great Falls, Montana, where the majority of the film was shot. The exploding building in one scene is the controlled demolition of the old Paris Gibson Junior High School. The Houston scenes were shot on a Hollywood back lot.

Filming in Great Falls began in February 1977. As Bronson exited the airport on February 13, 1977, a huge black limo waited for him at the curb with a swarm of

Filmed partly in Great Falls, *Telefon* was a bizarre spy thriller starring Charles Bronson (left) and Lee Remick (in the car).

autograph seekers crowded around it. According to one eyewitness, there were "throngs of fans." Some had placards that read "Charlie Bronson, Great Falls Loves You."

Telefon, released Christmas 1977, continued along the familiar pattern of Bronson films. With his slanted eyes and chiseled stoic face, Bronson made a credible Russian. Don Siegel, maker of *The Shootist* and scores of other action-packed dramas, directed the movie. Siegel was full of praise for Bronson, telling *Photoplay* in April 1978: "He is a very helpful actor in planning or staging a scene. He gets wonderful ideas, good practical suggestions and I enjoy his contributions. He's a positive force for good in this grinding work of making a film. He's patient when the work is difficult and he's never satisfied until he's convinced what's been done is right. He's my kind of actor, you might say. He's a true loner. After work he goes straight home to his wife and family; no pause for an after work drink or chitchat."

Charles' nephew Terry Buchinsky, who worked as his stand-in on *Telefon* and other movie sets, managed to shed a little light on the private actor. "My uncle is a very kind man," he said. "It's impossible to watch him on the screen and still believe he's the same person as the man who taught me to swim when I was a kid. I never saw anybody who loved kids so much." On the set of the film Bronson was asked about his mystique, and he said he had one hard and fast rule: "I guard my privacy…They can have my work but not my life."

Sequences of sabotage provided technical challenges. The first of these scenes depicted agent Harry Bascomb driving a truck full of explosives into an Air National Guard base and destroying an immense building in the blast. Great Falls was planning to tear down a local school, and the *Telefon* filmmakers arranged to incorporate its destruction into the filming.

Central High School in Great Falls opened in 1896. The gargantuan blocks of sandstone that formed the walls came from a quarry near Helena and rested on a founda-

In one scene in *Telefon*, a building is blown up. The actual building was the annex of the old Paris Gibson Junior High School in Great Falls, which had been scheduled for demolition anyway. A local crowd watched the fiery scene.

tion sixteen-feet thick in some places. In 1913, a brick annex with an auditorium and gymnasium doubled the size of the school. From 1930 to the 1970s, the school served as Paris Gibson Junior High. In 1977, it became the Paris Gibson Square Museum of Art. But just before this adaptive reuse, film crews blew up the annex.

Cinematographers filmed the sequence with seven cameras and embellished the demolition with fire effects. As with the Helsinki shoot, the Great Falls location "experienced sub-zero temperatures" during filming, and Siegel admitted he was "frightened" when the head of the demolitions team told him he had never "dropped" a building in conjunction with additional explosions and fire effects before and "was not sure how it would turn out." Stunt coordinator Paul Baxley drove Bascom's truck into the front of the school for the beginning of the shot, and when the explosions detonated with no one injured, Siegel became "choked up with emotion—a first for me."

Siegel originally intended to shoot the final blazing finale in downtown Los Angeles at the Bonaventure Hotel. The Bonaventure's owners rebuffed the offer. Siegel decided to film at San Francisco's Hyatt; the director had a positive experience filming *Dirty Harry* in the city.

Siegel purportedly had disagreements with Bronson while working on the San Francisco location. Bronson complained about what Siegel termed "the filth of Market Street" and the "city's homeless population," and when Siegel argued that at least San Francisco has excellent food, Bronson hit his own muscular stomach and remarked, "I don't eat."

Cue magazine skewered the espionage yarn, writing "the action moves from Moscow to various U.S. cities, and while the film is busy, it is also dull and ridiculous." *Films and Filming* took the hostility one step further: "I would suggest that if you take *Telefon* as a black comedy, everything will be fine. If you demand a more serious attitude to East-West relations, you would do best to stay away."

The Soviets quickly denounced the film, branding it as "naive and banal." *Telefon*, the Soviets claimed, attempted to "stoke up a psychosis against the Soviet Union in the Western countries reminiscent of days long since past." *Izvestia* called the film a predictable dirty trick from "notorious Western intelligence agencies." The Moscow-directed blast left Bronson unmoved. "I'm not offended by anything the Russians or anyone else said," Bronson said. "They simply didn't say anything offensive. I don't think there's anything wrong with being in the CIA or the FBI. I think they're doing a great job. I know some guys from the CIA and they're great guys." If such sentiments did not exactly turn on the liberal lights in the Hollywood hills or Capitol Hill, Bronson could not have cared less. Bronson's opinion of most of Hollywood's younger stars was quickly stated: They are "full of bull. They decorate themselves with affairs and politics. It's all bull."

The Ballad of Little Jo

CAST
Suzy Amis, Ian McKellen

DIRECTOR
Maggie Greenwald

LOCATION
Red Lodge area

1993

Red Lodge is nestled on the edge of the half-million acre Beartooth-Absaroka Wilderness Area. At the northern Great Plains intersection with the majestic Rockies, Red Lodge is a former coal mining town which today combines western ranching country and traditions with high-mountain scenery and recreation. Red Lodge is a unique synthesis of old and new—and a perfect movie setting.

Several productions have come to Red Lodge, most notably *The Ballad of Little Jo*, based a true story of a woman who disguises herself as a man to survive the hardships of the Old West. On the banks of Montana's Rosebud Creek, a surly Suzy Amis swings off her Appaloosa and uncorks a rifle shot. It's a scene from the nineteenth-century western filmed in wide-open Custer National Forest. Disgraced after bearing a child out of wedlock, Jo disguises herself as a man (yes, Amis hacks off her famous mane with a knife on-screen) and braves the western frontier. "I've always wanted to do a movie where I wear big period dresses and get to ride horse," said Amis.

In 1992, the independent film company Polygram started production of *The Ballad of Little Jo* in and around the Red Lodge area. It was the first feature film to be shot entirely on location in Red Lodge. Filming took about three months, and was centered along Rock Creek south of town and near the East Rosebud River. The period piece set in 1866 blended gritty visual realism with a contemporary feminist sensibility to tell the tale of Josephine Monaghan (Suzy Amis).

Shunned by her well-to-do family in the post–Civil War West after having a child out of wedlock, Josephine has left her baby with a sister and headed for parts unknown. Befriended by a seemingly benevolent tinker, Josephine barely escapes human slavery when the fellow tries to sell her to a couple of ruffians. Terrified of further depredations, she disguises herself in men's clothes, scarring her face with a straight razor to keep the predators away. She drifts into the rugged mining town of Ruby City, Montana, and begins her new life as a man. She had realized that, as a woman, her options are to be a wife or a whore; as a man, however, Little Jo soon becomes a respected if admittedly peculiar member of the community.

Jo adopts the life of a hermit, staking out a remote spread on which to raise sheep, and only coming to town for the essentials. The less she is subjected to male-dominated civilization, the less likely her secret will be exposed.

It's the true story of Josephine Monaghan of Buffalo, New York, a society girl who in 1866 became Little Jo Monaghan, an Idaho rancher, and lived out her life as a man. Jo was so convincing, her secret wasn't discovered until she died in 1903 and the shocked undertaker blurted out, "Little Jo—he was a woman!"

"She [Amis] has a face that can be believed as a boy," said director Maggie Greenwald. Amis learned to ride, wrangle sheep, dig for gold, shoot and—most difficult, she declared—wear a corset when she was Josephine. Her assessment of a woman's life on the frontier? "Hell," said Amis.

Montanan Walt Secrest had nine parts in this film, ranging from driver of a runaway horse and buggy to a man going to market with chickens and sacks of vegetables. But Walt's most interesting role in the film was when he assisted a naked prostitute. "I'm in an outhouse area and hear music outside," said Secrest. "I come outside buttoning my pants and there's a midget playing a little squeeze box leading a llama with a pack and a white horse with a naked prostitute on it. I led the horse to the saloon and the miners gathered around. He walked up three stairs to the saloon, and I help her off the horse."

Producer Brenda Goodman, who had a budget of $3.5 million, scouted four states and much of Montana before choosing the Red Lodge area. "We chose Red Lodge for its natural and diverse beauty as well as what the town and people have to offer," said Goodman. The population of the fictitious western town of Ruby City was about 60 souls.

Filming started on September 22 and ended November 15, 1992. "Ruby City," where most of the filming took place, was actually located outside Red Lodge, about 12 miles up the Beartooth Pass, near the M-K Campground and at the foot of Hell Roaring Plateau. The buildings of Ruby City, like Addie's Saloon, were built in the hangar of the Red Lodge Airport and trucked to the set. A construction crew built a cabin near Rosebud Lake for a scene there. Filming one day was done on the Meeteetse Trail. Another day, Grizzly Peak Realty in Red Lodge was turned into a studio. "Call Time"—the start of the work day at "Ruby City"—varied. Sometimes it was during the day. Quitting time was generally 3:30 A.M.

"To see a movie end is always a mixed feeling," said co-producer Brenda Goodman. "You're exhausted. You can't wait to get some rest. You can't wait to not have to get up at 5 and not have to stand out in the cold all day. But on the other hand it's been a great shoot. It's almost like postpartum depression when a movie ends. No matter how much you prepare for it, it happens every time."

"*The Ballad of Little Jo* had some really beautiful scenery around Red Lodge," said Chad Branham, the movie's on-set dresser: "We built a log cabin along the creek and built a prairie house in the prairie—half a shack. Essen-

tially, we had this whole Western town—an actual model—built at the base of the Beartooth Road. There was a back road at the bend, and we had three false fronts, a mining camp, and a whole bunch of stuff. Later, I went back to find that same location and it didn't look the same. Since it was on National Forest land, everything had to be removed.

"There is a scene with a dead sheep and one of the ranchers gave us an actual dead sheep and we put it in the freezer and saved it. I think a wolf killed it or something and we brought it to the set for the scene and thawed it out. We drug it over to where [the killing] was supposed to take place, sliced it open and pulled its innards out. One of art guys dumped a gallon of blood on it and it looked like a massacre. Three people from the New York production crew walked in and they weren't used to seeing dead critters. I don't think they ever forgot that."

Director Maggie Greenwald said she loves Westerns and always wanted to make one. "It is a white-male–dominated genre," said Greenwald. "The challenge for me was to find a story through which my point of view of the world could be expressed in this genre. Women—and blacks and Asians—played a pivotal role in settling the West, a fact that has been ignored in the film industry. "It is a story of a woman's life in the West, and there are almost no films about women in the West."

Entertainment Weekly declared *The Ballad of Little Jo* "an enchanting, plainspoken sleeper" before adding, "the cinematography is ravishing." *Daily Variety* credited Amis's "full-bodied performance" with making the film worthy and ended its review with this equally full-bodied endorsement of Montana movie magic: "Handsomely lensed by Declan Quinn in southern Montana, pic captures both the beauty and harshness of the vast uninhabited landscape and the indomitable spirit of one fearless woman."

A young John Wayne poses on the set of *The Big Trail*, filmed partly on the National Bison Range near Moiese. The part was Wayne's first leading role.

The Big Trail

Cast
John Wayne, Tyrone Power, Sr.

Director
Raoul Walsh

Location
Moiese, National Buffalo Range

1931

The Big Trail is a 1930 pre-code early widescreen movie shot on location across the American West, starring John Wayne in his first leading role and directed by Raoul Walsh.

Film crews passed through Missoula on July 16, 1930, on a special Fox film train en route to California, via Butte, from Moiese where they had been filming several buffalo scenes. Buffalo from the government range at Dixon were used in the scenes with the great Mission Range as a background. The scenes were among the final ones to be taken for the picture which had been shooting for several months. There were approximately 400 regular actors in the cast, 100 of which were on the train in Moiese. The others were engaged in filming final touches in other Western states.

Though only one-fourth of the artists engaged in making the picture were at Moiese for the several days of filming, all of the principal actors and actresses were in the group.

After the film was approved by the producers at Fox Studios in early 1930, Walsh offered the lead to Helena-born actor Gary Cooper, who couldn't accept it. Walsh then asked friend and fellow director John Ford for suggestions: Ford recommended a then-unknown kid from Iowa named John Wayne because he "liked the looks of this new kid with a funny walk, like he owned the world." When Wayne professed inexperience, Walsh told him to just "sit good on a horse and point."

The scene of the wagon train drive across the country was pioneering in its use of camera work and the depth and view of the epic landscape. An attempt was made to contribute authenticity to the movie, with the wagons drawn by oxen instead of horses—they were lowered by ropes down canyons when necessary for certain shots in tight valleys. Locations in five states, starting from New Mexico and ending in California, were used to film the caravan's 2,000-mile trek. Several scenes were filmed at the 18,500-acre National Bison Range in Moiese.

One of the principal parts of the intricate machinery used for pictures and sound in filming the picture at Moiese was a special machine known as the "grandeur production," having a larger scale of reproduction than other cameras. It was one of the most recent inventions in the moving picture world and was said to be used "only in three theaters in the country." Its use at Moiese was said to be "the first time for such work."

After shooting, the film was previewed to select audiences and released generally in October 1930. The movie quickly became a box office dud because it was released as a widescreen film during a time when theatres would not change over their standard screens due to the huge cost, and mainly because the Great Depression left so many exhibitors almost financially ruined. The film barely made its huge investment back. It would be almost 20 years before the concept of widescreen films would be put back into general production.

After completion of the film, Wayne found work only in low-budget serials and features until the 1939 film *Stagecoach* brought him to mainstream prominence.

In 2006, the United States Library of Congress deemed *The Big Trail* "culturally, historically, or aesthetically significant," and selected it for preservation in the National Film Registry, saying "the plot of a trek along the Oregon Trail is aided immensely by the majestic sweep provided by the experimental Grandeur widescreen process used in filming."

and pilgrimages in search of real-life Narnias in England, Northern Ireland, and New Zealand, where several key locations were filmed.

Fans of Narnia may add Montana to the list of magical places linked to the mythical world. "The principal shoot actually took place in New Zealand—the home of middle earth," said scout John Ansotegui. "But after filming was completed and they had begun postproduction in Los Angeles, they realized they needed more footage. The *Narnia* scout had remembered his time working on *Hidalgo* and suggested that Glacier National Park had everything they needed. Instead of flying everyone to New Zealand, they packed up a second crew and send them to Montana. Producers shot the missing scene in Montana. They actually hired a crew, shot scenes to double Montana as New Zealand and added the actors and lion in digitally in postproduction."

The Chronicles of Narnia: The Lion, The Witch and The Wardrobe

CAST
Georgie Henley, Skandar Keynes

DIRECTOR
Andrew Adamson

LOCATION
Glacier National Park, St. Ignatius,
and Helmville areas.

2005

The Devil Horse

CAST
Yakima Canutt, Rex the Wonder Horse

DIRECTOR
Fred Jackman

LOCATION
Hardin area

1926

Several second-unit scenes shot in Montana appear in the film. The second-unit is a small, subordinate crew responsible for filming shots of less importance, such as inserts, crowds, scenery, etc.

In Disney's blockbuster movie *The Chronicles of Narnia: The Lion, the Witch and the Wardrobe*, four young siblings use a wardrobe door to travel from wartime England to the fairy-tale landscapes of Narnia, the imaginary world made famous by British novelist C.S. Lewis. The celluloid version of Lewis' classic sparked related tours

"'Rex, the Devil Horse' Tells Story of Old West in Novel Manner," trumpeted the March 1926 issue of *Drama and Silver Screen*. The film was billed as the "last remaining evidence of the famous old West."

Promotional material for the film preserves the reverential parlance of the time: "The Buffalo has been corralled, the stage coach put away, the Indians quieted: and the pony express almost forgotten, but 'Rex—The Devil Horse,' plants the spirit anew in the breasts of those that have known and loved that great section of the country

One of the earliest movies made in Montana, *The Devil Horse* featured rodeo champion Yakima Canutt fighting to protect actress Gladys McConnell. The movie also starred Rex the Wonder Horse.

Rachael Leigh Cook starred in *The Hi-Line*, filmed in the Livingston area. PHOTO BY AUDREY HALL.

that has come to be known as the West. This horse plays a part that is most human and uncanny."

As the story unfolds, Rex had been the faithful companion of a small boy, the son of a pioneer. Boy and colt were inseparable. The rest of the plot is described by Hal Roach Studios press kit: "The Indians swooped down on the cavalcade one day and, after killing all the adults, stole the boy and drove the colt away into the mountains. The hatred born of the brutal treatment that he had received at the hands of the Indians made him known as the Devil Horse. Years later the boy, now grown to manhood, has been captured by enemies and is tied to a stake—ready to be burned."

The Devil Horse appears and the captors flee, but the horse senses something about this man that is familiar. Rex frees him from his bonds, and he and his newfound friend and master start on a campaign of vengeance·that has much to do with his story. A love story is wound into the picture and the Devil Horse also finds a mate.

"This is one of the truly great novelty pictures of years and was obtained by Hal Roach only after many months of painstaking work and worry," said the *Minneapolis Star Tribune*. While many scenes were filmed at the 500-acre Iverson Ranch in Chatsworth, California, the location site of hundreds of films and television shows from the 1910s to the late 1960s, several of the movie's visually exquisite shots come courtesy of the Little Big Horn River area.

"The entire production was filmed in the Indian country and for scenery never equaled," erroneously boasted *The Dallas Morning News*.

The Hi-Line

CAST
Ryan Alosio, Rachael Leigh Cook

DIRECTOR
Ron Judkins

LOCATION
Livingston area

1999

At age 20, Vera Johnson (Rachael Leigh Cook) is two years out of high school but still living with her parents Clyde and Laura. Passing time with a part-time job, she yearns for a life beyond the limits of her small town. Her wishes come true when a dubious 32-year-old liquor store clerk from the south side of Chicago (Ryan Alosio) arrives at her door with news of her true parentage. The scam artist convinces the naive young woman in fictitious Whitman, Montana, that she is to be given a job by a major Chicago discount store. However, her dad and mom see through the ruse and try to have him run out of town.

The man claims that he has a letter from a death-row inmate in Illinois who recently died in prison. The letter indicates that the young woman was fathered by him and a woman named Estelle and was placed in this couple's

Montana's wintry weather was very real for *The Hi-Line* stars Rachael Leigh Cook and Ryan Alosio, who nearly became hypothermic during filming. PHOTO BY AUDREY HALL.

care. This leads the young woman into a search for her real mother, who it turns out is a Blackfoot woman living on the Hi-Line, a sparsely settled area in northern Montana. Cook's character is the adopted daughter of Montana parents portrayed by Stuart Margolin and Margot Kidder. Kidder is a Paradise Valley resident who starred in the *Superman* movies of the 1970s.

"It's a real intimate story," said co-producer Colin Phillips.

"They didn't really work with us other than initial location info in the beginning and then some minor troubleshooting during production," said Montana Film Commissioner Lonie Stimac.

"I believe they actually filmed in the greater Livingston area, including Wilsall. At that time Livingston had a real buzz about it as a hip place to shoot. At the same time, because the diversity of landscape in a 90-mile radius, it was a logical place to base out of. Plus it made an easy sell to the money guys. How could they argue with the location that Robert Redford had chosen twice? Plus

Hollywood was familiar with it as a second home and vacation destination.

"Great Falls would have provided the same location opportunities and better logistics but it didn't have the same allure. While it was frustrating to those who knew better, and [despite] our bosses who wanted to see movies spread throughout the state, particularly as the movie's name was *The Hi-Line*, there really wasn't a reason to go there to film."

Christine Schuman, production designer on *The Hi-Line,* recalled the frigid days of filming, primarily around Livingston and Clyde Park in a cabin.

"There were days when it was twenty below zero and actor Ryan Alosio, he actually got hypothermia at night, at night working, during a scene, we tried to get him warm by putting the car inside the old garage on the north side of the railroad tracks," said Schuman. "The scene in which he took his coat off and is in short-sleeves, well, he got real sick that night. We were lucky he didn't get hypothermia. They got blankets to keep him warm and a vehicle. He had to get in and out, and in the movie it's an unheated car and the scenes were pretty long. When you see that scene, you would never think that was right at the moment of hypothermia."

"We put in long hours. I remember February 22 was one cold day. One of the things for me as production designer that seemed like a conundrum was that we had to put ice on the windows, to make an ice-crowded window. We are used to seeing ice and snow, but you still have to make it for movies. It has to be where and when they want to film it, so you have to scrape windows and then add it when they want it."

In addition to feeling the bitter cold, one of the other occupational hazards of filmmaking is sometimes being subjected to all kinds of harsh stenches. "We did one scene in the cabin up Rock Creek, out at Clyde Park," recalled Schuman. "We found an old house and the cows had been in it. We had to clean four feet of cow manure. We had to repair the old house [so] we did it, even the… ceilings. But a couple of days before we got in a skunk had gotten it. And the crew had to work through that."

Allison Whitmer, who worked as the film's property master, colorfully recalled the filming. "It was so bloody cold," said Whitmer. "During the shooting at the mother's cabin out on the prairie, we encountered a shack full of cow [pies] and it smelled like [it]. The dance sequences that were set in Chicago were filmed at the Gallatin Gateway Inn. It's the scene that is on the radio and they are listening to the broadcast from one of the big hotels, and later meet up in Chicago."

The budget was "well, well under" $500,000, according to Phillips. The project started out as a "credit card film," he said, but the strength of the script, and director Ron Judkins' connections to Steven Spielberg's production company, where he had worked as a sound man on a number of films, attracted help.

Reviews of *The Hi-Line* ranged from enthusiastic to laudatory, including this nod from the *Minneapolis City Pages*. "*The Hi-Line* has the feel of a Carson McCullers short story transplanted from the Southern environs to colder climes."

The *Austin Chronicle* noted the unique subculture of Montana the film attempted to depict. "Judkins paints his characters with respect, allowing them to hold on to their isolated world without losing their dignity. These are not smart people, but they're good people, and through the performances of the actors, we grow to care about them.

Although their story seems familiar, on closer inspection, it is entirely unique."

The *Hollywood Reporter* labeled the film "a tantalizing near-miss," but praised the production as "beautifully photographed and capably performed."

"Technically, the film is a small marvel, in particular the evocative, descriptive production design of Christine Schuman, the brooding cinematography of Wally Pfister and the fluid editing by Charlie Webber…Late in the film, a single pan that shifts the action from the barren Montana flatlands to Chicago's lakefront is haunting. It only points out the missed opportunities. Indeed, one leaves 'The Hi-Line' wishing the words lived up to the images."

The Horse Whisperer

CAST
Robert Redford, Kristin Scott Thomas, Sam Neill

DIRECTOR
Robert Redford

LOCATION
Big Timber and Livingston areas

1998

Beauty, vision, spirituality. Some films have a way of capturing the essence and meaning of life. From the pages of a script where carefully crafted words blend to create the stories of our lives, to the director who shapes those visions into action, a film is a confluence of hope and dreams. However, not even the best of stories, not even the most titanic of directors can bring together the cinematic process with the right location. For it is there, the place where the sun drops behind majestic mountains and the Earth brings with it a raw sense of nature, that a picture truly comes to life. Sometimes the location is integral, sometimes it is a bit player, but above all else, locations complement a film. For *The Horse Whisperer*,

For *The Horse Whisperer*, Montana could be considered one of the film's stars. Filmed mostly in the Livingston area, the movie was directed by Robert Redford, who also played one of the film's lead characters.

inspired by Nicholas Evans' novel, Montana could be considered one of the film's stars.

The story follows a family and its heartbreak following a riding accident that leaves daughter Grace disabled. To mend broken spirits and heal internal wounds, mother Annie and daughter travel to Montana, taking with them a tortured horse whose spirit has also been fractured. *The Horse Whisperer* character can be attributed to horse trainer Buck Brannaman, who was born in Wisconsin, grew up in Montana and Idaho, and worked as a technical advisor on the film. The film features Scarlett Johansson in an early role.

Principal photography began on location in Saratoga Springs, New York, with the filming of the accident sequence that opens the story. From there, the company moved to Manhattan for scenes in the MacLean family apartment, the exterior of Grace's school, and Annie MacLean's office.

Following the East Coast portion of filming and a brief hiatus to allow the snow to melt in the West, production resumed with the company moving to Park and Sweet Grass counties in Montana in early June. The runoff of melting snow was still substantial, and the crew faced flooded sets and soggy ground for several weeks, keeping an eye on the high water in neighboring rivers swollen above flood stage from the immense snowpack left behind by the winter of 1997.

"We were essentially chasing the seasons for most of the shooting schedule," said executive producer Patrick Markey. "Although it was one of the wettest summers on record in Montana, in a way, the weather served us very well." The production did have to compete with mercurial Montanaesque elements, including ground flooding, inexplicable bouts of thunder and lightning and hearty winds that knocked down tents and set elements.

"There is something about the combination of the drama of scale from the plains and the mountains that is unique to Montana," said production designer Jon Hutman. "For the opening of the film, we wanted to synthesize the East coast environment into something very spare and structured and minimal, in order to very succinctly define where Annie and Grace were journeying from. But as they made the transition, we were looking for a life-altering sense of space that would be initially overwhelming to these characters. The environment in Montana wasn't just a backdrop for the story, it embodied the power of Tom Booker [Robert Redford's role] and also the power of the land and place, which is also what the story is about."

"We looked at 300 ranches all the way from Nevada to British Columbia," said Markey of his search for the fictitious Double Divide Ranch. "We continued to narrow it down and ended up with a few choices in Colorado and few in Montana. One ranch on the Boulder River in Montana seemed to have it…it all came together there," said Markey. That location was close to where *A River Runs Through It* was filmed. "It was completely serendipitous. It's nice to go back," said Markey. "Whisperer" arrived in Montana in May and shot though September, with 70 percent of the Big Sky filming taking place on the ranch and the other 30 percent at locations within 100 miles of the ranch.

When a quick downpour caused a torrent of rain to gush through the set and damage construction materials, the production took it in stride, and looked at it from the bright side.

"All the wet and water gave us a lush, green look for the movie," said Markey. "Fourth of July starts to brown out from the lack of water. We were able to hold that green look of spring in September. What appeared to be a curse turned out to be this extra gift we were given."

The principal location was the working cattle ranch of the Engle family, southeast of Livingston, where the cast and crew were based. During production, the rigors and practices of daily life moved forward. "The Engles' ranch is a real working ranch that has been in their family for a couple of generations," said Hutman. "We chose it because of the river and the mountains and the vistas, and there is a look and a feeling of reality to that ranch. The land also has wonderfully varied qualities that allowed us to incorporate other nearby locations to create the complete environment."

"With today's filmmaking technology," said Robert Redford, discussing his approach to the cinematography with *Time*, "there are all kinds of ways you can make anything look good with filters and optical treatments and so forth The truth is that the real West is pretty powerful and quite beautiful just the way it is. I was more interested in trying to show it in a way that would make you feel it changing, to let the clouds come and go and color a scene accordingly."

"The visual style of the film played a huge role in the making of *The Horse Whisperer*. The visual aspect is very important to me because I was an artist, yet I didn't want to put it out there and brandish it or headline it. You want to make it sort of seamless in a way that the audience will be able to experience something and feel it, rather than feeling urged to comment on it."

Production designer Hutman chose to build a ranch house for the Booker family as well as the adjacent Creek House, both along a river. "In the story, there is a specific physical connection between the two buildings," said Hutman. "Building our own house also meant that we could make the rooms big enough to shoot in. It was like having the best of a real house with the best of a set. And constructing it on location allowed us to the freedom to incorporate the environment into the shots as we wished."

Hutman came to his design of the ranch house after scouting over 100 actual ranch houses as possible locations for the film. "We wanted to convey the quality or sense that several generations of the Booker family had lived in this house over a period of time, to give the environment a reality and weight and a rich history," he said. "So you see that there are original cabinets and then others remodeled in the '50s or '60s. The fireplace has a wood-burning stove inside it because that is just a more efficient update. For Tom Booker's room, we wanted to create a place that had an ascetic sparseness without making him monk-like."

The movie-makers devised a way to transform Big Timber into Hardin, at least the part near the Little Bighorn Battlefield (a stop along Annie and Grace's drive to Montana). They landscaped the Crazy Mountain Museum and the cemetery nearby to play the part in the movie of the cemetery near the battlefield. Trees, gates, bushes—"it cost a pretty penny," said film publicist Kathy Orloff—went up overnight.

Brannaman was a key model for the Tom Booker character in Nicholas Evans novel. Brannaman grew up in a foster home near Norris, Montana. He always wanted to be a cowboy. Inspired by his loving foster father, he began performing trick roping with his brother when he was six years old. In time he met famed horse clinician and trainer Ray Hunt, who became his mentor.

Brannaman's methods of dealing with young colts and difficult older animals earned him recognition. "When we started doing research, Buck's name kept coming to the top of the list," said Markey. "He is the third in a line of horse trainers who use this particular methodology. Tom Dorrance was the grandfather of the movement followed by Ray Hunt, who mentored Buck. Buck is the heir apparent to this training approach.

"Buck is all about establishing a very intimate and trusting relationship with the animal and then never violating that trust," added Markey, who, along with Redford, attended several of Brannaman's seminars. "He shows the owner of the animal how to get the best results from their horse by having the horse trust them, as opposed to being afraid of them. Without sounding too new-agey, people tend to pass on whatever is troubling them to their horse. The horse acts up as a result of them transferring this baggage. Buck shows them how to deal with that stuff themselves and how not to put it onto the horse. He unlocks those secrets from people's psyches all the time."

Costume designer Judy L. Ruskin tried to duplicate the authentic look of the modern cowboy. "The approach was in how to represent an American ranch in the contemporary West," said Ruskin. "The ranchers wear predominantly American-made clothing from Levis, Wrangler, Woolrich and Carhart, with Justin Boots and hats by Bailey. I believe that people working on ranches try to support American products, so that credibility is seen through the wardrobe.

"Don Edwards plays ranch hand Smokey and his clothing is very similar to everyone else's, but his style is very much his own. He makes his own ranch-hand crease, the way he's been wearing it for years. And the way he buttons up his shirts is very proper and old-fashioned and charming."

Legendary costume designer Bernie Pollack has designed Robert Redford's wardrobe for more than 20 films since 1965, including the westerns *Jeremiah Johnson* and *The Electric Horseman*. "In *The Horse Whisperer*, Tom Booker is pure, a man of the soil, but he's got another dimension to him in that he's a real healer," said Pollack. "For Tom Booker, I wanted to incorporate some distinctive style, but I was also careful to stay true to the essence of Booker's code as a rancher, a healer, and an intentionally simple man."

Pollack had much of Booker's horse-work clothing suited to the style he envisioned for the character and had most of the accessories custom-made in Montana. Redford's hats were made by John Morris of the Rocky Mountain Hat Company in Bozeman. Master saddle-maker Chas. Weldon, of Billings, created saddles, chaps and hand-tooled belts finished with sterling silver buckles.

Markey said that he was committed to an accurate presentation of horses and horse handling: "We wanted to approach horse training in the right way, just as we did with fly fishing in *A River Runs Through It*, so that when people who knew something about horses would go to see the movie, they would come away saying 'You know, those guys did a pretty good job with that horse work.' And for both films, we really sought out the best people we could find to instruct us and guide us, and to make sure we had our methodology correct."

Redford utilized five separate horses. "Redford could ride anything that we brought in," said head wrangler Mike Boyle. "Some of the other actors needed a little brushing up. I think Scarlett Johansson started out pretty scared, but she's one of those people who doesn't say she's scared or show fear. And she made a two hundred per cent change and improvement. She got to where I could put her on any horse on the set and she could just lope off and have fun."

Markey said that Brannaman developed a keen eye for filming angles and the horseman didn't hesitate to share his opinions, which was all for the better. "Buck and his number-one man, Curt Pate, started suggesting shots and ways of covering scenes," said Markey. "They saw different approaches to using the camera around horses, that sometimes ended up being more effective than what we had chosen to do, and they didn't know anything about our business before starting production."

"My day job is that I ranch a little bit on the side," said Brannaman. "But for real, I teach people how to work with their horses. I do colt-starting horsemanship clinics, work with problem horses, much the same as with the story in the movie, only I usually have to do it all in a weekend.

"What I have in mind when I'm working with a horse is to consider how the horse got into the situation he's in. If he's troubled or scared or worried or upset, I try to understand what got him there. Sometimes they just start out that way. Sometimes it's a result of poor handling. But if you can understand what got the horse in trouble, and you think of it from the horse's point of view, the solution is there as well. Every horse is an individual, just like every human. You really have to understand them from the inside, and then the outside kind of takes care of itself."

Brannaman, 54, who lives in Sheridan, Wyoming, rejects the term "Horse Whisperer." "It's hard to find someone who isn't a horse whisperer these days. I'm not offended by the term, but the way I see it, if I went around telling people that's what I was, I'd be a phony anyway. So I'll leave the labels to everyone else. I don't think I need that."

He, however, has no regrets jumping on board as technical advisor. "I felt like they were really interested in doing it right," said Brannaman. "They were so interested in it happening right that I really couldn't resist the temptation to help them tell the story. Movie audiences are very sophisticated, and a lot of horse people know good from bad. And I think it worked out well."

The Killer Inside Me

CAST
Susan Tyrell, Don Stroud, Tisha Sterling, Keenan
Wynn, Stacy Keach

DIRECTOR
Burt Kennedy

LOCATION
Butte

1974

From the opening scene at the Berkeley Pit and Stacy Keach's introduction to Central City, Montana, to actor Don Stroud's drunkenly shouting the name Butte while being hauled to jail, *The Killer Inside Me* is brined in the Mining City's sites and personality.

Shooting of *The Killer Inside Me* started in Butte in October 1974. Keach, 33 at the time, had prepared himself in earnest for a future in politics. He was studying law through extension courses and hoped to pass the California bar exam before he was 40. Determined to achieve his own goals, he had already directed his own television show, *Incident at Vichy*, written by Arthur Miller. He also directed a short film about a man living in a Southern prison, entitled *The Repeater*.

His father, Stacy Keach Sr., had produced and directed industrial films and was also an actor. Stacy began his career at 17, when a senior in high school in Los Angeles. He and some of his friends made their own horror films. They built some of their own equipment and even had their own screening room.

Twenty-four hours before Stacy arrived in Butte to begin filming *The Killer Inside Me*—a big-screen treatment of Jim Thompson's merciless and enthralling 1952 pulp novel about a psychotic West Texas sheriff—he was in Tennessee completing an ABC television Movie of the Week titled *All the Kind Strangers*. "I really suffered in the sweltering heat and humidity—it was a welcome relief to come to Butte," he said.

In the movie, Tisha Sterling portrays the innocent, loving girl friend of Lou Ford, played by Keach. The actress was no newcomer to Butte. Her first husband was born and reared there, and was a childhood friend of Evel Knievel. When they were first married, they hitchhiked from Los Angeles to Butte and bought an old Yellowstone Park touring bus to add to their collection of antique cars. The bus broke down near Helena, and Tisha recalled limping back to Butte in the vehicle at 10 miles per hour, stopping every five miles to make adjustments. The car dealer refused a refund, so Tisha flew back to Los Angeles while her husband had the bus repaired for the trip home.

Tisha's great-uncle, a Danish immigrant, had been a Billings resident for years, where he owned a bar before retiring. "I'm not a city person too much. I prefer to live in the country. I like nature things," she told the *Montana Standard*. Sterling began her theatrical career at 17, when she had a role in an Alfred Hitchcock television se-

Actors Stacey Keach (left) and Don Stroud talk during the filming of *The Killer Inside Me*. Filmed in Butte, the story is set in west Texas in the early 1950s.

ries. She then took a part in the play, *Chinese Prime Minister*, in New York. When the play closed, she returned to Los Angeles and worked there in movies, television and stage plays.

Character actor Keenan Wynn brought his considerable talent to bear in his role as Chester Conway. Steely eyed and flint-hearted, Conway is the gruff, pragmatic mayor and boss of the town's mining company. He rules town and company successfully with an iron will and hand. It's a strong part for a strong man, and Wynn seemed the perfect choice. "Acting in the movies is not B.S. today," growled Wynn to *Screen Magazine*, as "he stabbed the air with his forefinger."

"Movies are coming back to what they were 50 to 60 years ago. The emphasis is on reality. The phony mechanics are gone," he said. Wynn discussed Keach and his lead role. "Stacy is basically a character lead, like Spencer Tracy. He's an instinctive actor. He knows what's right. An actor who can display his emotions, like Brando can do, like Stacy can do, will move you. Stacy's role in *The Killer Inside Me* is a very difficult part, very difficult. He has to be truly schizophrenic."

Wynn said an instinctive actor has two things he uses constantly to convey his feelings—his eyes. Wynn turned to Montana's favorite star. "Gary Cooper was an embarrassed actor," said Wynn, friend and neighbor of Cooper before his death. "He didn't like to show emotion."

The Killer Inside Me, a decent representation of Thompson's novel, features some excellent footage of Butte, including sequences down in the Berkeley Pit, out on the flat near the Four Mile, and scenes around the School of Mines. While the original is so long on plot, character development and suspense that it could be considered tedious, the brash, fetishized violence of Michael Winterbottom's repulsive remake (2010) stands as a comparison of Hollywood's accelerated appetite for ultra-violence and coarseness.

The Last Ride

CAST
Mickey Rourke, Lori Singer, Aaron Neville

DIRECTOR
Michael Karbelnikoff

LOCATION
Bozeman area, Deer Lodge

1994

Set in present-day Montana, *The Last Ride* portrays a man trying to escape his criminal past and becoming involved with a woman born under a bad sign. Kalispell's Frank T. Wells (Mickey Rourke) is a newly-released ex-con looking for a few acres of freedom on the rodeo circuit. He has just been released after spending ten years in prison, the result of a manslaughter conviction stemming from an act of self-defense. Frank wants to rebuild his life and start his own ranch; to raise the money, he begins riding for pay.

While on the road, Frank meets a woman named Scarlet Stuart (Lori Singer), who has "F.T.W." tattooed on her hand (though it doesn't stand for "Frank T. Wells," but "F--- The World"); Scarlet was both part-

The Last Ride (shot under the working title F.T.W.) filmed at several Montana locations, including rodeo scenes at Wilsall and country dancing at Gallatin Gateway.

ner in crime and unwilling lover to her brother Clem, who recently died after shooting four people in a bank holdup. When Scarlet discovers Frank's initials are F.T.W., she believes it means that they were meant to be together, and they quickly fall into a relationship as Scarlet supports herself the way she knows best—armed robbery.

"*The Last Ride*—also known as "F.T.W"—is interesting," said Montana Film Commissioner Lonie Stimac. "HKM Productions was a company that came a lot to Montana and made several commercials in Montana. So they were familiar with Montana and they knew who to hire and what to do. But this was their first feature film. When they called about making a move instead of shooting commercials, the film wanted to know about union situation. We told them, 'You have to talk to the unions, if you are going to make a movie.' We said, 'If you think you can come in under the radar—just don't do it.' Lots of low-budgets movies shoot here. But they were too afraid or they did not want to make the deal with the unions. We told them that if they didn't, then don't look to film commission to protect you.

"But the company didn't follow labor law and when the Teamsters came and said, 'You have to talk to us,' the production called us to call off the Teamsters. They even wanted the governor to call out the National Guard so they didn't picket the movie. On top of that, they were shooting in Butte and asked for the National Guard—not a good idea."

Rourke wrote the 30-page screen treatment. It was Mickey Rourke's second movie in Montana. In 1979 he had an often-overlooked small role in Michael Cimino's *Heaven's Gate*. "I love Montana. I'd like to move here if I could afford it," he told producer Tom Mickel. "I've got an ex-wife and IRS problems." Saddle bronc back-up stunt rider Casey Fredericks of Great Falls said that Rourke was "really concerned about the riding." "He asked for our stunt riders' (Kevin Small and Chad Onstad) input because he wanted to get it right. He was really concerned with how it came off."

The movie filmed from August 9 to September 25, 1991. In addition to filming at Old Montana Prison, the Montana Power Company building and the courthouse in Deer Lodge, and locations in Butte, *The Last Ride* filmed three rodeo scenes in Wilsall. Wilsall, population 300, was chosen for its mountain scenery and rodeo grounds. After the filming there, the cameras moved to Montana State University and a warehouse in Bozeman. They then traveled to Three Forks, where the film crew shot some mud rodeo scenes for a prison rodeo sequence. To come up with good footage, they offered $100 extra to the cowboy who made the most spectacular fall into the mud. Extras in the film included rodeo watchers and cowboys and parts requiring specific casting including the prison scenes which called for "biker types" and the scene shot at Stacey's Bar in Gallatin Gateway requiring couples with "considerable country dancing skill."

"Cowboys, cons, and cars was literally what I was casting for," said casting director Tina Buckingham. "The movie shot five rodeos—a night, a mud rodeo, and they were all done in different places, including Wilsall, Livingston, Deer Lodge, and Three Forks, which was that mud rodeo. We casted extras as cons in Deer Lodge. Do you know how tough it is to cast shower scenes naked in a prison?

Mickey Rourke stayed in his trailer with entourage and little dog, but he was very professional. Rodney

Grant (who played Bucky Miller, Frank's best friend) of *Dances With Wolves* showed up with his hair cut off. He violated the first rule of casting: you don't change your look between being cast and showing up on the set."

The Northern Rodeo Association allowed filmmakers to capture the riding and roping activity. "I'm not into bull riding, I'm bull filming," said producer Tom Mickel. "I got some great stuff. I got some bad stuff too. I love shooting in Montana, any time of the year. What was important was finding the necessary rodeo and wilderness and a pool of cowboys to draw off." Screenwriter Michael Davis agreed. "I think this is where it was supposed to be," he said of the original Texas setting. "The production people had been here and Montana is one of the best places for rodeo."

The Park County Fairgrounds in Livingston was the site of several rodeo scenes. The general public was welcome to watch free of charge and be filmed in the grandstands for the movie. Occasionally the rodeo was delayed and the audience asked to be silent because scenes were being filmed behind the rodeo arena. Standing in front of the camera and beneath sound equipment to capture their every word and breath, Singer and Rourke talked. From afar, their lips moved silently before she grabbed him and they kissed passionately. Former rodeo champion Larry Mahan served as the film's technical adviser and set up the rodeo contests filmed on screen. A camera crew moved among the cowboys crowded behind the chutes, filming the bulls and bucking horses and the cowboys who climbed atop them. Walt Lockie, of Jordan, said the cowboys heard of the rodeo through a newsletter. He signed up because he thought it would "be kind of neat to see yourself in a movie."

In film, a scene that lasts about thirty seconds can take several hours to shoot. When a chase scene was filmed in Uptown Butte, it took five takes and almost three hours to get it right. For this scene, Singer's stunt double drives a late 1950s model Buick, and a stunt double for a cop drives one of the Butte police department's older cars. The Buick was parked adjacent to Harrington's Café on West Broadway, facing east. The cop car parked adjacent to an ice cream shop, also facing east. Singer's double slammed the Buick in reverse, heading west backwards, and the cop moves forward. When they meet in front of the Greyhound Bus Depot, Singer's double pulls a 180-degree turn, and the cop car squeezes a 45-degree turn. A shootout follows. After the shooting scene, they had a bank robbery scene to shoot in the La Toucan restaurant at Park and Main. "Places like this are good for shooting because of old abandoned buildings," said sound mixer Jim Thornton. "We can do what we want with the buildings to make them fit in with the scene."

Issues with picketing labor unions was but one of the movie's major problems. Besides bringing the viewer a paralyzing boredom, the movie looks rushed, sloppy, and glaringly inadequate. For starters, the theme of a man and a woman "running from their pasts" while trapped on a collision course with the future is hardly original. Either way, it failed to earn wide theatrical release under its original name *The Last Ride* and disappeared.

The Missouri Breaks

CAST
Marlon Brando, Jack Nicholson

DIRECTOR
Arthur Penn

LOCATION
Red Lodge, Billings, Virginia City

1976

Like many who sample Montana's pleasures once or twice, director Arthur Penn worked on a plan to return to the state that he had come to love. In 1975 he sealed a deal with United Artists to take Marlon Brando and Jack Nicholson to Montana. Filming began on *The Missouri Breaks*, a highly anticipated film with big stars, a successful director, a cutting-edge Montana scriptwriter, and real Montana settings. Trouble soon followed.

On Independence Day 1975, Marlon Brando and his teenage son, Christian, arrived at *The Missouri Breaks* encampment fifteen miles southeast of Billings, where director Arthur Penn was retouching the Virginia City sets he'd used five years earlier in *Little Big Man*. "How do you do? I'm Marlon Brando," the world's most famous actor

greeted each person as he lumbered toward Penn's trailer.

Scriptwriter Thomas McGuane of Livingston observed, "I got the feeling that people really liked Brando and [that] Jack [Nicholson] was a politician: a devious type."

The Missouri Breaks is a western set in the fine, high hill country of Montana in the 1880s. It is about a rich, literate rancher (he reads *Tristram Shandy* to relax) trying to cope with horse thieves who are stealing him blind. It's about the main horse thief (Nicholson) and his pals, who aren't bad fellows really, nor especially successful, just guys trying to make ends meet under increasingly difficult circumstances. It's also about the eccentric "regulator" or private gun (Brando) hired by the rancher to bring law and order to his territory.

To a lesser degree, it's about the rancher's pretty, bright, exceedingly bored daughter, who quotes Samuel Johnson and once seduces an outlaw by suggesting he get down off his horse. "What for?" says the outlaw, suddenly prissy. "We'll talk about the Wild West," says the girl, "and how to get the hell out of it."

According to *Film Comment* magazine, McGuane's offbeat Western was "a package waiting to happen when the producer Elliott Kastner [a former talent agent] juggled egos and money to get the green light from United Artists."

Unlike many film projects which can gestate for decades and still die at the moment of birth, *The Missouri Breaks* came together in only six weeks. In the words of *Screenplay*, it was "a half-baked product of the new and frequently faulty studio trend toward pairing stars with auteur directors, while worrying about such niceties as a coherent script after the fact."

"A picture doesn't cost much to make," observed *The Missouri Breaks* director Arthur Penn (*Bonnie and Clyde, Little Big Man*) in a 1997 interview. "What costs more is when there are either one, two, or three stars and all the perks that go with that. The accretions of staff, people, time, and nonsense have an inhibiting effect on production."

The Missouri Breaks opened May 19, 1976, in theaters nationwide. The *New York Times* said that in addition to Brando and Nicholson, the film had a cast of "superb supporting actors," including Kathleen Lloyd as the rancher's outspoken daughter, Harry Dean Stanton and Randy Quaid as two of Mr. Nicholson's more prominent partners in fumbled crime, and John McLiam as the rancher.

Then the *Times* ripped it: "'Rancho Deluxe,' which was also written by McGuane, was a much smaller, similarly wise-talking version of virtually the same story, though set in contemporary Montana. You might think that Mr. McGuane, by setting the same situation in the 1880s, would give us the romantic side of the story. Not at all.

"In the 1880s of 'The Missouri Breaks' the characters are just as bored, confused and directionless as they are in 1975, and they, too, look back to some dimly remembered period when the old days were good. Instead of being elegiac and funny, however, the anachronisms in 'The Missouri Breaks' too often seem like camp."

Critics principally blamed "the out-of-control performance given by Mr. Brando." He enters the film hidden behind a horse, which he at last peeks around, and then spends the rest of the movie upstaging the writer, the director, and the other actors. "Nothing he does (affecting the Irish accent he used earlier in *The Nightcomers* and wearing odd costumes, including frontierswoman drag at one point) has any apparent connection to the movie that surrounds him. He grabs our attention but does nothing with it," wrote *Film Comment*.

In their earlier films both Penn and McGuane had demonstrated a fondness for eccentric characters whose impulses have a kind of grandeur about them. There's no grandeur to Brando's character. Nor much mystery. On the set "he behaves like an actor in armed revolt," wrote photographer Mary Ellen Mark, who met Brando on the set of *The Missouri Breaks*. "One has no way of knowing whether *The Missouri Breaks* would have been a good film without this peculiar presence as its center, but there are so many arresting things in the rest of the movie that one can speculate—a raucous kangaroo-court sequence in which the defendant, a horse thief, becomes just as giddy and rowdy as the men trying him; a scene in a frontier whorehouse that, for once, looks depressingly grim; a marvelous caper in which several none too bright outlaws steal a corralful of horses from the Royal Canadian Mounties, who are otherwise occupied. They are in church singing 'Bringing in the Sheep.'"

The overarching response to the film was that it lacked continuity, cohesion and any semblance of flow. The *New York Times* had this critique: "It's one of the film's oddities that as *The Missouri Breaks* proceeds to its bloody climax, with the scenes of violence increasing in intensity until one man slits the throat of another, it becomes in-

Two of cinema's best actors collided in *The Missouri Breaks*. Jack Nicholson (left) said he was honored to be in a movie with his acting hero, Marlon Brando (right). Dueling egos and Brando's outlandish behavior disrupted the set.

creasingly trivial. The killing of a rabbit on screen earlier in the movie (which has been rated PG) is more brutal and more shocking than the climactic confrontation of the two superstars, which doesn't seem important at all."

The *San Francisco Chronicle* liked some of the film's components, just not Brando: "The film conveys a fine sense of place and period, of weather and mood and the precariousness of life, which are things that Nicholson responds to as an actor. Yet the plot, along with Brando, keeps intruding and throwing things out of balance."

At the time of shooting the film, Nicholson was fresh from an Oscar for *One Flew Over the Cuckoo's Nest*, his star in the ascendancy. And yet he appeared happy to cede center stage to his one-time acting idol. Nicholson saw *The Missouri Breaks* as his chance to team with— maybe even upstage—Brando on the big screen. Nicholson said, "It's a pleasure to be in the same sentence with him, no less in the same movie."

Brando did what he wanted. Improvising his lines

The Missouri Breaks was filmed in Virginia City and Red Lodge, and on a ranch near Billings. Here actors John McLiam (left) and Jack Nicholson rest on the set between scenes.

from beneath a series of comedy hats, he embarks on a merry dance from burlesque to menace and back again, while the picture frantically plays catchup behind him. In hindsight, *The Missouri Breaks* can be seen as the film that ended Marlon Brando's career as a serious actor. By the time the cameras rolled for *The Missouri Breaks*, the five-foot-ten-inch actor weighed in at 250 pounds and he no longer seemed concerned with his appearance. He was far more interested in sex, food, counterculture, and the future of the American Indian Movement (AIM).

Earlier that year, a firefight had broken out between AIM and the FBI on the Oglala Sioux reservation in South Dakota. By mid-afternoon, one Indian and two federal agents were dead, launching the biggest pre-September 11 manhunt in the Bureau's history. By summer's end, AIM fugitives Dennis Banks and Leonard Peltier would slip into L.A. to hide out at Brando's place, which was right next door to Nicholson's. But Brando wasn't on hand to greet them. That meeting would take place later, after Arthur Penn had put *The Missouri Breaks* to bed.

(An early supporter, Brando supplied AIM with money, sanctuary, and the power of his celebrity throughout the turbulent 1970s.)

Yet here, perhaps for the last time, there is a whiff of method to Brando's madness. He plays his hired gun as a kind of cowboy Charles Manson, serene and demonic, affecting a ripe Irish accent and discarding it at will. Towards the end he pops up (for no apparent reason) wearing a starched pinafore and a prairie woman's bonnet, quite out of control and peculiarly terrifying by the light of the bonfire. "Old granny's getting tired now," the actor mumbles—his last farewell before sailing off the map. After *The Missouri Breaks*, Brando would squander his talent with wild-eyed cameos and uninteresting supporting roles.

The Missouri Breaks cost $8 million to produce at a time when similar films cost half as much, but the most scandalous part of the budget was above the line. Its stars, Marlon Brando and Jack Nicholson, earned $1.25 million and $1 million, respectively, before they ever set foot

When he made *The Missouri Breaks*, Jack Nicholson had just finished his Oscar-winning performance in *One Flew Over the Cuckoo's Nest*.

on the set. In addition, Brando claimed 11.3 percent of the gross beyond $8.85 million, while Nicholson's payday—10 percent of the gross—kicked in once the film took in $12.5 million.

Sensing box office trouble a week before the movie opened, Nicholson hedged his bet by selling back 5 percent of his eventual gross to Elliot Kastner for $1 million in cash. Kastner agreed but didn't pay, prompting Nicholson to sue later that year. Brando claimed that *The Missouri Breaks* eventually earned him more than $16.5 million, a bigger payday than his legendary cameo as Christopher Reeves's father in *Superman*, which earned him $15 million for three days in front of the cameras. According to industry reports, *The Missouri Breaks* earned a domestic box-office gross of a mere $14 million.

Penn later criticized the American tendency to glorify actors as more precious than the actual content of the movies that they appear in. "On the other hand, that's very much a part of American filmmaking," he said. "American stars are the international stars. It's what makes American film an industry rather than an individual labor of love, but studios have come around to an awareness that stars don't necessarily guarantee a highly successful movie."

McGuane once joked that the movie might have been called *Dueling Egos in the Sun* because of the emotional turbulence between Brando and Nicholson, and between Penn and his stars. Soon enough, the production was past schedule, over budget, and out of control. Nicholson blamed Penn for caving in to Brando's indolence and careless caprice, but McGuane blamed them all. "Instead of being the ensemble thing that I had imagined, it now had to be a vehicle for two superstars," he said.

McGuane said he wrote *The Missouri Breaks* for "inexpensive" actor-friends of his, Warren Oates, Harry Dean Stanton, and Randy Quaid, with the idea of directing a low-budget movie himself. But Kastner, the producer, hired both Brando and Nicholson to be the stars and that changed everyone's plans. McGuane said Nicholson wanted to be in a movie with Brando, but Brando

Director Arthur Penn talks with Kathleen Lloyd, the female lead in *The Missouri Breaks*. The movie's screenplay was written by Montanan Thomas McGuane.

wasn't very interested in leaving his home in Tahiti. Kastner decided to trick Brando into becoming part of the cast. "Kastner hired a plumber to tell Brando that the plumbing in his house in Tahiti was bad and would cost $150,000 to fix," said McGuane. "When the producer offered Brando the job, he accepted."

McGuane said that he quickly lost any semblance of artistic oversight: "When I was first working with Arthur, I strongly felt his attention to the matters of the screenplay. As soon as the first movie star arrived, I was startled by how my status in the project just evaporated. I remember one day Arthur and I were talking about something that was intensely interesting to me, and Jack Nicholson came in, and suddenly Arthur seemed to be incredibly interested in how blue Jack's eyes were. And Nicholson's standing there like this little balding fireplug, and we're really trying to think about how blue his eyes were! At that point, my interest in the project literally went out the window. I said to myself, 'What am I going to do next, because I ain't gonna do this anymore.'"

"Nicholson felt that he never got to 'go through with anything'—that was his phrase—and that Brando had all the action stuff," McGuane said. "Jack was kind of intimidated by Brando. So when Brando left the scene, Jack suddenly came on strong and wanted changes, right now. Arthur Penn called me and asked me if I was willing to make changes on Jack's behalf, and I said no."

McGuane said Penn was a "control freak" who had trouble controlling the actions of his stars, particularly Brando. As the filming progressed, McGuane said, people on the set used to watch Penn grind his teeth in frustration.

McGuane also said Brando and Nicholson didn't get along well during the filming. "Nicholson felt overfaced by Brando," said McGuane. "Marlon had not much respect for Jack's acting."

Even Brando boasted: "Poor Nicholson was stuck in the center of it all, cranking the damned thing out while I whipped in and out of scenes like greased lightning."

McGuane didn't have kind words for the female lead, either. He said Kathleen Lloyd had done a great job of acting during her screen test, but she wasn't enthusiastic about trying to portray her character. "Either she was tooted out of her bird or she was having a magic moment during the screen test because she never looked like that again," McGuane said. "She had all the dramatic timing of a faulty starter's pistol."

McGuane said Brando changed everything about his part of bounty hunter, hit-man Lee Clayton. McGuane wrote the bounty-hunter character as eccentric, but by the end of the movie, Brando had fanned eccentricity into madness, merrily murdering each rustler while humming a tune or making a joke, going in and out of an Irish accent, and changing the costumes.

During one scene the crew watched in genuine horror when Brando plucked a live frog from the river, took a big bite, and then tossed the injured animal back into the water.

Photographer Mary Ellen Mark observed: "Marlon Brando's body was going through the motions, awaiting the return of his personality. It was miles away. He was reeling it in like a dancing sailfish.

"His van was parked by the trees in a grassy field. Inside it was quiet. The air conditioner diced the air. Minutes had passed since our introduction, but he just sat on the edge of the bed, hands in a drawer fumbling aimlessly with a hank of wires. He picked up a screwdriver and turned it over carefully. Here was a hero whose vanity had surrendered. Beneath those wide oak stump shoulders was a vast rippling cargo-hold of 240 pounds on a 5-foot-10 frame. It was neat enough in here, a small brown space piled high with books on solar energy and Indian history, and his two congas. Cupboards were stacked with fresh T-shirts, clean towels, and the icebox was filled with Tab.

"When at last he found what he was looking for, a cassette tape of Caribbean drum music, he eased across the bed and rested his head against the curtained window. The silvery blond hair rolled over his ears. That face. He

Lunchtime for the extras on the set of *The Missouri Breaks*.

looks an old medicine man. He appears as unmovable as the city planetarium…with that head balled up, like a clenched fist, that forehead all knotted and complicated. People were embalmed with awe. Beethoven must have had the same air."

Most days, Brando didn't even bother to learn his lines. "Marlon's still the greatest actor in the world, so why does he need those goddamned cue cards?" Nicholson complained.

"Brando's a strange cat to be around." McGuane observed. "He wakes up in a different world every day. Once he jumped out of a pine tree onto a horse's back and rode off. The next day he was afraid to ride a horse."

McGuane said he liked many of the changes Brando made. Still, as filming progressed, McGuane's control over the script lessened. He said the movie moguls wanted him to change the ending of the script so there would be a shootout between ranch owner Braxton and Nicholson's character. "I didn't want to write a traditional Western," said McGuane. "I wanted to take the Western and push it to its limits. I liked it [when it was]

fast, funny and evil." McGuane said the moguls couldn't get him to kill Braxton in a shootout, so they brought in Robert Towne, a popular script doctor, to do it. Towne wrote the shootout scene. McGuane later said that although changes were made, 85 percent of *The Missouri Breaks* was shot from his script.

Critics later blasted *The Missouri Breaks* for having five directors: Penn, its two stars, McGuane, and the United Artists production accountant.

When Nicholson was a high school kid in Neptune, New Jersey, his very last hero was Brando. At the time of filming the *Breaks*, they were next door neighbors in Beverly Hills. "It's a big problem," Nicholson said to a Canadian journalist. "I suddenly felt myself feeling an old symptom while working with Marlon, which is that he's so powerful, you fall so in love with what he's doing, that you want to do it yourself. I studied him then and I find myself now, even when I'm working with him, wanting to emulate him. [But] I made a very conscious choice not to do that, even though I might feel in my heart that Marlon and I were true soul brothers"

At less guarded times, Nicholson muttered that Brando "is telling us that what we [actors] are doing is [garbage]. He said the other day, 'This is kind of a silly way to make a living, but nothing pays as good.'"

Later, when actor Bruce Dern joked to Nicholson that he thought Brando stole *The Missouri Breaks* out from under him, Nicholson freaked: "I don't know who the [crazy] guy is! Lives up the hill from me. What do you want from me?"

Nicholson's hero worship of Brando never entirely faded. He couldn't blame Brando for upstaging him during *The Missouri Breaks*, so he took out his pique on Arthur Penn. "I was very hurt," said Nicholson. "The picture was terribly out of balance, and I said so. Well, an actor isn't supposed to care, I suppose. I mean, Arthur Penn doesn't talk to me anymore because I told him I didn't like his picture. The movie could've been saved in the cutting room, but nobody listened."

"When the movie first came out, I thought it was unrelieved, gloomy trash," said McGuane. But when he attended a showing of *The Missouri Breaks* in Bozeman in October 1984, he seemed to suffer a change of heart. "But I didn't hate it tonight," he told the audience during a question-and-answer forum.

When questioned about the film in later years, McGuane said he felt guilty about not doing more to change the outcome. "I'm sorry I didn't go over to the Red Lodge set and break a [profanity] chair over Robert Towne's head when he was in there wrecking the end of *The Missouri Breaks*. I'm sorry that I didn't tell Jack Nicholson that when you make deals like that, you deprive yourself of your own claims of being an artist—that you're just another filthy little hustler like the ones you complain about. I'm really sorry I didn't do it. But next time, I will do it. Next time, I'm gonna be absolutely right in people's faces, from A to Z. You have to care enough to do that."

Steven Seagal's *The Patriot* riled up Montana militia members who feared they would be portrayed badly in the movie. The Ennis-based film crew contacted the FBI after receiving threats from callers claiming to be militia members.

The Patriot

CAST
Steven Seagal, Gailard Sartain

Director
Dean Semler

LOCATION
Ennis area

1997

Casting directors for Steven Seagal's film *The Patriot*, set in Ennis, received 400 applicants for extra speaking parts. In fact, the Ennis casting office closed so directors could assess the pictures and packets they had received. Approximately 25 men would appear in the movie. Filming began on September 23, 1996, and ran through November 19. The plot featured an ex-military doctor, played by Seagal, who combats a virus introduced into the Ennis community by an anti-government bad guy.

Ennis, which plays itself, was chosen mainly because Seagal's real-life 15,000-acre Sun Ranch was nearby. In the story, a renegade government lab worker steals the toxin, which somehow falls into the hands of the anti-government militia, killing some militia members as well as townspeople.

The Patriot filmed at several public facilities, including the Ennis High School and Madison County Courthouse in Virginia City. In addition, some outdoor scenes took place along local streets and highways. Some of the extras played sick people; others would be involved in gun fighting.

"I'm in the beginning, the middle and the end of the movie—unless I end up on the cutting room floor," said Jim Miller, bartender at Ennis's Rustler's Roost. Miller, of West Yellowstone, answered a newspaper ad for extras and was featured as one of the bad guys, a militia member. "Since I didn't have any lines, I only got $100 a day and didn't have to get a Screen Actors Guild membership," said Miller. "But I might need one in the future because I'm going to look into getting into other movies…" Miller said he ate "the best I've eaten in six months. They were originally feeding us at a restaurant in Ennis but the food was so bad we started sneaking into the big tent and eating with the featured stars and other staff people. The food was great there."

Steven Seagal immediately came under fire from some Montana militia members. Casting director Tina Buckingham had been fielding calls from Militia of Montana leader John Trochmann. "Trochmann said he hoped we wouldn't portray the Militia as a bunch of wackos," said Buckingham. Buckingham had been fielding anonymous calls from people who said that they belonged to the militia. They threatened to infiltrate the film—either as extras or food service workers—to sabotage equipment or contaminate food. The film crew was concerned enough to call the authorities, including the FBI, because of the anonymous threats. Early press reports incorrectly said the script had the militia stealing the toxin and deliberately unleashing it on the town. And that had riled up militia supporters.

"They called my home several times and threatened me," recalled Buckingham. "My phone was public because I was looking for extras. I played the message for the line producer and next thing I know, there are two guys from New York, who looked like Mafia guys, placed in my office in Ennis as bodyguards. On another mes-

sage, [the caller] told me to tell the powers that be to get in touch with them; they wanted approval of the script. They said they would be sending infiltrators to the casting calls, and they did. There was a guy who later claimed that he had no Social Security number, who flat out told me, 'You'll hire me and I will be on that set'."

Lonie Stimac, then head of the state film office, said she was called by the producer about the threats. "We take this seriously because, of course, we take anything seriously that affects film production in the state," said Stimac. "We apprise the governor's office when something like this comes up. We don't want that image of Montana and we don't want film production threatened."

A member of a militia-affiliated group in Bozeman denied that anyone in her organization would threaten the filmmaking. "We might picket the film after it was out if we didn't like it," said Kamala Webb, whose group was known as Citizens for a Free America. "But anyone can say they belong to the militia and make a threat," said Webb.

A Militia of Montana leader who worried that militia members would be portrayed as a bunch of crazies said he planned to meet film officials to explain what the militia movement was all about. "If the script is incorrect, we'd like to make it correct," said John Trochmann of Noxon. He said he drove to Ennis to meet with *The Patriot's* producer and director. A spokesman for the film, Andy Lipschultz, said he knew nothing about a meeting between Trochmann and film officials. Referring to the script, in which Seagal rescues his town, Trochmann said, "I hope he [Seagal] will come to the rescue of America, to stop the encroachment of global government."

"We have no intention of disturbing the film," said Randy Trochmann of Noxon, who organized the Militia of Montana with his brother. "We're concerned about the story line," said Randy. "We're concerned that people will think real militia members would do such a thing." The media portrays militia members as the sort of radicals who commit violent acts, he said. "Stereotypes make you mad," said Randy. The 1997 Militia of Montana preparedness catalog offers a book written by the Trochmanns, titled *Enemies: Foreign and Domestic*. In it John Trochmann writes about surviving biological warfare and economic collapse, as well as other disasters.

The Patriot was shot over the eight weeks on Seagal's Sun Ranch at Ennis, in Virginia City, and for three days on the third floor of a Montana State University building transformed into a top secret, underground laboratory where Seagal would try to discover a cure for a deadly virus. MSU's steam tunnels were used to depict underground tunnels leading to the bunker. The last day was extremely busy. Down one long hall in the Engineering and Physical Science Building, lights and cables were strewn on the floor. Between takes, Seagal was in his white trailer on South Sixth Avenue. South Sixth was blocked to traffic between Grant and Garfield streets and lined with many trailers.

Snow fell in Virginia City Oct. 24 and 25 while the crew was filming and several movie scenes didn't include snow, so the crew had to remove it. "We had to melt it, sweep it, rake it, anything to get rid of it," said location manager Mark Zetler. The crew used weed burners to melt the snow and covered the white stuff with camouflage netting.

Bob Coppock of Bozeman, a fly fishing outfitter known as Captain Trout, was a stand-in for actor Gaillord Sartain, who played Floyd, the heavy. Coppock described Floyd as "the chief bad guy in the movie." Coppock was the first stand-in hired and the last to be let go because his character was needed for the whole movie.

Sixteen-year-old Philip Winchester of Belgrade had a good time on *The Patriot* set portraying "The Kid," an innocent teenager who got caught up with rough militia members. "He was hired for two days to say two words and he worked for four weeks at full actor's rates," said casting director Buckingham. "Winchester was a high-school senior in Belgrade and he was in agony over whether or not to vacate a performance at the school for the movie."

"I was told they liked what they saw and they felt they could give the character a little more depth," said Winchester, who later starred in a *Chicago Law* spinoff on NBC.

The Patriot overspent and the production confronted serious financial trouble.

"I've been involved with about 29 features, and the only movie I've worked on that was like a runaway train was *The Patriot*," said Zetler. "Movies have bonding companies and the bonding company will take a movie over. It's rare, but that's what happened. Seagal put more money into his ranch at the time and the bonding company stepped it. We closed Main Street in Ennis seven times and negotiated 30 to 40 businesses to shut down

for the day. Before the bonding company took over, we paid everyone $250 to $500. After the bonding company took over, there were no money restrictions, essentially coming from insurance. At one point, I had $50,000 in cash in my pockets and was stuffed with $100 dollar bills, like Santa Claus. The price went from $250 to a minimum of $2,500 each. Nobody in the bonding company showed restraint and the people in Ennis made a lot of money on it."

"Seagal at that time had donated money to the Dalai Lama and he received the title of reincarnated master, basically the buying of the Dalai Lama," said Whitmer. "He donated half a million and received that title. So every time he would come to the Ennis café, the monks would walk in and bless the café so he could enter. It was a sideshow. It is the last big movie he did. He also apparently took money from mob and the mob said, 'pay me'."

"It turned out that *The Patriot* was financed by the mob and Seagal had to testify in federal court as part of the government's case," said Allison Whitmer, the movie's local first assistant accountant and a film extra. "Whoever did the movie had the government against them. It turned out that the mob had been blackmailing Seagal and using the movie to launder $20 million or so. Either way, the movie sucked, and Seagal is an asshole. He had all of his Buddhist guys with him, and the Buddhists had to cleanse the set before he came out."

"He had a monk and then these girls came in," recalled Buckingham. "The girls, we called them the *monkettes*. I felt badly for Seagal. He could have had a good time. I felt sad for Seagal because he made himself so distant from everybody. He just didn't fit in. He was at the local rodeo, years before *The Patriot*, with his wife, and they looked so out place. But he left her for the nanny, who was also from Ennis. He left the nanny, too."

At the conclusion of filming, Seagal reportedly left for Nepal shortly after "to seek spiritual guidance and renewal from a Buddhist mentor." He did return to ride a horse and serve as marshal of the Ennis Fourth of July Parade in 1998. He kicked off the parade riding a horse down the same stretch of Main Street where Huey helicopters had landed one year earlier for a scene. "I am very happy to be here," said Seagal, sitting on a brown-and-white horse and wearing beaded leather with black hair pulled back in his usual pony-tail style. "It's a nice place."

Parade organizer Mary Oliver said she sent Seagal a

letter back in November 1997, asking if he would ride in the Fourth of July parade, especially given the title of his film. "He said he would be pleased to be part of our Fourth of July celebration," said Oliver. "This is the largest spectator crowd we've ever seen."

Seagal failed to drum up much enthusiasm for the film. "The movie has problems," he said. "I don't think they are done with it." As far as the militia men who were worried the film would portray them unfavorably: "Most of that was a bunch of hype," said Seagal. "Those people have respect for me, and I respect them."

On the bright side, "*The Patriot* took place during the fall," said Lonie Stimac. "We don't get a lot of movies that shoot here in the fall because people have a misconception that it turns from summer to winter and that there is no fall season. It went quite well for them in fall."

"My only recommendation for the movie is to watch it with the sound off," said Buckingham. "Dean Semler is the cinematographer. He was also the cinematographer of *Dances With Wolves*."

Steven Seagal finally ran into a foe that was too much to handle. In 1998, he decided to sell his Montana ranch rather than fight the knapweed that was overrunning the property and threatening native grasses. The actor, accused in multiple lawsuits of sex trafficking and hit with sexual harassment lawsuits, one filed as recently as 2015, continues to make ultra-violent third-rate action movies, primarily filmed and released in countries such as Romania.

The Real Thing, aka Livers Ain't Cheap

CAST
Rod Stieger, Pat Gallagher, Esai Morales, Gary Busey, James Russo, Jeremy Piven, Emily Lloyd

DIRECTOR
James Merendino

LOCATION
Deer Lodge

1996

Warning sirens from a prison escape were part of a movie known as *The Real Thing* filmed at the Old Montana Prison. Released under the title *Livers Ain't Cheap*, the entire film, except for the prison escape scene, was shot in L.A. with a cast of 32 actors and extras. Only the stars involved in the prison break scene were in Deer Lodge on July 17, 1995. The movie was shot in 30 days, with one day in Deer Lodge. The area around the Kelly Street Bridge was cordoned off for the filming, which began around dusk. The camera used a "one camera movement" technique, following the escapee (Dexter, played by Pat Gallagher) from the prison wall where he was dressed as a guard, out of the prison, across the bridge to a waiting car.

At the beginning of the film, Dexter is nabbed by police in downtown L.A. after blowing a paltry purse-snatching. In jail, as Dexter reveals to buddy Collin (Esai Morales) his plans to rob a ritzy nightclub to the tune of more than $1 million on New Year's Eve. He is overheard by young punk James Little, who soon tells his older brother and measly criminal Rupert (James Russo) about it. When the brash James is critically wounded in an attempt by a suspicious Collin to rub him out, the kid requires an expensive liver transplant that, Rupert presumes, only the New Year's heist can pay for. So the gang of usual slimeballs and losers is rounded up, including Dexter. The film itself is stylish, but the one-liners and shoot-outs feel a bit threadbare, handed down from older, better genre movies.

Originally released under the name *Livers Ain't Cheap*, the film was called everything from "preposterous" to "brutal" to "goofy." *Variety* had this to say about the violent low-budget attempt at film noir: "Coming at what is probably a trailing off of the ultra-violent crime cycle, pic reps a minor entry in the field, with a marginal theatrical life possible en route to homevid."

The Revenant's crucial, frigid scene at Kootenai Falls was actually shot during the summer, with plenty of professional kayakers on hand for filming, ferrying equipment, and making emergency rescues. Winter snow and ice (shot in Argentina) was overlaid on the Montana scene. PHOTO COURTESY OF BIRDS EYE OF BIG SKY.

The Revenant

CAST
Leonardo Dicaprio

DIECTOR
Alejandro González Iñárritu

LOCATION
Yaak River, Flathead Indian Reservation

2015

The Revenant stars Leonardo DiCaprio as American fur-trapper and frontiersman Hugh Glass in the 1820s. It is based on a novel about Glass and his extraordinary ex-periences in what are now South Dakota and Montana. Mauled by a grizzly bear, Glass was betrayed by another member of the crew of trappers he was traveling with and left to die. He didn't—and pursued the man who betrayed him.

The Revenant was shot by Academy Award-winning Director of Photography Emmanuel Lubezki, who won back-to-back Best Cinematography Oscars for *Gravity* and *Birdman*. The majority of the film was shot in the winter of 2014 in Alberta, Canada, but as the problem-atically lengthy project dragged on into spring and sum-mer, Lubezki still needed the right location for a gripping scene in which DiCaprio is washed down a turbulent river, survives in harsh winter conditions, and sets out for revenge.

The Revenant first scouted in Wyoming, Montana, and North Dakota, but decided to take the motion pic-ture to Alberta, Canada, and eventually Argentina because the production "ran out of winter" and required a more convincing, punishing cold. After returning to Los Angeles for post-production, the filmmakers needed to fill in some gaps with river scenery. Iñárritu's quest to find the perfect location for a survival drama's roiling river sequence led him to a far-flung corner of Montana and a setting that serves as the backdrop for one of the film's most epic scenes.

"Sometime around the spring of 2014, probably around May, is when *The Revenant* filmed some river stuff in Montana," said scout Rob Story. "I think they had every location guy in the country on it in for two weeks, being such a huge production. Originally, I thought the filming may have come out of Fort Union and the wild river stuff could be shot there, but there was too much sound, too much of the oilfields, and they even considered using the real Fort Union. But another issue was that the water level was not where they wanted it to be—and they needed a big run of whitewater.

"My favorite spot was south of the mouth of the Clark's Fork of the Yellowstone River, which I thought set well with the script—the frozen ice scenes. It was close to Cody, Wyoming, the Bureau of Land Management and Forest Service, and it seemed logistically and visually correct. I looked at the Bighorn Canyon area and bunch of other places and even down to the eastern part of the state, around where story took place. But the eastern part of the state looks very contemporary, fence and power lines, and railroads, not many pristine shots that could work."

After scouting locations across North America, Lubezki settled on Kootenai Falls near Libby, and film crews united on the terraced river and waterfall for a 10-day shoot in July 2014. Several Montanans were employed on the Libby crew, according to Deny Staggs, commissioner of the Montana Film Office. They included people from the Whitewater Rescue Institute in Missoula. *The Revenant* is set in winter, but stuntmen and stunt doubles filmed their dramatic scenes on hot July days.

Staggs said the scene was shot using "a technically complex camera array suspended by cable from a helicopter," and employed "a pair of stuntmen wearing bearskin coats over wetsuits" and a group of kayakers on safety patrol. DiCaprio and the other actors integral to the scene performed their parts in colossal water tanks back in Hollywood, and Lubezki used green screen technology to patch the shots together. Lubezki overlaid footage shot

in Argentina in the winter with the Kootenai Falls scene so that the Montana riverbanks look as if blanketed in snow and ice.

"They were looking for a water location that was dramatic and had character and could be fitting for this really incredible stunt, this action scene that this character has to go through to escape peril during an epic section of the movie," said Staggs. "They searched all over North America and the location manager came back and said 'we just want you to know that we looked at every water feature like this in North America and this is the most amazing place we've found.' So they were really dead set on being there." Staggs said he watched *The Revenant* on the big screen, and was impressed by the river sequence. "We were happy to get a little bit of the film made here in Montana, since a lot of the real story took place here," said Staggs. "It's a small part of the movie, but a beautifully epic part. I think it's one of the most spectacular scenes in the movie."

Cody Harris, director of Montana's Whitewater Rescue Institute (WRI), helped Hollywood capture footage of the water action. "We worked with them at one location on the Kootenai for about a week," said Harris. "I think in total the amount of time our shots take up in the movie is about 10 seconds. From ferrying equipment and personnel on jet boats to rafting below the falls with 400 pounds of camera equipment attached to the boat, it was pretty exciting. The main cast wasn't there; we worked with stunt doubles. They were excellent swimmers, but most of their experience came from the ocean environment. We provided transport via jet boat for close to 100 actors, crew and equipment. The jet boats were also used to film a sequence of a stunt double swimming a Class II [rapid].

The entire film was shot in the open air using only "natural light," meaning that the lion's share of the wilderness drama was constrained to a thin window of "magic time"—when the outdoor light is at its most vivid.

Yvonne Hill, who owns the Sandman Motel where *The Revenant* stunt crew spent their nights, said a stunt double for DiCaprio was twice injured while going over Kootenai Falls. "The first time I think a helicopter blew him off course and he missed the six-foot window he had, and after he went over the falls he hit so hard it crushed his heel," said Hill. "The movie people asked him if he could do another take, and he said yes. The second time he went over he shattered his leg…Nobody else has ever gone over Kootenai Falls and lived to tell about it." Alex Krimm, the stuntman, was taken by ambulance to Kalispell Regional Medical Center after the second mishap and has undergone four surgeries in the months since. While others have publicly corroborated Krimm's story, director Iñárritu repeatedly denied rumors that *The Revenant* had been dogged by hellish working conditions, crew defections and injuries on the set. Yet, Krimm's name has curiously been omitted from the film's credits.

The Revenant has another link to Montana: Michael Punke, who lived in Missoula from 2003 to 2009, wrote *The Revenant: A Novel of Revenge*, which was published in 2002. Punke is the United States ambassador to the World Trade Organization in Geneva, Switzerland. The job prevents him from speaking publicly and generating publicity for the novel or the movie. Leonardo DiCaprio (Best Actor), Alejandro González Iñánarritu (Best Director) and Emmanuel Lubezki (Cinematography) won Oscars.

The River Wild

CAST
Meryl Streep, Kevin Bacon, Charles Reilly

DIRECTOR
Curtis Hanson

LOCATION
Libby area, West Glacier area

1994

What started as an evening influenced by whiskey on the rugged banks of Montana's Smith River turned into a $30 million Hollywood production. Scriptwriter and co-producer Dennis O'Neil said the idea of making a movie came to him while on a fishing trip down the Smith River in the Lewis and Clark National Forest. The river's steep canyons and rugged whitewater make it a one way in, one way out river. O'Neil chronicled the trip in a series of articles for *Flyrod and Reel*. The series was a diary of the "mad floater" on his trip in 1986. While in the middle of the trip, O'Neil realized how horrific the float would be if they were being chased by crazed killers. "So I decided to write it down," said O'Neil.

The River Wild was shot in the summer of 1993 on the Kootenai River near Libby, Montana's Flathead River, and on Oregon's Rogue River. The movie is about a troubled family that goes on a rafting vacation to try to mend their relationship. But along the fictitious river, they encounter two shady characters and an increasingly dangerous river. Some of the movie's whitewater footage was shot at Bonecrusher rapids on the Middle Fork of the Flathead River, but the most harrowing scenes were filmed at Kootenai Falls, near Libby, which cinematographer Robert Elswit said was "unraftable in any real sense because the rapids and falls were lethal. If you went over these falls, you'd be killed." Special effects crews recreated Kootenai Falls in a flat area between the upper and lower falls by running a track to transport a raft through imitation rocks with water sprayed from large pipes. The production company had to mentally adapt the filmmaking process as an actual river-rafting endeavor.

Streep spent four months on location filming *The River Wild*, playing Gail, a character who sets a new standard for "supermoms"—a mother of two and a history teacher for the deaf who grew up as a river guide. As the movie progresses, Streep's character demonstrates incredible prowess at the oars of a raft.

"Meryl Streep," said director Curtis Hanson, "is like the Good Housekeeping seal of approval." Streep, a two-time Academy Award winner, did her own raft-steering down dangerous rapids in Oregon and Montana. "I was blessed with two natural wonders on this movie: the river and Meryl Streep," said Hanson on the set in 1993. "It'll be hard for me to ever replicate this experience."

Over 11 weeks of remote and treacherous filming, in which a fleet of helicopters transported actors and equipment from base camps, Hanson's primary obsession, he said, was safety for the cast and crew. Some suffered ankle injuries, but the worst moment involved Streep, early in the filming in Montana. The incident that almost killed her one August afternoon happened right after lunch. It was a little past 2 p.m. The Kootenai River was particularly angry that day, and Streep was particularly pooped. Up since the crack of dawn, she had been paddling her

The River Wild starring Meryl Streep and Kevin Bacon was filmed on the Kootenai River (and Kootenai Falls) near Libby and the Middle Fork of the Flathead River.

heart out all day. Streep didn't want to wimp out, really. Still, she told director Curtis Hanson that she couldn't go back in the water. "He needed just one more take," Streep recalled in the *Los Angeles Times*, "and, really, this particular stunt looked like nothing. All I had to do was paddle the raft into this hole where the water surges up between a few rocks." Streep powered her vessel as instructed. But then something went wrong. "The boat surfed down into the hole, rose and flipped over," said Streep. "And I went into the river. I remember sinking down to the bottom with this powerful and freezing water pulling me in deeper…My first thought was that if I died my husband would come to the set with a machete. Actually, I was really very quiet and not scared, which is not at all how I thought I'd react under these circumstances."

"Everybody on shore began screaming, 'Meryl's gone under,'" said Hanson. "I saw my life spinning before my eyes. I still think of it. I was responsible. One of the kayakers we had rushed over and hauled her up like a big

fish. She was conscious. She was banged up. And she was mad. But she was also pumped up with adrenaline."

Eventually, the river spit her out about 500 yards down from the frantic film crew. "When I got to the shore my legs actually went out from under me, but I still managed to get to Curtis," she said. "My heart was just pounding and I tried to be calm when I said, 'I really feel quite sure if I say that I'm too tired to do something that we have to assume I'm telling the truth.'" An extremely pale Hanson could only stammer, "Absolutely. That's how we'll do it from now on, Meryl."

"That was the defining moment for all of us," the director continued. "That could have been the end of my having the cooperation of the actors. To Meryl's tremendous credit, she did it again the next day. She got over it, she forgave me and, on the creative and physical level, she and the other actors trusted me. Nobody behaved like a movie star. If they had, it wouldn't have worked. It wouldn't be the same movie."

For Hanson, the film, which underwent extensive re-

Meryl Streep thought stunt doubles would do most of her rafting scenes in *The River Wild*, but the director wanted her in the shots. She almost drowned while filming one scene.

writes to build up the Streep character, has personal overtones. "I felt I knew these river rafters because of my years with surfers and beach-volleyball players," he said. "You know, they're similar. And they're people I knew really well and could deal with."

All told, Streep said she spent "four months on location" filming *The River Wild*. To prepare for her role, Streep had to do some things she hated. "'Like work out," she groaned to a writer from the *New York Times*, "shrugging off comments about how buff she looks with her Madonna-like arm muscles." "Please!" she said. "I worked out because I knew this river rafting would be tougher than the rowing machine at my gym, which, incidentally, I never use because I'm not really big on working out. I was trying to be strong because I was motivated by fear. Streep claims that when she accepted the role, she didn't think the river would be so wild. "I thought they would fake most of the rafting," she said.

"I thought I would have to do things like stand on the beach, waving. I thought that it would be somebody else on that raft, such as a stunt person. That's how they make movies, you know." But not *The River Wild*. "When Curtis said, 'I want it to really be you in that raft,' I think I just looked at him a bit quizzically."

She eventually agreed to do the stunts and, over the months, actually learned to appreciate the pure physical trauma. "I'd be on that river at 8 in the morning. This was so outside my experience as a woman who grew up in New Jersey and was a cheerleader and went to an Ivy League school. Soon I found myself living for the thrill. I wanted to have the ride and feel things that felt like life to me. At night I would fall into bed. It was the kind of tired that you couldn't even get up to go to the bathroom. And then the alarm would go off the next morning and I couldn't wait to get back outside and do it again."

Before the filming, Streep's only experience with whitewater rafting was as a passenger on a commercial rafting trip. But the physical aspects of the role came to her naturally, with the help of the "river unit," a group of whitewater experts who were always on hand during filming. Streep said she prepared for the role by rowing on a 38-mile trip on Oregon's Rogue River, under the guidance of Arlene Burns of the river unit. Then she discovered that Hanson wanted her to be involved in more of the whitewater scenes than she had anticipated. "I thought it would be a lot of (shots) very far away, with somebody else at the oars," said Streep. Instead, Hanson used Streep in about 90 percent of the river footage.

Streep said that before accepting the role, she had been inspired by the carefree, reckless nature of her four children, who were in Montana with her during filming. But when production started, she was inspired by the adventuresome nature of the river unit people. Streep's character has a line in the movie that plainly refers to the eternal adolescents who can be found on Montana rivers. "That's who they are. They live this real pure existence; they live for that descent down the river, and that's so much unlike me. I'm always intrigued by people who are not like me," she said.

Great Falls native Holly Sorensen had the opportunity to interview Streep on location for a story in *Premiere* magazine. "Meryl Streep was an amazing person," said Sorensen. "There's a person there who is the best in the world at what she does so she doesn't have to put up any airs. She was very authoritative and very present."

Streep had high praise for stunt double and whitewater rafter Kelley Kalafatich. "The river guides on the unit told me that very often the best guides are woman, because they don't try to overpower a current or situation. They'll read where the water is going, and a combination of manipulation and give and skill makes them powerful on the river," she said. Kalafatich, a world-class whitewater boater from Placerville, California, made a smooth run through Kootenai Falls as Streep's stunt double. "She epitomizes what the movie is all about. She's what Meryl Streep's character is supposed to be," said Wasson of Kalafatich. "She's just one of the best in the world, period."

Arlene Burns, a river-rafting guide hired by Universal Studios to train Streep for the dangerous activity of rowing a raft through whitewater: "We spent five days together in whitewater school, during which time she swam rapids and learned to read water, catch eddies, ferry and hop around on the raft like a seasoned river rat. I was amazed at her physical strength and stamina, a result of six months of training which included weight lifting, aerobics, stretching and yoga." To finish off training, Streep rowed 24 miles on Oregon's Rogue River in a day.

And it wasn't only Streep who faced river dilemmas. During one scene, the river pulled one of the oars into the whitewater. When it surfaced, the oar slammed into the stunt double playing one of the characters and threw him from the raft. That incident, improvised by the river and caught by the cameras, opened up several new creative possibilities and a new scene was worked around it. Editors Joe Hutshing and David Brenner were faced with the task of cutting the sequence into shape and looping some of the dialogue that had been obliterated by the noise of the water. "We cut out great whitewater things, stunts that didn't fit in because they were of a certain length," said Hutshing. "We could have made the Gauntlet scene an hour long. There was so much good stuff." Hutshing decided to add even more danger in postproduction. "Near the end [of the film] there is a big double waterfall," said Hutshing. "That was created by two waterfalls that were put together very carefully by a company called Digital Magic. They did a fabulous job. That gave it a really exciting finale."

One of the movie's major scenes stars the roaring "Gauntlet," the final whitewater obstacle that Streep's character must deal with. Except for scenes shot on the Rogue River, nearly all footage used for the Gauntlet was captured during intense filming with helicopters and almost 200 support personnel at Kootenai Falls near Libby. Hanson said that *The River Wild* was different

from other whitewater movies, such as *Deliverance*, because most of the dialogue takes place in a raft, on a river. Four scenes in the film are shot on the ground, rather than on a river. "There aren't very many river movies that have been done," said assistant director Tom Mack. "A lot of the techniques we've had to sort of invent as we go along. The difference between this movie and *Deliverance* is that *Deliverance* is an action movie that was filmed mostly from shore, while this movie is sort of a drama where most of the dialogue and a lot of the filming takes place on the river."

Filming on the river involved convoluted logistics problems. When the film was in its planning stage, the directors contacted John Wasson, a veteran rafter and kayaker from Idaho who had made first descents of numerous rivers in the United States and all across the world. Wasson contacted a network of a dozen seasoned whitewater guides, kayakers and rafters from across the western United States to help with the production. Wasson and his team provided advice and safety support, designed raft riggings for cameras and sound and helped develop unusual filming equipment, including a huge barge, complete with lights and cameras, that floated in front of the "hero raft" carrying the actors. The terraced falls are generally considered to be Class 6, unnavigable whitewater, but whitewater boaters on Wasson's unit found passages for rafts through the falls.

Capturing the dialogue required cameras mounted on rafts as well as the camera-equipped barge. In terms of stunts and logistical demands, filming at Kootenai Falls was the most difficult part of the movie. Streep and Joseph Mazzello, who plays her son, along with bad guys Kevin Bacon and John C. Reilly, made rushing approaches to the edge of the massive falls in a raft that was tethered by a cable. The sequence was completed by stunt doubles who went over the edge. Streep was at the oars during many of the sequences filmed in the huge hydraulics at the base of the falls. Besides Streep's accident, Bacon was thrown from a raft during filming and also was washed downstream. The safety crew could not spot him at first, but momentarily he was plucked from the river. Bacon later said he had absolutely no river experience, which suited his character. Hanson said seeing his stars disappear in a river was "terrifying." "But the actors became more cautious as the filming went along," said Hanson. "They became more aware of the force of the river."

Universal Pictures paid the Flathead National Forest $6,150 for a permit to film. The company also had permission for limited filming from the Glacier National Park side of the river. Under the federal Wild and Scenic River Act, there is a 10-horsepower motorboat limit on that stretch of the river. However, the forest lifted boat-motor regulations, allowing Universal to use a 40-horsepower outboard. Also, the crew worked behind gates normally locked to the public. "I don't think it's right," said a spokesman for a group called Montanans for Multiple Use. "The local people don't get all these exemptions." Some Montana environmentalists agreed. "It's hypocritical," said Stormy Good, vice president of the Flathead Chapter of the Montana Wilderness Association. "A movie called *River Wild* shouldn't be receiving exemptions from the Wild and Scenic River Act to run a 40-horsepower motor on the Middle Fork." Flathead forest recreation officials said that Universal was receiving no special favors, pointing out that big motors are commonly allowed for river searches and search-and-rescue training.

Universal Pictures produced the $42 million movie, and the approximately $3 million cash infusion from their production was enough to add some color to the anemic Libby economy. The community had been hard-hit by plant closures and downsizing in the late 1980s. About 300 people had lost their jobs when the ASARCO mine near Troy shut down, and more than 300 people lost their jobs when Libby's Champion lumber mill in Libby changed ownership. "It's been a tremendous benefit to Libby," said Donna Olson, administrative assistant at the Libby Chamber of Commerce. From the local pharmacy to the local equipment rental, Libby merchants felt the impact of the production. "I was glad to see them here," said Rick Gullingsrud, owner of Rick's Rental. "I know there's some people in town who aren't, but they don't want to see anything here, and they don't have a business."

Rick Jaqueth, a pharmacist at Gene's Pharmacy, said the crew had purchased everything from bee sting kits to prescription drugs to combination suntan lotion/insect repellent. Alan Baker, an employee at Libby Sports, said movie personnel had purchased personal items, and Universal Pictures had purchased prop items, such as boxes of ammunition, which were needed just for the boxes. "I think it's a very good thing," said Baker. "As far as tourists go, it's exciting for them to know that there's a movie in town. It adds a novelty aspect to the town."

Flathead County sheriff's vehicles appear in film chase scenes. Three off-duty deputies using a patrol car and two four-wheel drive units volunteered to work with the film crew. The studio paid the county $18 an hour for use of the vehicles. Deputies Phil Caperton, Gordon Barthel and Ernie Freebury contributed their personal time as impromptu movie actors in scenes shot in a rural area west of U.S. 93. At Ace Home Center in Libby, owner Ted Werner said Universal had kept him busy with some "soup to nuts" orders, but had had to do "some searching" to find specialty items. "Their orders are typically different than our regular orders," said Werner. "But we're glad to have them."

A platoon of reporters descended from all over the world on the Flathead Valley on the weekend of August 30, 1994, for a press screening, or "international press junket," probably the first ever to be held in Montana for the release of a major movie. Director Curtis Hanson said that he chose to hold the event in Montana since the cast and crew were in the state for most of the filming. "This was special," said Hanson. "On the flight into Kalispell, I told David (Strathairn) that I feel like I'm going to a reunion, and he said he felt the same way, because we had such a great time here. The beauty of this place and the rivers really became my collaborators in making this movie. So to come here and share the final product with the locals was an opportunity not to be missed." Cinematographer Elswit credited Hanson for pulling off such an ambitious project. "The logistical problems of the movie were overwhelming, but Curtis stayed calm throughout. He was always able to concentrate on the most important thing, which was telling the story. We were constantly scrambling up wet rocks and plunging into icy water. We all had three kinds of shoes. We had wet suits, dry suits, and every kind of outdoor gear made. It was the most physically demanding show I could imagine. The grips, camera assistants and electricians never gave up. I lost 20 pounds. It didn't seem like fun at the time, but now, in retrospect, it does."

Streep, dressed western style in blue jeans and boots, said the lead role gave her the chance to work in the western outdoors in an action movie—a type of a role she had never done in her diverse career. "The opportunity to be here for four months, outdoors, on the river, was a real big enticement. And I wanted to do something very physical," said Streep.

The first showing of *The River Wild* took place Thursday, September 29, 1994, at the Dome Theater in Libby, one day before it would be unveiled to moviegoers across the nation. A benefit reception and auction of film memorabilia followed at the Libby Eagles Lodge, items including a hat worn by Meryl Streep in the film and a prop nose used by Streep's stunt double. Governor Marc Racicot, a Libby native, congratulated his home community for its community spirit. "Many of the values I cherish today are those I learned growing up in this great community," said Racicot. "I'm pleased with the recognition this movie will be giving Montana and we hope it brings more good things to the Libby area and our state."

The film opened over the weekend as the top box-office draw, and to mixed reviews but almost universal acclaim for Hanson and Streep. While it grossed approximately $48 million domestically, selling the movie to audiences was unusually tricky. "It's the opportunity and the challenge," said Hanson. "These movies are always sold to the male audience. The typical action crowd tends not to like to see women who are strong and assertive. And what you might call the Meryl Streep crowd of women are not interested in seeing male-dominated action films." *Daily Variety* heralded Elswit's choice of landscape as "exceedingly handsome" and the on-water footage "exciting" and "rough-and-tumble as it could be."

The Shining

CAST
Jack Nicholson, Shelley Duvall

DIRECTOR
Stanley Kubrick

LOCATION
Glacier National Park

1980

The Going-to-the-Sun Road in Glacier National Park sets the opening scene in *The Shining* as the Torrance family drives to a mountain hotel to be winter caretakers—and where Jack Nicholson's character descends into homicidal madness.

Jack Torrance (Jack Nicholson) becomes winter caretaker at the isolated Overlook Hotel in Colorado, hoping to cure his writer's block. He settles in along with his wife, Wendy (Shelley Duvall), and his son, Danny, who is plagued by psychic premonitions. As Jack's writing goes nowhere and Danny's visions become more disturbing, Jack discovers the hotel's dark secrets and begins to unravel into a homicidal maniac hell-bent on terrorizing his family. Glacier National Park, more specifically, the eastern side of the Going-to-the-Sun Road, sets the opening scene for *The Shining* as the Torrance family drives to the haunted hotel. The aerial cinematography helicopter shots of Torrance driving to the Overlook were filmed by a second unit, running along the western shore of Goat Lake and Saint Mary Lake.

"I believe they used a shot of a little Volkswagen coming down through Logan Pass and they brought in a basic crew of grips, cameramen, a producer and director," recalled Montana Film Commissioner Garry Wunderwald. "Going-to-the-Sun Road was shot for second unit scenes and those are some of the most spectacular scenes in the country."

"Smaller second units were sent to Montana to film the opening scenes of the horror classic," said Montana film scout John Ansotegui. "The road leading up to the lodge was filmed in Montana; the exterior of the lodge itself was the Timberline Lodge in Oregon, and the interior of the lodge was a large set in London."

Ryan Gosling played the teenage hero of *The Slaughter Rule*, a well-received independent film written and directed by Montana brothers Alex and Andrew Smith, and filmed in Montana. PHOTO COURTESY ALEX AND ANDREW SMITH.

The Slaughter Rule

CAST
Ryan Gosling, David Morse

DIRECTOR
Alex and Andrew Smith

LOCATION
Great Falls area

2000

Alex and Andrew Smith wrote *The Slaughter Rule* and directed the independent low-budget film about teen angst and football. The movie scored among critics and entered their names into the world of moviemaking. The twins' sense of aesthetics was shaped in large part by their upbringing at Potomac, Montana, a forested haven criss-crossed with mountains. For the record, Alex is twelve minutes older. The brothers graduated from Missoula's Hellgate High School. Their dad, Dave, died in 1974, when the twins were six.

"Potomac was beyond provincial back then," said Andrew Smith. "Now it's sort of a bedroom community for Missoula. Years ago, it was a working-class, lumber-oriented, timber-oriented community, and we were at the end of the road and we were basically left to our own devices. Mom was a widow and she was working. Alex and I were able to play in the woods and subsist out there. We didn't have a TV and I think that helped a lot. We had comic books, literature, outdoor play, and films. My mom was a cinephile and we would go into town every weekend."

"Our dad passed when we were little," added Alex, "so we had to fill that role when we were little—fixing fences, chopping wood, working with horses, and going to school. It was the classic *Little House on the Prairie* experience and we were out in the elements a lot, and that's something that we think plays in our films and resonates to us."

David Smith was a literature professor, lover of films, and aspiring screenwriter. His widow Annick Smith led by example, showing her two sons that art required passion, inquisitiveness, and sacrifices.

"She worked first on a series of documentaries on Native American customs, and we were with her when she was shooting a lot of these docs," said Alex. "We remember going to a lot of powwows and to reservations and we were exposed to a lot of fascinating rituals. Once, she was editing a doc about Richard Hugo and they were editing it in our house. We could hear Hugo's poetry run forward and backwards. Back in the day, they would run the sound forward and backwards, and we were able to recite his poems backwards."

Annick forged a successful career as a writer and filmmaker, directing *Heartland* (1979), a stark, rugged saga of frontier life based on the actual diaries of a pioneer woman, which won the Golden Bear Award at the Berlin Film Festival. "I can remember being on the set of *Heart-*

land," said Andrew. "I think we were ten when we visited Harlowton, and we went for a couple of days, and it was a very exciting, a very immersive film and environment. It was very influential and it stuck."

Not only has moviemaking allowed the siblings to creatively exorcise some of their difficult memories, but it has fostered the rebirth of their own cultural awareness. Indeed, the state's stern, poised visage and durable residents are a far cry from the easy smiles and contagious laughs of a Hollywood back lot.

"We are definitely interested in people on the edge," said Alex. "We are interested in people on the fringes, the marginalized. We like those stories of people who struggle, and a good story to use is one where someone struggles really hard and overcomes that struggle in some capacity. Montanans overcome a lot of adversity. The state is no joke. It makes for a certain hearty, stoic person who can handle anything."

The twins attended different colleges, but both ended up with Master of Fine Arts degrees in writing. They worked on *The Slaughter Rule* script for almost six years, including the time in 1998 when they worked on it at the Sundance Institute, Robert Redford's incubator for promising films. The film was accepted into the influential Sundance Film Festival. *Village Voice* said it was "the most impressive feature by far in the dramatic competition at Sundance."

The title comes from the former "mercy rule" in six-man football, by which a game is called if one team runs up a 45-point lead. Through the story of a cross, frustrated teen and the moody, volatile man who befriends him, the brothers Smith emphasize that there is "no mercy rule in life." One reviewer said the film "hits you like a 250-pound linebacker."

The Smiths co-directed filming in Montana in the winter of 2000. "When filming *The Slaughter Rule*, we hit a record cold snap in Great Falls and it shows up on screen," said Alex. "It was almost too cold to shoot, but it's amazing because…you can see the actors' breath, you can hear the crackle, you see people shivering. I believe that it made the film even more intense. Winters are fierce—and they are long. Every season is robust and has its challenges. We are not after a postcard. We are not after the ideal Montana. We are after the real Montana."

The film company spent $500,000 in the Great Falls area. Low budget wasn't all bad, said Alex Smith. No studio ties translates to autonomous control. "We keep the creative control." The Smiths decided to tackle a challenging subject matter—the relationship between men and the boys they mentor. The boy, played by Ryan Gosling, is Roy Chutney, a high school senior in Blue Springs, Montana. Roy is cut from his rural Montana high school football team by a coach who tells him, "You ain't angry enough," shortly after his estranged father passes away. In need of a male role model, he is approached by an eccentric loner, Gideon (David Morse), who taps him to quarterback an independent league's six-man squad. The Renegades compete in a league with small outlying schools that don't have enough boys to field eight- or 11-man teams. Emboldened by the aggressive play, Roy disregards the rumors swirling around Gideon and his enigmatic history with boys.

"The movie is actually semi-autobiographical and comes from a fellow we knew in Missoula," said Alex Smith. "We both graduated from Hellgate High School in 1985. We were cut from our high school basketball team and recruited to play men's league by this coach in this small town we grew up. There were kids that said he was an unusual guy, or strange, and someone you needed to stay away from. Nothing ever became of it, but the guy—the character, the coach, the subject to lots of rumor and hearsay—stayed in our mind. We were interested in the complexity.

"It's funny because we went to separate colleges and later I was writing a story about the coach and Andrew was writing a short film about the coach, unbeknownst to me," said Alex. "We decided to collaborate on this experience."

At times the story shifts from Roy's initiation by Gideon as a football player and ferociously aggressive team leader, and to his relationship with older barmaid, Skyla (Clea Duvall), with whom he has his first affair. At the same time he struggles to maintain his friendship with Tracy Two Dogs, a Blackfeet Indian with his own roster of troubles.

David Morse, one of the finest and most underrated actors of our day, has made a career out of depicting morally dubious characters. Andrew Smith referred to Morse as "a mensch." "It took us nine years to get film made to the end of production, and it was five years after we saw *The Crossing Guard*, and we were blown away by his performance. He was sympathetic but weary. But we knew we needed David to be Gideon. We met at Sundance in 2000, and he hadn't read the script. He was an intense and intimidating guy at first. He checks you out to make sure you are bona fide. He humored us and he slowly got interested in it. He has twin sons and I think he was intrigued by working with twins."

"*The Slaughter Rule* was filmed during the coldest November in 100 years," recalled Morse later. "I think it was 10 below all night long and I had frostbite on my ears. There were times when I didn't have to be out there, but I felt some obligation to be out there with them—after all, Gideon almost dies in snow. I can tell you that my ears were white and numb for two months afterward.

"The scripts by the Smith Brothers are wonderful poetry and there is a humor to them and there is obviously drama in their stories, and that's what I'm drawn to [Morse also appeared in *Winter in the Blood*]. Too much of the stuff you receive as an actor, there are characters that aren't there to evolve the plot, and are one-dimensional, and you have to do a lot of work to make them human beings. In the Smith Brothers' films, there are rich characters and you'd want to play any of them. One of the things I loved about playing Gideon was that he didn't even know himself and he didn't know what his own nature was. He'd spent time in the oil fields and he had a tough life, a damaged, confused guy, and I love that combination. Being that it was based on some of their own experience growing up, the brothers were real sensitive to that original person who was being presented."

Critics noted that *The Slaughter Rule* was "beautifully photographed" by Eric Edwards and "well designed" by John Johnson, the realistic Montana landscapes and character-revealing sets evoking a maturity that belies the filmmakers' youth. One commented that as the movie ambles along, it finds "its own eccentrically impressionistic style."

The *Los Angeles Times* had this to say: "Scenes and images (some of them blatantly symbolic) bleed together into what feels like a thick, messy scrapbook of live-action snapshots. The dialogue is rough and twangy and sometimes sounds too muddy to be intelligible…And the movie seems to support a view that in western Montana the unceasing battle with the elements is often a losing one, culminating in self-destruction."

Of 35 speaking roles, all but six would be cast in Montana. The Smiths never played six-man football themselves. "It's a wide-open game," said Alex Smith. "Everybody is an eligible receiver. There's a lot of scoring, because if you miss your tackle, it's almost an automatic

six points." While on location, the brothers watched area six-man games at Highwood, Brady, and other nearby towns in which scores ran up as high as 71-60.

On a December day outside Augusta High School, the brothers filmed a six-man game between the fictional Renegades and the real Elks. Cars and trucks were parked in strategic positions along the edge of the football field. Three chickens huddled in a pen, waiting in the wings, for their cue to run across the field. A few days earlier, the film crews had shot an ice fishing scene at Bean Lake.

Carroll College's Kim Delong plays a supporting role. As Alex Smith told people, "It isn't *The Mighty Ducks*," comparing his six-man football movie to the PG-rated Disney hockey films of the 1990s. The movie was rated R for its violence and profanity. "It's locker room talk," said Cody Harvey, a Great Falls man who acted in the movie. "You might not feel comfortable watching it with your mother."

Ryan Gosling, the movie's most recognizable name, has gone on to star in several blockbusters. "Ryan Gosling," said Alex Smith, "when we cast him, we had never seen him before and had seen up to 200 boys prior to that in auditions. We could tell from a handshake that he was our Roy. In preproduction we had lost another actor we had cast. We flew from Montana to L.A. to cast for that character and it was magic. With Ryan, preparing for an early scene in which Roy is supposed to drinking mezcal, he had never experienced mezcal and the prop master got him some to taste it. After much deliberation, we allowed him to taste it, and we didn't know that tasting it meant drinking one-third of the bottle."

"We all knew when he auditioned that Ryan was a great choice," said Morse. "I was in LA at the time and the movie had worked with five other actors they had chosen, but eventually it was Ryan. On-screen, I pushed Ryan and he pushed back. There was a quality to him that was deep, sure of himself, and he had all that Mouseketeer background, and he had a tough background, a single mother in Canada, and he had to fight. I told him he had the quality of the best actors I've worked with. It's no surprise people recognized what he was about."

Members of the cast also received coaching in the Blackfeet language from Arlene Grant of Browning. An exchange in Blackfeet between Tracy Two Dogs, played by Lakota actor Eddie Spears, and Waylon Walks Along, played by Noah Watts, an enrolled Crow, is translated into English subtitles. Great Falls–area locations are recognizable, including Great Falls High School and First Peoples Buffalo Jump State Park near Ulm, and the Peoples brothers avoided dating the film by not using any sport utility vehicles or cell phones.

"I think *The Slaughter Rule* is a timeless piece," said Andrew. "It's anytime between 1960 and now. There are no cell phones or computers or anything. It's the underlying theme of what is a man or what does it take to become a man. And the whole film is really about trust."

"We wanted it to be authentic to the West," said Alex Smith. "It is obvious that it is Montana, but the town was fictional." The brothers said that they were pressured to film their story elsewhere, but they declined. "We just couldn't do this anywhere but Montana," said Alex. "There were a lot of exteriors, and we probably had on the most layers of clothing during any film ever shot in the US. We made T-shirts at the end that said, 'We Survived *The Slaughter Rule*'."

The Stone Boy

CAST
Robert Duvall, Frederick Forrest, Glenn Close,
Wilford Brimley

DIRECTOR
Chris Cain

LOCATION
Great Falls, Cascade area

1984

About 95 percent of *The Stone Boy* was shot in the Cascade and Great Falls area, with the remainder shot in either Reno or Las Vegas, Nevada. Much of the filming was done in July 1983 on a ranch east of Cascade. Other filming locations include the town of Cascade, Bair's Truck Stop northwest of Great Falls, an area cemetery, and the Great Falls bus station. Interior shots comprised about half of the filming, including a pair of farm houses.

Actress Gail Youngs (left) starred in *The Stone Boy* made in the Great Falls and Cascade area.

The Stone Boy was released in several cities around the nation, but quickly pulled off screens. "The reviews all said great acting, great this, great that, but…extremely depressing," said Dean Ostrander, district manager of Carisch Theatres in Great Falls.

The Stone Boy is the tale of a family in the rural Midwest struggling to stay together as it is torn apart in the wake of a tragic accident. Robert Duvall plays the father of a young boy who retreats behind a mental wall of stone after he accidentally kills his older brother on an early morning hunting trip.

But this is really about ordinary people: farmers who have to cope with tragedy using strength from within and have no help from professional shrink. Director Chris Cain shows enormous talent as he leads the actors through tricky territory. Arnold (Jason Presson) and Eugene Hillerman (Dean Cain, the director's son) are brothers living on a farm. They rise early to go duck hunting, but their happy plans soon turn tragic as Eugene is accidentally shot by Arnold's gun. Arnold becomes quiet, doesn't know what to do. His brother is dead and he realizes he'll have to tell everyone what happened, but he can't face the fact right away.

When he finally returns home to break the terrible news to his parents (Robert Duvall and Glenn Close), he is immediately left outside of their sorrow. Since Arnold is not in tears or hysterical, his father misreads that as his not caring. His mother also can't fathom Arnold's tranquil behavior, but she is less stern. In the center of an emotional whirlpool, Arnold gets quieter and quieter, becoming a "stone boy" who cannot be part of the madness of a family in chaos. *Film Magazine* summed it up this way: "A languorous movie with little of the tear jerking and often obvious sequences one might have expected, *The Stone Boy* pulls no punches and makes very few statements. All it seems to do is present the story very simply and let the audience decide what's right and what's wrong."

Both Great Falls and Cascade residents were hired as extras in the film, which was shot primarily on the vacant Hillerman Ranch. A production crew spent more than a week at the ranch painting and furnishing the house and grooming the yard before filming began June 28. The house had been abandoned, and production designer Joe Pacelli said he was only given eight days to get the place in shape for filming. Pacelli said his chores included cutting "waist-high grass and weeds," completely painting and furnishing the house interior, and putting new doors on the old barn, then having a special artist use "Hollywood tricks" to age the doors to match the building.

Pacelli said all the furnishings were rented from area shops and that local painters and carpenters were hired to get the buildings in shape. "With only eight days, I didn't think we'd make it," said Pacelli. "But they got it done. I think the thanks go primarily to the hard work of the people, the locals."

One of the biggest filming events was in Cascade, where a street was blocked off and a carnival—complete with rides, games, and refreshments—was set up. Locals were allowed to attend the carnival and many had fill-in roles in the movie. Actress Glenn Close passed time between shooting scenes by working on a needlepoint project.

As with all films, some segments had to be reshot because of problems. On the first day of shooting, after the deputies' car came roaring into the farmyard at top speed, smoke started pouring from under the hood. There was a delay until the radiator was cooled and refilled. The crew faced frequent rain and unexpected thundershowers that postponed work several times.

Labor problems in mid-July also delayed production of the film. Three labor business-managers from Hollywood came to Montana and threatened to yank union members from the job unless certain conditions were met. In a hurried bargaining session with the film's attorney, the main points were hammered out and shooting at the Hillerman ranch continued.

Allen Knauber, editor of the *Cascade Courier* newspaper, said townspeople had mixed reactions about the movie being filmed in and around their community. Knauber said many people were excited and wanted parts in the film, while others tended to ignore it. But he said such events as the café filming drew big crowds. "The bars were doing excellent business," said Knauber. "It was a wild time in Cascade for the moment." Knauber said the film makers didn't release much information about their local shooting schedule. "They're trying to keep the local, mundane, day-to-day color," he said.

In Great Falls, an apartment scene was shot downtown and other filming was done at Bair's Truck Stop and the Bar S Saloon, as well as at the city bus station. The interior of the Sportsman's Club café in Cascade was also used in several sequences. Local waitresses Sharon Edwards and Denise Deshner, as well as cook Joann Erickson, had parts in the scene. The café was not changed much for the filming, except that a hole in one wall was resurfaced and painted. While there were some scenes filmed in Reno, "for the most part, it'll look like Montana—that's for sure," said director Chris Cain. Cain scouted several set locations in other states, but chose Montana. "The story was written for the Wyoming/Montana area," said Cain. "When that's the case, I think you've got to film there—not on some Hollywood back lot. I looked around in Colorado, but the colors were wrong. You've got to have the right textures, the right atmosphere. And sounds are very important."

Cain said the Cascade sites were cinematic in the same sense that some people are photogenic—they looked good on film. When the movie was being filmed near Cascade, the script called for a garden in full bloom. Trouble was it was April. How do you get tomatoes and peas on the vine in April? The movie company hired a local gardener to start seedlings early and raise them in her greenhouse. "By the time they were ready to film we had a garden you wouldn't believe, big ripe tomatoes and everything," said Montana Film Commissioner Gary Wunderwald.

During production, Cain said *Stone Boy* would be in the same genre as films such as *On Golden Pond, Kramer Versus Kramer*, and *Chariots of Fire*—films with more emotional impact than action-packed violence or sex. "This is an actor's piece, and I think we've got one of the finest groups of actors in the world to make it," said Cain.

Because of child labor laws, the 12-year-old star of the film, Jason Presson, was only allowed on the set for six hours a day, which limited when certain scenes could be shot. Cain's 17-year-old son, Dean, made his acting debut as the brother who was killed. But Cain said he hadn't encouraged his children to get into the film business. "I'm not sure it's good for some kids to act," he said. "There are some things more important. We encourage them in athletics, and scholastics more." But he said Presson, the film's star, was definitely one child who should be before a camera. "It's like therapy for him," said Cain. "When he's acting he shows emotion I don't think he's comfortable showing in his own life."

"It is a beautifully-made movie but it is conveying a very difficult subject," said Cary Jones, sales manager for Twentieth Century-Fox's specialized films division. "Audiences would rather go see a movie with all the hoopla around it, like *All of Me*."

New York Times film critic Vincent Canby had the following to say when the film opened in New York April 4: "*Stone Boy* is about a grief so special and so private that the film has the effect of seeming to force us to invade its privacy, making us feel more uncomfortable than moved."

"We decided to pull it because it was difficult to compete against the summertime films, like *Ghostbusters* and *Gremlins*," said Jones. "The response was 'soft,' as we like to say."

The Thing From Another World

CAST
Margaret Sheridan, Kenneth Tobey, Robert Cornthwaite, James Arness

DIRECTOR
Christian Nyby

LOCATION
Glacier National Park

1951

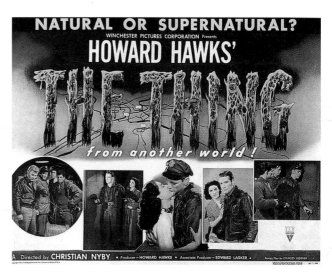

Glacier National Park subbed for the North Pole in legendary director Howard Hawk's *The Thing from Another World*.

In this horror classic, the crew of a remote Arctic base fights off a murderous monster from outer space. While most of *The Thing From Another World* was filmed in Los Angeles, several outdoor scenes were filmed in the wintery confines of Glacier National Park. *The Thing From Another World* (which was remade in 1982 by John Carpenter) functions as both a tight science-fiction thriller and a revealing snapshot of the Cold War paranoia beginning to sweep the country in post-WWII America. The story, about the battle between a group of stranded military personnel and an alien creature fueled by human blood, is a model of economic storytelling. At the time, it was considered one of the most terrifying motion pictures ever made.

A group of soldiers led by Captain Patrick Hendry (Kenneth Tobey) travel to the North Pole to examine an aircraft crash located near a scientific outpost. What they discover is a flying saucer and a sole extraterrestrial pilot, whom they bring back to the lab, frozen in a block of ice, for further study. It's not long before the Thing (James Arness)—essentially a super-intelligent vegetable man with the ability to both regenerate lost limbs and reproduce through spreading seeds—thaws out and begins to wreak havoc, although Nyby wisely maintains tension by keeping the creature hidden from view and focusing on the clash between mad scientist Dr. Arthur Carrington (Robert Cornthwaite) and Captain Hendry.

Carrington deduces that the Thing feels no emotional or sexual pleasure and, thus, is "our superior in every way," while Captain Hendry sees the visitor as merely

The "Thing" from *The Thing from Another World.*

a monster bent on harvesting the planet for mankind's blood.

Newspapers warned that the motion picture was not recommended by the management to those persons who frighten easily. The *Dallas Morning News* cited as an example J.P. Harrison, city manager for Interstate Theatres in Denton:

"*The Thing* has been produced with such realism that it seems to crawl from the screen almost as if it were in third-dimension, ever appearing as though it were all around the viewer ready to strike all during the running time of the film."

The Untouchables

CAST
Kevin Costner, Sean Connery, Robert De Niro

DIRECTOR
Brian De Palma

LOCATION
Cascade area

1987

Former Montana Film Commissioner Garry Wunderwald was adept at finding what directors and producers needed, including antique cars, railroad beds, carnivals and waterfalls. A tame bull elk, a hawk that flies on command, an antique airplane—these are a few other things.

One August afternoon in 1986, he fielded an especially challenging request. He was asked to find a 1930-period bridge—but it couldn't be just any 1930-period bridge. On this bridge, Prohibition-era whiskey runners would clash with lawmen as part of Paramount Production's *The Untouchables*.

"The movie was being filmed in Chicago and they called and said that they needed to do a scene and they'd be out in two days," recalled Garry Wunderwald, who served for more than 15 years as Montana film commissioner, from the mid-1970s to 1990.

What the filmmakers needed was a bridge that connected two distinctly different geological formations, a setting that would suggest a border crossing between Canada and the United States. It had to be low enough that a man could fall from it and survive, and it had to look like Canada on the far side. Wunderwald found several bridges that didn't quite fit the bill before scouting out the two-lane Hardy Bridge, which crossed the Missouri River about 50 miles north of Helena.

"Most of the bridges the company looked at in the Midwest were too close to Chicago in an area where modern bridges were within view," Wunderwald said, "so they came to the Northwest and looked in four states as well as Canada. Actually, we looked at three bridges in the state before settling on the Hardy Bridge over the Missouri.

"One, at Thompson Falls, was beyond repair, making it unsafe for equipment. The Dearborn Bridge, on the back road to Augusta, also was considered for possible use, but lost out because of lack of water in the Dearborn River. One of the bridges was too narrow. I had another bridge in mind between Red Lodge and Billings, but it had way too much traffic on it. We were on the last bridge that they had time to scout in Montana before they were heading to Washington."

Producers liked Wunderwald's final suggestion, selecting Hardy Bridge, located on the frontage road between Cascade and Wolf Creek. The Hardy Bridge, built in 1930, was closed to traffic during filming, from October 6 to October 20, 1986. The scene involved a shootout between Al Capone's gangsters and Prohibition agent

The Hardy Bridge over the Missouri River north of Craig became a Canadian border crossing in *The Untouchables*, a prohibition-era film starring Kevin Costner and Sean Connery.

Eliot Ness (played by Kevin Costner) and his Untouchables, played by Sean Connery, Andy Garcia and Charles Martin Smith. Like the early television series of the same name, *The Untouchables* portrayed the criminal activities of bootleggers under mobster Capone, as well as the government agents working to stop them.

Paramount sent a crew of nearly 100 people to shoot the bridge segment. About 25 area residents were cast to ride horseback as red-coated Royal Canadian Mounted Police during the scene in which the lawmen try to capture Capone's bootleggers. The extras playing Mounties didn't need their own horses. Paramount, with a strict eye for detail, wanted all the horses to look similar, in keeping with the Mounties' custom.

There was another major detail: sometimes filming isn't a case of locating things but of concealing them.

When the crew of *The Untouchables* decided to use the Hardy Bridge, they had to make cabins and summer homes along the river temporarily vanish. They did so by using 50,000 square feet of olive-drab canvas and camouflage netting, plus 600 trees that were all planted in a day and a half. "I called every company in Montana that could conceivably provide this canvas and netting, but no one had such large amounts in stock," Wunderwald said, so a firm in Chicago provided the material.

The trees, however, were state-raised, and brought in from the Lincoln and Kalispell areas. The movie company paid about $25,000 for the additional greenery. "It was a wild thing to see these Christmas trees out there," Wunderwald recalled. Wunderwald helped obtain several 1920s- and 1930s-era Fords and Ford Model-Ts from a group of ranchers from Conrad who restored old Ford

Sean Connery gets instructions from director Brian De Palma on the set of *The Untouchables.* Of De Palma's 29 films, it's the only one to win an Oscar—for Connery's supporting performance.

the lead role as Eliot Ness, organizer of the group of U.S. government agents known as the Untouchables. Connery played Jim Malone, a tenacious Irish beat cop from Chicago who is Ness's first recruit as a Prohibition agent.

The production crew allowed people to watch the filming from a nearby field, and to use cameras. Hundreds of people showed up during the first weekend of filming. Connery treated well-wishers and fans "openly and cordially," Wunderwald said.

As happened in the case of *The Untouchables,* Wunderwald said, he generally had little advance notice from scouts. In more than 10 years of pitching and promoting, his preparedness and quick-thinking led to the use of many production sites in Montana. He "lost a few along the way," he said, but rejection and competition were part and parcel of the Hollywood hunt. "If the scouts or companies don't find what they need in 24 hours they politely exit," he said. "You have to be cool and level-headed and patient. You can't let it get to you."

Opinion was unaminously favorable. Indeed, of De Palma's 29 films, it's the only one to win an Oscar—for Sean Connery's supporting performance. De Palma reflected on the film in 2016 to *Entertainment Weekly,* "Beautifully photographed, beautifully scored, fantastic locations. Every once in a while it all comes together."

bodies as a hobby. Several Great Falls area folks who provided period autos were paid $300 a day. The person hired to maintain the vehicles received $50 a day.

"The film crew marked them up to appear as if they were all shot up—Hollywood-style," Wunderwald said. "We figure close to $1 million was spent in Great Falls in the two weeks they took to shoot the film. And of course there was the prep work, too. One carpenter said he made $4,500 in that time."

Actual filming in Montana took approximately 10 days, but the production staff reserved the bridge for enough time to allow for production delays. "Everything went smoothly," Wunderwald said. "The train master in Helena even agreed not to run trains through at the time of the shooting."

Robert DeNiro, who played Al Capone, did not appear in the Montana-filmed sequence. Costner played

Thousand Pieces of Gold

CAST
Rosalind Chao, Chris Cooper

DIRECTOR
Nancy Kelly

LOCATION
Nevada City, Butte, Ennis

1991

Marginally based on a true story, *Thousand Pieces of Gold* is about a young Chinese immigrant woman who lands

Thousand Pieces of Gold is about a young Chinese woman who lands in America during the Gold Rush of the 1880s and is sold into marriage.

in America during the Gold Rush of the 1880s and is sold into marriage. Mother Lode Productions contacted 35 film commissions looking for an authentic-looking gold rush town. From California to Canada, too many of the towns had been "prettied up," restored into cute little shops, said co-producer Kenji Yamamoto. "They needed a town with actual authentic feel," said Yamamoto.

Yamamoto and the production, well, struck location gold with Nevada City's 114 historical buildings assembled as an old mining town. While the script called for scenes in Northern China, San Francisco's Chinatown, and a livery stable in Lewiston, Idaho, the movie was filmed entirely in Montana—in Nevada City, Ennis and Butte. Filming took place during three months in the spring of 1989.

At first glance Nevada City looks like a typical tourist ghost town. Old hand-hewn log buildings flank muddy streets; snow melts on worn wooden boardwalks as an old sign creaks in the wind.

But by the end of April 1989, the town's population jumped from two to more than 60. Wagons, horses, and actors filled the streets and the 1870s returned. Saws buzzed as an old building became an 1870s saloon. Artists mixed colors to make the remodeled buildings match the rustic ones. The crew restored the floor of a billiards hall for boarding house scenes, pushed a leaning cabin upright for a star's residence and turned the Criterion Hall into a saloon with moveable walls that allowed the saloon to also become a bedroom and kitchen.

A little Chinese village of nomadic yurts was built on a grassy hillside near Nevada City while an alley near the Peking Noodle Parlor in Butte was transformed into a scene from San Francisco in the 1870s.

"Looking at photographs you notice that Mongolia is not too much different than Montana," said location manager Mark Zetler. "The shots required large tracts of land with no fences or telephone poles and a place where you could still get a crew in there. We shot outside of Ennis and created China. And 1870s San Francisco which we shot behind the Peking Noodle Parlor."

"There is a Chinatown on the outskirts of Nevada City," said director Nancy Kelly. "That's very typical of a mining town. It works very well for the story." In-

The cast and crew of *Thousand Pieces of Gold* celebrate filming at Nevada City. While the script called for scenes in China, San Francisco, and Idaho, the entire movie was shot in Montana.

side one of the buildings in Nevada City's Chinatown were a variety of artifacts: metal tins, abacuses, baskets, paper lanterns, Buddha figures, canned goods labeled with Chinese characters, old photos—even sugar lotus roots—a sweet candy-like treat.

Rosalind Chao depicts Polly Bemis (Chinese name: Lalu Nathoy), an iron-willed young Chinese woman determined to keep her dignity and self-esteem intact. The film opens in northeast China, circa 1880, where a frightened Lalu is being sold into slavery by her despairing, poverty-stricken father. Taken in chains across the Pacific Ocean to San Francisco, she's promptly auctioned off to a Chinese trader known as Jim.

Lalu slowly falls in love with Jim, whose Chinese name is Li Po and who, eight years earlier, had arrived in the U.S. as a virtual slave-laborer for the railroad: he was an indentured worker who eventually worked off his debt and earned his freedom. Though Jim apparently yearns

to return Lalu's affection, he is weak in the face of what he perceives to be his duty: namely, the transportation of Lalu from San Francisco to the isolated mining town of Warren's Diggens, Idaho, where she is to work as a prostitute for Hong King, the local would-be entrepreneur and saloon manager, the man who gave Jim the money to purchase a Chinese slave. Hong King's plans for Lalu include exploiting her as an exotic change-of-pace from the town's white whores.

Unwilling to permit her body to be used or abused by the rough and rowdy mining camp drunkards, Lalu contemplates suicide before fate intervenes in the form of Charlie Bemis, the saloon's actual owner. Charlie gives Lalu tips on how to save herself from her seemingly hopeless fate. Following a confrontation with Charlie, Hong King grants Lalu her wish to work off her debt via hard labor. Charlie's fondness for Lalu blossoms into devotion and years later Lalu returns his affection.

Documentarian Nancy Kelly's theatrical directorial debut was co-produced with her film-editor husband, Kenji Yamamoto. Even though the film reportedly cost less than $2 million, it frequently has the look of a much more expensive film. Yamamoto discovered Nevada City from an article in *Sunset* magazine. There are shades of the grandeur of a classic John Ford–style Western, even though much of this film (unlike Ford's frequent spectacular vistas in Monument Valley) is played out in confined, intimate quarters. When the picture opens, the scenery is magnificent, thanks to cinematographer Bobby Bukowski, who never fails to make the best possible use of the Montana wilderness that serves as both northern China and Idaho.

Kelly has warm—and chilly—memories of directing *Thousand Pieces of Gold* in Montana in 1989. "We had six weeks of pre-production during which it snowed every single day," said Kelly. The day the crew shot the opening scene, "Take one, it was sunny. Take two, it was cloudy. Take three, it was snowing."

Along with finding a location, another challenge was casting oriental actors in Montana. "Amazingly we're finding a lot of Chinese for parts," said Kelly. They drew from Chinese visiting professors and students across the state. The film features a number of Montana and Missoula actors, including Jianli Zhang and Weili Fan, who play the heroine's parents. The two were students from Beijing, studying at the University of Montana, when Kelly and Yamamoto recruited them for the project. Since many western gold-rush towns are tourist stops now, with busy shops and traffic, it was no easy task choosing the right location to shoot this period piece. "Everywhere we looked was going to be really expensive, or in the wrong place," said Kelly. When the couple checked out Nevada City, "it was perfect."

Yamamoto and Kelly did extensive research on the American Gold Rush and found that the true story their film details "was quite common." "Thousands of Chinese women were sold by their families and ended up enslaved or in brothels. Most of these women died from their ordeals." By contrast, their heroine, Polly Bemis, "lived into her eighties and was revered as one of the great legends of the Pacific Northwest."

The movie was filmed in the spring. "Everyone said the most stable weather was in the fall, but we couldn't wait that long," said Kelly. "I kept saying, 'Oh, it's in the banana belt of Montana, it's all right.'" Filming took

In *Thousand Pieces of Gold*, San Francisco's Chinatown was actually an alley behind the Peking Noodle Parlor in Butte.

place throughout May, a mercurial month for Montana weather. However, when they really needed Mother Nature to come through, she did. "We didn't have a lot of money, and we needed some seasonal transition stuff," said Kelly. "We needed fake snow, but could only afford about two boxes. On the first week we were shooting, it snowed. It looked like the dead of winter, and we got our winter footage. Our production designer Dan Bishop said to me, 'This is more than $10,000 worth of snow that's falling from the sky!'"

Actress Rosalind Chao, who portrays Bemis in the movie, said Bemis's story taught her "a lot about surviving and not giving up."

"It also broke a lot of stereotypes about Asian women. This woman was really a pioneer." Chao said she retained positive feelings about working in Montana. "Montana couldn't have provided a better backdrop," said Chao. "The location was the star."

The crew's headquarters was the Nevada City hotel, but at night they retired to an Ennis motel. "The vegetarians have had a terrible time," said Kelly. "Within a few days we ate all the spinach in Ennis." But Yamamoto said the crew had been well received. "Montana people are great. They are real helpful."

Made by a group from Maine, the small, independent movie *Three Priests* was filmed at Choteau because one of the filmmakers' grandmothers lived there.

Three Priests

CAST
Michael Parks, Olivia Hussey, Wes Studi

DIRECTOR
Jim Cole

LOCATION
Choteau area

2007

A romantic rivalry strains the bonds of an already fragile family relationship in this independent drama. Jake Sands (Michael Parks) runs a ranch on the plains of Montana with his wife Rachel (Olivia Hussey). Jake and Rachel have two grown sons; Joe is a dutiful young cowboy who helps his father look after the cattle, while Dusty is an emotionally nomadic rodeo rider with an eye for the ladies and a knack for locating trouble. Jake makes no secret of the fact he doesn't approve of Dusty's wild ways, and he dotes on his younger and more devoted son.

Familial tension simmers beneath the surface when Dusty comes home for a visit, but the rivalry between the two brothers explodes when Joe learns that he and Dusty have both been dating Abby, a local beauty they've known since childhood. When Joe and Dusty's anger explodes into deadly violence, Jake is forced to make some painful choices. From the opening scenes of Parks and actor Wes Studi driving nails atop a roof, to that on the dark, shadowy bluffs where Dusty ultimately meets his death at the hands of his brother, *Three Priests* is rife with splendid visuals. One of the movie's highlights: the character-actor Parks in a Choteau baseball cap.

"*Three Priests* was filmed on a family ranch or a connection to the director outside of Choteau, so I was along for the ride as far as scouting," said John Ansotegui. "It was a pretty self-contained production."

Three Priests was shot on a budget of approximately $300,000. "*Three Priests* was produced by guys out of Maine, and I believe that one of the guys' grandmother lived in Choteau," said unit production manager Allison Whitmer. "The production office was an apartment and the guys lived in the grandmother's house. We had less than half a million as a budget and we used abandoned houses where people were cooking meth. We found these meth houses on these farms. We found a nice house but it was a meth house and eventually it was condemned and torn down after we left. Choteau was in the grips of it at that point. The movie is about a guy who loses his [head]—and it happens. The people were super nice. It won some festivals in Maine.

Thunderbolt and Lightfoot

CAST
Clint Eastwood, Jeff Bridges

DIRECTOR
Michael Cimino

LOCATION
Livingston, Great Falls

1974

Filmmakers have aimed their lenses at central Montana for decades. Its wide-open prairies and rugged peaks seem well-suited to storytelling that embraces the individual, the loners and seekers, people looking to get away from something—or find it. And for these reasons, the area has played host to some of the biggest names in the business.

The historic Fort Benton Bridge overlooks the Missouri River—and a film location in *Thunderbolt and Lightfoot* that featured two of Hollywood's biggest stars: Clint Eastwood (a veteran bank robber) and Jeff Bridges (his free-spirited sidekick).

In a cloud of Sunday dust, the shabby old Cadillac swoops into the churchyard. Out of the car steps the stranger. He stands there, wiping sweaty grime off his sloping forehead. Then impatient, he steps through the door of the one-room church. He opens fire. Bullets whiz. Machine gun bullets shatter the altar. The minister, his cover blown, scoots out the back door and sprints off across a flat Montana wheat field. And the wild chase begins, in Big Sky Country.

In 1974's *Thunderbolt and Lightfoot*, Eastwood and Bridges play a pair of drifters who fall into friendship and joint criminal enterprise. *Thunderbolt and Lightfoot* brought director Michael Cimino to Hollywood after a successful career in East Coast advertising.

As an anti-hero, Eastwood's character is known as Thunderbolt for his exploits (he broke into the State Armory with a cannon, getting away with thousands), hides out in rural Montana as a minister while angry cohorts seek his death. They think he turned in his pals for the loot—hidden somewhere in Montana.

Set in and around Great Falls, the film uses landscape as a character in its own right, as the duo makes repeated escapes into Montana's mountains while fleeing from police, fellow hoods, and civilization. George Kennedy (as Red) lends his role a live-wire, bare-knuckle intensity and an unexpectedly tender sort of grace.

Why Kennedy has been trying to kill the two for half the movie is finally revealed: he thinks Eastwood pulled one over on him in a long-ago heist, but Eastwood explains that he didn't get the goods, either. So they head for Great Falls and plan a finale, the mother of all robberies to cap their careers.

Fort Benton and its historic trestle bridge frame host a pivotal scene, and the film's bittersweet ending occurs at a scenic overlook above the Missouri River near Cascade.

Originally, several parts of the film were supposed to be completed in Idaho. Instead, after the filming ended in Great Falls, the movie crew traveled to the Gates of the Mountains area on the Missouri River 15 miles north of Helena for completion. The decision not to go to the Lewiston, Idaho, area on the Snake River made the movie an all-Montana product. Production manager Abner Singer said that filming the final scenes near the Gates of the Mountains saved money. The replica of an old Ravalli County schoolhouse used in the movie was set up at a rest stop on Interstate 15 north of Craig and was there for a month. It was sold to a land-development firm which moved it to a site just off the Dearborn exit of the interstate (for use as an office).

The St. John's Lutheran Church in Hobson used in *Thunderbolt and Lightfoot* was relocated to Troy, Montana, in 1981. Choteau's Grain Terminal association can be seen in the background in the scene in which Bridges steals a car off the dealer's lot. Bridges and Eastwood park their Trans Am at Diversion Lake after Eastwood, the preacher, is run out of the Hobson church. Folks will also recognize the Intermountain Bus Depot in the scene where Eastwood searches for a bag full of cash inside one of its lockers; and when the two drifters hop on the "Idaho Dream" boat, it transports them through the distinctly identifiable mouth of Gates of the Mountains. Several of the scenes of the Trans Am were filmed in areas near Gates of the Mountains, where there was no road access and the movie crew had to transport the vehicle by boat.

Other recognizable points of interest include the Meadowlark Elementary School in Great Falls and 56 Dearborn River Road, the site of the schoolhouse built for the film and dismantled afterward. Bridges and East-

Jeff Bridges (left) and Clint Eastwood (right) play a pair of drifters who fall into friendship and criminal enterprise in *Thunderbolt and Lightfoot*. Here the actors prepare for a scene at Gates of the Mountains on the Missouri River.

wood chat amiably in the Fort Benton park where the statue of the brave dog Shep was erected. Bridges dies in a Cadillac driven by Eastwood on I-15 at Tower Rock State Park.

When filming was completed, United Artists ran a large ad in the Great Falls newspaper thanking the people of the community for their cooperation and a wonderful stay. A *New York Times* Hollywood columnist subsequently reported that Eastwood and most of the cast were relieved to "Leave the location 'in the wilds of Montana'."

"*Thunderbolt and Lightfoot* was an exciting movie," said Jeff Bridges decades afterward. "I was a young guy and Eastwood was producing [along with Robert Daley] and he was giving Michael Cimino his first shot, his first

editorial job. It was filmed partly in Helena, at the Gates of the Mountains. I fell in love with Montana, I bought a Harley Davidson, and there was no better place to buy a bike and ride around. My friend Gary Busey was also in the film and I had a wonderful time to share with him. Clint Eastwood is famous for not wanting to do more than one take of a scene, but Clint was patient with Cimino and he would say, 'Give the kid another shot.' It was all a wonderful experience. The light, the mountains, and the people—everything just struck a chord in me."

For his role in *Thunderbolt and Lightfoot*, Jeff Bridges received an Oscar nomination for Best Supporting Actor. Bridges has been a resident of Montana for 40-plus years.

Timberjack

CAST
Sterling Hayden, Vera Ralston

DIRECTOR
Joseph Kane

LOCATION
Missoula area, Polson, Glacier National Park

1955

Missoula has not been selected for a world premiere of a Hollywood feature film since February 4, 1955. That night, pencils of brilliant blue light traced the snowy skies above the Garden City. Some of Hollywood's more recognizable idols were greeted by flashbulbs and microphones as they arrived at the Fox Theater (opening in 1949 and demolished in the late 1970s) for the world premiere of *Timberjack*. It was the climax of "Timberjack Days," a joint celebration with the U.S. Forest Service's golden anniversary, which included a festive afternoon parade down Higgins Avenue.

The cast and production crew had been in Montana the previous summer to shoot scenes in the Bonner-Blackfoot area, in Polson and in Glacier National Park. The Florence Hotel was headquarters for the filming. Locals, including Bonner School students, mixed with the stars. Star Sterling Hayden didn't return to Montana for Timberjack Days. Neither did jazz composer and pianist Hoagy Carmichael, who played the part of piano-playing Jingles in the movie. A native of Indiana, Carmichael had spent most of a year, circa 1910, in Missoula as a boy, attending Lowell School and entering the red-light district not far from his family's tiny home on West Pine Street to, as he later recalled, "listen to the piano players."

Carmichael sent a telegram to Missoula Mayor James Hart expressing his disappointment over his inability to attend due to "a serious illness." "Let it be known," the wire said, "that I just now stood up in bed and toasted all of you from my teacup. P.S., maybe I should have stayed in the healthy country." The Missoula entourage included co-star Vera Ralston, a native of Czechoslovakia

and that country's national figure skating champion before moving to the U.S. in 1940, and her husband Herbert Yates, president of Republic Pictures, *Timberjack*'s producer. Others were David Brian, the villainous Montana lumber baron Croft Brunner in the movie; Adolphe Menjou, a World War I veteran whose film career had started in the silent movie era, and Chill Wills, the lively character actor who played hero Steve Riika in *Timberjack*. Also along to lend his name to the promotion was Rex Allen, the singing Arizona cowboy who was at the height of his fame in the early 1950s.

They arrived on Wednesday and spent the next two days making appearances at luncheons and banquets. They were joined by Dan Cushman, who drove over from his home in Great Falls. Cushman (1909-2001) wrote the 1953 novella that the movie was based on. Though he grew up and still lived in Montana, he'd set his *Timberjack* in the woods of Canada. Cushman would have "a seat of honor" with Ralston in one of the lead convertibles in the Friday afternoon parade.

The winter parade had more than 100 entries, which included, according to one contemporary newspaper account, "Forest Service trucks carrying saws, axes, picks and shovels from the old days, and chain saws and other mechanized equipment from the modern era." A pack train of white mules "clopped down the street" in front of a "mechanical mule"—described as "a one-wheeled power device used to haul material on mountain trails." The University of Montana marching band was joined by half a dozen high school bands from around the region, including one from Polson, "75 members strong," that would return home for another "Timberjack Day" parade the following day.

The climax was the premiere showings of *Timberjack* at 6:20 p.m. at the Fox, on the northwestern end of the Orange Street Bridge, and at 7:25 p.m. at the Roxy on South Higgins. Fireworks exploded when the stars and executives arrived at the Fox.

Allen emceed a short program at intermission and sang a few numbers, including Carmichael's *Lazy River*. When they finished at the Fox, the entourage drove over to the Roxy to do it all again. Then it was over. The Hollywood crowd flew back to California and Cushman went home to Great Falls.

The Anaconda Copper Mining Company mill in Bonner lent the studio their shay engine for the movie, which is now at the Historical Museum at Fort Missoula.

The Bonner history center, a small museum next to the Bonner Post Office, is teeming with a large collection of *Timberjack* memorabilia. "I think we're really fortunate to be able to bring these items back to Bonner," said Judy Matson, a volunteer at the Bonner history center. "So many people here have fond memories of the filming of the movie, and I think it really helps to give a sense of place to the new people who are here."

The stars are all dead now, and locomotive No. 7 that was brought out of retirement to co-star in the movie is at rest at the Historical Museum at Fort Missoula.

of a Man Called Horse." He said that shooting locations were studios and locations in Mexico. "If there was any photography in Montana, then on the one hand, I simply don't recall it. On the other hand, I am sure it would have not involved any actors, but rather, something like wide shots for the editing. I know firsthand it would be easier to send two young ambitious camera people to grab masters than it would be to purchase stock footage." And apparently that's what happened.

Triumphs of a Man Called Horse

CAST
Richard Harris, Michael Beck

DIRECTOR
John Hough

LOCATION
Cooke City, Red Lodge

1983

True Colors

CAST
James Spader, John Cusack, Mandy Patinkin

DIRECTOR
Herbert Ross

LOCATION
Big Sky Resort

1991

In 1967, Ireland-born Richard Harris ranked alongside Sean Connery and Michael Caine as one of the more rugged men in international cinema. Harris's movie career continued to rise with the release of his best known film of the '70s, *A Man Called Horse* (1970). This was a violent western in which he played an English aristocrat who is first tortured, then eventually adopted by the Sioux. The film was a major hit, and spawned two sequels. *Triumphs of a Man Called Horse* is the tepid third entry in the trilogy. The films are built around the exploits of aristocratic Englishman Lord John Morgan, played in all three features by Richard Harris, and his rejection of Euro-American culture for the life of an Indian warrior.

Producer Donald P. Borchers who "was involved in that film from top to bottom" said that he has "never set foot in the great state of Montana, nor did *Triumphs*

True Colors is a movie about two University of Virginia law students whose friendship comes apart as their lives intersect on Washington's fast track. Tim Garrity (James Spader) is an overachieving, finely-bred preppie who dates the daughter of a liberal senator and goes on to work for the Department of Justice. He's the principled one. Peter Burton (John Cusack), Tim's roommate, drops out of law school to work as the senator's aide. His aim: To replace the senator within 10 years. Along the way, he manages to swipe the daughter Diana, cut a crooked campaign-finance deal with a real-estate shark, and alienate just about everybody.

The Washington Post summed up *True Colors* as a "movie in a hurry, a movie on the go, an overstuffed drama about bent ethics, a globe-trotting wake-up call for us money pigs."

The movie follows the boys' friendship for nearly a decade. It highlights Montana's Big Sky ski resort in a short segment of the film. During a winter vacation in Montana, the two men fight it out like a couple of mountain rams on skis. Peter is gravely injured and Tim nobly bows out, agreeing to be the best man at his wedding to Diana.

Big Sky was chosen as a location when the script called for steep and deep skiing terrain for the crucial scene between Spade and Cusack. The dramatic skiing segment was filmed off the Challenger lift on the experts-only A-Z Chutes. Cusack and Spader had Warren Miller stand-ins for the skiing stunts who had to repeatedly perform a thrilling "accidental" fall.

Film critic Roger Ebert described the scene in detail: "In no time at all Cusack has angled himself onto the senator's staff and into the daughter's bed, and then Cusack and Spader go on a ski holiday together, where Cusack confesses his infidelity, providing a lame excuse for the two of them to have a ludicrous fight on skis."

Ebert had no qualms gloriously expanding on just how much he hated the remainder of the film. "*True Colors* requires more than the willing suspension of disbelief; it demands a willful abandonment of incredulity."

Under Siege 2: Dark Territory

CAST
Steven Seagal, Eric Borgosian

DIRECTOR
Geoff Murphy

LOCATION
Missoula area

1995

It's not a ridiculous degree of complexity that Steven Seagal's fans are seeking in the action film star. In the 1992 film, *Under Siege*, Seagal played a heroic loner who subverts a group of nuclear terrorists at sea. The movie earned $156 million at the box office, enough to justify a sequel, on a similarly thin premise. Former U.S. Navy SEAL Casey Ryback (Seagal) has left the armed forces to lead a quiet life as a chef in Denver. While taking time off from his new job, Ryback decides to go on a cross-country train trip with his niece Sarah. When the arrival of brilliantly demented Travis Dane (Eric Borgosian) and an international team of hijackers interrupt their scenic journey through the majestic Rocky Mountains, Ryback must liberate the day. Much of what comes next in *Under Siege 2* feels determined to keep the audience straightforward and engaged, to uneven results.

Despite reviews for the film being largely unfavorable, *Under 2 Siege* raked in more than $100 million. Although, noted critic Roger Ebert said that he was "amused" by the film, "It isn't as good as the original *Under Siege*, but it moves quickly, has great stunts and special effects, and is a lot of fun." Most of the movie was filmed in Colorado, but Montana manages to haul in a tiny bit of screen time.

"*Under Siege 2* shot on the trestle outside of Missoula," recalled ex-Montana Film Commissioner Lonie Stimac. "They did a small amount of filming in April 1995 near Highway 93 going toward Kalispell on Evaro Hill. There is a large train trestle on a bluff there. They [Paramount Pictures] didn't really work with us all that much."

Big Sky-born filmmakers Alex (left center) and Andrew (right center) go over directions on the set of *Walking Out*, their third film made in Montana. PHOTO COURTESY ALEX AND ANDREW SMITH

Walking Out

DIRECTOR
Andrew Smith, Alex Smith

CAST
Matt Bomer, Josh Wiggins, Bill Pullman

LOCATION
Paradise Valley, Livingston, Bozeman

2016

Grand mountains, rolling plains covered with fields of wheat and barley, a romantic myth of cowboys and Indians and the mystique of the West. These images are what people conjure up when thinking of Montana. Few people immediately think of drought, hardship, social isolation, alcoholism, aloofness, and a set of cold, distant variables understood only through the lens of uncommon insularity. But those who know the history of Montana know both the good and bad are part of its sprawling heritage.

After representing Montana's disposition twice on the big screen (*The Slaughter Rule, Winter in the Blood*), Big Sky–born filmmakers Alex and Andrew Smith found that the third time was a charm in 2016 with the film *Walking Out*. Filmed on location in Paradise Valley, Livingston and Bozeman, *Walking Out* earns the "Made-in-Montana" label. Indeed, the Smith twins revere their art as the act of sharing a point of view of both visual and emotional truth; landscape, topography and scenery are sacrosanct intermediaries, depictions deserving to be set on celluloid. "For us," said Alex, "landscape is the character, and we don't want the setting to ever feel as if it were generic. For us, it's really crucial, especially when you are

Walking Out actors Matt Bomer and Josh Wiggins portray a father and son on a hunting trip that goes awry. PHOTO COURTESY ALEX AND ANDREW SMITH.

dealing with a piece of literature that is set in Montana [*Winter in the Blood* and *Walking Out* are adaptations of Montana stories], to shoot it in Montana."

"I think that one of the keys to shooting in Montana is that you need to be in the right space at the right moment," said Andrew. "You need to be flexible and antici-pate what's going to happen. The production values that Montana gives us are incredible.

"This morning, we had snow coming down on our ac-tors as if they woke up from a camp in the snow. When the snow was really happening, the cameras and the ac-tors pick up that energy. We also said going in that we were going to embrace what the day gives us. We were not going to try to challenge the film gods, but embrace what they give us. If they give us snow, we can throw in a line about snow. Actors get there easier if they believe in the space that's around them. When we put actors into our world—the real world—we are not settling for easier shots."

Producer Brunson Green agreed that *Walking Out* played out better in its natural environment. "We shot it in the fall and the winter and I have to admit I didn't think or know if I'd be able to handle the winter," said Green. "But the snow and the weather was cooperative and everyone survived, and the film has its own unique character that importantly best tells and shows where the story takes place. And those sunny mornings in the Para-dise Valley—the orange and red—were unlike anything I've ever seen."

While the scale is greater than before, the brothers' belief that Montana tales are much too complicated for tidy, generic, or ordinary resolutions hasn't vacillated. "I think that if you look at the sort of weird cross-genres that we've made," said Andrew, "there is a football movie (*The Slaughter Rule*), a Native American Western (*Win-ter in the Blood*), and now this (*Walking Out*) is in the hunting genre, in each case we are trying to get past a cliché. We are trying to get past a stereotype of, say, what kind of a person is a hunter and what kind of a person plays football. We've tried to find stories that are inside that seemingly known world and find stories about real lives and the people who are living it." *Walking Out* has not yet been released.

War Party

CAST
Billy Wirth, Kevin Dillon, M. Emmet Walsh

DIRECTOR
Franc Roddam

LOCATION
Choteau, Browning, Cut Bank, Glacier Park

1988

Set in the jagged mountains and box canyons of Montana, *War Party* illustrates the tension between whites and Indians. The reenactment of a battle between the cavalry and the Blackfeet was filmed on the Blackfeet Indian Reservation.

Tim Sampson, a full-blood Creek Indian from Okmulgee Agency, Oklahoma, got his start in the film industry. He viewed *War Party* as an indication that the new Hollywood was looking at what really happened to American Indians. "There's a lot of interest in Vietnam now," said Sampson in 1989. "People want to know what happened there. People are not as tunnel-visioned as they used to be. *War Party* should make people think about the Indians."

Sampson, who plays Warren Cutfoot, said the film paints a truer picture of American Indians than earlier films did. The son of the trail-blazing Indian actor Will Sampson, who died in 1988, Tim said that while the film doesn't get into Native American issues such as broken treaties, he viewed it as a starting point. "We can get into issues later," said Sampson. "In *War Party*, 90 percent of the cast is Native American. Nowadays, if it calls for an

American Indian, they use one. It's not just some guy putting on a wig."

Sampson said it was hard to call it work, riding horseback through early autumn in and near the Rockies. One of the fondest memories he took with him from the 14 weeks spent filming in Browning was learning to square dance. "It was [culture shock] to see a bunch of Indians square dancing."

The film was produced by the Hemdale Film Corporation, a large independent filmmaker with a reputation for taking chances on controversial films. Hemdale produced *Platoon*, which received four Oscars, including Best Picture. Directed by Franc Roddam, *War Party* is a contemporary story about four young Indians in the fictional town of Binger. The mayor of Binger persuades tribal leaders of the bordering Blackfeet reservation to stage a mock battle between reservation Indians dressed as warriors, and whites in 19th century U.S. Cavalry garb. *War Party* opens with a scene from 100 years ago at the Milk River in Montana, where a party of Blackfeet, led by Chief He-Who-Kills-Crows, clashed with cavalry troops and was systematically wiped out.

In the near present, the chief's descendant Sonny Crowkiller, portrayed by Billy Wirth, lives on a reservation at Binger. But when Calvin Morrisey, a local resident with a grudge against one of the Indians, loads his rifle for the mock battle with real bullets and kills a man, Sonny infers he too is a target and shoots Morrisey in self-defense. Then Sonny and a group of his friends flee to the hills.

Writer Spencer Eastman said he was intrigued by modern-day Native Americans. "I was always struck with how Indians were defeated in the films," said Eastman, "and I wanted to write something where the Indians were victorious. I also wanted to show the younger kids regaining some of their tribal identity." According to Sampson, Eastman did a creditable job on the screenplay because he did a considerable amount of research in Browning. "But Indians carry a certain amount of bitterness inside, and white men have trouble portraying it."

"This film is more special than just an ordinary action film," said producer John Daly. "It's contemporary but tells a story of what happened to the Indians. This film brings back dignity to Indians." During the 10 weeks of filming in Montana, more than 5,000 extras also were used. Film commissioner Garry Wunderwald was even invited to play a doctor in a scene that was later trimmed.

One of the more scenic locations used was Chief Mountain in Glacier Park.

Montana has a special attraction for Sampson, who said he enjoys every excuse to visit or work in the state. While he was working on *War Party*, he was adopted into the Blackfeet Tribe. "No matter where I'm going, I seem to keep coming back to Montana. It's kind of like walking through the kitchen: You always stop at the ice box," said Sampson.

War Party is a movie about prejudice, but most Browning residents who had varying roles in the movie found it inoffensive and, in fact, enjoyable. More than 250 Browning residents traveled to Great Falls for the premiere. Some of the Browning delegation appeared in *War Party* as extras. Others had speaking parts. Still others worked behind the scenes, providing horses, props, and locations.

Three members of the Blackfeet tribe, however, living off the reservation in California, found the movie racist and urged Indians to boycott it. Jay Harwood, Marilyn LaPlant St. Germaine, and Betty New Breast Cooper urged people to boycott the movie because of the way it portrayed Indians. "Indians have been shown in a negative way throughout history, and I guess we were hoping maybe that had changed," said St. Germaine. "The movie was a slap in the face."

She said she contacted Blackfeet Tribal Councilman Darryl Horn after she saw the film and asked for the council's assistance in urging people not to see the movie. Horn said that the council would not take a stand on the matter. "As far as we're concerned, it's just a movie, not something we have to get involved with," said Horn. "People will develop their own opinions after they see it."

All three Californian Blackfeet were distressed by the portrayal of the tribal medicine man as the town drunk. "A medicine man would certainly not be that type of character," said Harwood. "They're very self-disciplined and strict with their own behavior."

"I have this deep concern that if a young audience sees it," said Cooper, "it will generate and support that kind of behavior—all that drug use and alcohol and violence." St. Germaine said she was disturbed by the portrayal of the tribal council and tribal police as inept and unable to deal with the mounting conflict.

Harwood said he was also appalled at the portrayal of the tribal chairman by Indian activist Dennis Banks. "Dennis has a long history of controversy, including time

Chief Mountain on the Rocky Mountain Front served as the backdrop for a scene in the contemporary western, *War Party*. During ten weeks of filming in Montana, more than 5,000 extras were used.

spent in jail," said Harwood. "Not all Indian people see him as a hero and a lot of people just plain disagree with him. They could have chosen a more appropriate person to play that role."

The three said they resented the constant tension and battles between Indians and non-Indians in the film. "It was just laced with racism—scene after scene after scene of how whites hate Indians and Indians hate whites," said Cooper. "It brought back a lot of personal feelings and experiences I had growing up on the reservation. We know there are problems, but we also know there are good things on the reservation. None of those were shown. But maybe that won't sell tickets."

Browning Indians stressed that prejudice was a fact of their lives and *War Party* was, after all, only a fictional movie. "The impact of this movie is its awareness of prejudice that truly happens—not just on the reservation but all over America," said Cynthia Kipp. "Boys really are killed like that over a game of pool." Prejudice flared during the making of the movie, said Kipp. "Extras had to be bused to Choteau for the scene at the courthouse because Choteau wouldn't rent rooms to the Browning Indians. Prejudice lives. No movie can change that, but I think it's good to show that prejudice exists." Kipp said that she didn't approve of the portrayal of the medicine man as the town drunk. "That's totally out of character for a medicine man," said Kipp.

Kipp said she knew the movie wouldn't win an Academy Award, "but you can't beat the scenery. Chief Mountain is our sacred mountain and to see it on the screen is breathtaking." Julene Kennerly, who was mayor of

Browning during filming, echoed Kipp's praise for the movie's use of Montana scenery. She emphasized the positive aspect of the medicine man's portrayal. "By portraying our sacred man as an alcoholic, the movie shows that anyone can have the disease," said Kennerly.

Darnell Rides Out The Door, who produced *Indian Country*, a public service program, said he was pleased that, although the story was fictional, Roddam had depicted the Blackfeet as "real people, not 10 tribes combined into one….the movie portrays real people in real settings with real problems." Earl Old Person, then chief of the Blackfeet Tribe, said he was pleased that the movie makers actually came to the reservation to make a movie about reservation Indians.

Wanda Bear Medicine Peterson said the movie was fiction and should be enjoyed as such. "If people want to raise issues about life on the reservation, they should come to the Concerned Pikuni (Piegan) Committee. That's what it's for."

War Party was also part of a controversy of a different sort, one that in part led to the creation of the Montana Film Office. The problem began when the Glacier County Assessor tried to make the company filming the movie pay $3,400 in property taxes. Although the tax on movie company equipment hadn't been levied in years, a later attorney general's opinion showed that the assessor's action was legal. The movie company ultimately paid the taxes, although one employee publicly criticized the state and county for charging the taxes, then was fired for her comments.

Montana was the only state charging such a tax. "As a consequence," said State Promotion Director John Wilson, "it's hard for us to get them up here to look at our locations." Senator Bob Brown, a Whitefish Republican, drafted Senate Bill 392, which exempted movie companies filming in Montana from property taxes.

Nonetheless, Sampson said that even today he is still happy with the film. "I believe the film is pretty true to life. Being a Native American, you're faced with this kind of thing every day."

Another take on Custer's Last Stand, *Warpath* featured battle scenes along the Yellowstone River that are impressive even today. Edmond O'Brien (left) starred as a Cavalry sergeant.

Warpath

CAST
Edmond O'Brien, Dean Jagger

DIRECTOR
Byron Haskin

LOCATION
Billings area, Crow Reservation

1951

Western historical events, especially the Battle of Little Bighorn, have been displayed vividly on the big screen with the visual crutch of Montana's scenic rivers, bluffs, and open prairies. Hollywood has never felt particularly compelled to film its representations of Brevet Major General George Armstrong Custer's last battle anywhere in or where the actual epic 1876 battle occurred. But several cinematic Custers and Sitting Bulls actually recreated their battles before the cameras at various locales between the Rocky Mountains and the muddy waters of the Missouri River.

Custer's failed attack has created a film world of its own. Perhaps the very first Custer film, William Selig's *Custer's Last Stand* (1909), utilized footage of a reenactment shot near the real Montana battle site, intercut with scenes done in Selig's Chicago studio. But it didn't take long for early producers to discover the sunny and balmy climate of Southern California. Of the subsequent film and television representations of Custer, only a few were filmed in southeastern Montana or South Dakota, the real-life haunts of the Seventh Cavalry and their Sioux and Cheyenne adversaries.

In the 1910s Montana began to attract filmmakers because of the numerous Indian tribes there, and Montana was the site of many filmic Indian battles. In 1913, the Edison Film Company made the documentary *Camping with the Blackfeet*, depicting tribal life on the reservation on the eastern slope of the Rocky Mountains. It was one of several factual films about western life released in 1913. *Indian Life*, issued in 1918 and re-released as *Before the White Man Came* in 1920—shot on the Crow Indian Reservation—features an all-Indian cast: Cheyenne and Crow from their reservations southeast of Billings.

Bob Hampton of Placer (1920) did an unusual combination of filming on the Blackfeet Reservation near Glacier National Park and Fort Huachuca in southern Arizona, where the all-black enlisted men of the famed Tenth Cavalry stood in for the Seventh Cavalry in vast panoramic shots filmed from high atop a hovering signal balloon.

The U.S. government decided to allow the production to shoot at Glacier National Park. Chief Two Guns White Calf from the Blackfoot Reservation appeared in the film and in its publicity. Directed by Marshall Neilan, starring James Kirkwood and Noah Beery, it depicts the escapades of Bob Hampton (Kirkwood) that bring him into involvement with General George Custer, who has plans for a raiding party on the Sioux camp near the Little Bighorn River.

Cecil B. De Mille's 1936 epic, *The Plainsman*, staged most of the film's large-scale battle scenes with a second unit near the Tongue River in Montana, only to see most of that footage then used as back projection for principal scenes filmed at sound stages on the Paramount lot in Los Angeles.

When Paramount revisited the Little Big Horn battle with a Technicolor western called *Warpath* in 1951, the same Tongue River area was used again, along with a partial reconstruction of Fort Abraham Lincoln at the Montana State Fairgrounds in Billings.

Starring Edmond O'Brien and Forrest Tucker, the film follows personal conflicts among soldiers set against events leading up to Custer's debacle (James Millican portrays Custer.) Cinematographer Ray Rennahan brings real excitement to the clashes between the Indians and the cavalry, shot in the Billings area, Pryor, Broadview, Laurel, and Yellowstone County.

The Nat Holt production was filmed in Technicolor for Paramount at location settings along the Yellowstone river, on the Crow Indian reservation and elsewhere in the vicinity of Billings. Producer Holt brought with him from Hollywood 23 leading actors with speaking roles and 20 additional stunt riders and a full-scale technical crew of 95 persons. At the time it was the largest film troupe ever to visit Montana and the first full-length feature to be shot in Montana in its entirety.

"Billings fills the bill in every way," Nat Holt told the *Billings Gazette*. "The city has ample hotel facilities to take care of our large company. These scenic locations are practically on the outskirts of the city. That prevents waste of valuable time in getting actors and technical crews from their hotels to the locations and back again at the end of each day's shooting."

Interiors and the Old Fort Abraham Lincoln (home post of the Seventh near Bismarck, Dakota Territory) exteriors were filmed at the Midland Empire fairgrounds. Hundreds of local people were employed as townsfolk. Scores of Montana riders were employed as well as hundreds of Crow Indians.

The battle scenes along the Yellowstone River are tremendous even today. The company sent a Technicolor camera unit to a remote section of the Crow reservation to film scenes among the 800 buffalo that comprised what was said to be "the nation's largest herd." Although the script of *Warpath* didn't call for buffalo, the locale of the picture was in buffalo country and a large herd of bison, against the background of colorful Big Horn Canyon, added much to a Technicolor production. The three-day trip into some of the least accessible country in the Montana mountains resulted in 780 feet of film. Out of this footage was chosen about 100 feet—enough for a little more than a minute on the screen.

The picture was released in 1951, 75 years after the historic Battle of the Little Big Horn. It is estimated that between $225,000 and $250,000 was spent in Billings between August 21 and September 18, 1950. Several of the expenditures made by the Nat Holt corporation were "salaries to Indians and extras, $6,510; salaries to other

Midland Empire extras, $6,570; horses, hay and grain expense, $7,500; hotels, $15,150; cost of lunches served on the set, $10,000; breakfast and super meals for Hollywood cast and staff, $20,150."

In *Warpath*, the story and scenario by Frank Gruber have Edmond O'Brien, the vengeful hero, tracing his fiancée's murderers to the Seventh Cavalry outpost. He joins up, gets the goods on Forrest Tucker, his merciless first sergeant, and on Dean Jagger, the storekeeper-father of his new love, a pretty redhead played by Polly Bergen. The traditional Nat Holt finale has the battered principals fleeing the warring Sioux to warn General Custer of a potential massacre. The culprits are picked off along the way.

The New York Times gave qualified praise: "Ray Rennahan has done an excellent job of photographing some fetchingly tinted terrain and Byron Haskin's direction is alert, if not particularly forceful. But it is chiefly Mr. O'Brien's portrayal of a hard-bitten, inherently decent cavalryman that gives 'Warpath' color and makes it seem better than it is—or was meant to be."

The world premiere for *Warpath* was held in the Fox and Babcock theatres in Billings, July 13, 1951.

What Dreams May Come

CAST
Robin Williams, Cuba Gooding Jr.

DIRECTOR
Vincent Ward

LOCATION
Glacier National Park, Blackfeet Reservation

1998

When Hollywood set out to find a "magical, mythical place," they arrived, perhaps appropriately, in Glacier National Park. Interscope Communications and Metafilmics Inc. descended on the park on June 30, 1997 and

Using Glacier's scenery and mind-bending visuals such as this scene with Robin Williams in a flower-bordered pool of purple goo, *What Dreams May Come* won an Oscar for Best Visual Effects.

continued filming in Glacier and the surrounding area through much of July. "It's like an invasion," movie publicist Michael Umble said of the production company's arrival in East Glacier. Hotels, motels, restaurants, rental agencies and caterers were kept busy with Hollywood in town. Most of the rooms at the Glacier Park Lodge as well as rooms in smaller hotels were appropriated by the more than 150 people involved in filming. Some rented small homes in the area.

Based on the novel by famed fantasist Richard Matheson, *What Dreams May Come* is a grand journey which explores the idea that the dead actually grieve for the living, much in the thread of Italian poet Dante's thoughts on the afterlife. The mythical romance costars Robin Williams and Annabella Sciorra as soul mates before and after death. The movie centers on Chris Nielsen (Williams), who is killed by a speeding car while assisting at the scene of an accident. He awakens in heaven to find that heaven, for him, exists in the form of a painting created by his wife Annie (Sciorra.) Distraught by her husband's death, Annie commits suicide and Chris must go through hell—literally—to find her and bring her back to heaven.

The production of *What Dreams May Come* came during a high point of Williams' film career. Two of his most successful movies, Jumanji and The Birdcage, had opened in theaters over the two preceding years, and filming had recently wrapped up on *Good Will Hunting*, a movie for which Williams would win a best supporting actor Oscar in 1998.

Cuba Gooding Jr. portrays Williams' mentor, guiding him through life. "In the book, after you die, you create your own world," said Umble. "It's an ideal world with no threats." Producer Steven Simon acquired rights to the book 19 years earlier but held onto it until he felt the time was right. "The world was not ready until now," said Simon in July 1997. "People's attitudes about the afterlife are different now. It's a subject whose time has come." Simon never had Glacier National Park in mind, but film scouts convinced him that the park's scenery was indeed heavenly. Filming was done on the east side of the park at Two Medicine, St. Mary, Many Glacier, and several locations on the Blackfeet Indian Reservation.

Indeed, it's easy to visualize the stunning vistas of Glacier National Park doubling as heaven, but it's more difficult to visualize the park's Lower Two Medicine Lake serving as a stand-in for the River Styx, the passageway into hell. But it did. Thanks to Mother Nature, the portrayal was brutally accurate, said Mark Van Artsdale of Kalispell, the film's "boat wrangler." Van Artsdale was co-owner of the Glacier Park Boat Co. In Hollywood vernacular, the boat wrangler is in charge of the film's boats and other floating objects, both on the set and off.

"It was pretty exciting," said Van Artsdale. In the 'hell' scene, Williams' character is being guided in a small sailboat down the river toward hell. Unfortunately, the Rocky Mountain Front's notorious winds came up, capsizing the boat and providing for a realistically hellish experience in the cold water. "The boat was upside-down three or four times," said Van Artsdale. "The sailboat was good for a 10-knot wind, but they were trying to shoot in 30 knots."

In the opening scene, Chris and Annie encounter each other while boating on a lake in Switzerland (actually Swiftcurrent Lake in Many Glacier.) Sciorra's "sailboat" is a converted skiff built by Bill Rice of Kalispell, who operated the Two Medicine Lake boat concession with his wife, Peg, for Van Artsdale's company. Williams' character lolls in a wooden driftboat built by former Whitefish resident Jason Cajune, Peg Rice's son. Van Artsdale said Sciorra didn't have to learn how to sail. An electric motor was attached to the boat's tiller and was operated by a technician lying in the bottom of the boat, out of sight of the cameras. However, Van Artsdale and his crew did build several floating platforms that camera crews used for shooting on the water, including a pontoon-boat platform converted to allow cameras to shoot at the water line, with half the frame submerged. The crew also handled a 50-foot-square floating platform with a buoy-

In the surreal *What Dreams May Come*, Glacier National Park doubled as both heaven (the majestic vistas) and hell (the park's Lower Two Medicine Lake was the River Styx, the passageway into hell).

ancy control that enabled it to be lowered just below the surface of the water. That platform was used in a scene in which Albert (Gooding Jr.) demonstrates to Chris how easy it is to walk on water. The platform allowed Gooding to stroll leisurely around the surface of St. Mary Lake in about 3 inches of water. "The illusion of him standing on the lake was pretty cool," said Van Artsdale.

However, he said, the final version of the movie was disappointing because of the amount of computer manipulation used. For example, the world of Annie's painting, which makes up so much of Chris' heaven, was computer enhanced to combine Two Medicine Lake, Sinopah Mountain, an island that somewhat resembles Wild Goose Island on St. Mary Lake, and Niagara Falls. Another scene, in which Williams' character awakens in heaven "was almost unrecognizable" as being on the shore of St. Mary Lake, said Van Artsdale. "A lot of the stuff was augmented synthetically so much that I don't know why they came to Montana, actually," he said. "I think a lot could have been done in a studio." Van Artsdale said he found some of the logistical aspects of the movie, such as moving an immense amount of camera, lighting and sound equipment across a lake and floating it on a platform for an on-the-lake shot, much more interesting than actually working with the actors. "It's amazing the amount of gear that goes along with a shot," said Van Artsdale.

One scene was filmed on land owned by local ranchers, Bud and Geri Broadhurst of Ledger, 14 miles northwest of Browning near Kiowa Camp. The Broadhursts truck cattle to their ranch every spring and graze them there during the summer months. Filming began at their ranch on June 23, 1997. The base camp for the 150 member cast and crew complete with caterers from L.A. was set up there also. Trucks, semis, and four wheelers dotted the landscape. Thirty cars drove in, with one person driving each car. One truck at the camp carried $5 million worth of camera equipment.

There was activity at the ranch for three weeks. "They paid very little for using the land, but did improve our road," said Geri. The scene which took place on Broadhursts' ranch was of Williams' character flying and running through a field of bright red poppies the crew had created from an entire truckload of fabric flowers. Masses of blue and purple silk flowers, peacocks and fawns were blended to create a blissful scene of the afterlife. One twenty-second scene took four hours to complete.

Other production houses had proposed more traditional approaches such as shooting actors against green screen and compositing them into digital landscapes. "Director Vincent Ward wanted Heaven to be as absolutely real, complex, and dynamic as the world we're used to," said visual-effects producer/supervisor Ellen M. Somers. "Vincent wanted to shoot in a very normal, naturalistic style. Go to location, shoot it any way you want, and we'll use the actual morphology and the vegetation in the plates as the basis for our effects."

The landowners were invited to eat with the crew, where they met Robin Williams, who thanked them for the use of their land and shook hands with their grandson, and even made one of his signature funny faces. "He was extremely polite and kind and his reputation for great humor holds true," said Geri. The Broadhursts were invited to a pre-filming party at the Lodge at Glacier in early July, where their daughters took photos with Gooding. The filming on the Rocky Mountain Front lasted six weeks.

"*What Dreams May Come* had to convince people that Glacier National Park could double for heaven," said Sten Iversen. "It was hard to work out with the hellish parts—the burned out areas of forest fires, on top of Beartooth Pass. But all of Switzerland and heaven would be here in Montana. We had to figure out a place where Robin Williams could step into a painting, partly digital and partly a practical effect, and finding a place on the shore of St. Mary Lake. We needed to get permission to basically put a hot-tub-like structure on the edge of the lake and have it filled full of a paint-like goo. The folks at Glacier were worried about even a little trail and worried about the environmental hazard of spilling goo into pristine St. Mary Lake. The greensman on the film turned a section of the regular park into silk flowers, and dressed silk in the trees. He was festooning the trees and the grass with silk and Williams with a trench coat stepped into a tub of goo."

Parts of the movie were filmed near Many Glacier Lodge, the park's largest lodge (built in 1915), sprawled along the shores of Swiftcurrent Lake and surrounded by towering massifs just miles from the Canadian border. "It's been beautiful," said producer Steven Simon in July 1997. "Personally, it's going to be very hard to leave. When I went from here to pick up my children in Kalispell at the airport, it was almost culture shock." Another movie producer, Barnet Bain, said the Blackfeet conducted a special face-painting ceremony to welcome the Hollywood contingent. "They've been incredible hosts, and the Park Service has been unbelievably kind," said Bain. Many Blackfeet residents worked as extras, security guards and set builders for the production. Director Ward, a New Zealand native, said the mountain terrain was a challenge for the crew. "It's a wind-blown paradise," said Ward. "It's harder to move things, and it's not as accessible as Sunset Boulevard. But the results are extraordinary."

Williams was 47 at the time of filming. "I remember *What Dreams May Come* was shooting at Many Glacier Lodge and in between takes, Williams would basically do standup for the tourists in the balcony of the hotel," Iversen recalled. "He had such a comedic personality and what was impressive was that he could go from serious acting and quickly turn to telling jokes, instead of going to his trailer to rest."

Craig Iron Pipe, who worked as a stunt man specializing in horseback scenes, was a part of the production crew that helped make the Montana segments happen. "I worked for the movie company's transportation department," he said. "I drove the set-up crews and some of the stunt people around, so I'd run into all the main actors all the time and get to visit with them now and then." According to Iron Pipe, Williams never ignored the common people around him. In the final days of *What Dreams May Come*, Williams on a break from filming took a red bus tour through the park and, before the cast and crew left, he paid for a party out of his own pocket and invited everyone to it. Then he stuck around and greeted all his guests, regardless of whether they were Hollywood stars or temporary hires.

"For him to do that—to fork out the money to hire a caterer and put on a nice meal and entertain the whole cast and crew—that was something special," said Iron Pipe. "He was there mingling with everybody. It wasn't just like some millionaire who got a caterer and then went off and did something else. He was right there. It was welcoming and it was something heartfelt. You could see it in his eyes and in the attention he would give you. He was a very kind soul."

Williams even took a few minutes to greet Iron Pipe personally and to meet his wife and daughter. The event was a special one for 2½-year-old Lily Iron Pipe.

"Her favorite movie at the time was *Mrs. Doubtfire,*" Iron Pipe said. "At the party, I introduced my wife, Billie Jo, to Mr. Williams and I told my daughter, 'This is Mrs. Doubtfire.'" The little girl looked up dubiously at the strange man in front of her, who was not in costume and looked suspiciously unlike the Scottish nanny from the hit movie. "I told Mr. Williams that *Mrs. Doubtfire* was her favorite movie, so he immediately went into character for a few minutes," Iron Pipe said. "You should have seen her eyes brighten up. It was just amazing for her. That was her hero at the time, and there he was right in front of her. It was awesome."

Film critics Gene Siskel described What Dreams May Come as "one of the great visual achievements in film history." The film won an Oscar for Best Visual Effects. When Robin Williams was asked in October 1999 by National Geographic *Traveler* to name his favorite personal spaces, he named Hayman Island off Australia and Glacier National Park.

"Another place that's soul-inspiring is Montana's Glacier National Park," Williams said. "I've never seen anything like it. If it isn't God's backyard, He certainly lives nearby."

One man with a thousand voices brought joy to millions—but could not sustain it in himself. In 2014, struggling with depression, anxiety, and the early stages of Parkinson's disease, Williams committed suicide. He was 63.

Winds of Autumn

CAST
Jack Elam, Jeanette Nolan

DIRECTOR
Charles B. Pierce

LOCATION
Kalispell

1976

Among the more colorful participants in the assembly line that fed the 1970s drive-in circuit was Charles Bryant Pierce, a Hollywood set decorator who moonlighted as an auteur of schlocky low-budget features. The independent filmmaker's movies have become minor cult classics. In 1972, while working in advertising, Pierce created a semi-documentary film first titled *Tracking the Fouke Monster,* later renamed *The Legend of Boggy Creek.* Pierce shot the movie—about a Sasquatch-like creature reportedly sighted in the vicinity of Fouke, Texas—with a homemade camera. Much of the movie was filmed in Fouke and Texarkana with local residents and students as actors and crew. Estimates place the cost of making the eighty-seven-minute film at about $165,000. Becoming popular as a drive-in horror feature around the country, it became one of the top ten highest-grossing movies of the year, earning over $20 million. In an interview with the *Tulsa World,* Daniel Myrick, director of the jolting 1999 hit movie, *The Blair Witch Project,* cited Pierce's semi-documentary style *Boggy Creek* as an influence.

Pierce's earliest films were primarily made in Arkansas with local actors and drew their inspiration from Arkansas themes. However, in the course of three years, three low budget westerns in Montana: *Winterhawk* (1975), *Winds of Autumn* (1976), and *Grayeagle* (1977). While Pierce evinced a measure of cinematic skill—for instance, his compositions are almost always pleasing to the eye— his storytelling ranged from, as one writer from *Movie Magazine* put it, "the basically competent to the hilariously inept." Pierce acted in several of his films, including *Winds of Autumn.*

Winds of Autumn, shot in the Kalispell area, is a dated

piece of drudgery. The haphazard plot is a flatline of inert drama, with long scenes of windy exposition interrupted by the occasional well-staged if ridiculous fight sequence. Bill Kuney, owner of the Outlaw Inn in Kalispell, and later a scout for the Montana Film Office, recalled Charles B. Pierce as "into himself." "He had that success with that first movie, *Winterhawk*, that he made and he was a bit demanding after that. He came back and did *Winds of Autumn*. Pierce wasn't too strict, I guess. I noticed in one of the scenes in *Winds of Autumn*, I could see the power lines in the background. He was not too careful."

And Pierce wasn't fastidious about his debts, either. "There was always talk circulating that he was behind on payments," said Garry Wunderwald. "The budgets to his films weren't high and he was slow on payments. Unfortunately, when people would call the film office, we'd have to remind that we weren't a collection agency."

Winter in the Blood

DIRECTORS
Alex and Andrew Smith

CAST
Chaske Spencer, David Morse, Julia Jones

LOCATION
Havre, Chinook

2013

The film *Winter in the Blood* is based on the first novel by James Welch. The author, who died of a heart attack at age 62 in 2003, was a product of the Hi-Line, born in Browning on the Blackfeet Reservation of a Blackfeet father and Gros Ventre mother, and raised on the Ft. Belknap Reservation (home to Gros Ventre and Assiniboine people). Published in 1974, *Winter in the Blood* tells the story of a young Native American who violently grapples with his heritage and his life. The story has been translated into eight languages and remains in print.

Winter in the Blood is based on the first novel by Montana writer James Welch. The movie's male star, Chaske Spencer of "Twilight Saga" fame, spent part of his childhood on the Fort Peck Reservation. PHOTO COURTESY ALEX AND ANDREW SMITH.

Welch wrote extensively about contemporary and historical Indians of northern Montana in his later novels, *The Death of Jim Loney*, *Fools Crow* and *The Indian Lawyer*, but he poured everything he knew about the area and about modern Native American life into *Winter in the Blood*.

"James Welch is the Native American writer, a writer at the epicenter of Native American culture," said writer and filmmaker Sherman Alexie, who worked on *Winter in the Blood*. "The book was the first thing I ever read where I identified with a character. He was the first practitioner of Native American realism. He wrote about the every-day, especially of reservation life. There were no talking animals or no references to the four winds."

"There are so many themes in the book," said actress Julie Jones, "a layered, nuanced piece of writing. I would think that anybody could benefit from it."

The story was brought to the screen by its co-directors, Montana natives Alex and Andrew Smith. The Smith brothers had been close to Welch for as long as they could remember. "We just grew up knowing him. He was one of the constants in our lives," said Andrew. A friend of the boys' parents, Welch even met his future wife, Lois, at a party at the Smiths' house. "After our dad, Dave, died (of a heart attack, in 1974, when the twins were six), we looked around at men and wondered, 'Would he have been a good dad?' and Jim was always high up in that category."

Once the brothers read *Winter in the Blood* in high school, said Alex, "It was, 'Whoa, this guy who's been so sweet at Thanksgiving and Christmas has this sadness, this depth he didn't display all the time.' He became someone we admired."

The Smiths decided to stay in Montana to film *Winter in the Blood*. "We were told we were crazy not to shoot in Canada," said Andrew. "The tax incentives were much greater, and we considered it." For the film, citing his family's respect for Welch's novel, then-Governor Brian Schweitzer offered to make his plane available to fly in potential investors. Eventually the Montana community embraced the film financially through the online fundraising site Kickstarter, and *Winter in the Blood* was filmed in Havre and Chinook during the summer of 2011.

The film crew transformed the towns back to 1975, decorating storefronts and downtown Chinook with props and period cars from that era. Havre was used because it was little changed from that era. "The last 30 years haven't been very kind to Havre and the area," said Alex Smith. "Knowing we had a big challenge and little money and that we had to cover two periods, the 1950s and 1970s, it would have been impossible to build all that." Chinook's Powell Ranch, on the rolling plains outside of town, was used as the fictional First Raise ranch.

The film is artfully made, with evocative cinematography and highly detailed production design. The score is striking, and the performances bellow authenticity.

Sixty of the crew members were Montanans, and 100 extras were Montanans. The film's cast includes 21 Montanans, several of them first-time actors from the Fort Belknap and Rocky Boy's Indian reservations.

The film's star Chaske Spencer is Lakota Sioux and grew up on reservations, spending part of his childhood in Poplar on the Fort Peck Reservation. Spencer is prob-

Directed by Alex and Andrew Smith, *Winter in the Blood* was filmed entirely in Montana, mostly in the Chinook and Havre areas. Photo courtesy Alex and Andrew Smith.

ably best known for playing werewolf leader Sam Uley in the *Twilight* movies.

"A lot of the cast were native cast," he said, "and we were able to bring that into the production. And, you know, [the Smith's] are really cool directors. They're really good guys. So they were very open about suggestions and stuff [for] how would this scene happen for that particular tribe."

"I grew up in Montana and I've grown up along Highway 2, on the Hi-Line," said Spencer. "The most authentic you can get is Havre, it's a complete throwback to the 1950s."

Alex Smith praised Spencer's commitment: "I was so consistently blow away by what Chaske was willing to do for the project. Where he was willing to go with it. Dark and damaged places. Such an involvement there. He can go there and get out. You shoot out of sequence, and sometime he had to be at the bottom of the barrel and other times he had to be loving life."

Alex Smith addressed the cultural nuances of the project. "It was written by a Montanan about Montana, and we are Montanans," he said. "I believe it would have been almost sacrilegious to shoot elsewhere for this particular novel. We had to keep it here. We are not Native Americans, we are Jewish Swedes. But there is universality of what Jim put on the page, about the challenges and the struggles. About losing family."

Alex said the brothers always knew that as non-Native Americans they had to tread carefully on Native American material. Andrew added that they relied on their mostly Native American actors to keep them honest. "We thought of ourselves as being a conduit between Jim [Welch] and the performers, and we cast 80 percent or over Native American, and we cast very specifically to be

Veteran character actor David Morse depicted the cryptic "Airplane Man" in *Winter in the Blood*. Photo courtesy Alex and Andrew Smith.

faithful and to be accurate to the book and to the experience," Andrew said. "And we were so fortunate to find and it was the first person we wanted—Chaske Spencer to play [Virgil]. And we just handed it over to him. He could bring so much more personal experience into it."

Throughout the film, Spencer's character Virgil First Raise struggles with who he is and where he belongs. After a brief prelude, the story begins with Virgil waking up drunk in a ditch. His wife (Julia Jones) has left him and taken some of his stuff, and he wants it back. He heads out in search of his wife and the beloved rifle she stole from him, and winds up finding himself. The story captures a slipstream of memory and regret, interweaving past and present and what is happening in Virgil's mind as he reflects on lost family and lost chances.

The sense of reality and the storytelling meld together in the film's locations, including the remote ranch outside Chinook, a place where the Milk River winds through classic Big Sky countryside. An abandoned farmhouse among whispering cottonwood trees was restored by production designer David Storm. The Smiths said it was "eerily similar" to the homestead where Welch was raised not 40 miles away.

"The people of Havre were resourceful and they were great," said Storm. "They gave us free props, free cars, and let us borrow things. It was the perfect thing to be in Havre because it's a high, rugged, desert prairie and people there are working through hard times and Havre is a hard-time area."

The cast included David Morse who starred in the Smiths' 2002 Montana-movie *The Slaughter Rule.*

"[*Winter in the Blood* is] a book that has meant a lot to different people," said Morse at the time. "If we are successful enough with this movie—to reach an audience big enough to expose more people to James Welch's writing—that would be the greatest gift." He added that "Alex and Andrew Smith have some terrific, interesting, creative people around them and it's good to be a part of."

Montana actress Lily Gladstone was provided the opportunity to break new ground creatively, as well as circumnavigate the stereotypically stoic roles Native American actresses are commonly offered. Gladstone played Marlene, an aimless, hard-drinking local girl who was Virgil's beer-swilling companion.

"As natives, we know that we are mixed and diverse," said Gladstone. "Most natives get pigeonholed, based on appearance first and talent second. But we are seeing more scripts written and filmed by natives.

"*Winter in the Blood* relied so heavily on the Montana community, so many locals, and so many people who have a strong connection with the legacy of the novel. Montana has seven reservations and 12 tribal nations, and we have strong Native American populations. It was such a labor of love, and people come out for that in Montana."

Gladstone, like author Welch, was born and raised on the Blackfoot reservation near Browning. Shuttling back and forth as a child between the reservation and a new home in Seattle, Gladstone remembered how strongly she identified with the plight of the novel's protagonist who is half-Native American, half-white. "I felt as distant from myself as a hawk from the moon," said Gladstone, quoting a potent line from the book.

The film stirred different reactions, noted Gladstone, who minored in Native American Studies at the University of Montana. "There are some who are troubled by all the scenes of alcoholism and poverty, and the abuses in Indian communities. But there is a reason stories like that are told so much."

Gladstone works with a Native American youth theatre program based in Seattle called Red Eagle Soaring. Still, her connection to the land of her childhood, the Blackfeet Reservation, is everlasting, dominant. Her first eleven years were spent primarily in Browning and East Glacier, and her family maintains a house in East Glacier.

Instead of rattling off a litany of deep-seated problems, Gladstone speaks affectionately about her ancestral land, to which she returns occasionally.

"The reputation of Browning depends on who you talk to," said Gladstone. "There are some incredibly ugly things that happen but shouldn't. But you have to look deeper into why things are the way they are. At the foundation of my life, there is community and family. There is poverty, violence, substance abuse, and unemployment everywhere. But there is so much love in that community. What unites people there is a love of family, a love of land."

Patty Limerick, a historian and director of the Center of the American West at the University of Colorado in Boulder, said *Winter in the Blood* adds an important dimension to Native American characters on screen. She points to the old blind man in the film who says several times that people have mistakenly thought he was dead: "That is a very intense and aimed commentary on the notion that the American people expect the film to go the way that films go, which is, 'Well, they were quite noble and now they're gone.'"

"They're still there," Limerick said. "They're haunted, they're troubled, they're not a world apart from anguished white people, of which we have seen in many, many movies….And if we didn't have anguished white people, we wouldn't go see movies about them because the anguish is really what makes audience's feelings come into play. So, in some ways, it's just that the complexity of human character finally got extended to Indian people [in *Winter in the Blood*]".

Alex Escarcega, who played the young Virgil, saw the movie as a boost of self-esteem: "You really don't see a lot of Native Americans in movies. They play extras. But we like to make the movies like *Powwow Highway*, and *Smoke Signals*, and *Winter in the Blood* to show people what we have…to let people know how we live."

How did the alternative and mainstream press react to this hallucinatory film centered around a Native American man whirling through reality and fantasy in a small Montana town?

The Los Angeles Times, which called the movie "in some ways a tale of simple, raw struggle and survival among a small-town Native American community," saw it as potent debut from a pair of brothers no doubt bursting at the seams with talent: "'Winter in the Blood' is a difficult film to get a handle on, not least because it often feels like it should be easier to dismiss. But then it locks onto a moment that is unexpectedly arresting and little jabs of poetic meaning or hard-earned truths reel a viewer back in. Whether this film provides some new start for the brothers Smith will remain to be seen, but this film sets them free of convention and, like its wandering hero, on a path perhaps all their own."

Winterhawk

CAST
Leif Erickson, Denver Pyle, Michael Dante

DIRECTOR
Charles B. Pierce

LOCATION
Kalispell area

1975

The second of the three of Charles B. Pierce's Montana productions, *Winterhawk* was shot in the Kalispell area (and Durango, Colorado, for the scenes which required snow), featuring Michael Dante as a Blackfeet chief who is treated badly and in revenge abducts a woman and her small brother. *Winterhawk* cost an estimated $1.1 million and dropped about $700,000 on the Kalispell area. Between 600 and 700 Blackfeet Indians were used. "The plot is basically about a Blackfoot Indian after the decimation of the tribe by smallpox around the 1840s," said Scott Warden, director of Montana's advertising unit—a precursor to the Montana Film Office. "They trade furs with mountain men who are having a fur rendezvous. They are getting the furs down river."

Pierce produced the movie on an eight- to ten-week schedule with headquarters at the Outlaw Inn in Kalispell. Warden said that the movie had been announced for Jackson Hole, Wyoming. "A former Helena public relations employee named Pat Mathews put in a pitch for Montana and the Pierce people flew up here," said Warden. "We took guys around and got great cooperation

Italian-American actor Michael Dante, who appeared in more than 100 television shows and films, starred as a vengeful Blackfeet warrior in *Winterhawk*, filmed in Kalispell.

from the Kalispell Chamber of Commerce. The people fell in love with the Kalispell area," said Warden.

As far as the movie, it's essentially a genre cliché, "a limiting piece of work that makes Dante look stiff," according to one review. Dante, a lifelong professional actor, had his first and only title role in *Winterhawk*.

During the filming, Dante suffered torn ligaments when the horse he was riding caught its foot between some logs and then reared up. This caused Dante to slide off as the horse bolted. They had to shoot without him during his ten-day recovery.

"I enjoyed working in Kalispell," said Dante at age 84. "I loved the background and the authenticity, the scenery, and the wildlife. It could not have been a better location, the access to horses, and working with the Native Americans. The Blackfeet journeyed from Browning to work on the film and were able to put them to work on the movie. That was honorable. The language in the picture—the language I spoke as Winterhawk—was 100 percent Blackfeet and approved by the Blackfeet. They wanted it perfect and we wanted it perfect, and we got it perfect.

"We started filming on September 2, 1975—my birthday. As far as the fall, there were rocks and trees that were cut down and there were all these splinters. It was very ominous; if you fell you could puncture your lungs. We set up by the riverbank and I relaxed on the horse. I had one foot in the stirrup and the horse got caught between two logs and got spooked and reared up. I fell off the back. The horse was half-Arabian, half-thoroughbred and we had to wear him down for two hours so we could work with him all day. He never [before] worked in front of a camera. He came from a ranch in Kalispell—an Appaloosa, black and white leopard, 17 hands, big and powerful."

Unfortunately, the show around Dante doesn't fare much better. *Winterhawk* rode through freshly cut grain fields and later through plowed, trimmed grain fields; he rode by barbed wire fences, telephone lines, and even, at one point, a blue pickup truck. In one scene, an airplane can be seen in the background.

Indian encampments were built along the banks of the Swan River near Bigfork. Ace Powell, a well-known western artist, played the part of Red Calf, Winterhawk's father. Governor Thomas L. Judge visited Kalispell during the filming and the governor spoke with Pierce concerning Montana's desirability as a movie location.

The world premiere of *Winterhawk* took place in Kalispell on May 1, 1975, at the Liberty Theater. Pierce said of *Winterhawk*, "I think this is my best film yet."

"I think we had the best cast of any of the western genre films ever," said Dante recently, who has appeared in approximately 30 films and 150 television shows. "Leif Erickson. Woody Stroud. Elisha Cook. Dennis Fimple. Arthur Hunnicutt. Dawn Wells. Denver Pyle. What a collection."

The trajectory of Pierce's life is worth noting: after moving to California in the 1980s, Pierce befriended Clint Eastwood while living in Carmel, where the actor-director was elected mayor in 1986. Pierce wrote the fourth movie in the *Dirty Harry* series, *Sudden Impact* (1983), and is credited with one of the most famous lines in cinematic history, spoken by Clint Eastwood's Dirty Harry character: "Go ahead, make my day." The line was based on something his father said when he was growing up: "When I come home tonight and the yard has not been mowed, you're going to make my day." Pierce died on March 5, 2010, at a nursing home in Dover, Tennessee.

Wolf Summer

CAST
Julia Boracco Braaten, Niklas James Knudsen

DIRECTOR
Peder Norlund

LOCATION
Bozeman area

2003

The ability to film with actual wolves and experienced animal handlers was a major factor in this Norwegian's production choosing to film in Montana. *Wolf Summer* or *Ulvesommer* is the story of an unusual partnership and an even more unusual friendship between a child and a wild animal. When a summer course in outdoor climbing is canceled, 12-year-old Kim decides that she will solo climb "the East Wall"—a mountain ridge near the Norwegian-Swedish border—as her late father did when he was 12. Kim has a fall, is badly injured, and wakes up to a dramatic encounter with a wolf. Frightened and helpless, she is trapped in a wolf's den with a starving wolf cub. This is the beginning of an exceptional friendship.

In *Wolf Summer*, the Livingston area depicts Norway and the logistics of the shoot required that Montana Film Commissioner Sten Iversen be creative and patient. "The director (Peder Norlund) came here to scout and he spent about a month here scouting. He loved Montana."

"The hard part was dealing with the immigration service and getting the cast and crew into the country was a nightmare," he recalled. "They needed special B-1 visas, work visas, special visas for performers. I remember having to go to the INS office, and standing at the bulletproof glass window, sliding forms through a slot, next to the farm workers and sheepherders. The look on their faces. Norwegian film crew? Really? But I flew to Nebraska to the main regional office of the INS to hand-deliver the application.

"The crew on the ground here during shooting was about half Montanans, half Norwegians. Norlund is one of the biggest producers in Norway, and he spent a lot of

The ability to film with trained wolves and experienced animal handlers was a major factor in making this Norwegian film in Montana. *Wolf Summer*, or *Ulvesommer*, became one of the most popular children's films in Norway.

time in Bozeman and Livingston, and he found it fascinating that Montana had so many people of Norwegian descent. It was something he was shocked to find. He came back the next summer and shot a documentary on Norwegians who ended up in Montana."

Animals of Montana—a "full service wildlife-casting agency" located near Bozeman—provided the wildlife for on-location filming.

"Animals of Montana had the trained wolves and a bear—at least 4 wolves were trained—and that's an interesting thing to deal with," said Iversen. "The set had to be contained and the Forest Service was concerned about wolves getting free, and they had to have enclosures. Because there were no trained wolves in Norway and they could use the animals in Montana, we got the film. Most of the first half of the movie is with wolves. We didn't have any of the restrictions that the Norwegian people had. It's important to remember that the old wolf with the girl—the teeth are digital teeth."

While some of the similarities between Montana and Norway are obvious, the doubling required more than natural scenery. "We needed to duplicate vehicles and the street signs and all kinds of stuff, bottles, cans, and food, to double as Norway. We worked with the local Ford dealership to retrofit a vehicle to a Norwegian standard, with five different marker lights."

"As interesting project as a project as *Wolf Summer* was, I remember most was that in Norway they don't tip," said location manager Mark Zetler. "That's an American thing. We would go out to a nice restaurant and there would be 25 people eating and the Norwegians would have an $800 tab and they didn't tip. So I ended up tipping for every big meal. It would cost me like 300 bucks a meal, because I knew all of the waitresses and restaurant owners in Livingston."

The fastidious eye to detail—and honorable compensating for meal service—paid off. *Wolf Summer* stands as one of the most popular children's films in Norway.

There was a special screening of the family adventure film at the Empire Theater in Livingston, the only U.S. screening of the production. Producer Kaare Storemyr introduced the film and conducted a question and answer session afterward. Storemyr returned to Montana to film a documentary on the Wilsall rodeo and Norwegians in Montana.

Academy Awards and Nominations for Montana Movies

A River Runs Through It (1992)
Won
BEST MUSIC, ORIGINAL SCORE: Mark Isham
BEST WRITING, SCREENPLAY BASED ON MATERIAL PREVIOUSLY
    PRODUCED OR PUBLISHED: Richard Friedenberg
Nominated
BEST CINEMATOGRAPHY: Philippe Rousselot

Forrest Gump (1994)
Won
BEST PICTURE: Wendy Finerman, Steve Starkey, Steve Tisch
BEST ACTOR IN A LEADING ROLE: Tom Hanks
BEST DIRECTOR: Robert Zemeckis
BEST WRITING, SCREENPLAY BASED ON MATERIAL PREVIOUSLY
    PRODUCED OR PUBLISHED: Eric Roth
BEST FILM EDITING: Arthur Schmidt
BEST EFFECTS, VISUAL EFFECTS: Ken Ralston, George Murphy,
    Stephen Rosenbaum, Allen Hall
Nominated
BEST ACTOR IN A SUPPORTING ROLE: Gary Sinise
BEST CINEMATOGRAPHY: Don Burgess
BEST ART DIRECTION-SET DECORATION: Rick Carter, Nancy Haigh
BEST SOUND: Randy Thom, Tom Johnson, Dennis S. Sands,
    William B. Kaplan
BEST EFFECTS, SOUND EFFECTS EDITING: Gloria S. Borders, Randy
    Thom
BEST MAKEUP: Daniel C. Striepeke, Hallie D'Amore, Judith A.
    Cory,
BEST MUSIC, ORIGINAL SCORE: Alan Silvestri

Little Big Man (1970)
Nominated
BEST ACTOR IN A SUPPORTING ROLE: Chief Dan George

Nebraska (2013):
Nominated
BEST MOTION PICTURE OF THE YEAR, ALBERT BERGER: Ron Yerxa
BEST PERFORMANCE BY AN ACTOR IN A LEADING ROLE: Bruce Dern
BEST PERFORMANCE BY AN ACTRESS IN A SUPPORTING ROLE: June
    Squibb
BEST ACHIEVEMENT IN CINEMATOGRAPHY: Phedon Papamichael
BEST ACHIEVEMENT IN DIRECTING: Alexander Payne
BEST WRITING, ORIGINAL SCREENPLAY: Bob Nelson

Runaway Train (1985)
Nominated
BEST ACTOR IN A LEADING ROLE: Jon Voight
BEST ACTOR IN A SUPPORTING ROLE: Eric Roberts
BEST FILM EDITING: Henry Richardson

The Revenant (2015)
Won
BEST PERFORMANCE BY AN ACTOR IN A LEADING ROLE: Leonardo
    DiCaprio
BEST ACHIEVEMENT IN DIRECTING: Alejandro G. Iñárritu
BEST ACHIEVEMENT IN CINEMATOGRAPHY: Emmanuel Lubezki
Nominated
BEST MOTION PICTURE OF THE YEAR: Arnon Milchan, Steve Golin,
    Alejandro G. Iñárritu, Mary Parent, Keith Redmon
BEST PERFORMANCE BY AN ACTOR IN A SUPPORTING ROLE: Tom
    Hardy
BEST ACHIEVEMENT IN FILM EDITING: Stephen Mirrione
BEST ACHIEVEMENT IN COSTUME DESIGN: Jacqueline West
BEST ACHIEVEMENT IN MAKEUP AND HAIRSTYLING: Sian Grigg,
    Duncan Jarman, Robert A. Pandini
BEST ACHIEVEMENT IN SOUND MIXING: Jon Taylor, Frank A.
    Montaño, Randy Thom, Chris Duesterdiek
BEST ACHIEVEMENT IN SOUND EDITING: Martín Hernández, Lon
    Bender
BEST ACHIEVEMENT IN VISUAL EFFECTS: Richard McBride, Matt
    Shumway, Jason Smith, Cameron Waldbauer
BEST ACHIEVEMENT IN PRODUCTION DESIGN: Jack Fisk (production
    design), Hamish Purdy (set decoration)

The Untouchables (1987):
Won
BEST ACTOR IN A SUPPORTING ROLE: Sean Connery
Nominated:
BEST ART DIRECTION-SET DECORATION: Patrizia von Brandenstein,
    William A. Elliott, Hal Gausman
BEST COSTUME DESIGN: Marilyn Vance
BEST MUSIC, ORIGINAL SCORE: Ennio Morricone

Thunderbolt and Lightfoot (1974)
Nominated
BEST ACTOR IN A SUPPORTING ROLE: Jeff Bridges

What Dreams May Come (1998)
Won
BEST EFFECTS, VISUAL EFFECTS: Joel Hynek, Nicholas Brooks, Stuart
    Robertson, Kevin Scott Mack
Nominated
BEST ART DIRECTION-SET DECORATION: Eugenio Zanetti, Cindy
    Carr

INDEX

Actors, Directors, Writers and Film Crews

Locations and Places

ABOUT THE AUTHOR

Brian D'Ambrosio lives in Helena, Montana, where he writes for a variety of publications. His favorite subjects: history, architecture, biography, boxing, NHL tough guys, photography, forgotten inventors, and obscure American poets and authors. D'Ambrosio may be reached at dambrosiobrian@hotmail.com